Somatoform dissociation

Praise for *Somatoform Dissociation*

"Following in the footsteps of Janet, Ellert Nijenhuis's book on somatoform dissociation expands our understanding of dissociation and illuminates its historical connection with hysteria. Drawing on an empirical base of research, Nijenhuis links aspects of clinical dissociation with freezing in the presence of a predator illustrating the fundamental role of dissociation defenses in the face of overwhelming fear and danger. This book brings important new information together with a conceptual synthesis of prior work that stimulates our thinking and advances the field."

—Frank W. Putnam, M.D., Professor of Pediatrics and Psychiatry, Children's Hospital, Cincinnati

"We have tended to dissociate mind from body, ignoring ample evidence that psychological stress has somatic effects. Therefore, Nijenhuis's work on somatoform dissociation is especially important, in that it provides rigorous evidence that mental and physical stress are interactive. His approach to the issue is both theoretically and methodologically sophisticated. He makes a significant contribution to the field, linking, somatoform symptoms to dissociation and trauma. I recommend it."

—David Spiegel, M.D., Professor of Psychiatry and Behavioral Science, Stanford University School of Medicine

A Norton Professional Book

Somatoform Dissociation

Phenomena, Measurement, and Theoretical Issues

E.R.S. Nijenhuis

W. W. Norton & Company
New York • London

The research on behavior of this book was made possible with the financial support of:
De Open Ankh, Soesterberg, The Netherlands

For information about permission to
reproduce selections from this book, write to
Permissions, W. W. Norton & Company, Inc.,
500 Fifth Avenue, New York, NY 10110

Production Manager: Leeann Graham
Manufacturing by Haddon Craftsmen

Library of Congress Cataloging-in-Publication Data

Nijenhuis, E. R. S. (Ellert R. S.).
Somatoform dissociation : phenomena, measurement, and theoretical issues / E. R. S. Nijenhuis.—1st American ed.
p.   cm.
"A Norton professional book"—P.
Includes bibliographical references.
ISBN 0-393-70460-2 (pbk.)
1. Dissociative disorders.   2. Somatoform disorders.   I. Title.

RC553.D5N535   2004
616.85′23—dc22   2004043394

W. W. Norton & Company, Inc., 500 Fifth Avenue, New York, N.Y. 10110
www.wwnorton.com

W. W. Norton & Company Ltd., Castle House, 75/76 Wells St., London W1T 3QT

1   3   5   7   9   0   8   6   4   2

Table of Contents

I   Introduction   1

PART I THE SOMATOFORM DISSOCIATION QUESTIONNAIRE   9

II   Somatoform Dissociative Phenomena: A Janetian Perspective   11
     Introduction   11
     Mental Stigmata and Mental Accidents   13
     Mental Stigmata: Negative Dissociative Symptoms   14
        Anesthesia   15
        Amnesia   16
        Motor Disturbances   16
        Suggestibility   17
     Mental Accidents: Positive Dissociative Symptoms   17
        Subconscious Fixed Ideas and Hysterical Accidents   17
        Hysterical Attacks: Reexperiences of Traumatic Events   19
        Somnambulisms: Complex Dissociative (Identity) States   19
        Deliriums: Dissociative Psychotic Episodes   20
     Case Example   20
     Lisa's Mental Stigmata: Negative Dissociative Symptoms   21
        Anesthesia   21
        Amnesia   22
        Motor Disturbances   22
     Lisa's Mental Accidents: Positive, or Intrusion Symptoms   22
        Subconscious Fixed Ideas   22
        Hysterical Attacks   22
        Somnambulisms: Complex Dissociative (Identity) States   23
     Conclusion   23
     References   23

III The Development and Psychometric Characteristics of the
     Somatoform Dissociation Questionnaire (SDQ-20)   26
     Introduction   26
     Methods   28

Instrument Development   28
Subjects and Procedure   29
Instruments   29
Data Analysis   30
Results   30
Discussion   32
References   34
Appendix A   38
Appendix B   39

IV   The Development of the Somatoform Dissociation Questionnaire
(SDQ-5) as a Screening Instrument for Dissociative Disorders   41
Introduction   41
Material and Methods   43
Instrument Development   43
Subjects and Procedure   44
Instruments   45
Data Analysis   45
Results   47
Implications for Screening and Clinical Use of the SDQ-5   49
Discussion   49
References   51

V   Psychometric Characteristics of the Somatoform Dissociation
Questionnaire: A Replication Study   54
Introduction   54
Methods   56
Subjects and Procedure   56
Instruments   57
Data Analysis   58
Results   59
Discussion   60
References   62
Appendix 1   65

VI   Somatoform Dissociation Discriminates among Diagnostic
Categories over and above General Psychopathology   66
Introduction   66
Methods   70
Subjects   70
Instruments   71
Procedure   72
Data Analysis   72
Results   72
Discussion   75
Conclusion   77
References   78

VII Dissociative Disorders and Somatoform Dissociation: Effects of
     Indoctrination? A Correspondence in the British Journal of
     Psychiatry   82
     I. Dissociative Pathology Discriminates Between Bipolar Mood
     Disorder and Dissociative Disorder   82
     References   83
     II. Merskey's Response   83
     References   84
     III. Somatoform Dissociation is Unlikely to be a Result of
     Indoctrination by Therapists   84
     References   85

PART II TRAUMA, SOMATOFORM DISSOCIATION, AND DEFENSE   87

VIII Degree of Somatoform and Psychological Dissociation in
      Dissociative Disorder is Correlated with Reported Trauma   89
      Introduction   89
      Methods   91
          Subjects   91
          Instruments   92
          Scoring and Data Analysis   93
      Results   94
          Prevalence of Specific Traumatic Experiences   94
          Trauma Composite Scores   94
          Relationship of Trauma Composite Scores to Somatoform and
          Psychological Dissociation   96
          Age at Onset of Trauma, its Duration, Perpetrators, and
          Posttraumatic Support   98
          Repeated Analyses with Women Only   99
          Comparisons Between Dissociative Disorder Patients with and
          Without Reported Corroborative Evidence of Traumatic
          Memories   99
          Repeated Analyses Deleting Subjective Estimation of Impact from
          the Composite Scores   99
      Discussion   99
      References   103

IX   Animal Defensive Reactions as a Model for Trauma-induced
     Dissociative Reactions   108
     Introduction   108
     Animal Defensive States   109
         Pre-encounter Defense   110
         Post-encounter Defensive Behavior: Flight, Freeze, and Fight   110
         Circa-strike Defense: Analgesia, Emotional Numbing, and the
         Startle Response   111

Post-strike Behavior: Pain and Recuperation   111
Inescapable Shock   112
Defense in Social Conflict Situations, and Pain   113
Early Availability and Rapid Maturation of Defensive Responses in
Animals   113
Symptoms of Traumatized Individuals and Those with Dissociative
Disorders as Related to Animal Defensive and Recuperative
Response-sets   114
Freezing   115
Analgesia, Anesthesia, and Emotional Numbing   116
Pain   116
Early Availability and Maturation of Human Defense   116
Summary and Discussion   118
References   119

X   Somatoform Dissociative Symptoms as Related to Animal Defensive
Reactions to Predatory Imminence and Injury   125
Introduction   125
Methods   129
Participants and Procedure   129
Instruments   130
Data Analysis   131
Results   131
Discussion   137
References   141

XI   Evidence for Associations Among Somatoform Dissociation,
Psychological Dissociation, and Reported Trauma in Chronic Pelvic
Pain Patients   146
Introduction   146
Methods   149
Subjects   149
Measurements   149
Procedure   151
Data Analysis   151
Results   152
Discussion   156
References   158

XII   Peritraumatic Somatoform and Psychological Dissociation in
Relation to Recall of Childhood Sexual Abuse   161
Introduction   161
Current and Peritraumatic Psychological Dissociation
and Trauma   162
Current and Peritraumatic Somatoform Dissociation and Threat to
Bodily Integrity   163
Peritraumatic Dissociation and Recall of Trauma   164

Methods   165
   Participants   165
   Instruments   165
   Procedure   167
   Data Analysis   167
Results   168
   The SDQ-P   168
   Prevalence of Types of CSA Recall and the Relationship of Recall
   with Peritraumatic Dissociation   168
   Prevalence of Trauma, Composite Trauma Scores, and Types
   of Recall   169
   Composite Trauma Scores and Peritraumatic Dissociation   169
   Peritraumatic Dissociation and Reported Severity of Childhood
   Sexual Abuse: Interview Data   171
   Peritraumatic Somatoform Dissociation, Reported CSA, and
   Reported Physical Abuse   171
   Corroboration of Reported Childhood Sexual Abuse   171
Discussion   172
References   174

XIII The Psychometric Characteristics of the Traumatic Experiences
   Checklist (TEC): First Findings Among Psychiatric
   Outpatients   179
   Introduction   179
   Methods   182
      Demographics   182
      Instruments   182
      Procedure   185
      Data Analysis   185
   Results   185
      TEC Reliability   185
      Reported Trauma Among Men and Women   186
      TEC Concurrent Validity   187
      TEC Criterion-Related Validity   188
      TEC Trauma Area Presence Scores   188
      Trauma Area Severity Scores   189
   Discussion   189
   References   191

XIV Summary, Discussion, and Future Directions   195
   Part I   195
      The Somatoform Dissociation Questionnaire   195
      Somatoform Dissociation in Various Diagnostic Categories and
      Among Various Cultures   198
      The SDQ-20 as a Therapy Evaluation Instrument   201
      Somatoform Dissociation and Iatrogenesis   201

Part II   201
    Somatoform Dissociation and Trauma   201
    Somatoform Dissociation and Defense   202
    Chronic Pelvic Pain, Somatoform Dissociation, and Reported
    Trauma   205
    Dissociation: A Dimensional or Typological Phenomenon?   207
    Are Dissociative Symptoms State-Dependent?   210
Conclusion   211
References   212

Appendices
    1. Somatoform Dissociation Questionnaire (SDQ-20)   216
    2. Somatoform Dissociation Questionnaire (SDQ-5)   220
    3. Traumatic Experiences Checklist (TEC)   223

Index   231

I
Introduction

*"Nature, as if in ridicule of the attempts to unmask her,
has in this class of diseases, reconciled contradictions,
and realised improbabilities, with a mysterious versatility
which inspires the true philosopher with diffidence,
and reduces the systematist to despair."*
Ferriar (1795, cited in Mace, 1992)

"Hysteria is a general disease which modifies the whole organism," wrote the French physician Briquet in 1859. His empirical study on the condition in a large sample of patients – the first of its kind – showed that hysteria is both characterized by multiple medically unexplained and often chronic physical complaints, and by psychological disturbances. A prominent symptom of the latter kind concerns psychogenic amnesia, hence *Briquet's syndrome* – given the contemporary label of *somatization disorder* (American Psychiatric Association, APA, 1994) – includes this disturbance of consciousness.

Known from Pharaonic Egypt (Veith, 1965), hysteria long had been considered a disease of somatic nature and origin. However, the theory of somatic origin was abandoned in favor of Sydenham's recognition of emotional causation in 1697. This, combined with Briquet's observation of psychological disturbances in hysteria, set the stage for the conceptualization of hysteria as a *mental* disease by the neurologist Charcot in 1877. He recognized that hysteria essentially involved disturbances of perception and control. As he maintained, hysterics somehow were unable to intentionally and consciously feel, see, or hear what they are supposed to perceive, and they lack the usual control over bodily movements. Apart from these losses, hysterical patients also suffer intrusion phenomena, such as pain that can not be accounted for in a physical sense. Partly adhering to a somatic explanation of the condition, Charcot yet thought that "dynamic or functional lesions," as induced by emotional causes, were responsible for these kinds of symptoms (1887/1888).

In paying tribute to Briquet, Janet (1893) particularly stressed involvement of both mind and body: "If it disturbs nutrition and all the physiological functions, it disturbs also the psychological phenomena which are one of the functions of the organism." Janet concurred with Briquet and Charcot that hysteria related to hereditary weakness and induction by emotional, frequently traumatic events, but he did not invoke physical lesions as an organic cause. While acknowledging that neurophysiological processes one day should be involved in explaining the symptoms that plague hysterics, Janet primarily pointed to two narrowly related psychological phenomena that characterize the disturbance: *retraction of the field of consciousness* and *dissociation*. He maintained that hysterics display a retraction of the field of consciousness, such that perceptions are not assimilated into normal consciousness and personality. That is, they are not synthesized into personal perceptions and memory stores. This *dissociation* of psychological phenomena does not result in their disappearance. Quite to the contrary, non-assimilated mental phenomena *are* perceived and stored; escaping control of normal consciousness, they may start to lead some life of their own. As Janet saw it, retraction of the field of consciousness is a mental phenomenon paralleled by dissociation. Whereas Moreau de Tours (1845) introduced the descriptive concept of dissociation, Janet undoubtedly was the author who most profoundly studied its manifestations. He observed that dissociative processes as a rule affect the whole organism; they find expression in somatoform disturbances of sensation, movement, speech, vision, and hearing, as well as in disturbances of consciousness, memory, and identity.

It is well known that the contributions of 19th century French psychiatry and especially Janet's intellectual legacy were to be disregarded for years. Presently these important works have experienced a revival, foremost with thanks to Ellenberger (1970), Hilgard (1977), and Van der Hart (1991; Van der Hart & Friedman, 1989; Van der Kolk & Van der Hart, 1989). Quite remarkably, this renewed interest has largely been restricted to psychological manifestations of dissociation, such as dissociative amnesia, depersonalization and derealization, as well as confusion and fragmentation of identity. According to the presently most influential psychiatric classificatory system at present, the *Diagnostic and Statistical Manual of Mental Disorders, fourth edition* (*DSM-IV*, 1994), the essential feature of dissociative disorders is a disruption in the usually integrated functions of consciousness, memory, identity, and perception of the environment. This emphasis on psychological dissociative phenomena seems to overlook the 19th century observation that a wide range of somatoform symptoms and disturbances troubling hysterical (i.e., dissociative) patients may also be dissociative in nature. Some of these phenomena were addressed by Charcot and Janet hysteria's *mental stigmata*, that is, symptoms present in most of the cases. As Janet earlier strove for acceptance of the psychological manifestations of hysteria, presently it seems necessary to call for renewed recognition of its somatoform expressions.

Some researchers explored the prevalence of physical complaints and symptoms of dissociative patients, and found them to be abundantly present (Ross, Heber, Norton, Anderson, & Barchet, 1989; Saxe et al., 1994). However, contrary to Janet's point of view, these phenomena have not been explicitly understood in relationship to dissociation. Another classificatory system, the *International Classification of Diseases, tenth edition* (ICD-10, WHO, 1992) states that dissociation may apply to a partial or complete loss of the normal integration of immediate sensations and the control of bodily movements. In this classification, the dissociative disorders include *dissociative disorders of movement and sensation*. However, this view has not yet led to contemporary empirical studies on what we propose to call *somatoform dissociation*, even though some clinical and theoretical attention has been paid to the phenomenon (Kihlstrom, 1992, 1994; Nemiah, 1990; Nijenhuis, 1990; Van der Hart & Op den Velde, 1991). The present work aims to study the validity of these early views of Briquet and Janet on somatoform dissociation, which to an extent have been again acknowledged in the ICD-10.

Objectives of This Study

Several objectives will be persued. A primary goal is the development of a self-report questionnaire aiming to measure somatoform dissociative phenomena, the *Somatoform Dissociation Questionnaire, SDQ*. If Charcot (1887) and Janet (1893) were correct in their opinion that particular psychological and somatoform dissociative phenomena are characteristic of hysteria, then contemporary cases should also display them.

Several self-report questionnaires and interview schedules intending to measure *psychological* dissociation have recently been developed. The two best studied questionnaires are the *Dissociative Experiences Scale, DES* (Bernstein & Putnam, 1986) and the *Dissociation Questionnaire, DIS-Q* (Vanderlinden, Van Dyck, Vandereycken, & Vertommen, 1993). These instruments contain subscales that also constitute the main areas of investigation of the *Structured Clinical Interview for DSM-III-R/-IV Dissociative Disorders, SCID-D* (Steinberg, Cichetti, Buchanan, Hall, & Rounsaville, 1993): dissociative amnesia, depersonalization, derealization, identity confusion and identity fragmentation.

If the presence of a range of somatoform dissociative phenomena would likewise be characteristic of dissociative disorder patients, then it might be feasible to develop a somatoform dissociation questionnaire measuring the *construct* of somatoform dissociation using these patients. Beginning with 19th century clinical material and moving up to contemporary clinical observations of somatoform dissociative phenomena, it would be possible to study which – if any – of these symptoms are particularly characteristic of dissociative disorder patients, as well as discriminative between these patients and those with other psychiatric disorders.

It would also be possible to study whether a subset of the items of this questionnaire might serve as a *screening instrument* for the assessment of dissociative disorder. Such a clinical tool might have certain advantages. Psychiatric patients generally seem more inclined to admit to somatoform symptoms than to psychological ones, which may delay rapid and proper assessment of their true condition. It apparently is the rule, rather than the exception, that they initially present themselves with somatoform symptoms in primary care (Bradlow, Coulter & Brooks, 1992; Bridges & Goldberg, 1985; Craig, Boardman, Mills, Daly-Jones, & Drake, 1993). While in some cases the somatic complaints evidently are part of the clinical manifestation of a psychiatric disorder, such as an affective or an anxiety disorder (Kellner, 1992), in others the nature of the symptoms remains unidentified (Kroenke, Arrington, & Mangelsdorff, 1990). Some psychiatric patients may be falsily suspected of malingering or presenting with a factitious disorder. Others erroneously are thought to suffer from physical disease. It has been reported that such was the case in 40% to 60% of patients with some type of somatoform psychiatric disorder (Ford & Folks, 1985; Goodyer, 1981; Lazare, 1981). Cases with unexplained somatic symptoms are frequent in general hospital outpatient clinics (Kellner, 1991; Kroenke et al., 1990; Mayou, 1993) and pain clinics (Keefe, Dunsmore, & Burnett, 1992). There are indications that a relatively small group uses disproportionate and very considerable amounts of consultations, laboratory investigations, costly surgical procedures and other forms of hospital care over long periods of time (Barsky, Wyshak, & Klerman, 1986; Kellner, 1990; McFarland, Freeborn, Mullooly, & Pope, 1985).

As many dissociative patients report, they (initially) seek frequent somatic care, and often reveal that they, their physicians, and medical specialists could not explain the varied and "strange" symptoms that come and go for seemingly inexplicable reasons. Boon and Draijer (1993) found that the patients with dissociative identity disorder (DID) they studied had received an average of 2.8 different diagnoses before being diagnosed as having DID, 37% received a neurological diagnosis in an earlier stage, and 82.9% reported a history of recurrent somatic complaints. Dissociative patients may also display denial of psychological dissociative phenomena (Putnam, 1989). Some fear being assessed as psychotic. Others are afraid of being disbelieved, ridiculed, or involuntary institutionalized (Cohen, Giller, & W., 1991).

In these instances, cases may not be detected by instruments that are designed to assess psychological dissociation, such as the DES and DIS-Q. It might prove true that these patients are more willing to acknowledge somatoform dissociative symptoms. Also, it could be that combined scores on psychological and somatoform dissociation questionnaires better predict caseness than do these scales separately. Finally, the development of instruments measuring psychological dissociation has resulted in increasing acknowledgement and recognition of the existence of dissociative phenomena and the dissociative disorders. This effect could perhaps also emerge with respect to somatoform dissociation in quarters of primary and secundary care.

Part I (Chapters II to VII) concerns the development and psychometric characteristics of two versions of the Somatoform Dissociation Questionnaire. Chapter II highlights a range of somatoform dissociative phenomena as encountered in 19th century patients with hysteria, and focuses on what Janet observed to be the markers of hysteria: *mental stigmata* and *mental accidents*. As hysteria prominently encompassed the current dissociative disorders, it was logical to study whether somatoform dissociative symptoms would also be prominent in a contemporary patient with DID. These and similar clinical observations inspired the formulation of a large pool of items that constituted the initial version of the SDQ.

Chapter III provides data on the relative prevalence of each of these somatoform phenomena with dissociative patients and psychiatric patients with other

DSM-IV diagnoses. More essentially, it describes the development and psychometric characteristics of the *SDQ-20,* a self-reporting questionnaire designed to measure the construct of somatoform dissociation. If dissociative disorders indeed affect the whole organism, as 19th century French pioneers such as Briquet and Janet claimed, then concomitant presence of somatoform and psychological dissociative symptoms should be found. To evaluate this hypothesis, the concurrence is analyzed between both phenomenological areas, as measured by the DIS-Q and the SDQ-20.

In this study, as well as in the studies on somatoform dissociation described in other chapters of this book, the SCID-D (Steinberg, 1993; Steinberg et al., 1993) is used as the "golden standard" to assess DSM-IV dissociative disorders (APA, 1994). As the SCID-D is unlikely to be a perfect instrument, some false positives and false negatives could be selected. In some cases it can be difficult to disentangle factitious dissociative disorder and cases of malingering from true dissociative disorder, or to diagnose dissociative disorder when the patient is denying his or her dissociative symptoms (Boon & Draijer, 1995). However, based on the excellent reliability and validity of the SCID-D, we assume that in the vast majority of cases, careful use of this instrument yields true positives and true negatives.

Beginning with the SDQ-20, an analysis is performed to determine whether a subset of items optimally predicted caseness of dissociative disorder. The development and psychometric characteristics of the resulting dissociative disorder screening instrument, the SDQ-5, are presented in chapter IV. Chapter V presents an SDQ-20 and SDQ-5 cross-validation study.

In Chapter VI the severity of somatoform dissociation in various diagnostic groups is examined. Amongst others, it involves a test of the hypothesis that among patients with *DSM-IV* somatoform disorders, which include somatization disorder and conversion disorder, somatoform dissociation is a prominent symptom. Some critics have argued that dissociation instruments do not assess severity of dissociation, but rather severity of general psychopathology. In order to assess whether this criticism applies to the SDQ-20, Chapter VI presents an assessment of whether this instrument discriminates between various *DSM-IV* diagnostic categories over and above differences in general psychoneuroticism. This chapter essentially involves assessment of the criterion-related and discriminative validity of the SDQ-20. In addition, this study includes an assessment of the proportions of patients from these various groups which obtain SDQ-5 and DES scores exceeding the cutoff values of these scales in the screening for dissociative disorders.

Chapter VII is dedicated to the hypothesis of Merskey (1992) that dissociative disorders are actually misdiagnosed bipolar mood disorders, or bipolar disorder iatrogenetically shaped to present as "dissociative disorder." The chapter includes two letters of ours to the Editor of the British Journal of Psychiatry, and describes Merskey's response to our first letter.

Several theories of dissociation state that in many cases dissociation is induced by exposure to traumatic events, and represents a way of coping with overwhelming events which may have certain advantages when threat is ongoing, but which, in the longer run, may become a pathological adaptation. *Part II* (Chapters VIII to XI) is dedicated to the theme of trauma, (somatoform) dissociation, and defense. Chapter VIII focuses on the hypothesized relationship of self-reported trauma with somatoform and psychological dissociation, and involves patients with dissociative disorders and patients with other *DSM-IV* diagnoses.

There is evidence suggesting that dissociation involves extreme state-dependency (Putnam, 1997) and that traumatic events exert harmful and desintegrating influences relative to their intensity, duration, repetition (Draijer & Boon, 1993; Janet, 1909), as well as the age of the victim at onset (Boon & Draijer, 1993). Extreme state-dependency is also characteristic of animal defense to predatory threat and injury. This defensive system consists of a series of discrete substates which are tuned to meet various stages of predatory imminence and injury. Starting from these observations, in chapter IX a model is presented which maintains severe and chronic childhood trauma, in particular, may induce basic, evolutionary developed, defensive substates which are adapted to meet particular stages of threat and attack. In this view, particular somatoform dissociative state-dependent responses would be similar to animal defensive state-dependent responses. In Chapter X several hypotheses derived from this model are empirically evaluated.

One of the SDQ-20 items evaluates (medically unexplained) genital pain occurring apart from sexual intercourse. In some cases, this pain may relate to (sexual) trauma, and possibly to presence of dissociative disorder as well. Since a substantial number of psychiatric patients first present for medical care with somatic symptoms (see above), it seemed worthwhile to study to what extent patients presenting in a gynecology outpatient department of a general hospital with chronic pelvic pain report somatoform and psychological dissociative phenomena, and trauma. It also seemed important to investigate to ability of the SDQ-5 to select cases of dissociative disorder among this population. This study is the subject matter of Chapter XI.

Chapter XII provides a summary, discussion and indications for future research. The appendices present the English and Dutch versions of the SDQ-20, the SDQ-5, and the Traumatic Experiences Checklist (TEC; Nijenhuis, Van der Hart & Vanderlinden, 1994). A Dutch version of chapter XII is included as well.

References

American Psychiatric Association (1994). *Diagnostic and statistical manual of mental disorders, 4th edn. (DSM-IV)*. Washington DC: Author.
Bernstein, E., & Putnam, F.W. (1986). Development, reliability, and validity of a dissociation scale. *Journal of Nervous Mental Disease, 102*, 280-286.
Barsky, A.J., Wyshak, G., & Klerman, G.I. (1986). Medical and psychiatric determinants of outpatients medical utilization. *Medical Care, 24*, 548-563.
Boon, S., & Draijer, N. (1993). *Multiple personality disorder in the Netherlands: A study on reliability and validity of the diagnosis*. Amsterdam/Lisse: Swets & Zeitlinger.

Boon, S., & Draijer, N. (1995). *Screening en diagnostiek van dissociatieve stoornissen* [*Screening and assessment of dissociative disorders*]. Amsterdam/Lisse: Swets & Zeitlinger.

Bradlow, J., Coulter, A., & Brooks, P. (1992). *Patterns of referral: A study of referrals to out-patient clinics from general practices in the Oxford Region.* Oxford: Oxford Health Services Research Unit.

Bridges, K.W., & Goldberg, D.P. (1985). Somatic presentations of DSM-III psychiatric disorders in primary care. *Journal of Psychosomatic Research, 29*, 563-569.

Briquet, P. (1859). *Traité clinique et thérapeutique de l'hystérie* (2 vols.) [Clinical and therapeutic treatise of hysteria]. Paris: J.-P. Baillière & Fils.

Charcot, J.-M. (1887). *Leçons sur les maladies du système nerveux faites à la Salpêtrière, Tome III.* Paris: Progrès Médical en A. Delahaye & E. Lecrosnie. English edition: Clinical lectures on certain diseases of the nervous system. Detroit: Davies, 1888.

Cohen, B.M., Giller, E., & W., L. (eds.)(1991). *Multiple personality from the inside out.* Baltimore: Sidran.

Craig, T.K.J., Boardman, A.P., Mills, K., Daly-Jones, O., & Drake, H. (1993). The South London somatization study. I: Longitudinal course and the influence of early life experiences. *British Journal of Psychiatry, 163*, 579-588.

Ellenberger, H.F. (1970). *The discovery of the unconsciousness: The history and evolution of dynamic psychiatry.* New York: Basic Books.

Ford, C.V., & Folks, D.G. (1985). Conversion disorders: an overview. *Psychosomatics, 26*, 5, 371-373.

Goodyer, I. (1981). Hysterical conversion reactions in childhood. *Journal of Child Psychology and Psychiatry, 22*, 2, 179-188.

Hilgard, E.R. (1977). *Divided consciousness: Multiple controls in human thought and action.* New York: John Wiley & Sons.

Janet, P. (1893). *L'Etat mental des hystériques: Les stigmates mentaux* [The mental state of hystericals: The mental stigmata]. Paris: Rueff & Cie.

Janet, P. (1898), *Névroses et idées fixes* (Vol 1) [Neurotics disorders and fixed ideas]. Paris: Félix Alcan. Reprint: Société Pierre Janet, Paris, 1990.

Janet, P. (1909). *Problèmes psychologiques de l'émotion* [Psychological problems of emotion]. *Revue de Neurologie*, 1551-1687.

Keefe, F.J., Dunsmore, J., & Burnett, R. (1992). Behavioral and cognitive-behavioral approaches to chronic pain: Recent advances and future direction. *Journal of Consulting and Clinical Psychology, 60*, 528-536.

Kellner, R. (1990). Somatization: the most costly comorbidity. In I.D. Maser & C.R. Cloninger (eds.), *Comorbidity of mood and anxiety disorders* (pp. 239-252). Washington, DC: American Psychiatric Press.

Kellner, R. (1991). *Psychosomatic syndromes and somatic symptoms.* Washington, DC: American Psychiatric Press.

Kihlstrom, J.F. (1992). Dissociative and conversion disorders. In D.J. Stein & J. Young (eds.), *Cognitive science and clinical disorders* (pp. 247-270). San Diego/New York: Academic Press.

Kihlstrom, J.F. (1994). One hundred years of hysteria. In S.J. Lynn & J.W. Rhue (eds.), *Dissociation: Clinical and theoretical perspectives* (pp. 365-395). New York: Guilford.

Kluft, R.P. (1993). Treatment of dissociative disorder patients: An overview of discoveries, successes and failures. *Dissociation, 6*, 2/3, 87-101.

Kroenke, K., Arrington, M.E. & Mangelsdorf, D. (1900). Common symptoms in medical out-patients and the adequacy of therapy. *Archives of International Medicine, 150*, 1685-1689.

Lazare, A. (1981). Current concepts in psychiatry: conversion symptoms. *New English Journal of Medicine, 305*, 13, 745-748.

Mayou, R. (1993). Somatization. *Psychotherapy and Psychosomatics, 59*, 69-83.

McFarland, B.H., Freeborn, D.K., Mulloolo, J.P., & Pope, C.R. (1985). Utilization patterns among longterm enrollees in a prepaid group practice health maintenance organization. *Medical Care, 23*, 1221-1233.

Moreau de Tours, J.J. (1845). *Du hachisch et de l'aliénation mentale: Etudes psychologiques.* Paris: Fortin, Masson & Cie. English edition: Hashish and mental illness. New York: Raven Press, 1973.

Nemiah, J.C. (1991). Dissociation, conversion, and somatization. In A. Tasman & S.M. Goldfinger (eds.), *American Psychiatric Press Annual Review of Psychiatry, Vol. 10.* Washington, DC: American Psychiatric Press.

Nijenhuis, E.R.S. (1990). Somatische equivalenten bij dissociatieve stoornissen [Somatic equivalents in dissociative disorders]. *Hypnotherapie, 12*, 139-142.

Nijenhuis, E.R.S., Van der Hart, O., & Vanderlinden, J. (Unpublished data). The Traumatic Experiences Questionnaire. [This instrument was recently renamed the Traumatic Experiences Checklist (TEC); see Chapter XI].

Putnam, F.W. (1989). *Diagnosis and treatment of multiple personality disorder.* New York: Guilford.

Putnam, F.W. (1997). *Dissociation in children and adolescents: A developmental perspective.* New York: Guilford.

Ross, C.A., Heber, S., Norton, G.R., Anderson, G., & Barchet, P. (1989). The Dissociative Disorder Interview Schedule: A structured interview. *Dissociation, 2*, 169-189.

Saxe, G.N., Chinman, G., Berkowitz, M.D., Hall, K., Lieberg, G., Schwartz J. & Van der Kolk, B.A. (1994). Somatization in patients with dissociative disorders. *American Journal of Psychiatry, 151*, 1329-1334.

Steinberg, M., Rounsaville, B.J., & Cichetti, D.V. (1990). The Structured Clinical Interview for DSM-III-R Dissociative Disorders: Preliminary report on a new diagnostic instrument. *American Journal of Psychiatry, 147*, 76-82.

Steinberg, M., Cichetti, D.V., Buchanan, J., Hall, P., & Rounsaville, B. (1993). Clinical assessment of dissociative symptoms and disorders: The Structured Clinical Interview for DSM-IV Dissociative Disorders. *Dissociation, 6*, 3-16.

Van der Hart, O. (ed.) (1991). *Trauma, dissociatie en hypnose* [Trauma, dissociation and hypnosis]. Amsterdam/Lisse: Swets & Zeitlinger.

Van der Hart, O., & Friedman, B. (1989). A reader's guide to Pierre Janet on dissociation: A neglected intellectual heritage. *Dissociation, 2*, 1, 3-16.

Van der Hart, O., & Op den Velde, W. (1991). Traumatische herinneringen [Traumatic memories]. In O. Van der Hart (ed.), *Trauma, dissociatie en hypnose* [Trauma, dissociation, and hypbosis] (pp. 91-125). Amsterdam/Lisse: Swets & Zeitlinger.

Vanderlinden, J., Van Dyck, R., Vandereycken, W., & Vertommen, H. (1993). The Dissociation Questionnaire: Development and characteristics of a new self-reporting questionnaire. *Clinical Psychology and Psychotherapy, 1*, 21-27.

Veith, I. (1965). *Hysteria: History of a disease.* Chicago: University of Chicago Press.

World Health Organization (1992). *The ICD-10 Classification of Mental and Behavioural Disorders. Clinical descriptions and diagnostic guidelines.* Geneva: Author.

PART I

THE SOMATOFORM DISSOCIATION QUESTIONNAIRE

II
Somatoform Dissociative Phenomena: A Janetian Perspective*

*"It is through the study of mental stigmata
that the malady of hysteria must be diagnosed and understood.
Each of them shows very well that
the subject has sustained a loss in his personality
and that he is no longer master of his own thought."*
Pierre Janet, 1901, p. 222.

Introduction

The observation that dissociation and the dissociative disorders affect a wide range of mental and physical functions was basic to 19th century views on hysteria. Janet defined hysteria as: "A form of mental depression characterized by the retraction of the field of personal consciousness and a tendency to the dissociation and emancipation of the systems of ideas and functions that constitute personality" (Janet, 1907, p. 332). Such "systems of ideas and functions" could either belong to psyche or soma.

Contemporary North American views on dissociation tend to be more restrictive, and completely or partially disregard the alterations in somatoform functions and reactions that according to Janet and other 19th century psychiatrists also could be manifestations of dissociation. For example, the *DSM-III-R* defined the essential feature of the dissociative disorders as "a disturbance or alteration in the normally integrative functions of identity, memory, or consciousness" (APA, 1987, p. 269). In the *DSM-IV* (APA, 1994) it was added that this disturbance could also affect perception of the environment. Consequently, in this diagnostic system, somatoform symptoms, considered to be dissociative by 19th century French psychiatrists, are diagnosed instead as disorders not understood or classified as dissociative in nature, such as somatization disorder, pain disorder, conversion disorder, sexual disorder, or body dysmorphic disorder. In contrast, the latest edition of the International Classifi-

* This chapter is an adapted version of: Nijenhuis, E.R.S., & Van der Hart, O. (1999). Somatoform dissociative phenomena: A Janetian perspective. In J.M. Goodwin & R. Attias (eds.), *Splintered reflections: Images of the body in trauma* (pp. 89-127). New York: Basic Books.

cation of Diseases, that is, the ICD-10 (WHO, 1992), recognizes that dissociation may affect somatoform functions and reactions: "the common theme shared by dissociative disorders is a partial or complete loss of the normal integration between memories of the past, awareness of identity and immediate sensations, and control of bodily movements." (p. 151) However, even this current international definition is more restrictive than what Janet had in mind. As defined in ICD-10, *dissociative disorders of movement and sensation* involve only *loss* of sensations and *loss* of, or *interference* with, movements. Disorders involving *additional* sensations such as pain are to be included in the somatoform disorders, and somatization disorder is not classified as a dissociative disorder.

Janet (1901, 1907) distinguished between two major categories of hysterical symptoms, that is, the *mental stigmata* and the *mental accidents*. The mental stigmata reflect functional losses, that is, losses of sensation (anesthesia), memory (amnesia), motor control, will (abulia), and character traits (modifications of character). The mental accidents involve intrusions, e.g., additional sensations, movements, and perceptions, up to the extremes of complete interruptions of the habitual state of consciousness through reactivations of dissociative *secondary existences*. These dissociative states display psychological and somatoform features which diverge from those characteristic of the habitual state.

Interestingly, Janet's dichotomy does not follow a mind-body distinction. Both categories apply equally to psyche and soma, which he insisted, should not be radically divided (Janet, 1901). However, *phenomenologically* the two types of dissociation can be categorized separately (Kihlstrom, 1992, 1994). In order to gain a clearer view on the matter, imagine a two by two table categorizing dissociative symptoms according to the double dichotomy described above (Table 1). The first dichotomy divides *psychological* and *somatoform dissociation*.

Somatoform dissociation designates dissociative symptoms that phenomenologically involve the body. The adjective "somatoform" indicates that the physical symptoms suggest, but can not be explained by a medical condition, or by the direct effects of a substance. Hence, we will use the adjective "somatoform" instead of "somatic" unless we describe symptoms which could perhaps be an expression of a somatic disease. "Dissociation" describes the existence of a disruption of the normal synthesis between "systems of ideas and functions that constitute the personality" (Janet, 1907, p. 332). This disruption relates to mental and neurophysiological processes still not completely understood. The second dichotomy divides *negative dissociative symptoms* (mental stigmata) from *positive dissociative symptoms* (mental accidents). Accordingly, "somatoform dissociation" includes negative and positive somatoform manifestations of disrupted mental synthesis.

Several clinicians have emphasized the need to return to Janet's pioneering studies in order to further understanding of the somatoform aspects of dissociation (Kihlstrom, 1992, 1994; Nemiah, 1974, 1990; Nijenhuis, 1990; Van der Hart & Friedman, 1989; Van der Hart & Op den Velde, 1991). Consistent with these clinically based opinions, several recent studies have shown that patients with *DSM-III-R* (or *DSM-IV*) dissociative disorders suffer from many somatoform symptoms (Pribor, Yutzy, Dean, Wetzel, 1993; Ross, Heber, Norton & Ander-

Table 1. A phenomenological categorization of dissociative symptoms.

	Psychological dissociation	Somatoform dissociation
Mental stigmata, or negative dissociative symptoms	Amnesia Abulia Modifications of character (loss of character traits, predominantly affects) Suggestibility	Anesthesia (all sensory modalities) Analgesia Loss of motor control (movements, voice, swallowing, etc.)
Mental accidents, or positive dissociative symptoms	Subconscious acts, hysterical accidents, and fixed ideas	Subconscious acts, hysterical accidents, and fixed ideas: singular intrusive somatoform symptoms which influence the habitual state
	Hysterical attacks	Hysterical attacks: complexes of somatoform symptoms which influence the habitual state
	Somnambulism	Somnambulism: alterations of state, which involve complex somatoform alterations
	Deliriums (dissociative psychosis)	Deliriums: alterations of state, which involve grotesque somatoform alterations and enduring failure to test reality

son, 1989; Saxe et al., 1994). It has also been found that patients with particular somatoform disorders, for instance, pseudoseizures (Bowman & Markand, 1996) and chronic pelvic pain (Walker, Katon, Neraas, Jemelka, & Massoth, 1992) show elevations on measures of psychological dissociation (as on the Dissociative Experiences Scale, DES [Bernstein & Putnam, 1986]). While ICD-10 recognizes pseudoseizures as a dissociative disorder, in North America these various somatoform phenomena have generally not been grouped with dissociative disorders (Bowman & Markand, 1996).

In this chapter, we will first detail the Janetian classification of mental stigmata and mental accidents. Next, we will show that the negative and positive somatoform symptoms which characterized the 19th century hysterical patients can be clinically observed in a contemporary traumatized patient with dissociative identity disorder (DID).

Mental Stigmata and Mental Accidents

According to Janet (1901, 1907; cf. Van der Hart & Friedman, 1989), the mental stigmata are the general markers of hysteria. He distinguished two classes of mental stigmata: (1) *proper* stigmata, which appear exclusively in hysteria; and (2) *common stigmata*, which are shared by hysteria and other mental disorders, notably psychasthenic neuroses. Janet understood "common stigmata" to be related to a *lowering of the mental level*; these symptoms included lapses of all the mental functions, the lack of feeling and of will (abulia), and the inability to begin and end activities. Hysteria's "proper stigmata" relate to the *retraction of the field of consciousness*, and include suggestibility and unconscious acts, absent-mindedness and alternations of symptoms. Somatoform mental stigmata include anesthesia, analgesia, and movement disorders. Mental accidents are hysteria's acute, transient features which appear briefly or intermittently, and include subconscious acts, fixed ideas, hysterical attacks, somnambulistic states (altered states of consciousness, memory and identity), and deliriums (dissociative psychotic episodes).

In our view, the mental stigmata and mental accidents of hysteria can be described in terms of negative and positive symptoms, respectively. The mental stigmata, as negative symptoms, are directly based on the dissociation and emancipation of the "systems of ideas and functions that constitute personality." Normally, these systems of ideas and functions are *synthesized* among each other to form coherent mental structures and then these are integrated into previous synthesized mental structures (Janet, 1909). Examples of non-synthesized systems range from a simple image, memory, or thought together with attendant feelings, bodily manifestations, and a rudimentary but alternate sense of self, to a complex dissociative identity state (Breuer & Freud, 1955; Janet, 1889; McDougall, 1926). The phenomena belonging to dissociated systems are not perceived or processed by personal consciousness. This is what produces mental stigmata, the gaps in perception and function that we call negative symptoms. When a memory system remains chronically dissociated, it may take on a life of its own, and can uncontrollably intrude on personal consciousness. These intrusive parallel perceptions and parallel existences are what we call positive dissociative symptoms.

According to Janet, both the stigmata and accidents that hysterical patients manifest are extremely *changeable*, because they are highly dependent on the mental state (ego center or identity) which dominates consciousness at that particular point in time. Rapid changes of symptoms may be based on transitions from one state to another. These symptoms also are *contradictory*, as it can be demonstrated by a patient who, for instance, displays visual (hysterical blind-ness), auditory (hysterical deafness), or kinesthetic anesthesia (hysterical insensi-bility pertaining to touch), and at the same time does see, hear, or feel. Janet maintained that this peculiar characteristic is based on simultaneously active dissociative states.

Mental Stigmata: Negative Dissociative Symptoms

As stated above, mental stigmata include a wide range of functional losses. Here we present an overview of these symptoms.

Anesthesia

Anesthesia refers to the absence or diminution (more properly called *hypoesthesia*) of normal sensibility. All sensory modalities (propriocepsis, kinesthesia, nocicepsis [perception of pain], vision, audition, as well as the sense of smell and taste) may be disturbed by it, separately, or simultaneously. Janet distinguished *localized*, *systematized*, and *generalized* anesthesia.

Localized anesthesia presents at a particular, localized area of the body, for instance the left side of the body (hemianesthesia), or the face, or sharply defined spots. Systematized anesthesia follows a single subconscious idea or a system of ideas which determine what will and will not be perceived. For example, the subject may see all the persons or objects in a room, but may fail to see or hear a certain person or object. Generalized anesthesia affects a sense in general, as in cases of hysterical blindness, deafness, or the inability to feel touch, temperature, texture, and pain in all bodily regions.

Janet maintained that, in contrast to somatically determined anesthesias, hysterical anesthesias are often ignored and unreported. Like the other mental stigmata, anesthesias are typically state-dependent (Janet, 1889, 1898, 1907).

- *Analgesia.* This frequent hysterical symptom (Janet, 1889, 1901) is defined as insensibility to pain, with the sense of touch remaining unimpaired.
- *Organic anesthesia.* Janet (1901) gave this name to "the loss of those vague sensations that are informing us of the presence and life of our organs" (p. 56). Some patients not only cease feeling the touch of their limbs, but lose the consciousness of their existence as well. In extreme cases these phenomena resemble parietal lobe syndromes with parts of the body being rejected as ego alien and/or experienced as foreign bodies not part of the self. Janet added that the sensations of hunger, thirst, fatigue, and the desire to urinate may also be lost. Genital sensations may also be completely or intermittently lacking.
- *Kinesthetic anesthesia.* Janet distinguished between anesthesias for movements that are self-initiated (active) and anesthesias for movements that are caused by someone else manipulating the body (passive). Anesthesia often implies *ataxia*, that is, the inability to direct one's movements with eyes closed. *Lasègue's syndrome*, a classic hysterical variant, involves difficulties in initiating movement and unawareness of movement without the help of sight.
- *Tactile anesthesia.* Hysterical patients may lack the sense of touch. They then are unable to identify objects which are placed in their hands with the eyes closed, and they will not sense being touched. In these cases, awareness of being touched is mediated by visual perception.
- *Visual anesthesia.* Retraction of the visual field may phenomenologically appear as "tunnel vision" or perceiving only parts of the body, persons or objects. According to Janet, the symptom tends to depend on state, but is also influenced by physiological variables, such as rest, alcohol, and menstrual periods, as well as psychological variables, such as emotions, and stress.

Visual anesthesia may be localized. An example is provided by patients who seem to have totally lost the vision of one eye. As all the other mental stigmata, this symptom is of a contradictory nature in that it can be experimentally shown that visual stimuli projected to the affected eye still are processed, although subconsciously. Visual anesthesia can also be of a systematized nature. As Janet explains, while remaining in a dissociative state a patient may only see a certain category of objects that relate to ideas of special significance to that state.

Like the other anesthesias, visual anesthesias are mobile. For example, Janet's patient Bertha usually was generally hemianesthetic on the left side, and her visual field was extremely contracted on both sides. However, after a hysterical attack, she became totally anesthetic and at times blind for some hours.

- *Auditory, gustatory, and olfactory anesthesia.* Much of what has been said with respect to other sensory modalities, is equally applicable to the auditory, gustatory, and olfactory senses.

Amnesia

Hysterical amnesia involves state-dependent inaccessibility of memories for present and past events (Janet, 1889, 1901), and thus is a mobile phenomenon. As more than one state can be concomitantly reactivated, amnesia is also contradictory in its presentation: the patient can, although unwittingly, still be influenced by apparently lost memories. In a word, dissociative barriers are far from absolute.

According to Janet (1889), dissociated knowledge predominantly involves autobiographical memory, but can also include state-dependent inaccessibility of motor and other skills. Such skills are regarded today as manifestations of implicit memory, that is, knowledge which is unavailable to consciousness, but which affects performance. Janet saw movements as the outward manifestation of certain images, holding that hysterical paralyses are the outward expression of the amnestic loss (inaccessibility) of these images about movement. Such paralyses usually are of a systematized type involving a particular group of movements and skills, for example, standing and walking (*astasia-abasia*), writing, or sewing, while leaving many others unaffected.

Motor Disturbances

Janet observed that voluntary movements of hysterical patients tend to be slackened, undecided, and ill-directed. These patients may have difficulty performing complex acts which necessitate simultaneously several different movements, resulting in a simplification of voluntary movement. In his view, such disturbances resulted from anesthesia and a retraction of the field of consciousness. According to Janet, the observed weakening of voluntary movement is more related to *abulia*, a common mental stigma pertaining to a defect of the will and of conscious attention. When Lasègue's syndrome is present, motor disturbances are usually more pronounced.

Catalepsy is another motor disturbance related to amnesia. The patient's limbs can be easily moved about by another person, but when a limb is put into some position, it will tend to stay in that position for a long time, as if the patient had completely forgotten the member.

Contractures may also relate to anesthesia and forgetting the body. For example, Maria had a tendency to hyperflexion on the anesthetic left side of her body, but not on the still sensitive right side. Upon the disappearance of the anesthesia, the motor contractures vanished with it. In Janet's mind, both catalepsy and contracture are determined by a retraction of the field of personal consciousness with a concomitant dissociative loss of the relevant motor images.

Suggestibility

According to Janet (1907), the increased suggestibility of hysteric patients strongly relates to their *absent-mindedness* in which critical cognitive functions are suspended. Both negative and positive symptoms may be induced in these patients with relative ease, and this effect is not dependent on induction of a hypnotic state.

Yet, this suggestibility is a complex matter: some hysterical patients are less suggestible than others and all resist suggestions at certain times. As he observed, it is extremely difficult to induce a suggestion in a person who has already received a suggestion or who has a fixed idea (powerful ideas which often are trauma-induced, and which are to be discussed shortly). Thus, it is very difficult to use suggestion to change dissociative symptoms and fixed ideas.

According to Janet hysteria is not a result of suggestion, as some 19th century authors believed and as several contemporary authors also maintain. As he remarked (i) patients, as a result of their restricted fields of consciousness, are often not aware of or indifferent to hysterical stigmata, which precludes an autosuggestive origin of the symptoms; (ii) hysterical stigmata are perfectly regular and have remained the same since the Middle Ages in all countries in which they have been observed; and (iii) while the disposition to suggestibility is not complete at the beginning of the disorder, mental stigmata show themselves very soon (Janet, 1901, pp. 357-358).

In summary, Janet suggested that the synthetic function of personal consciousness can be disrupted. Sensations, perceptions of the environment, memories, affects, will, and character traits may to a greater or lesser extent escape normal synthesis and assimilation into the habitual personality.

Mental Accidents: Positive Dissociative Symptoms

In Janet's view, the mental accidents are acute, transient features of hysteria, which tend to be intermittently present and are usually experienced as distressing or painful.

Subconscious Fixed Ideas and Hysterical Accidents

Subconscious fixed ideas are thoughts or mental images which take on exaggerated proportions, and have a high emotional charge (Janet, 1901; cf. Van der

Hart & Friedman, 1989). They are formed without the patient's conscious control or awareness under the influence of traumatic events, fatigue, or severe illness. Because dissociated states are the carriers of these ideas, as a rule, dissociative patients in their habitual personality state are unable to account clearly for fixed ideas that beset them.

Fixed ideas are present during waking hours, but may also be expressed during sleep and dissociative episodes in which trauma is reexperienced. The reactivation of fixed ideas may occur through partial representations or much more inclusive representations of traumatic events and responses. Janet (1901) labeled the former *hysterical accidents*, and the latter *hysterical attacks* (which are discussed below). Whereas a partial reexperience of trauma leaves room for the appreciation of present circumstances, during more or less total traumatic reexperiences the orientation to the present is lost. Fixed ideas may involve all sensory modalities and a wide range of other somatoform responses as well. Following are several examples.

- *Dysesthesia (intrusive, non-painful sensations)*. Perceptual alterations may relate to fixed ideas, as was evident in the case of Janet's patient Bertha, who found the color red repugnant, because it is the color of blood, reminding her of the tragic death of her father.
- *Hyperesthesia (pain)*. Pain symptoms of hysterical (dissociative) patients may be an expression of subconscious fixed ideas. Janets patient Colinm., the victim of a serious railway accident, recovered from a serious abdominal wound. However, upon drinking alcohol, he reexperienced the accident and concomitant abdominal pain. Six years later, Colinm. experienced violent emotions related to the death of his wife and child, due to which he became morbidly sad, and suffered intense abdominal pain. Pressing the scar would evoke reexperiences of the accident.
- *Audition*. Auditory hallucinations of hysterical patients appear to stem from communications of dissociative states that are perceived as voices, or as a peculiar type of thoughts. The utterances of these dissociative (identity) states may reveal fixed ideas.
- *Motor disturbances*. Fixed ideas may also relate to motor disturbances, for instance, paralyses, contractures, problems of speech, tics, and tremors (Janet, 1907). Dissociative states are either organized around one main fixed idea (monoideism) or around a limited set of related fixed ideas (polyideism), directing thoughts, emotions, perceptions, sensations, and actions (Janet, 1901, 1907). Thus various states may have widely diverging ideas, precipitating struggles among dissociative states. As a result, movements of all types may be postponed, prevented, undermined, abolished, or implemented.
- *Nutrition*. Hysterical patients often have problems with eating, which may relate to fixed ideas. Thus, Janet's patient Isabelle refused to eat anything for six weeks because of such a fixed idea (Janet, 1901). During hysterical attacks, Isabelle's deceased mother "appeared," blaming her for a fault she had committed, and telling her that she was not worthy to live, and that she ought to join her (mother) in heaven. To achieve this, mother's "manifestation" ordered Isabelle not to eat. The "fault" that Isabelle felt mother was accusing

her of related to a fixed (but erroneous) idea that she had murdered her sister (who in fact had died of natural causes).

Hysterical Attacks: Reexperiences of Traumatic Events

Hysterical patients may intermittently seem to lose consciousness, becoming unresponsive to external stimuli (Janet, 1907). During such dissociative episodes they may writhe with great, irregular, apparently meaningless movements, become completely inert and immovable, or display combinations of both types. The attacks are acute phenomena of relative short duration (not lasting longer than a few hours at most), but repetitive nature (tending to occur daily, or even several times a day). To the extent that the habitual state of consciousness remains activated, it experiences, or suffers from these somatoform and emotional symptoms as well.

Attacks, or fully reactivated traumatic memories as we would now term them, involve enlarged, disfigured, and inferior expressions of emotions pertaining to fixed, trauma-related ideas (Janet, 1901), which are repeatedly evoked by reminders of traumatizing events. In contrast with normal *narrative* memories, traumatic memories are predominantly expressed in a somatosensory way: the subject repeats acts and emotions, as well as visual, kinesthetic, auditory, and other somatoform perceptions pertaining to past trauma, as if the event is unfolding itself in the present (Janet, 1889, 1898, 1904, 1928; cf. Van der Kolk & Van der Hart, 1991). Traumatic memories need not entirely match historical facts, because they pertain to impressions these events once evoked (Janet, 1932).

Somnambulisms: Complex Dissociative (Identity) States

"... Hystericals may at certain moments pass into abnormal psychological states, the first characteristic of which is to appear strange, extraordinary, very different from the normal psychological state of the subject," Janet (1901, p. 413) remarked. These states were called *somnambulisms*: abnormal states, distinct from the normal life of the subject, "in which the patient possesses particular recollections, which he finds no longer when he returns to his normal state." (p. 415) These memories, which amongst others pertain to fixed ideas and traumatic recollections, tend to be rather directly available in these "second existences," which currently are often called dissociative identity states.

During an hysterical attack patients are absorbed in traumatic fixed ideas, while losing awareness of, and adaptation to, the current reality. However, in somnambulistic states they remain perceptive of the present, and are able to adapt their behavior accordingly. Although less exclusively dominated by fixed ideas than during the hysterical attacks, somnambulistic states are still organized around one main fixed idea (*monoideism*) or around a limited set of related fixed ideas (*polyideism*), directing thoughts, emotions, perceptions, sensations, and actions (Janet, 1901, 1907).

After switching to a complex dissociative state, some patients could be free from symptoms such as anesthesias, amnesias, motor disturbances and the like, which were present in the habitual personality state. As remarked before, these body symptoms are state-dependent, mobile, and contradictory. What is not sensed, perceived, or controlled by one state of consciousness, is processed by one or more other states. This produces a capricious symptomatic picture, which caused some to argue that hysteria is nothing but a condition of simulation and suggestion, notably Babinski (1901, 1909).

Deliriums: Dissociative Psychotic Episodes

Some hysterical (dissociative disorder) patients tend to get caught in brief or more prolonged reactivations of somnambulistic states, in which they are poorly oriented to the present and are predominantly undergoing a hysterical attack. Such a condition was formerly called hysterical psychosis, and was more recently termed *reactive dissociative psychosis* (Nijenhuis, 1995; Van der Hart, Witztum, & Friedman, 1993). During such an episode specific somatoform dissociative symptoms may manifest.

In summary, while mental stigmata apparently involve *functional losses,* mental accidents can be regarded as positive symptoms, pertaining to *intrusions* of more or less developed dissociative mental structures into the habitual state of consciousness. In Janet's view, these intrusions stem from fixed ideas, dissociative relivings of traumatic events and responses (hysterical attacks), reactivations of dissociative identity states (somnambulisms), and dissociative psychotic states (deliriums). It thus may be said that in the Janetian perspective mental accidents are intrusions, reflecting manifestations of lost personal mental contents, which are dissociatively processed, stored, and reactivated.

The following case example illustrates that according to clinical observation contemporary DID patients may, like 19th century hysterical patients, manifest a multitude of somatoform symptoms that can be understood as an integral part of their severely dissociative condition.

Case Example

In addition to the psychological dissociative phenomena that justified the DID diagnosis, Lisa (38) suffered a profusion of somatoform symptoms. Apart from rather common somatic complaints, Lisa had unusual symptoms. These included the perception that parts of her body had gone and an intermittent inability to move. Lisa was continually surprised by these symptoms appearing "out of the blue", and disappearing unpredictably within minutes, hours, or days.

Lisa had frequented the family doctor for many years, who remained unable to make a suitable diagnosis. Medication proved ineffective. Lisa became gradually aware that the course of her "real" somatic symptoms differed from that of the "strange" ones. The first were generally of a more stable character, and covered a longer time-span, whereas the latter appeared intermittently, were of relatively short duration, and could go away as unexpectedly as they came. Finally she realized that these curious symptoms rarely lasted for more than two or three days, and she consequentially decided that only when symptoms lasted longer than that span of time she would ask for medical help. Despite these precautions she was repeatedly sent to medical specialists, and was hospitalized more than once.

Like many DID patients do, Lisa recalled severe and chronic sexual, physical, and emotional abuse, as well as emotional neglect. She had been able to find documents and to interview collateral informants that confirmed, or were consistent with, significant parts of these recollections.

As the following discussion suggests, Lisa's somatoform symptoms can be described in terms of mental stigmata and mental accidents.

Lisa's Mental Stigmata: Negative Dissociative Symptoms

Anesthesia

Lisa had several types of anesthesia. *Tactile anesthesia* was evidently present as her body felt partly or completely numb at times. If anesthetic areas were touched, she would become aware of this only by looking, and even then she did not feel the touch (*Lasègue's syndrome*). Lisa also had difficulty directing her own movements, due to that condition described above as *kinesthetic anesthesia*. For example, without looking at her limbs, Lisa had difficulty knowing their position in space, or controlling their movements, as when knitting, sewing, or writing. She frequently placed objects inches away from the place she had in mind (*ataxia*). Upon eye closure, Lisa experienced her body as an assembly of unrelated and disconnected elements.

It also happened that at times an arm, a leg, or some other part of the body developed a thing-like quality. In this context, Lisa might also lose her sense of ownership of that limb or the entire body. At times, Lisa felt like a robot, a condition she also described as having no body, as being pulled into action by commands of unknown sources, or as being a puppet on a string. At other times, Lisa had the experience that the body, or a part of it, had vanished. This disappearance phenomenon affected most often her hands, breasts, and pelvic area. She saw (*visual anesthesia*) and experienced "holes" (*organic anesthesia*) where those members should have been.

Visual anesthesia also presented in other forms, such as tunnel vision (*retraction of visual field*) and temporary blindness (*generalized visual anesthesia*). Sometimes the problem with vision could be traced to anticipatory fear of perceiving a traumatic scene (e.g., when she felt socially obliged to watch the news, or thrillers on television).

The way in which Lisa apprehended her body was state-dependent. In each dissociative identity state, she experienced a divergent body schema, which systematically altered the visual and kinesthetic perception of herself.

State-dependent anesthesia applied to other sensory modalities as well. *Analgesia* had been present in the context of previous self-mutilation, but also appeared at other times, especially when she felt threatened. Then, it was often accompanied by concomitant stiffening of the body and inability to move.

Amnesia

Lisa's dissociative amnesias affected both past and recent experience, and involved autobiographical memory, as well as implicit memory. Implicit memory loss manifested through state-dependent losses and gains of skills. For example, in her normal condition, Lisa was able to perform motor skills which, upon a transition to a child state, were instantaneously lost. In child states, she could neither write as an adult, nor perform even simple tasks.

Dissociations of autobiographical memory also involved the body. For example, the "forgetting" in some states of certain body parts seemed to coincide with amnestic gaps in those identity states for reported childhood aversities that had injured those parts of the body.

Motor Disturbances

Apart from ataxia and Lasègue's syndrome, Lisa's motor disturbances involved occasional immobility as a response to threat, paralyses, and contractures. Lisa also experienced total loss of bodily control, as when overtaken by a dissociative state.

Lisa's Mental Accidents: Positive, or Intrusion Symptoms

Subconscious Fixed Ideas

Lisa's subconscious fixed ideas affected a wide range of senses, somatoform (re)actions and functions, and emotions. These ideas included *dysesthesias* (i.e., intrusive, non-painful sensations) which were often related to dissociated traumatic experiences involving touch. Fixed ideas also led to *hyperesthesia* (pain) and sudden changes of taste and food preferences. Many localized pain symptoms related to reported traumatic events. Fixed ideas might present as *pseudo-hallucinations*. For example, under the influence of a fearful child state, Lisa "saw" her mother in the office of the therapist.

Motor disturbances related to fixed ideas caused intermittent inability or disability to act or move (partial or complete *catalepsy; contractures*), eat, swallow, or speak (*aphonia; dysphonia*), as well as leading to the involuntary performance of motor acts. For example, upon the reactivation of particular fearful child states, her body grew stiff, or became immobile. At such times, she might experience sudden inability to move or speak.

Hysterical Attacks

Hysterical attacks involved many somatoform symptoms and related to the reactivation of traumatic memories and various fixed ideas. For example, when reliving exiles to a freezing cold barn, Lisa shivered intensely, and became immobile.

Somnambulisms: Complex Dissociative (Identity) States

Lisa's dissociative identity states, which showed all the characteristics of somnambulism, displaying intricate ties between psychological and somatoform functioning. For example, a particular dissociative identity state contained a lifetime of bad memories about menstruation. Amongst others, as a young girl, Lisa had not been allowed by mother to use pads or bandages. Later in life, when her monthly period was due, the state that felt persistently "dirty" took control, bought excessive quantities of pads and new underwear, and washed the body excessively. Until therapy, Lisa was amnestic for these behaviors.

Conclusion

According to Janet and contemporary clinical observation – as exemplified in the present case – dissociation affects both soma and psyche. It seems that a lack of mental synthesis can result in a wide range of somatoform reactions and functions, as well as psychological reactions and functions. As these observations in fact suggest that somatoform dissociative phenomena may belong to the essential symptoms of dissociative disorders, this hypothesis warrants systematic study.

The case example is consistent with Janet's observation that somatoform and psychological dissociation are highly intertwined phenomena, indicating that both may stem from a common source. According to Janet, two processes are involved: a retraction of the field of consciousness, and a lowering of the level of mental functioning, which jointly favor the formation of dissociative mental structures.

Somatoform dissociative symptoms, as well as psychological dissociative symptoms, can be described in terms of Janet's classificatory distinction between mental stigmata and mental accidents, or, as we have proposed to label these categories, negative and positive dissociative symptoms. These negative and positive symptoms impress us also as closely related phenomena. For example, localized anesthesias may be tied to subconscious fixed ideas. In the same vein, amnestic episodes can represent shadows left by interruptions of normal consciousness by hysterical attacks, somnambulistic, or dissociative psychotic states. In combination, these losses and intrusions suggest parallel distribution of information processing by two or more mental states, causing the capricious and contradictory phenomenology of hysteria.

References

American Psychiatric Association (1987). *Diagnostic and statistical manual of mental disorders, 3rd rev. ed.*. Washington DC: Author.

American Psychiatric Association (1994). *Diagnostic and statistical manual of mental disorders, 4th edn.* Washington DC: American Psychiatric Association.

Babinski, J. (1901). Définition de l'hystérie. *Revue Neurologique, 9*, 1074-1080.

Babinski, J. (1909). Démembrement de l'hystérie. *La Semaine Médicale, 9*, 3-8.

Bernstein, E., & Putnam, F.W. (1986). Development, reliability, and validity of a
     dissociation scale. *Journal of Nervous Mental Disease*, 102, 280-286.
Bowman, E.S., & Markand, O.N. (1996). Psychodynamics and psychiatric diagnoses of
     pseudoseizure subjects. *American Journal of Psychiatry*, 153, 57-63.
Breuer, J., & Freud, S. (1955). On the psychical mechanism of hysterical phenomena.
     In J. Strachey & A. Strachey (eds.), *Standard edition of the complete psychological works
     of Sigmund Freud* (pp. 1-181). London: Hogarth.
Janet, P. (1889). *L'Automatisme psychologique*. Paris: Félix Alcan. Reprint: Société Pierre
     Janet, Paris, 1973.
Janet, P. (1898). *Névroses et idées fixes*, Vol. 1. Paris: Félix Alcan.
Janet, P. (1901). *The mental state of hystericals*. New York: Putnam & Sons. Reprint:
     University Publications of America, Washington DC, 1977. Original editions: *L'Etat
     mental des hystériques: Les stigmates mentaux*. Paris: Rueff & Cie., 1893, and *L'Etat
     mental des hystériques: Les accidents mentaux*. Paris: Rueff & Cie., 1894.
Janet, P. (1904). L'Amnésie et la dissociation des souvenirs par l'émotion. *Journal de
     Psychologie*, 1, 417-453.
Janet, P. (1907). *Major symptoms of hysteria*. London: Macmillan. Reprint: Hafner,
     New York, 1965.
Janet, P. (1909). *Les névroses*. Paris: Flammarion.
Janet, P. (1911). *L' Etat mental des hystériques*, 2nd extended edition. Paris: Félix Alcan.
     Reprint: Lafitte Reprints, Marseille, 1983.
Janet, P. (1928). *L'Evolution de la mémoire et de la notion du temps*. Paris: A. Chahine.
Janet, P. (1932). Les croyances et les hallucinations. *Revue Philosophique*, 113, 278-331.
Kihlstrom, J.F. (1992). Dissociative and conversion disorders. In D.J. Stein & J.E.Young
     (eds.), *Cognitive science and clinical disorders* (pp. 248-270). San Diego: Academic
     Press.
Kihlstrom, J.F. (1994). One hundred years of hysteria. In S.J. Lynn & J.W. Rhue (eds.),
     Dissociation: Clinical and theoretical perspectives (pp. 365-394). New York: Guilford
     Press.
McDougall, W. (1926). *An outline of abnormal psychology*. London: Methuen.
Nemiah, J.C. (1974). Conversion: Fact or chimera? *International Journal of Psychiatry in
     Medicine*, 5, 443-448.
Nemiah, J.C. (1991). Dissociation, conversion, and somatization. In A. Tasman & S.M.
     Goldfinger (eds.), *American Psychiatric Press Annual Review of Psychiatry*. (Vol 10
     pp. 248-260). Washington DC: American Psychiatric Press.
Nijenhuis, E.R.S. (1990). Somatische equivalenten bij dissociatieve stoornissen [Somatic
     equivalents in dissociative disorders]. *Hypnotherapie*, 12, 139-142.
Nijenhuis, E.R.S. (1995). Dissociatie en leertheorie: trauma-geïnduceerde dissociatie als
     klassiek geconditioneerde defensie [Dissociation and learning theory: trauma-induced
     dissociation as classically conditioned defense]. In K. Jonker, J. Derksen, & F. Donker
     (eds.), *Dissociatie: een fenomeen opnieuw belicht [Dissociation: A phenomenon illuminated
     afresh]* (pp. 35-61). Houten: Bohn Stafleu Van Loghum.
Pribor, E.F., Yutzy, S.H., Dean, J.T., & Wetzel, R.D. (1993). Briquet's syndrome,
     dissociation, and abuse. *American Journal of Psychiatry*, 150, 1507-1511.
Ross, C.A., Heber, S., Norton, G.R., & Anderson, G. (1989). Somatic symptoms in
     multiple personality disorder. *Psychosomatics*, 30, 154-160.
Saxe, G.N., Chinman, G., Berkowitz, R., Hall, K., Lieberg, G., Schwartz, J., & van der
     Kolk, B.A. (1994). Somatization in patients with dissociative disorders. *American
     Journal of Psychiatry*, 151, 1329-1334.

Van der Hart, O., & Friedman, B. (1989). A reader's guide to Pierre Janet on dissociation: A neglected intellectual heritage. *Dissociation, 2*, 3-16.

Van der Hart, O., Witztum, E., & Friedman, B. (1993). From hysterical psychosis to reactive dissociative psychosis. *Journal of Traumatic Stress, 6*, 43-64.

Van der Hart, O., & Op den Velde, W. (1991). Traumatische stoornissen [Trauma-induced disorders]. In O. van der Hart (ed.), *Trauma, dissociatie en hypnose* [Trauma, dissociation and hypnosis] (pp. 71-90). Lisse: Swets & Zeitlinger.

Van der Kolk, B.A., & Van der Hart, O. (1991). The intrusive past: The flexibility of memory and the engraving of trauma. *American Imago, 48*, 425-454.

Walker, E.A., Katon, W.J., Neraas, K., Jemelka, R.P., & Massoth, D. (1992). Dissociation in women with chronic pelvic pain. *American Journal of Psychiatry, 149*, 534-537.

WHO (1992). *The ICD-10 Classification of Mental and Behavioral Disorders. Clinical description and diagnostic guidelines.* Geneva: World Health Organization.

III
The Development and Psychometric Characteristics of the Somatoform Dissociation Questionnaire (SDQ-20) [*]

"... due to a retraction of the field of personal consciousness a certain number of elementary phenomena, sensations and images, cease to be perceived and appear suppressed by personal perception; the result is a tendency to a complete and permanent division of the personality, to the formation of several groups independent of each other; these systems of psychological factors alternate some in the wake of the others or coexist; in fine, this lack of synthesis favours the formation of certain parasitic ideas which develop completely and in isolation, protected against the control of the personal consciousness, and which manifest themselves by the most varied disturbance, apparently only physical."
Janet, 1893, pp. 527-528.

Introduction

Dissociative disorder patients, as a rule, have many somatic symptoms (Ross, Heber, Norton, & Anderson, 1989a; Saxe et al., 1994), and somatization disorder is a frequent and serious comorbid disorder among them (Saxe et al., 1994). According to 19th century (Janet, 1893, 1907) and contemporary clinical observations (Kihlstrom, 1992, 1994; Nemiah, 1991; Nijenhuis, 1990; Van der Hart & Op den Velde, 1991), these somatic symptoms may reflect somatoform dissociative phenomena. Research that systematically evaluates their presence in dissociative and other psychiatric patients is, however, lacking.

Janet's dissociation theory (1889/1973, 1893, 1901/1907; *cf.* Van der Hart and Friedman, 1989) postulates that parallel to a retraction of the field of consciousness, both somatoform and psychological components of experience, reactions and functions may be stored in memory and identity structures that are not integrated in the personality at large. Janet argued that dissociative

* This chapter has previously been published as: Nijenhuis, E.R.S., Spinhoven, P., Van Dyck, R., Van der Hart, O., & Vanderlinden, J. (1996). The development and psychometric characteristics of the Somatoform Dissociation Questionnaire (SDQ-20). *The Journal of Nervous and Mental Disease, 184*, 688-694. The study was supported by a grant of the Stichting Dienstbetoon Gezondheidszorg, Soesterberg, Netherlands, number 11.92.

disorders, at the time subsumed under the label "hysteria," are predominantly characterized by the presence of "mental stigmata" and "mental accidents," which pertain to both psychological and somatoform dissociative phenomena. He considered the mental stigmata as symptoms that are essential of hysteria (Janet, 1893). These permanent symptoms all involve losses of perceptions and of control over functions, and, thus, seem to reflect negative dissociative symptoms, as we propose to call them. They include several kinds of anesthesia (loss of proprioceptual, visual, auditive, gustatory, and olfactory perception), amnesia (loss of the capacity to retrieve stored knowledge), loss of control over motor responses, abulia (loss of will-power), and state-dependent restriction of the range of emotional experiences and expressions. According to Janet (1901/1977, 1907/1965), the mental accidents as generic phenomena are evenly characteristic of hysteria, but they are transient, or at most, periodical, and their specific expressions vary. Mental accidents intermittently intrude or even interrupt the apparently normal state of consciousness, memory, and identity, and, thus, may be said to reflect positive dissociative symptoms, as we propose to call them. They pertain to reactivations of fixed ideas, somnambulistic states, and deliriums. Janet stated (1901/1977, 1907/1965) that fixed ideas, as a rule, constitute state-dependent traumatic, or trauma-associated responses, which upon their reactivation may intrude normal consciousness (partial dissociation). They may involve somatoform reactions: for example, localized pain, a particular movement, some smell, or taste. In a somnambulistic state, a dissociated part of the personality has taken full control over behavior and consciousness; somnambulism, thus, refers to a full dissociative state switch (Putnam, 1988). In contrast to fixed ideas, these dissociative states are more intellectually developed and adaptive to their surroundings. They tend to encompass a complex system of fixed ideas, including various somatoform responses, which, apart from taking full control, may also intrude into and, thus, influence other dissociated states and the normal state. In a delirium, or hysterical psychosis, or reactive dissociative psychosis, as Van der Hart, Witzum, and Friedman (1993) state, perception, consciousness and behavior are fully controlled for an extended period of time by a dissociated state that is completely dominated by one or more fixed ideas and has almost lost all sense of reality. For example, in a reactive dissociative psychotic state, which lasted for approximately 2 weeks, a patient was completely dominated by the idea of being an assaulted little girl and was only able to walk in the way her handicapped and sexually abusive grandfather had. In this state, she was fully unable to adapt her conduct to the actual environment (Nijenhuis, 1995b). Janet, thus, maintained that dissociation, which he regarded as a mental characteristic, affects both mind and body.

Most items of self-reporting questionnaires that measure psychological dissociative phenomena (Dissociative Experiences Scale [DES]; Bernstein & Putnam, 1986; Dissociation Questionnaire [DIS-Q]; Vanderlinden, Van Dyck, Vandereycken, Vertommen, & Verkes, 1993) and structured clinical interviews for *DSM-IV* dissociative disorders (Dissociative Disorders Interview Schedule [DDIS]; Ross, Heber, Norton, Anderson, & Barchet, 1989b; Structured Clinical Interview for *DSM-IV* Dissociative Disorders [SCID-D]; Steinberg, 1993; Steinberg, Cichetti, Buchanon, Hall, & Rounsaville, 1993) indeed refer to negative and positive symptoms. For example, the factor structure of the DIS-Q (Vanderlinden et al., 1993), consists of four factors that were interpreted as loss of control, amnesia (most items of both subscales pertain to losses, e.g., inaccessability of autobiographical information), identity confusion and fragmentation (most items refer to intrusion phenomena, e.g., the idea of being influenced by someone else inside), and absorption (some items refer to intrusion phenomena, e.g., reliving former experiences). We are not aware of instruments that measure somatoform dissociation.

If psychological and somatoform dissociative symptoms predominantly characterize dissociative disorders, both mental stigmata (negative dissociative symptoms) and mental accidents (positive dissociative symptoms) should be as highly prevalent in contemporary cases as they were in 19th century patients. Also, these symptoms should be far less common in patients with other psychiatric disorders. Further, if psychological and somatoform dissociative symptoms stem from a common mental process, but represent phenomenologically different aspects of that process, they should be highly related but not identical phenomena.

This study was performed to construct a somatoform dissociation questionnaire. The dimensional structure and reliability of the somatoform dissociative items that best discriminate between dissociative disorder patients and controls were assessed. A further aim was to establish the construct validity of the somatoform dissociation questionnaire: convergent validity was studied by analyzing the association between somatoform dissociation questionnaire scores and scores on a scale of psychological dissociation (DIS-Q), whereas criterion-related validity was studied by comparing somatoform dissociation questionnaire scores of dissociative identity disorder (DID) patients versus cases of dissociative disorder not otherwise specified (DDNOS) or depersonalization disorder (DP). Because DID is a more complex dissociative disorder than DDNOS and DP, the somatoform dissociation questionnaire scores of DID patients should exceed those of patients with DDNOS or DP.

Methods

Instrument Development

A pool of 77 items was formulated based on clinically observed manifestations of somatoform dissociation, defined as dissociative state-dependent somatoform responses that in clinical settings had appeared upon reactivation of particular dissociative states and that could not be medically explained. The items, which pertained to negative and positive phenomena, were supplied with a Likert-type 5-point scale. To evaluate face-validity, the items were submitted to six clinicians experienced in dealing with dissociative disorders. An item was included if four to six experts judged that it possibly reflected a somatoform dissociative symptom. As a result, two items were removed.

Subjects and Procedure

Psychiatric outpatients suspected to suffer from a dissociative disorder were interviewed by experienced clinicians using the SCID-D (Steinberg, 1993; Steinberg et al., 1993). All were trained in the administration and interpretation of the instrument. Fifty patients who presented with a dissociative disorder were selected (21 with DDNOS, 27 with DID, and 2 with DP). The mean age of this group (44 women and 6 men) was 34.8 (SD = 9.7 years; range 20 to 57).

The comparison group consisted of 50 psychiatric outpatients with other *DSM-IV* diagnoses (American Psychiatric Association, 1994) who scored < 2.5 on the DIS-Q (Vanderlinden, 1993, Vanderlinden et al., 1993). Diagnoses included axis I anxiety disorders (social and specific phobia, panic disorder with and without agoraphobia, obsessive compulsive disorder and posttraumatic stress disorder; n = 29), depressive disorder (n = 5), eating disorders (n = 8), hypochondriasis (n = 1), body dysmorphic disorder (n = 1), conversion disorder (n = 1), adjustment disorder (n = 5), and alcohol abuse (n = 3). Some patients presented with other conditions described in *DSM-IV* that warranted clinical attention: bereavement (n = 2), problems of relationship (n = 2) and phase of life problems (n = 1). Axis II diagnoses included borderline personality disorder (n = 2), narcissistic personality disorder (n = 1), dependent personality disorder (n = 2), and personality disorder nos (n = 1). Twenty-six patients displayed traits of personality disorder, predominantly dependent personality disorder. The mean age of the comparison group (39 women and 11 men) was 34.7 (SD = 12.7 years; range 16 to 79).

Informed consent was obtained from all subjects involved in the study.

Instruments

The SCID-D (Steinberg, 1993; Steinberg et al., 1993) is a diagnostic instrument developed for the assessment of dissociative disorders. It covers five dissociative symptom areas (amnesia, depersonalization, derealization, identity confusion, and identity fragmentation). Severity ratings of the symptom areas range from 1 to 4 (absent to severe). The total score ranges from 5 to 20. Good to excellent reliability and validity have been reported both in the United States and in The Netherlands (Boon and Draijer, 1993; Steinberg, 1993; Steinberg et al, 1990; Steinberg et al., 1993).

The DIS-Q (Vanderlinden, 1993; Vanderlinden et al., 1993) is a 63-item self-reporting questionnaire that measures psychological dissociation. The scale consists of four empirically derived factors labeled identity confusion and fragmentation, loss of control, amnesia, and absorption. The DIS-Q reliability rates are good to excellent, scores are stable over time, and the DIS-Q differentiates between patients with dissociative disorders and normals and psychiatric subjects with other diagnoses (Vanderlinden, 1993). The DIS-Q highly correlates with another self-reporting dissociation questionnaire, the DES (Bernstein and Putnam, 1986). Scores range from 1.0 to 5.0. The mean score of DID patients is 3.5 (SD = 0.4), and of DDNOS patients 2.9 (SD = 0.6). A cutoff score of 2.5

has been advised for purposes of case-selection of patients with a dissociative disorder (Vanderlinden, 1993).

Data Analysis

The 75 symptoms of the original item pool were entered in separate logistic regression analyses (p to enter < .05) to evaluate their ability to discriminate between dissociative disorder patients (DD) and comparison patients. Next, the predicted probabilities of caseness were compared to observed outcomes and the ratio between predicted caseness (PC) in both groups was calculated as a discriminant index (DI) using the formula:

$$DI = \frac{PC / N_{\text{Dissociative Disorder Patients}}}{PC / N_{\text{Comparison Patients}}}$$

Symptoms with a discriminant index of ≥ 4.0 were selected for further analysis. However, items that were gender-specific ($n = 8$) or related to particular characteristics that did not apply to all subjects (wearing visual correctives, use of medication and alcohol; $n = 6$) were excluded a priori. A nonparametric Mokken scale analysis for polytomous items was used to evaluate scalability on an unidimensional latent scale (Loevinger's general scalability coefficient H and the scalability coefficient for individual items $H_g ≥ 0.40$ and $p < .05$). The model assumptions of monotone homogeneity and double monotonicity of the scalable items were evaluated, and the reliability of the resulting Somatoform Dissociation Questionnaire (SDQ) scale was assessed.

The association of SDQ-20 scores with biographical variables was assessed with t-tests for independent samples (gender) and Pearson product-moment correlation coefficients (age) for dissociative disorder and comparison patients separately. Pearson correlation coefficients were also employed to evaluate the interrelatedness of SDQ-20 scores with total and subscale scores on the DIS-Q. Considering the absence of a normal distribution, as indicated by the sizable differences of standard deviations, differences on the SDQ-20 between SCID-D dissociative disorder cases and comparison patients, as well as cases of DID versus cases of DDNOS or DP were analyzed with Mann-Whitney U test for independent samples.

Statistical analyses were performed with SPSS-PC 6.0 (SPSS INC., 1993) and Mokken Scale analysis for Polytomous items (Molenaar, Debets, Sytsma, & Hemker, 1994).

Results

The discriminant indices of all 75 items analyzed, and p-values of B between dissociative disorder patients ($n = 50$) and comparison patients ($n = 50$) are shown in Appendices A (items interpreted to reflect negative somatoform dissociative symptoms) and B (positive somatoform dissociative symptoms).

Table 1 Somatoform Dissociative Symptoms of Dissociative Disorder Patients and Comparison Patients with Discriminant Indices ≥ 4.0

Symptom	Dissociative disorder patients (n = 50)		Comparison patients (n = 50)		Discriminant indices
	M*	SD	M*	SD	
It sometimes happens that:					
it is as if my body, or a part of it, has disappeared	2.5	1.5	1.0	.14	30
I am paralysed for a while	1.9	1.2	1.1	.6	24
I cannot speak (or merely with great effort) or I can only whisper	2.6	1.4	1.1	0.6	12.3
my body, or a part of it, is insensitive to pain	2.9	1.5	1.1	.5	12
I have pain while urinating	1.9	1.2	1.0	.2	12
I cannot see for a while (as if I am blind)	1.9	1.3	1.1	.4	10.5
I have trouble urinating	2.2	1.3	1.1	.5	9.3
I cannot hear for a while (as if I am deaf)	2.5	1.3	1.1	.5	9
I hear sounds from nearby as if they come from far away	2.7	1.3	1.2	.5	7.6
I grow stiff for a while	2.7	1.4	1.3	1.0	7.4
I do not have a cold but yet am able to smell much better or worse than I usually do	1.9	1.3	1.1	.3	7
I feel pain in my genitals (apart from sexual intercourse)	2.6	1.4	1.1	.5	6.8
I have an attack that resembles an epileptic fit	1.5	1.1	1.0	.2	6.5
I dislike smells that I usually like	2.0	1.2	1.1	.4	6.2
I dislike tastes that I usually like (women: apart from pregnancy or monthly periods)	2.1	1.2	1.1	.4	6.2
I see things around me differently than usual (for example as if looking through a tunnel, or seeing merely a part of an object)	2.8	1.4	1.2	.5	5.1
I cannot sleep for nights on end, but remain very active during daytime	2.9	1.5	1.5	.9	4.7
I can not swallow, or only with great effort	3.1	1.5	1.5	1.0	4.6
people and things look bigger than they actually are	2.4	1.5	1.1	.3	4.5
my body, or a part of it, feels numb	3.1	1.2	1.6	.9	4.4

* Range of mean scores is 1 (not applicable) – 5 (highly applicable).

These differences reached significance for 66 items. Table 1 presents the univariate associations of the 20 symptoms to caseness significant at $p < .05$ and with a discriminant index of 4.0 or higher. These items were selected for further analysis.

Mokken scale analysis showed that the 20 items were strongly scalable (H = .50). Items met assumptions of monotone homogeneity and double monotonicity. The reliability of the 20-item scale was excellent (Cronbach's α = .95).

Men (n = 11) and women (n = 39) without a dissociative disorder did not reach significantly different SDQ-20 total scores (range of possible scores, 20 to 100; mean for men 23.8 [SD = 3.0]; for women 23.4 [SD = 4.2], t-test: ns), nor did men (n = 6) and women (n = 44) with such a disorder (men 40.8 [SD = 11.0]; women 49.1 [SD = 15.6]; t-test: ns). Using all 100 subjects, Pearson correlation coefficients between the SDQ-20 total score and age (r = -.027) proved not significant.

Criterion-related validity was demonstrated by the fact that, as computed with Mann-Whitney U test, the SDQ-20 score strongly discriminates between dissociative disorder patients (48.14, SD = 15.24) and comparison patients (23.5, SD = 3.97; z = -8.24, $p < .0001$; see Table 2) as computed with Mann-Whitney U-test. Patients with DID (51.81, SD = 12.63) reached significantly higher SDQ-20 scores than patients with DDNOS or DP (43.83, SD = 7.11; Mann-Whitney U test, z = -2.17, $p < .05$).

Table 2

Intercorrelations between Somatoform (SDQ-20) and Psychological Dissociation (DIS-Q) of Dissociative Disorder Patients (n = 50) and Comparison Psychiatric Patients (n = 50)*

	SDQ-20
DIS-Q total	.76
DIS-Q identity-confusion/identity fragmentation	.73
DIS-Q loss of control	.70
DIS-Q amnesia	.71
DIS-Q absorption	.46

* All p-values = <.0001

The intercorrelations between the SDQ-20 score and the DIS-Q total score as well as three of the four factor scores were high (.71 < r < .76, $p < .0001$). The intercorrelation with the absorption scale was more moderate (r = .46, $p < .0001$). Overall, these data support the convergent validity of the SDQ-20.

Discussion

The present results confirm the findings of 19th century French psychiatrists (Briquet, 1859; Janet, 1893) and more recent studies (Ross et al, 1989a; Saxe et al., 1994) which found that dissociative disorder patients suffer from a wide range of somatoform symptoms. It seems, however, that some of them are more characteristic of dissociative disorder than others. It is striking that most of the SDQ-20 items pertain to negative and positive dissociative phenomena. The list contains several kinds of sensory losses, including analgesia ("my body, or a part of it, is insensitive to pain"), and kinesthetic anesthesia ("my body or a part of it feels numb;" "it is as if my body, or a part of it, has disappeared"). The phenomenon of "not being able to sleep during nighttime, but remaining very active during daytime" can be seen as an indirect measure of kinesthetic anesthesia, in that the subject lacks kinesthetic feedback that indicates tiredness. Anesthesia also applies to vision ("I cannot see for a while [as if I am blind]"; I see things differently than usual [for example, as if looking through a tunnel or only seeing a part of an object]) and audition ("I hear sounds from nearby as if they come from far away"). Other negative dissociative symptoms pertain to losses of motor control appearing as inhibitions: not being able to swallow, speak, or move. General paralysis and pseudo-epileptic fits seem to relate to far fetching losses of motor control. Several items refer to positive dissociative symptoms, which apply to alterations of vision, audition, taste, and smell, as well as to pain symptoms in the urogenital area, and difficulty urinating.

The selection of items that best discriminate dissociative disorder patients and patients with other psychiatric diagnoses seems to constitute a scale of sound psychometric quality. According to Mokken analysis, they are strongly scalable, and the reliability is high. The resulting scale was interpreted to measure somatoform dissociation, and we, therefore, named it the SDQ-20.

In support of the divergent validity of the SDQ-20, age and gender did not appear to influence the SDQ-20 scores of dissociative disorder and comparison patients. The sample contained few male dissociative disorder patients ($n = 6$), limiting the power of the contrast between males and females with dissociative disorder on the SDQ-20.

As hypothesized, the intercorrelations between the SDQ-20 and the DIS-Q total and subscales scores were high, a finding supporting the SDQ-20 convergent validity. The correlation with the DIS-Q absorption scale was more moderate. In a previous study (Vanderlinden et al., 1993) the intercorrelations between the DIS-Q absorption factor and total score, as well as the three other DIS-Q subscale scores, were also more moderate. It seems that the absorption scale is relatively less indicative of pathological dissociation than the other DIS-Q factors and the SDQ-20. In the same vein, none of the DES absorption subscale items (Ross, Joshi, & Currie, 1991a) entered the DES-T, an 8-item version of the DES (Bernstein and Putnam, 1986) that measures pathological dissociation (Waller, Putnam, & Carlson, 1996). The construct validity (criterion-related validity) of the SDQ-20 was further supported by the finding that patients with DID obtained higher scores than patients with DDNOS or DP.

As many of the symptoms the SDQ-20 items address previously were not generally known or recognized by the field at large as essential markers of complex dissociative disorders (cf. American Psychiatric Association, 1994), it seems unlikely that these phenomena are the result of suggestion by therapists. For example, few would have guessed that intermittent change of taste and smell preference, pain while urinating and not being able to speak and swallow would reach such high discrimination indices. Moreover, even if therapists had known of these facts, it seems equally unlikely that the therapists would have gone to any lengths to suggest all phenomena involved. As Janet (1893) put it, self-suggestion also seems a very crude interpretation of the systematic presence of quite specific somatoform phenomena in complex dissociative disorders. How could patients have gained the knowledge needed to perform this feat? Why would they unwittingly respond in most comparable ways to their 19th century companions in distress? Moreover, it seems hard to self-suggest those types of extensive and enduring analgesia and anesthesia, which are induced by the release of endogenous endorphins (Van der Kolk, 1994; Van der Kolk, Greenberg, Boyd, & Krystal, 1985). The phenomena of freezing, analgesia, and anesthesia are known outcomes of animal and human traumatization (cf. Fanselow and Lester, 1988; Nijenhuis, 1995a; Nijenhuis, Vanderlinden, & Spinhoven, in press; Siegfried et al., 1990; Van der Kolk, 1994; Van der Kolk & Greenberg, 1987; Van der Kolk, Greenberg, Orr, & Pitman, 1989). They often are present in posttraumatic stress disorder induced by validated trauma (Van der Kolk et al., 1989), whereas traumatic memories are very frequently present in dissociative disorder patients (Boon & Draijer, 1993; Hornstein & Putnam, 1992; Putnam, Guroff, Barban, & Post., 1986; Ross et al., 1991b). Hence, we postulate that a traumatogenetic interpretation of somatoform dissociative symptoms seems more adequate.

Future research with the SDQ-20 should include cross-validation of its dimensional structure and reliability with an independent sample of patients. Also, considering a traumatogenetic explanation of pathological somatoform dissociation, demonstration of a relationship between SDQ-20 scores and reported trauma would further strenghten the construct validity of the SDQ-20. Next, the relationship between somatoform and psychological dissociation warrants extended investigation. More specifically, study as to whether somatoform and psychological dissociation independently contribute to the prediction of caseness of dissociative disorder must be performed. To that end, it first should be studied whether a subset of SDQ-20 items could constitute a screening instrument for dissociative disorders.

References

American Psychiatric Association (1994). *Diagnostic and statistical manual of mental disorders, 4th edn. (DSM-IV).* Washington DC: Author.

Bernstein, E., & Putnam, F.W. (1986). Development, reliability, and validity of a dissociation scale. *Journal of Nervous Mental Disease, 102,* 280-286.

Boon, S., & Draijer, N. (1993). *Multiple personality disorder in the Netherlands: A study on reliability and validity of the diagnosis.* Amsterdam/Lisse: Swets & Zeitlinger.

Briquet, P. (1859). *Traité clinique et thérapeutique de l'hystérie* (2 vols.). [Clinical and therapeutic treatise of hysteria.] Paris. J.-P. Baillière & Fils.

Fanselow, M.S., & Lester, L.S. (1988). A functional behavioristic approach to aversively motivated behavior: Predatory imminence as a determinant of the topography of defensive behavior. In R.C. Bolles & M.D. Beecher (eds.), Evolution and learning (pp. 185-212). Hillsdale NJ: Lawrence Erlbaum Associates.

Hornstein, N.L. & Putnam, F.W. (1992). Clinical phenomenology of child and adolescent disorders. *Journal of the American Academy of Child and Adolescent Psychiatry 31*, 1077-1085.

Janet, P. (1889). *L'Automatisme psychologique.* [Psychological automatism.] Paris, Félix Alcan. Reprint: Société Pierre Janet, Paris: 1973.

Janet, P. (1893). *L'Etat mental des hystériques: Les stigmates mentaux.* [The mental state of hystericals: The mental stigmata.] Paris: Rueff & Cie.

Janet, P. (1901). *The mental state of hystericals: A study of mental stigmata and mental accidents.* New York: Putnam. Translation into English of *L'Etat mental des hystériques: Les stigmates mentaux,* which also contains an additional part on mental accidents: The mental state of hystericals. A study of mental stigmata and mental accidents. New York: Putnam, 1901. Reprint University Publications of America, 1977.

Janet, P. (1907). *The major symptoms of hysteria.* London/New York: Macmillan. Reprint of second edition Hafner: New York, 1965.

Kihlstrom, J.F. (1992). Dissociative and conversion disorders. In D.J. Stein & J. Young (eds.), *Cognitive science and clinical disorders* (pp. 247-270). San Diego/New York: Academic Press.

Kihlstrom, J.F. (1994). One hundred years of hysteria. In S.J. Lynn & J.W. Rhue (eds.), *Dissociation: Clinical and theoretical perspectives* (pp. 365-395). New York: Guilford.

Molenaar, I.W., Debets, P., Sytsma, K., & Hemker, B.T. (1994). *User's manual MSP. A program for Mokken Scale analysis for polytomous items. Version 3.0.* Groningen: iec ProGAMMA.

Myers, C.S. (1940). *Shell shock in France 1914-18.* Cambridge: Cambridge Unversity Press.

Nemiah, J.C. (1991). Dissociation, conversion, and somatization. In A. Tasman & S.M. Goldfinger (eds.), *American Psychiatric Press Annual Review of Psychiatry* (Vol 10, pp. 248-260). Washington, DC: American Psychiatric Press.

Nijenhuis, E.R.S. (1990). Somatische equivalenten bij dissociatieve stoornissen [Somatic equivalents of dissociative disorders], *Hypnotherapie, 12,* 4, 10-21.

Nijenhuis, E.R.S. (1995a). Dissociatieve stoornissen als gevolg van incest [Dissociative disorders as a consequence of incest]. In H. Baartman (ed.), *Op gebaande paden. Tien jaar incesthulpverlening in Nederland en Vlaanderen* [On paved roads: Ten years of incest-assistance in the Netherlands and Flanders] (pp. 61-85). Utrecht: SWP.

Nijenhuis, E.R.S. (1995b). Dissociatie en leertheorie: Trauma geïnduceerde dissociatie als klassiek geconditioneerde defensie [Dissociation and learning theory: Trauma-induced dissociation as classically conditioned defense]. In K. Jonker, J.J.L. Derksen, & F.J.S. Donker (eds.), *Dissociatie: een fenomeen opnieuw belicht* [Dissociation: A phenomenon illuminated afresh] (pp. 35-60). Houten: Bohn Stafleu Van Loghum.

Nijenhuis, E.R.S., Vanderlinden, J., Spinhoven, P. (in press). Animal defensive reactions as a model for trauma-induced dissociative reactions. *Journal of Traumatic Stress, 11,*243-260.

Prince, M. (1924). *The unconsciousness.* New York: MacMillan.

Putnam, F.W. (1988). The switch process in multiple personality disorder. *Dissociation, 1,* 24-33.

Putnam, F.W., Guroff, J.J., Silberman, E.K., Barban, L., & Post, R.M. (1986). The clinical phenomenology of multiple personality disorder. *Journal of Clinical Psychiatry, 47,* 285-293.

Ross, C.A., Heber, S., Norton, G.R., & Anderson, G. (1989a). Somatic symptoms in multiple personality disorder. *Psychosomatics, 30,* 154-160.

Ross, C.A., Heber, S., Norton, G.R., Anderson, G., & Barchet, P. (1989b). The Dissociative Disorder Interview Schedule: A structured interview. *Dissociation, 2,* 169-189.

Ross, C.A., Miller, S.D., Bjornson, M.A., Reagor, P., Fraser, G.A., & Anderson, G. (1991). Abuse histories in 102 cases of multiple personality disorder. *Canadian Journal of Psychiatry, 36,* 97-102.

Ross, C.A., Joshi, S., & Currie, R. (1991). Dissociative experiences in the general population: A factor analysis. *Hospital and Community Psychiatry, 42,* 297-301.

Saxe, G.N., Chinman, G., Berkowitz, M.D., Hall, K., Lieberg, G., Schwartz J. & Van der Kolk, B.A. (1994). Somatization in patients with dissociative disorders. *American Journal of Psychiatry, 151,* 1329-1334.

Siegfried, B., Frischknecht, H.R., & Nunez de Souza, R. (1990). An ethological model for the study of activation and interaction of pain, memory, and defensive systems in the attacked mouse: Role of endogenous opioids. *Neuroscience and Biobehavioral Reviews, 14,* 481-490.

SPSS PC: SPSS Inc/M.J. Norušis (1993). SPSS for Windows Release 6.0. Chicago: SPSS Inc.

Steinberg, M. (1993). *Structured Clinical Interview for DSM-IV Dissociative Disorders (SCID-D).* Washington DC: American Psychiatric Press.

Steinberg, M., Rounsaville, B.J., & Cichetti, D.V. (1990). The Structured Clinical Interview for DSM-III-R Dissociative Disorders: Preliminary report on a new diagnostic instrument. *American Journal of Psychiatry, 147,* 76-82.

Steinberg, M., Cichetti, D.V., Buchanan, J., Hall, P., & Rounsaville, B. (1993). Clinical assessment of dissociative symptoms and disorders: The Structured Clinical Interview for DSM-IV Dissociative Disorders. *Dissociation, 6,* 3-16.

Van der Hart, O., & Friedman, B. (1989). A reader's guide to Pierre Janet on dissociation: A neglected intellectual heritage. *Dissociation, 2,* 1, 3-16.

Van der Hart, O., & Op den Velde, W. (1991). Traumatische herinneringen [Traumatic memories]. In O. Van der Hart (ed.), *Trauma, dissociatie en hypnose* [Trauma, dissociation, and hypnosis] (pp. 91-125). Amsterdam/Lisse: Swets & Zeitlinger.

Van der Hart, O., Witzum, E., & Friedman, B. (1993). From hysterical psychosis to reactive dissociative psychosis. *Journal of Traumatic Stress, 6,* 1, 43-65.

Van der Kolk, B.A. (1994). The body keeps the score: Memory and the evolving of posttraumatic stress. *Harvard Review of Psychiatry, 1,* 253-265.

Van der Kolk, B.A., Greenberg, M.S., Boyd, H., & Krystal, J. (1985). Inescapable shock, neurotransmitters and addiction to trauma: Towards a psychobiology of posttraumatic stress. *Biological Psychiatry, 20,* 314-325.

Van der Kolk, B.A., & Greenberg, M.S. (1987). The psychobiology of the trauma response: hyperarousal, constriction, and addiction to traumatic reexposure. In B.A. Van der Kolk (ed.), *Psychological Trauma* (pp. 63-89). Washington: American Psychiatric Press.

Van der Kolk, B.A., Greenberg, M.S., Orr, S.P., & Pitman, R.K. (1989). Endogenous opioids, stress induced analgesia, and posttraumatic stress disorder. *Psychopharmacalogy Bulletin, 25,* 417-422.

Vanderlinden, J. (1993). *Dissociative experiences, trauma, and hypnosis: Research findings and clinical applications in eating disorders.* Delft: Eburon.

Vanderlinden, J., Van Dyck, R., Vandereycken, W., Vertommen, H., & Verkes, R.J. (1993). The Dissociation Questionnaire: Development and characteristics of a new self-reporting questionnaire. *Clinical Psychology and Psychotherapy, 1,* 21-27.

Waller, N.G., Putnam, F.W., & Carlson, E.B. (1995). Types of dissociation and
    dissociative types: A taxometric analysis of dissociative experiences. *Psychological
    Methods, 1*, 300-321.

Appendix A

Negative Somatoform Dissociative Phenomena of Dissociative Disorder (n = 50) and Comparison Psychiatric Patients (n = 50): p-Values of B and Discriminant Indices

	p-Value of B*	Discriminant Index
Motor inhibitions/loss of motor control		
General paralysis	.0033	25.3
Inability/difficulty speaking	< .0001	12.3
Stiffening of the body	< .0001	7.2
Inability/difficulty swallowing	< .0001	4.6
Inability/difficulty walking	.0001	3.1
Inability/difficulty writing	< .0001	3.6
General cramp states of body parts	< .0001	3.1
Immovability of extremities	.0003	2.7
Kinesthetic anesthesia/analgesia		
Body (or parts of it) missing	.0034	20.0
Analgesia	< .0001	12.0
Numbing	< .0001	4.4
Visual anesthesia/perceptual alteration		
(Intermittent) blindness	.0039	10.5
Restriction of visual field	< .0001	5.1
Variable visual acuity	< .0001	3.7
Blurred vision	.0002	2.2
Auditive anesthesia		
(Intermittent) deafness	< .0001	9.0
Auditive distancing	< .0001	7.6
Intermittent reduced acuity	< .0001	2.3
Olfactory alteration		
Change in acuity	.0021	6.0
Gustatory alteration		
Change in acuity	.0030	3.0
Loss of function		
Difficulty urinating	.0002	9.3
Pseudo-epileptic attacks	.0293	6.5
Inexplicable tiredness	< .0001	3.8
Loss of appetite and inability to eat	< .0001	2.5
Impotency	*ns*	-

* Separate logistic regression analysis

Appendix B
Positive Somatoform Dissociative Phenomena of Dissociative Disorder Patients (n = 50) and
Comparison Psychiatric Patients (n = 50): p-Values of B and Discriminant Indices

	p-Value of B	Discriminant Index
Pain symptoms		
Pain while urinating	.0009	12
Genital pain apart from intercourse	< .0001	6.9
Vaginal or penal pain during or after intercourse	.0005	4.4
(results of two gender-specific items combined)		
Extremely heavy menstrual pain	.0012	3.8
Rapidly intermitting joint-pain	.0001	3.7
Pelvic pain (apart from menstruation)	< .0001	3.0
Inexplicable pain symptoms	< .0001	3.0
Rapidly intermitting stomachache	< .0001	3.0
Rapidly intermitting headache	< .0001	2.8
Stomachache	.0009	2.5
Intermittent back-pain	.0002	2.5
Joint-pain	< .0001	2.4
Headache	.0001	2.2
Localized headache	.0004	1.9
Tension headache	.0009	1.7
Migraine-type headache	.0016	1.6
Back-pain	.0035	1.6
Anal pain/cramps with intercourse	ns	-
Movement		
Uncontrollable movements (trembling/shaking)	< .0001	3.9
Vision		
Enlargement of the perceived	.0002	4.5
Shrinkage of the perceived	< .0001	3.9
Double vision	.0002	3.3
Taste/smell alterations		
Intermittent change of smell-preference	.0004	6.2
Intermittent dislike of preferred tastes		
(apart from pregnancy or menstruation period)	.0003	6.1
Intermittent attraction to otherwise disliked tastes		
(apart from pregnancy or menstruation period)	ns	-
Intermittent attraction to otherwise disliked smell	ns	-

	p-Value of B	Discriminant Index
Gastro-intestinal symptoms		
Vomiting	.0001	2.9
Sickness	.0001	2.5
Stomach-/intestinal cramps with diarrhoea	.0052	1.6
Vomiting during full pregnancy-period	.0388	1.3
Other functions		
Uncontrolled (bulimia type) eating	.0002	2.9
Irregular menstruation	.0001	2.7
Extremely heavy menstruation	.0124	2.3
Intermittent skin allergy	.0002	2.0
Intermittent food allergy	ns	-
Interrupted menstruation	ns	-
Other state-dependent responses		
High level of activity notwithstanding chronic lack of sleep	< .0001	4.7
Affective state-dependent responses to medication	.0031	3.0
Impredictable responses to alcohol (apart from having eaten or not)	.0014	2.6
Variable responses to medication	.0005	2.4
Impredictable response to medication	.0118	2.0
Variable responses to alcohol	.0022	1.9
Without exertion		
Variable levels of blood pressure	.0388	3.0
Fainting	.0276	2.9
Dizzyness	.0001	2.4
Palpitations	.0108	2.1
Headache	.0047	2.1
Hyperventilation	ns	-
Shortness of breath	ns	-

* Separate logistic regression analysis.

IV

The Development of the Somatoform Dissociation Questionnaire (SDQ-5) as a Screening Instrument for Dissociative Disorders[*]

> *"Examination of recorded cases shows ...that besides mental memories, physiological functions may be involved in dissociation. Thus, there may be a loss of sensation in its various forms, and of the special senses, or the power of movement (paralysis), or visceral functions (gastric, sexual, etc.). Dissociation may, then, involve quite large parts of the personality, including very precise and definite physiological and psychological functions."*
> Prince, 1924, p. 548.

Introduction

In recent years a revival of the concept of dissociation has been evident (Van der Kolk & Van der Hart, 1989). However, this interest has largely been restricted to psychological manifestations of the phenomenon, e.g. dissociative amnesia, depersonalization, and fragmentation of identity. Janet's (1893) original observations and definition of the concept indicated that somatoform functions and reactions can also be subject to dissociation. In this context, Janet paid much attention to disturbances of the functions of sensation, movement, speech, vision, and hearing that frequently troubled his hysterical patients. Nevertheless, modern definitions of dissociative disorders generally lack reference to somatoform dissociation. For example, in the *Diagnostic and Statistical Manual of Mental Disorders fourth edition* (American Psychiatric Association, 1994), it is stated that the essential feature of these disorders is a disruption of the usually integrated functions of consciousness, memory, and identity, or perception of the environment. Yet in clinical practice it is observed that somatoform symptoms may relate to dissociated somatic reactions and functions (Kihlstrom, 1992, 1994;

* This chapter has previously appeared as: Nijenhuis, E.R.S., Spinhoven, P., Van Dyck, R., Van der Hart, O., & Vanderlinden, J. (1997). The development of the somatoform dissociation questionnaire (SDQ-5) in the screening for dissociative disorders. *Acta Psychiatrica Scandinavica, 96,* 311-318. The study was supported by a grant of the Stichting Dienstbetoon Gezondheidszorg, Soesterberg, The Netherlands. Grantnumber: LK 11.92.

Nemiah, 1991). Much like dissociated emotions and knowledge, somatic sensations, motor and other somatoform responses could be core aspects of dissociated memory/identity states. Dissociative disorder patients generally report many somatoform symptoms, and often satisfy the *DSM-IV* (American Psychiatric Association, 1994) criteria of somatization disorder and conversion disorder (Boon & Draijer, 1993; Pribor, Yutzy, Dean, & Wetzel, 1993; Ross, Heber, Norton, & Anderson, 1989; Saxe et al., 1994). Patients with somatization disorder tend to display amnesia (Othmer & DeSouza, 1985), which in *DSM-IV* (APA, 1994) is regarded as one of the markers of dissociative disorder.

The somatoform symptoms that now are categorized under the headings of somatoform disorder (*DSM-IV*; APA, 1994) or dissociative disorder (*International Classification of Diseases tenth edition;* World Health Organization, 1992) once received the label of *hysteria.* Janet regarded these somatoform symptoms as dissociative phenomena induced by psychological trauma, severe illness, or fatigue (Janet, 1893). Freud initially held that hysteria is induced by sexual trauma (Breuer & Freud, 1974), but he later became convinced that sexual fantasy and forbidden wish fulfilment are involved. He then regarded somatoform symptoms as the result of a process of conversion, that is, the transformation of an unacceptable idea into a somatic symptom. Other authors used the term *somatization* (Stekel, 1908). Since the beginning of this century several definitions of somatization have been proposed, but they generally refer to a postulated transformation of psychological problems into somatoform symptoms (Mayou, 1993). After World War I, the dissociative and conversion disorders were categorized together under the heading of *conversion hysteria* (Kihlstrom, 1992, 1994). With each new version of the *DSM* – the first version was edited in 1952 (APA, 1952) – the conversion, somatization, and dissociative disorders have been differently categorized. Sometimes they were joined (*hysterical neurosis: conversion type and dissociative type, DSM-II*) (APA, 1968), sometimes they were separated (*DSM-I* [APA, 1952], *DSM-III[-R]* [APA, 1980, 1987], *DSM-IV* [APA, 1994]: *somatoform* and *dissociative disorders*). The *DSM-IV* (1994) contains a section on somatoform disorders, which includes somatization disorder and conversion disorder. Although it is stated that somatization disorder may encompass dissociative symptoms (amnesia, which pertains to psychological dissociation, is mentioned as an example), and that conversion and dissociative symptoms may occur in the same individual, the somatoform symptoms are not described as dissociative symptoms. In contrast, the existence of somatoform dissociation is partly recognized in the ICD-10 (WHO, 1992), which includes dissociative disorders of movement and sensation (formerly conversion disorder) in the dissociative disorders. Thus, while in due course of psychiatric history relationships between dissociation, conversion, and somatization have been indicated or suggested, there is continuing lack of consensus regarding their status.

Current interest in psychological aspects of pathological dissociation is reflected in the contents of newly developed instruments that are designed to measure the phenomenon. They include self-reporting questionnaires, such as the *Dissociative Experiences Scale* (DES) (Bernstein & Putnam, 1986) and the

Dissociation Questionnaire (DIS-Q) (Vanderlinden, 1993), and clinical interviews, such as the *Structured Clinical Interview for DSM-IV Dissociative Disorders* (SCID-D; Steinberg, 1993; Steinberg, Cichetti, Buchanan, Hall, & Rounsaville, 1993). The questionnaires include items that pertain exclusively to psychological phenomena, and the SCID-D measures dissociative amnesia, depersonalization, derealization, identity confusion and identity fragmentation. These instruments are extremely helpful devices in psychiatric practice. However, dissociative disorder patients may deny or be unaware of psychological dissociative phenomena, and may be among the cases with unexplained somatic symptoms that are frequently encountered in general hospital outpatient clinics (Kellner, 1991; Mayou, 1993) and pain clinics (Keefe, Dunsmore, & Burnett, 1992). They probably are part of the relatively small group which uses disproportional and very considerable amounts of consultations, laboratory investigations, costly surgical procedures and other forms of hospital care over long periods of time (Kellner, 1990). For example, Saxe et al. (1994) found a strong correlation between somatization, dissociation, and number of medical hospitalizations and consultations. If, indeed, somatoform dissociative phenomena are among the markers of dissociative disorders, attempting to measure somatoform dissociation may help to identify dissociative disorders in patients who do not present with psychological dissociative phenomena, or who present in medical care with somatoform symptoms.

In conclusion, the primary aim of the present study was to develop a brief self-report instrument to detect these cases of pathological dissociation (Yates & Nasby, 1993). More specifically, the capacity of a short list of somatoform dissociation items to discriminate between dissociative disorder patients and those with other psychiatric diagnoses was assessed.

Material and Methods

Instrument Development

A pool of 77 items was formulated, based on clinically observed manifestations of somatoform dissociation in patients with a dissociative disorder. These manifestations were defined as physical symptoms suggesting a general medical condition that had appeared upon the reactivation of particular dissociative states, but that could not be explained by a known medical condition, or by the effects of a substance. Most of these dissociative state-dependent somatoform symptoms caused clinically significant distress or impairment in social, occupational, or other areas of functioning. The items were supplied with a Likert-type five-point scale. To evaluate face validity, the items were submitted to six clinicians experienced in dealing with dissociative disorders. An item was included if four of six experts judged that it possibly reflected a somatoform dissociative symptom. As a result, two items were removed. Items which were gender-specific ($n = 8$) or related to particular characteristics that did not apply to all subjects (wearing visual correctives, use of medication and alcohol; $n = 6$) were excluded from the analyses.

Subjects and Procedure

In phase I, psychiatric outpatients with a suspected dissociative disorder were interviewed by experienced clinicians using the SCID-D (Steinberg, 1993; Steinberg et al., 1993). All of the clinicians were trained in the administration and interpretation of the instrument. In total, 50 cases were collected that presented with a dissociative disorder (21 cases with DDNOS, 27 cases with DID, and 2 cases with depersonalization disorder). The mean age of this group (consisting of 44 women and 6 men) was 34.8 (SD = 9.7 years; range 20 to 57).

The comparison group consisted of a sample of 50 psychiatric outpatients who were receiving psychiatric treatment, predominantly behavior therapy, with a non-dissociative *DSM-IV* (APA, 1994) diagnosis, and who scored below the cutoff score (< 2.5) on the DIS-Q (Sainton, Ellason, & Ross, 1993; Vanderlinden, 1993). Diagnoses included Axis I anxiety disorders (n = 29) (social and specific phobia, panic disorder with and without agoraphobia, obsessive compulsive disorder and posttraumatic stress disorder), depressive disorder (n = 5), eating disorders (n = 8), hypochondriasis (n = 1), body dysmorphic disorder (n = 1), conversion disorder (n = 1), adjustment disorder (n = 5), and alcohol abuse (n = 3). Some patients presented with conditions described in *DSM-IV* that warranted clinical attention, namely bereavement (n = 2), relationship problems (n = 2) and phase-of-life problems (n = 1). Axis II diagnoses included borderline personality disorder (n = 2), narcissistic personality disorder (n = 1), dependent personality disorder (n = 2), and personality disorder NOS (n = 1). Signs of personality disorder were displayed by 26 patients, and predominantly included dependent personality disorder. The mean age of the comparison group (consisting of 39 women and 11 men) was 34.7 (SD = 12.7 years; range 16 to 79).

The patients with putative dissociative disorder completed the SDQ-items and the DIS-Q (described below), and were interviewed by their attending clinicians using the SCID-D as part of their clinical assessment. Informed consent for use of relevant data in the present study was obtained. The patients in the comparison group completed the self-report questionnaires after their informed consent had been obtained. It was explained to patients that completing the items would help clinicians to provide assistance to victims of disagreeable and/or painful events (that may be remembered with difficulty) more quickly and effectively.

Phase II included patients who would serve as an independent sample for cross-validation of the screening test. The sample consisted of a group of 33 patients (32 women and 1 man; mean age 32.7 (SD = 10.1 years; range 22 to 50) who, according to their attending psychotherapists or psychiatrists, all of whom are experts in the assessment and treatment of dissociative disorders, had a dissociative disorder. In total, 16 patients had been formally diagnosed with the SCID-D by their attending clinicians, and all of them completed the initial SDQ items and the DIS-Q. In addition, a group of 42 psychiatric outpatients who consecutively presented at a psychiatric outpatient department (24 women, 18 men; mean age 33.6 (SD = 14.0 years, range 18 to 62) completed the initial SDQ and the DIS-Q upon first contact. Checking of their records at a later stage revealed that none was assigned a *DSM-IV* dissociative disorder diagnosis. Therefore they could be used as comparison patients. Informed consent was obtained from all cross-validation group subjects.

Instruments

The *Structured Interview for DSM-IV Dissociative Disorders* (SCID-D; Steinberg, 1993; Steinberg et al., 1993) is a diagnostic instrument developed for the assessment of dissociative disorders. It covers five dissociative symptom areas (amnesia, depersonalization, derealization, identity confusion and identity fragmentation). Severity ratings of the symptom areas range from 1 to 4 (absent to severe). Good to excellent reliability and validity have been reported both in the USA and in The Netherlands (Boon & Draijer, 1993; Steinberg et al., 1993).

The Dissociation Questionnaire (DIS-Q) (Vanderlinden, 1993; Vanderlinden, Van Dyck, Vandereycken, Vertommen, & Verkes, 1993) is a 63-item self-report questionnaire measuring psychological dissociation. Four factors were extracted, and these were labeled identity confusion and fragmentation, loss of control, amnesia, and absorption. The DIS-Q reliability rates are good to excellent, the scores are stable over time and the DIS-Q differentiates between patients with dissociative disorders, normal subjects and psychiatric subjects with other diagnoses (Vanderlinden, 1993). As was found by Vanderlinden (1993) and Sainton et al. (1993), the DIS-Q correlates strongly with another self-report dissociation questionnaire, namely the DES (Bernstein & Putnam, 1986). Scores range from 1.0 to 5.0. The mean score of DID patients was 3.5 (*SD* = 0.4), and that of patients with DDNOS was 2.9 (*SD* = 0.6). A cutoff score of 2.5 has been suggested for purposes of case-selection of patients with a dissociative disorder (Vanderlinden, 1993).

Data Analysis

The 61 symptoms of the original item pool were entered into separate logistic regression analyses (*p* to enter < .05) in order to evaluate their ability to discriminate between patients with dissociative disorder and comparison patients. The predicted probabilities of caseness were then compared with the observed outcomes and the ratio between predicted caseness (PC) in both groups was calculated as a discriminant index (DI) using the formula:

$$DI = \frac{PC / N_{\text{Dissociative Disorder Patients}}}{PC / N_{\text{Comparison Patients}}}$$

Symptoms with a discriminant index of ≥ 4.0 were preselected for further analysis. These 20 items were entered in a stepwise logistic regression analysis using forward selection (*p* to enter < .05) and backward elimination (*p* to remove > .10) based on likelihood ratio estimates. In order to test the discriminant ability of the unweighted sum score of the final selection of items, a predicted probability of caseness was calculated for each individual using logistic regres-

Table 1 Somatoform Dissociative Symptoms of Patients with Dissociative Disorder and Comparison Patients with Discriminant Indices ≥ 4.0

Symptom	Dissociative disorder patients (n = 50)		Comparison Group (n = 50)		Discriminant Index
	M*	SD	M*	SD	
It sometimes happens that:					
It is as if my body, or a part of it, has disappeared**	2.5	1.5	1.0	0.1	30
I am paralysed for a while	1.9	1.2	1.1	0.6	24
I cannot speak (or merely with great effort) or I can only whisper**	2.6	1.4	1.1	0.6	12.3
My body, or a part of it, is insensitive to pain**	2.9	1.5	1.1	0.5	12
I have pain while urinating**	1.9	1.2	1.0	0.2	12
I cannot see for a while (as if I am blind)	1.9	1.3	1.1	0.4	10.5
I have trouble urinating	2.2	1.3	1.1	0.5	9.3
I cannot hear for a while (as if I am deaf)	2.5	1.3	1.1	0.5	9
I hear sounds from nearby as if they come from far away	2.7	1.3	1.2	0.5	7.6
I grow stiff for a while	2.7	1.4	1.3	1.0	7.4
I do not have a cold but yet have a much better or worse sense of smell than I usually do	1.9	1.3	1.1	0.3	7
I feel pain in my genitals (apart from sexual intercourse)	2.6	1.4	1.1	0.5	6.8
I have an attack that resembles an epileptic fit	1.5	1.1	1.0	0.2	6.5
I dislike smells that I usually like	2.0	1.2	1.1	0.4	6.2
I dislike tastes that I usually like (women: other than during pregnancy or menstrual periods)	2.1	1.2	1.1	0.4	6.2
I see things around me differently from normal (for example, as if looking through a tunnel, or seeing only a part of an object)**	2.8	1.4	1.2	0.5	5.1
I cannot sleep for nights on end, but remain very active during daytime	2.9	1.5	1.5	0.9	4.7
I cannot swallow, or only with great effort	3.1	1.5	1.5	1.0	4.6
People and things look bigger than they actually are	2.4	1.5	1.1	0.3	4.5
My body, or a part of it, feels numb	3.1	1.2	1.6	0.9	4.4

* Range of mean scores is 1 (not applicable) – 5 (highly applicable).

sion. The discriminant ability was expressed in terms of sensitivity and specificity of the score with regard to observed caseness. Thereafter, the sensitivity and specificity of the final selection of items using the same cutoff level was tested in an independent cross-validation sample. Statistical analyses were performed with SPSS-PC 6.0 (SPSS Inc., 1993).

Results

Table 1 presents the univariate associations of the 20 symptoms to caseness significant at $p < .05$ and with a discriminant index of ≥ 4.0. In the stepwise logistic regression analysis, these 20 items were evaluated for their independent contribution to a discrimination between dissociative disorder and comparison patients. The following five symptoms contributed independently to the discrimination between cases and non-cases: (i) having pain while urinating; (ii) experiencing insensivity to pain in the body, or a part of it; (iii) seeing things differently than usual (e.g., looking as if through a tunnel, or seeing merely a part of an object); (iv) noticing that one's body or a part of it seems to have disappeared; and (v) being unable to speak (or only able to speak with great effort), or only being able to whisper. The reliability of this five item Somatoform Dissociation Questionnaire (SDQ-5) was 0.80 (Cronbach's coefficient alpha).

Table 2

Sensitivity, Specificity, Predictive Values (All Expressed as Proportions) and Likelihood Ratios of the SDQ-5 at Essential Cutoff Scores Discriminating between Patients with DSM-IV Dissociative Disorder (n = 50) and Psychiatric Patients without a Dissociative Disorder (n=50)

Cutoff Score	Sensitivity	Specificity	Positive Predictive Value	Negative Predictive Value	Predictive Value Estimated at Prevalence of				Likelihood Ratio	
					10%		15%*			
					Pos.	Neg.	Pos.	Neg.	Pos.	Neg.
≥ 11	0.62	1.00	1.00	0.72	1.00	0.96	1.00	0.94	∞	0.4
≥ 10	0.74	0.98	0.97	0.79	0.80	0.97	0.87	0.95	37.0	0.3
≥ 9	0.82	0.96	0.95	0.84	0.69	0.98	0.78	0.96	20.5	0.2
≥ 8	0.94	0.96	0.96	0.94	0.72	0.99	0.81	0.99	23.5	0.1
≥ 7	0.96	0.88	0.89	0.96	0.39	0.99	0.58	0.99	8.0	0.0

* Since in another study (Draijer & Boon, 1993) an estimated dissociative disorder prevalence rate of 15% was included, for the sake of comparability we also provide data relevant to that percentage.

The diagnostic reliability of the predicted probability of caseness on the basis of the unweighted SDQ-5 sum score (range of possible scores 5 to 25) was first tested on the same data from which the model was derived ($OR = 4.05$; 95% $CI = 7.35 - 2.24$; $p < .0001$). Of the dissociative disorder patients, 94% (47/50) had a score > 7 (sensitivity), and of the comparison patients 96% (48/50) had a score of ≤ 7 (specificity) (Table 2). The positive predictive value was 96% (47/49) and the negative predictive value was 94% (48/51). The total percentage of correct classification was 95% (95/100). The corresponding values of the 20 item scale were somewhat more moderate, in particular the sensitivity, the positive predicitive value, and the positive likelihood ratio (Table 3).

Table 3

Sensitivity, Specificity, Predictive Values (All Expressed as Proportions) and Likelihood Ratios of the SDQ-20 Scores Discriminating between Patients with DSM-IV Dissociative Disorder (n = 50) and Psychiatric Patients without a Dissociative Disorder (n = 50), Calculated by Logistic Regression Analysis

Sensitivity	Specificity	Positive Predictive Value	Negative Predictive Value	Predictive Value Estimated at Prevalence				Likelihood Ratio	
				10%		15%*			
				Pos.	Neg.	Pos.	Neg.	Pos.	Neg.
0.88	0.94	0.94	0.89	0.62	0.97	0.70	0.96	14.7	0.2

* Since in another study (Draijer & Boon, 1993) an estimated dissociative disorder prevalence rate of 15% was included, for the sake of comparability we also provide data relevant to that percentage.

The level of specificity was reproduced in the cross-validation sample, but at a slightly higher cutoff point (Table 4). At a cutoff value of ≥ 8 it was 88% (37/42), and at a cutoff value of ≥ 9 it was 93% (39/42). The sensitivity at cutoff values of ≥ 8 and ≥ 9 was 82% (27/33).

Table 4

Sensitivity, Specificity, Predictive Values, and Likelihood Ratios of the SDQ-5 at Essential Cutoff scores Discriminating between Clinically Assessed Dissociative Disorder Patients (n = 33) and Consecutive Psychiatric Patients without a Dissociative Disorder (n = 42)

Cutoff Score	Sensitivity	Specificity	Positive Predictive Value	Negative Predictive Value	Predictive Value Estimated at Prevalence of				Likelihood Ratio	
					10%		15%*			
					Pos.	Neg.	Pos.	Neg.	Pos.	Neg.
≥ 11	0.51	1.00	1.00	0.72	1.00	0.95	1.00	0.92	∞	0.5
≥ 10	0.67	1.00	1.00	0.79	1.00	0.96	1.00	0.94	∞	0.3
≥ 9	0.82	0.93	0.9	0.87	0.57	0.98	0.67	0.97	11.7	0.2
≥ 8	0.82	0.88	0.84	0.86	0.43	0.98	0.55	0.97	6.8	0.2
≥ 7	0.91	0.76	0.75	0.91	0.3	0.99	0.38	0.98	4	0.1

Sensitivity, specificity, and predictive values are expressed as proportions.

* Since in another study (Draijer & Boon, 1993) an estimated dissociative disorder prevalence rate of 15% was included, for the sake of comparability we also provide calculations relevant to this percentage.

High sensitivity and specificity of a test do not yield high predictive power when the prevalence is low (Rey, Morris-Yates, & Stanislaw, 1992). The prevalence of dissociative disorders in a psychiatric population has been estimated to be about 15% (Horen, Leichner, & Lawson, 1995; Saxe et al., 1993). Little is known about the prevalence of dissociative symptoms in other psychiatric disorders. When corrected for prevalence conservatively estimated at 10%, at a cutoff value of ≥ 8, the positive predictive value was 72% and the negative predictive value was 99% in the original sample. Using the same cutoff in the cross-validation sample, these values were 43% and 99%, respectively.

Implications for Screening and Clinical Use of the SDQ-5

Screening of dissociative pathology in a random psychiatric population requires high sensitivity and a high positive predictive value, since it aims to select all patients who have the disorder being studied. The likelihood that unselected cases do not have the disorder should be maximal. According to the results of the samples studied, a cutoff score of ≥ 8 yields a sensitivity of 94% and a corrected positive predictive value of 72% at an estimated prevalence rate of 10%, meaning that 72% of the patients with positive scores can be expected to have a dissociative disorder. The likelihood ratio for disease at that value is 23.5. However, using the cross-validation sample, the positive predictive value was more modest (43%). As inspection of Tables 2 and 3 shows, based upon the present findings for case-finding purposes among psychiatric patients a cutoff score of ≥ 8 is to be recommended.

If one wishes to select cases that are very likely to have a dissociative disorder, the cutoff score should be raised further. However, as will be clear, doing this implies an increase in the number of cases that are missed. For example, at a cutoff score of ≥ 10 in the original and the cross-validation sample the sensitivity dropped to 74% and 67%, respectively. In both samples, at a cutoff score of ≥ 11 the positive predictive value reached 100%.

Discussion

The SDQ-5 discriminates with good to high sensitivity and specificity between dissociative and non-dissociative psychiatric outpatients, and its reliability was satisfactory. Because of the limited prevalence of dissociative disorders in the psychiatric population, the positive predictive value, corrected for prevalence, conservatively estimated at 10% in random psychiatric groups, decreases from 96% to 72% in the original sample, and to 43% in the cross-validation sample (at a cutoff score of ≥ 8). Compared with the positive predictive value of the DES, which at this prevalence rate and at the optimal cutoff score of 25 was 42% (Draijer & Boon, 1993), the SDQ-5 performs equally well. In both samples studied, the specificity of the SDQ (96%/88%) was also comparable to the specificity of the DES (86%). Patients with SDQ-scores above the cutoff value of ≥ 8 warrant further assessment with the SCID-D to eliminate false positives.

The SDQ-5 was derived from the 20 items which constitute the SDQ-20

(Nijenhuis, Spinhoven, Van Dyck, Van der Hart, & Vanderlinden, 1996). As is described by Nijenhuis et al. (1996), the SDQ-20 measures the dimensional construct of somatoform dissociation. The 20 items are strongly scalable on a latent unidimensional scale, the reliability of this SDQ-20 is very satisfactory (Cronbach's alpha = 0.94), and there is a strong intercorrelation with the DIS-Q. The sensitivity, positive predictive value, and positive likelihood ratio for disease of the SDQ-20, compared with the corresponding values of the SDQ-5, were more moderate. Since the SDQ-5 has the additional advantage of being very short, this instrument is suitable for use as a screening instrument for dissociative disorders.

The sensitivity and specificity of the SDQ-5 at a cutoff score of ≥ 8 were more modest in the cross-validation sample than in the original sample, and these results may have been influenced by several factors. All cases of dissociative disorder of the original sample, but only 16 of the 33 cases of the cross-validation sample, were interviewed using the SCID-D. Next, the comparison group of the original sample was obtained using the DIS-Q (cutoff score of 2.5) as a selection criterium, a criterium that was not used to select the cross-validation comparison group. Furthermore, the latter group included consecutive patients who completed the questionnaires during their first visit to a psychiatric outpatient department, whereas the comparison group of the original sample consisted of patients who were already receiving psychiatric treatment.

The items of the SDQ-5 pertain to those symptoms that, according to Janet (1893), characterized "hysteria", the diagnostic category that in former times indicated dissociative disorder. It seems that the 19th century hysterical symptoms are also characteristic of contemporary dissociative disorder patients. They include insensitivity to pain (analgesia), the sensation of disappearance of body or parts of it (kinesthetic anesthesia), retraction of the visual field (visual anesthesia), and difficulty in speaking or inability to speak (motor disturbance), as well as a specific symptom, that is, pain while urinating (probably related to sexual trauma). Janet related these symptoms to retraction of the field of consciousness of hysterical patients and to dissociation, that is, the lack of assimilation and synthesis of experiences and perceptions into personal consciousness (Janet, 1893). Thus dissociative patients are both characterized and identifiable by psychological and somatoform dissociation. Our findings support the early clinical notions regarding these disorders and suggest that, apart from psychological dissociative phenomena, somatoform dissociative symptoms constitute core symptoms in dissociative disorder.

The next stage of development of the SDQ-5 as a screening device for dissociative disorders will involve further validation. It has to be tested whether the SDQ-5 is able to identify cases of dissociative disorders among general hospital outpatients and inpatients with (un)explained somatic symptoms. Examples would be patients with epileptic and pseudo-epileptic seizures, organic and nonorganic pelvic pain, and other groups of pain patients.

It would also be important to study the extent to which the SDQ-5 selects *DSM-IV* somatization and conversion disorder patients with and without dissociative disorder. As dissociative disorder, somatization disorder (Briquet's syndrome) has its roots in hysteria. Briquet's 1859 study of hysteria revealed that his patients were suffering from amnesia, a psychological dissociative symptom, and an abundance of somatoform symptoms (Briquet, 1859). Recent studies also indicate that dissociation and somatization are very closely related. For example, Saxe et al. (1994) found that two-thirds of the patients who fulfilled the DSM-III-R (1987) criteria for a dissociative disorder also fulfilled the criteria for somatization disorder. Ross et al. (1989) found that 7 of 20 patients with DID met the criteria of somatization disorder, while only 1 of 20 eating disorder subjects, 2 of 20 panic disorder subjects, and none of 20 schizophrenics did so. Moreover, of the subjects who also had somatization disorder, those with DID had more somatoform symptoms than patients with other types of comorbidity. Saxe et al. (1993) estimated that approximately 8% of psychiatric patients fulfil the criteria for both dissociative disorder and somatization disorder. The somatoform symptoms studied by Ross et al. (1989) and Saxe et al. (1994) included several DSM-IV conversion symptoms.

Finally, it would be valuable to study the incremental validity of the SDQ-5 and other psychological screening devices such as the DIS-Q (Vanderlinden, 1993) and the DES (Bernstein & Putnam, 1986) with respect to each other. As has already been found, there may be a considerable overlap in the range of DES (Draijer & Boon, 1993) and DIS-Q (Vanderlinden, 1993) scores of patients with various types of dissociative disorder, as well as of patients with other diagnoses. However, it is conceivable that incremental validity depends on characteristics of particular subgroups of dissociative disorder, the setting in which the patient remains, the timing of assessment, and comorbidity.

References

American Psychiatric Association (1952). *Diagnostic and statistical manual of mental disorders*. Washington, DC: American Psychiatric Assocation.

American Psychiatric Association (1968). *Diagnostic and statistical manual of mental disorders, 2nd edn*. Washington, DC: American Psychiatric Association.

American Psychiatric Association (1980). *Diagnostic and statistical manual of mental disorders, 3rd edn*. Washington, DC: American Psychiatric Association.

American Psychiatric Association (1987). *Diagnostic and statistical manual of mental disorders, 3rd rev. edn*. Washington, DC: American Psychiatric Association.

American Psychiatric Association (1994). *Diagnostic and statistical manual of mental disorders, 4th edn*. Washington DC: American Psychiatric Association.

Bernstein, E., & Putnam, F.W. (1986). Development, reliability, and validity of a dissociation scale. *Journal of Nervous and Mental Disease, 102*, 280-286.

Boon, S., & Draijer, N. (1993). *Multiple personality disorder in the Netherlands. A study on reliability and validity of the diagnosis*. Amsterdam: Swets & Zeitlinger, 1993.

Breuer, J., & Freud, S. (1974). *Studies on hysteria*. Harmondsworth: Penguin Books.

Briquet, P. (1859). *Traité clinique et thérapeutique de l'hystérie* [Clinical and therapeutic treatise of hysteria]. Paris: J.-P. Baillière & Fils.

Draijer, N., & Boon, S. (1993). The validation of the Dissociative Experiences Scale against the criterion of the SCID-D, using receiver operating characteristics (ROC) analysis. *Dissociation, 6*, 28-38.

Horen, S.A., Leichner, P.P., & Lawson, J.S. (1995). Prevalence of dissociative symptoms and disorders in an adult psychiatric inpatient population in Canada. *Canadian Journal of Psychiatry, 40*, 185-91.

Janet, P. (1893). *L'Etat mental des hystériques: Les stigmates mentaux.* Paris: Rueff & Cie, 1893. Translated into English as: The mental state of hystericals: A study of mental stigmata and mental accidents. New York: Putnam, 1901.

Keefe, F.J., Dunsmore, J., & Burnett, R. (1992). Behavioral and cognitive-behavioral approaches to chronic pain: recent advances and future direction. *Journal of Consulting and Clinical Psychology, 60*, 528-536.

Kellner, R. (1991). *Psychosomatic syndromes and somatic symptoms.* Washington, DC: American Psychiatric Press.

Kellner, R. (1990). Somatization: the most costly comorbidity. In I.D. Maser & C.R. Cloninger (eds.), *Comorbidity of mood and anxiety disorders* (pp. 239-252). Washington, DC: American Psychiatric Press.

Kihlstrom, J.F. (1992). Dissociative and conversion disorders. In D.J. Stein & J. Young (eds.), *Cognitive science and clinical disorders* (pp. 247-270). New York: Academic Press.

Kihlstrom, J.F. (1994). One hundred years of hysteria. In S.J. Lynn & J.W. Rhue (eds.), *Dissociation: Clinical and theoretical perspectives* (pp. 365-395). New York: Guilford.

Mayou, R. (1993). Somatization. *Psychotherapy and Psychosomatics, 59*, 69-83.

Nemiah, J.C. (1991). Dissociation, conversion, and somatization. *Annual Review of Psychiatry, 10*, 248-260.

Nijenhuis, E.R.S., Spinhoven, P., Van Dyck, R., Van der Hart, O., & Vanderlinden, J. (1996). The development and psychometric characteristics of the Somatoform Dissociation Questionnaire (SDQ-20). *Journal of Nervous and Mental Disease, 184*, 688-694.

Othmer, E., & DeSouza, C. (1985). A screening test for somatization disorder (hysteria). *American Journal of Psychiatry, 142*, 1146-1149.

Pribor, E.F., Yutzy, S.H., Dean, J.T., & Wetzel, R.D. (1993). Briquet's syndrome, dissociation and abuse. *American Journal of Psychiatry, 150*, 1507-1511.

Prince, M. (1924). *The unconsciousness.* New York: Macmillan.

Rey, J.M., Morris-Yates, A., & Stanislaw, H. Measuring the accuracy of diagnostic tests using Receiver Operating Characteristics (ROC) analysis. *International Journal of Methods in Psychiatric Research, 2*, 39-50.

Ross, C.A., Heber, S., Norton, G.R., & Anderson, G. (1989a). Somatic symptoms in multiple personality disorder. *Psychosomatics, 30*, 154-160.

Sainton, K., Ellason, J., Ross, C.A. (1993, November). Reliability of the new form of the Dissociative Experiences Scale (DES) and the Dissociation Questionnaire (DIS-Q). Proceedings of the 10th International Conference on Multiple Personality/Dissociative States (p. 125). Chicago.

Saxe, G.N., Chinman, G., Berkowitz, M.D., Hall, K., Lieberg, G., Schwartz J., Van der Kolk, B.A. (1994). Somatization in patients with dissociative disorders. *American Journal of Psychiatry, 151*, 1329-1334.

Saxe, G.N., Van der Kolk, B.A., Berkowitz, R., Chinman, G., Hall, K., & Lieberg, G. (1993). Dissociative disorders in psychiatric inpatients. *American Journal of Psychiatry, 150*, 1037-1042.

SPSS PC (1993). SPSS Inc. SPSS for Windows Release 6.0. Chicago: SPSS Inc., 1993.

Steinberg, M. (1993). *Structured Clinical Interview for DSM-IV Dissociative Disorders (SCID-D).* Washington DC: American Psychiatric Press.

Steinberg, M., Cichetti, D.V., Buchanan, J., Hall, P., Rounsaville, B. (1993). Clinical assessment of dissociative symptoms and disorders: The structured clinical interview for DSM-IV dissociative disorders. *Dissociation, 6,* 3-16.

Stekel, W. (1908). *Nervöse Angstzustände und ihre Behandlung* [Nervous mental states and their treatment]. Berlin: Urban und Schwarzenbach.

Van der Kolk, B.A., & Van der Hart, O. (1989). Pierre Janet and the breakdown of adaptation in psychological trauma. *American Journal of Psychiatry, 141,* 187-190.

Vanderlinden, J. (1993). *Dissociative experiences, trauma, and hypnosis: Research findings and clinical applications in eating disorders.* Delft: Eburon.

Vanderlinden, J., Van Dyck, R., Vandereycken, W., Vertommen, H., & Verkes, R.J. (1993). The Dissociation Questionnaire: development and characteristics of a new self-reporting questionnaire. *Clinical Psychology and Psychotherapy, 1,* 21-27.

World Health Organization, Division of Mental Health (1992). *The ICD-10 Classification of mental and behavioral disorders: Clinical descriptions and diagnostic guidelines.* Geneva: World Health Organization, 1990.

Yates, J.L., & Nasby W. (1993). Dissociation, affect, and network models of memory: An integral proposal. *Journal of Traumatic Stress, 6,* 305-327.

V

Psychometric Characteristics of The Somatoform Dissociation Questionnaire: A Replication Study[*]

"... the effect of such dissociation and repression should not be regarded as confined merely to the realm of memory, but as also involving motor and sensory loss of control and even reflex disturbances, the functional 'somatic' symptoms forming part (or being an expression) of the 'psychical' dissociation which has produced the 'apparently normal' personality."
Myers, 1940, p. 68.

Introduction

According to the *Diagnostic and Statistical Manual of Mental Disorders* (*DSM-IV*; American Psychiatric Association, 1994), the essential feature of dissociative disorders is a disruption of the usually integrated functions of memory, consciousness, identity and perception. This definition ignores that the body, and bodily functions may also be subject to dissociation. Clinical observations, however, confirm the view prevailing in 19th century French psychiatry that somatoform symptoms may constitute somatic manifestations of dissociation (Janet, 1901, 1907; Kihlstrom, 1992, 1994; Nemiah, 1989; Nijenhuis, 1990; Van der Hart & Op den Velde, 1990). Examples include kinesthetic and visual anesthesia, motoric inhibitions, intermittent pain symptoms, variable smell and taste preferences, and dissociative loss of consciousness. We propose to use the term *somatoform dissociation* for such symptoms that in the 19th century were subsumed under the label of hysteria, and that in the *DSM-IV* (APA, 1994) are categorized as symptoms of conversion, somatization, pain, or sexual disorder. In the ICD-10 (WHO, 1992), some of these symptoms are categorized as expressions of dissociative disorders of movement and sensation.

---

* This chapter has also appeared as: Nijenhuis, E.R.S., Spinhoven, P., Van Dyck, R., Van der Hart, O., & Vanderlinden, J. (1998). Psychometric characteristics of the Somatoform Dissociation Questionnaire: A replication study. *Psychotherapy and Psychosomatics, 67,* 17-23. Supported by a grant of the Stichting Dienstbetoon Gezondheidszorg, Soesterberg, The Netherlands. Grantnumber: LK 11.92.

In order to systematically study somatoform dissociation, we developed two versions of a self-report questionnaire, that is, the Somatoform Dissociation Questionnaire. The SDQ-20 (Nijenhuis, Spinhoven, Van Dyck, Van der Hart, & Vanderlinden, 1996; Appendix I) evaluates the severity of somatoform dissociative phenomena, and the SDQ-5 (Nijenhuis et al., 1997; Appendix I) is a screening instrument for dissociative disorders.

The SDQ-20 was constructed using patients with dissociative disorders (n=50), diagnosed with the Structured Clinical Interview for Dissociative Disorders (SCID-D; Steinberg, 1993; Steinberg, Cichetti, Buchanan, Hall, & Rounsaville, 1993), and patients with other *DSM-IV* (APA, 1994) disorders (n=50). These patients completed a list of 75 items that according to clinical experience and the judgment of experts in dissociation could reflect instances of somatoform dissociation. Somatoform dissociation was defined as dissociative state-dependent somatoform responses that in clinical settings had appeared upon the reactivation of particular dissociative states, and that could not be medically explained. Separate logistic analyses and determination of discriminant indices per item revealed 20 items that best discriminated between cases and non-cases. Mokken scale analysis (Mokken, 1971; Molenaar, 1986) showed that these items are strongly scalable on a unidimensional latent scale, interpreted to measure somatoform dissociation. The internal consistency of the SDQ-20 was high, and the scores were not dependent on gender or age. The convergent validity of the SDQ-20 was supported by high intercorrelations with the Dissociation Questionnaire (DIS-Q; Vanderlinden, 1993; Vanderlinden, Van Dyck, Vandereycken, & Vertommen, 1993) which measures psychological dissociation. Higher SDQ-20 scores of patients with dissociative identity disorder (DID; APA, 1994) in comparison to patients with dissociative disorder NOS (DDNOS; APA, 1994) demonstrated criterion-related validity (Nijenhuis et al., 1996).

From the SDQ-20 a shorter version (SDQ-5) was derived for screening purposes. The SDQ-5 provided optimal discrimination between cases of dissociative disorders and psychiatric patients with other *DSM-IV* disorders, and yielded high sensitivity (94%) and specificity (96%). At a conservatively estimated prevalence rate of dissociative disorders of 10% among psychiatric patients (Horen, Leichner, & Lawson, 1995; Loewenstein, 1994; Saxe, Van der Kolk, Berkowitz, Chinman, Hall, & Lieberg, 1993) positive predictive value would be satisfactory (72%), and negative predictive value was excellent (99%). Cross-validation in an independent sample largely corroborated the first findings (Nijenhuis et al., 1997).

As the SDQ-5 was derived from the SDQ-20, and the SDQ-20 was derived from a much larger pool of items, it is necessary to study the psychometric characteristics of the SDQ-20 and SDQ-5 when administered as separate scales. It is also important to study whether the SDQ-5 scores are influenced by the context of measurement, that is, the SDQ-5 as embedded in the SDQ-20 compared to the SDQ-5 presented as an independent scale. These objectives constituted the primary aim of the present study.

The original studies could be improved on a few points. The initial comparison patients were not consecutively gathered, which may have introduced some bias (although the independent sample used in the cross-validation of the SDQ-5 did include consecutive comparison patients). Furthermore, in order to avoid the selection of false positive comparison patients, patients with non-dissociative *DSM-IV* diagnoses (APA, 1994) who scored above the recommended DIS-Q cutoff point in the screening for dissociative disorders (Vanderlinden, 1993) were excluded in the earlier study. This exclusion may be criticized, considering that non-dissociative disorder patients displaying substantial psychological dissociative phenomena were prevented from entering the comparison group. Another criticism is that in the SDQ-5 study, the cross-validation sample included 31 patients with dissociative disorders, but 15 of them had not been diagnosed using the SCID-D as a criterion. For these reasons, it was decided to include in this replication study only patients with *DSM-IV* dissociative disorders as diagnosed using the SCID-D, and consecutive comparison patients meeting the criteria of non-dissociative *DSM-IV* disorders, irrespective of their DIS-Q scores.

Methods

Subjects and Procedure

Psychiatric outpatients displaying symptoms suggestive of dissociative disorders were interviewed by experienced clinicians using the SCID-D (Steinberg, 1993; Steinberg et al., 1993) as part of their clinical assessment. In most cases ($n = 22$), this interview was performed upon the referral to a psychiatric outpatient service by a diagnostician ($n = 8$), or a diagnostician/therapist ($n = 14$). In other cases, clinicians without a special investment or interest in dissociative disorders had in the course of treatment observed considerable dissociative symptoms in patients with non-dissociative *DSM-IV* diagnoses. These observations had given these clinicians serious doubts about the accuracy of the previously assigned diagnoses. They, therefore, had requested diagnostic revaluations by experts in dissociative disorders, which included the administration of the SCID-D. In some cases ($n = 9$), a dissociative disorder was detected. All SCID-D interviewers were trained in the administration and interpretation of this instrument. In total, thirty-one cases were collected that presented a dissociative disorder (16 with DDNOS, 15 with DID). The mean age of this group (28 women, 3 men) was 32.1 years ($SD = 10.3$ years, range 18 to 53).

A subgroup of these patients with dissociative disorders had been diagnosed and had received treatment of their dissociative condition in advance of obtaining their responses to the SDQ-20, SDQ-5, and DIS-Q (these self-report questionnaires are further described below). This group included 10 patients with DID, and 3 with DDNOS. Five patients with DID, and 13 with DDNOS completed these questionnaires as a part of their clinical (re)assessment. In all cases informed consent with use of relevant data in the present study was obtained.

The comparison group consisted of 45 psychiatric outpatients, consecutively presented at a psychiatric outpatient service with a non-dissociative

DSM-IV diagnosis. Diagnoses were assigned by clinicians using DSM-IV criteria, and included Axis I anxiety disorders (n = 20) (social and specific phobia, panic disorder with and without agoraphobia, obsessive compulsive disorder and posttraumatic stress disorder), depressive disorder (n = 14), eating disorders (n = 1), somatization disorder (n = 1), adjustment disorder (n = 10), alcohol abuse (n = 1), polysubstance dependence (n = 1), and schizophrenia (n = 1). Some patients presented with other conditions described in DSM-IV that warranted clinical attention: bereavement (n = 2) and problems of relationship (n = 3). Axis II diagnoses included borderline personality disorder (n = 3), avoidant personality disorder (n = 2), dependent personality disorder (n = 2), and personality disorder NOS (n = 2). Personality disorder traits were displayed by 8 patients, and included traits of dependent, histrionic, borderline, and narcissistic personality disorder. The mean age of the comparison group (27 women and 18 men) was 34.6 years (SD = 10.1 years, range 19 to 53). The comparison patients completed the SDQ-20, the SDQ-5, and the DIS-Q after their first visit to the outpatient service, and the acquisition of informed consent.

Instruments

The Structured Interview for DSM-IV Dissociative Disorders (SCID-D; Steinberg, 1993; Steinberg et al., 1993) is a diagnostic instrument developed for the assessment of dissociative disorders. It covers five dissociative symptom areas (amnesia, depersonalization, derealization, identity confusion, and identity fragmentation). Severity ratings of the symptom areas range from 1-4 (absent-severe). The total score ranges from 5-20. Good to excellent reliability and validity have been reported both in the US and in the Netherlands (Boon & Draijer, 1993; Steinberg et al., 1993).

As described above, the Somatoform Dissociation Questionnaire (SDQ-20; Nijenhuis et al., 1996) is a 20-item self-report questionnaire measuring somatoform dissociation. The items are supplied with a Likert-type five point scale. The range of scores is 20 to 100.

The SDQ-5 (Nijenhuis et al., 1997) is a five-item dissociative disorders screening instrument (range of scores 5 to 25), and was introduced above. The recommended cutoff point is ≥ 8.

The Dissociation Questionnaire (DIS-Q; Vanderlinden, 1993; Vanderlinden et al., 1993) is a 63-item self-report questionnaire measuring psychological dissociation. Four factors were extracted and were labeled: identity confusion and fragmentation, loss of control, amnesia, and absorption. The DIS-Q reliability rates are good to excellent, scores are stable over time, and the DIS-Q differentiates between patients with dissociative disorders and normals and psychiatric subjects with other diagnoses (Vanderlinden, 1993). As was found by Vanderlinden (1993) and by Sainton, Ellason, and Ross (1993), the DIS-Q highly correlates with the Dissociative Experiences Scale (DES; Bernstein & Putnam, 1986), another widely used self-report dissociation questionnaire. Scores range from 1.0 to 5.0. The mean score of DID patients is 3.5 (SD = 0.4) and of DDNOS patients 2.9 (SD = 0.6). A cutoff score of 2.5 has been advised for purposes of case-selection of patients with a dissociative disorder (Vanderlinden, 1993).

Sixty-nine patients completed, apart from the SDQ-20 which includes the items of the SDQ-5, the SDQ-5 as a separate scale. Thirty patients completed the instruments in the order SDQ-5, DIS-Q, SDQ-20, and 39 completed these scales in the reverse order.

Data Analysis

A nonparametric Mokken scale analysis for polytomous items (Molenaar, 1986) was used to evaluate SDQ-20 scalability on a unidimensional latent scale (Loevinger coefficient of homogeneity and the Mokken coefficient of homogeneity ≥ 0.30).

A Mokken model is used in order to construct hierarchical, unidimensional scales (Mokken, 1971). The model assumes the existence of an underlying continuum represented by a homogeneous set of dichotomous items related to this continuum. In this model the function describing the relation between the probability of a positive response and the latent scale value is defined nonparametrically and is called the item characteristic curve or item response function. It is assumed that the probability of a positive response to an item is a monotonely nondecreasing function of a particular value of a subject on this latent scale. Besides this assumption of single monotonicity, a further requirement is that of double monotonicity. This means that an item with a higher difficulty than another item has a lower probability or an equal probability of eliciting a positive response. The hierarchical ordering of items in a scale is based on this requirement that all items should have different proportions of positive responses. Molenaar (1986) has proposed an extention of Mokken's model from dichotomous to polytomous items (i.e., items with at least three ordered response categories) and in this study the program MSP (Mokken Scale analysis for Polytomous items) based on this generalized model was used to test the scalability of the polytomous SDQ-items. The model assumptions of single and double monotonicity of the SDQ-20 items were evaluated, and the internal consistency (Cronbach's alpha) of the SDQ was also assessed.

As no more than three male patients with dissociative disorders were included, the association of SDQ-20 scores with gender was assessed with t-test for independent samples (gender) for comparison patients only. The association of SDQ-20 scores and age was evaluated using Pearson product moment correlation coefficients. Pearson correlation coefficients were also employed to evaluate the interrelatedness of the SDQ-20 scores with total and subscale scores of the DIS-Q. Considering the absence of a normal distribution, differences on the SDQ-20 between dissociative disorders patients and comparison patients, as well as cases of DID versus cases of DDNOS were analyzed with Mann-Whitney U test for independent samples.

In order to test the effect of the context of measurement of the SDQ-5, Pearson correlation coefficients were used to compare the SDQ-5 scores when administered as a separate scale, or as embedded in the SDQ-20. To test the discriminant ability of the unweighted SDQ-5 sum score, a predicted probability of caseness was calculated for each individual using logistic regression. The discriminant ability was expressed in terms of sensitivity and specificity of the score with regard to observed caseness. As the predictive power of a test depends on prevalence (Rey, Morris-Yates, & Stanislaw, 1992), positive and negative predictive values were calculated using a correction for an estimated dissociative disorders prevalence rate among psychiatric outpatients of 10% (Horen et al., 1995; Loewenstein, 1994; Saxe et al., 1993). Statistical analyses were performed with SPSS-PC 6.0 (1993).

Results

A Mokken scale analysis (Molenaar, 1986) showed that the items of the SDQ-20 were strongly scalable (Loevinger coefficient of homogeneity = 0.56). One item (Mokken coefficient of homogeneity = 0.28) failed to reach the lowerbound (≥ 0.30), but its exclusion only marginally affected the Loevinger coefficient of homogeneity (increasing to 0.58). The Mokken coefficients of homogeneity of the other items ranged from 0.40 to 0.63. The items met the assumptions of single and double monotonicity. The internal consistency of the SDQ-20 was excellent (Cronbach's alpha = 0.96).

Males ($n = 18$) and females ($n = 28$) without a dissociative disorder did not obtain significantly different SDQ-20 scores (males $M = 22.5$; $SD = 3.4$; females $M = 23.1$, $SD = 4.3$). Using all 76 subjects, Pearson correlation coefficients between the SDQ-20 score and age ($r = .0421$) were not significant.

Criterion-related validity was demonstrated by the fact that, as computed with Mann-Whitney U test, SDQ-20 scores strongly discriminate between dissociative disorder patients ($M = 50.7$, $SD = 14.7$) and comparison patients ($M = 22.9$, $SD = 3.9$) ($z = -7.24$, $p < .0001$). Patients with DID ($M = 57.3$, $SD = 14.9$) reached significantly higher SDQ-20 scores than patients with DDNOS ($M = 44.6$, $SD = 11.9$) ($z = -2.30$, $p = .021$).

The intercorrelations between the SDQ-20 and the DIS-Q total score ($r = .82$), and the correlations between the SDQ and the four DIS-Q factor scores (identity fragmentation factor $r = .81$; loss of control ($r = .72$); amnesia ($r = .80$); absorption $r = .60$) were high (all $p < .0001$). These data support the convergent validity of the SDQ-20.

Assessment of the diagnostic reliability of the predicted probability of caseness on the basis of the unweighted SDQ-5 sum score (range of scores 5 to 25) revealed that of the dissociative disorders patients 94% (29/31) had a score above 7 (sensitivity), and of the comparison patients 98% (44/45) had a score of 7 or lower (specificity). At this cutoff point, the positive predictive value was 97% (29/30) and the negative predictive value was 96% (44/46). The total percentage of correct classification was 96% (73/76). According to the results of the samples studied, a cutoff score of ≥ 8 yields a corrected positive predictive value of 84% at an estimated prevalence rate of 10% (Horen et al., 1995; Loewenstein, 1994; Saxe et al., 1993), meaning that 84% of the patients with positive scores can be expected to have a dissociative disorder. The likelihood ratio for disease at that value is 47. As inspection of table 1 shows, based upon the present findings for case-finding purposes among psychiatric patients, a cutoff score of ≥ 8 is to be recommended.

Table 1
Sensitivity, Specificity, Predictive Values and Likelihood Ratios of the SDQ-5 at Essential Cutoff Scores Discriminating between DSM-IV Dissociative Disorder Patients (n = 31) and Psychiatric Patients without a Dissociative Disorder (n = 45)

Cutoff score	Sensi-tivity	Speci-ficity	Positive Predic-tive Value	Negative Predic-tive Value	Predictive value estimated at prevalence 10%		Likelihood ratio	
					pos.	neg.	pos.	neg.
10	0.77	0.98	0.96	0.86	0.81	0.97	38.5	0.23
9	0.87	0.98	0.96	0.92	0.83	0.98	43.5	0.13
8	0.94	0.98	0.97	0.96	0.84	0.99	47.0	0.06
7	0.97	0.89	0.86	0.98	0.49	0.99	8.8	0.03

Sensitivity, specificity, and predictive values are expressed as proportions.
Positive predictive value (corrected for prevalence) = [sensitivity x prevalence] / [(sensitivity x prevalence) + (1 − specificity) x (1 − prevalence)]
Negative predictive value (corrected for prevalence) = [specificity x (1 − prevalence)] / [specificity x (1- prevalence) + (1- sensitivity) x prevalence]
Likelihood ratio (positive) = sensitivity / 1 − specificity
Likelihood ratio (negative) = 1 − sensitivity / specificity

The intercorrelation between the SDQ-5 score calculated by summation of the relevant five SDQ-20 items and the independent SDQ-5 score was high (Pearson's $r = 0.92$). The order in which these scales were administered did not affect the SDQ-5 scores considering that the intercorrelations were $r = 0.93$, respectively $r = 0.92$. Using the independent SDQ-5 scale, or the SDQ-20 embedded SDQ-5 scores, yielded highly comparable estimations of sensitivity (0.96, respectively 0.94) and identical estimations of specificity (0.98). The SDQ-5 scores thus were not dependent on the context of measurement.

Discussion

In concordance with the findings of Nijenhuis et al. (1996), according to a Mokken analysis, the items of the SDQ-20 are strongly scalable, and the internal consistency is high. Gender and age do not affect SDQ-20 scores. However, both samples contained few male dissociative disorder patients (previous study n = 6, the present study n = 3). Convergent validity was corroborated by the replication of high intercorrelations between the SDQ-20 and the DIS-Q total and subscore scales. Criterion-related validity was corroborated by the replicated finding that the patients with dissociative disorders obtained higher SDQ-20 scores than comparison patients, and that patients with DID scored higher compared to patients with DDNOS. As in the original SDQ-20 study these 20 items were embedded in a far larger pool of items, it may be concluded that our first findings were not an effect of this context.

No indications were found that SDQ-5 scores are influenced by the order of administration and the presence or absence of the remaining SDQ-20 items. In both contexts, the SDQ-5 performed well as a dissociative disorders screening instrument, as it did in our original study (Nijenhuis et al., 1997). Sensitivity and specificity, as well as positive and negative predictive value corrected for prevalence were very satisfactory. This time the positive predictive value (84%) was higher than in the original study (first sample 72%; independent cross-validation sample 43%). In comparison with the Dissociative Experiences Scale (DES; Bernstein & Putnam, 1986), which at an estimated prevalence rate of 10% and at the optimal cutoff of 25 reached a positive predictive value of 42% (Draijer & Boon, 1993), the SDQ-5 does very well as a screening instrument for dissociative disorders.

These results suggest that the SDQ-5 may distinguish patients with dissociative disorders and other psychiatric disorders better than the DES. The higher positive predictive value of the SDQ-5 could perhaps relate to the finding that the DES measures dissociation, as well as absorption/imaginative involvement. Using the DES, Waller, Putnam, and Carlson (1996) found taxometric evidence for the existence of two types of experiences, which they labeled "non-pathological dissociative experiences," and "pathological dissociative experiences," such as dissociative amnesia, depersonalization, derealization, and identity alteration. The evidence suggested that the first are manifestations of a trait, whereas the latter are manifestations of a latent class variable. Non-pathological dissociation, which involves absorption, would thus be dimensional in nature, whereas pathological dissociation would be a typological, "taxonic" construct. Consistent with this perception, subjects with dissociative disorders were identified best by 8 of the 28 DES items measuring pathological dissociation, which Waller et al. referred to as the DES-T(axon). We remark that labeling absorption "non-pathological dissociation" empties the dissociation concept of meaning. Therefore, it would be best to distinguish between absorption/imaginative involvement and dissociation.

The higher positive predictive value of the SDQ-5 could also indicate that somatoform dissociation is even more specific for dissociative disorders than the dissociative phenomena as measured by the DES/DES-T. In order to address these questions, it would be of value to compare the dissociative disorders screening ability of the SDQ-5 and the DES/DES-T. Considering our previous (Nijenhuis et al., 1996, 1997) and present findings, and the findings of Waller et al., one would expect stronger correlations between the SDQ-5 and the DES-T, than between the SDQ-5 and the DES-items that measure absorption/imaginative involvement. Consistent with this prediction, in this study, as well as in our previous study (Nijenhuis et al., 1996), we have found that the intercorrelation between the DIS-Q absorption factor and the SDQ-20 is lower than the intercorrelation between the DIS-Q total and the other DIS-Q subscale scores versus the SDQ-20 scores.

The present results confirm that the SDQ-20 and the SDQ-5 are scales of sound psychometric quality, and that somatoform dissociative phenomena constitute core symptoms in dissociative disorders. The SDQ-20 can be used to evaluate the severity of somatoform dissociative phenomena. Further study should test the divergent validity of the SDQ-20, and should assess the severity of somatoform dissociation in various psychiatric disorders, in particular somatization disorder, *DSM-IV* conversion disorder/ICD-10 dissociative disorders of movement and sensation, chronic pain disorder, and eating disorder. In view of the observed associations between somatization, psychological dissociation, and reported as well as verified trauma (Boon & Draijer, 1993; Darves-Bornoz, 1997; Hornstein & Putnam, 1992; Kinzl, Trawager, & Biebl, 1995; Marmar et al., 1994; Ross, Heber, Norton, & Anderson, 1989; Walker, Gelfand, Gelfand, Koss, & Katon, 1995), the instrument can also be used to investigate to what extent somatoform dissociation is associated with trauma.

The SDQ-5 is useful as a dissociative disorders screening instrument. However, it is not a diagnostic tool. Patients with a SDQ-5 score ≥8 should be subjected to a structured diagnostic interview for the (*DSM-IV*) dissociative disorders, such as the SCID-D, or the Dissociative Disorders Interview Schedule (DDIS; Ross, Heber, Norton, Anderson, Anderson, & Barchet, 1989), in order to eliminate false positives.

Somatization is neither a discrete clinical entity, nor the result of a single pathological process (Kellner, 1994). Somatoform dissociation constitutes a subset of medically unexplained, or insufficiently explained somatoform phenomena. There are indications that presently a substantial number of dissociative disorder cases remains undiagnosed, and this may partly be due to a lack of recognition of somatoform dissociation. For example, Jantschek, Rodewig, Von Wietersheim, and Muhs (1995) found that only 50% of 129 diagnosticians at 13 psychiatric centers correctly assigned dissociative disorder. One can assume that in medical care many more cases will be missed. Evaluation of somatoform dissociation and screening for dissociative disorder using the SDQ may be helpful to ameliorate this state of affairs.

References

American Psychiatric Association (1994). *Diagnostic and statistical manual of mental disorders, 4th edn.* Washington DC: American Psychiatric Association.

Bernstein, E. & Putnam, F.W. (1986). Development, reliability, and validity of a dissociation scale. *Journal of Nervous and Mental Disease, 102,* 280-286.

Boon, S. & Draijer, N. (1993). *Multiple personality disorder in the Netherlands: A study on reliability and validity of the diagnosis.* Amsterdam/Lisse, Swets & Zeitlinger.

Darves-Bornoz, J.-M. (1997). Rape-related psychotraumatic syndromes. *European Journal of Obstetrics & Gynecology, 71,* 59-65.

Draijer, N. & Boon, S. (1993). The validation of the Dissociative Experiences Scale against the criterion of the SCID-D, using receiver operating characteristics (ROC) analysis. *Dissociation, 6,* 28-37.

Horen, S.A., Leichner, P.P., & Lawson, J.S. (1995). Prevalence of dissociative symptoms and disorders in an adult psychiatric inpatient population in Canada. *Canadian Journal of Psychiatry, 40,* 185-191.

Hornstein, N.L., Putnam, F.W. (1992). Clinical phenomenology of child and adolescent disorders. *Journal of the American Academy of Child and Adolescent Psychiatry, 31*, 1077-1085.

Janet, P. (1901). *The mental state of hystericals.* New York: Putnam and Sons. Reprint: University Publications of America, Washington DC, 1977.

Janet, P. (1907). *The major symptoms of hysteria.* London/New York: Macmillan. Reprint of second edition: Hafner, New York, 1965.

Jantschek, G., Rodewig, K., Von Wietersheim, J., & Muhs, A. (1995). Concepts of psychosomatic disorders in ICD-10: Results of the research criteria study. *Psychotherapy and Psychosomatics, 63*, 112-123.

Kellner, R. (1995). Psychosomatic syndromes, somatization and somatoform disorders. *Psychotherapy and Psychsomatics, 61*, 4-24.

Kihlstrom, J.F. (1992). Dissociative and conversion disorders. In D.J. Stein & J. Young (eds.), *Cognitive science and clinical disorders* (pp. 247-270). San Diego/New York, Academic Press.

Kihlstrom, J.F. (1994). One hundred years of hysteria. In S.J. Lynn & J.W. Rhue (eds.), *Dissociation: Clinical and theoretical perspectives* (pp. 365-395). New York: Guilford.

Kinzl, J.F., Traweger, C., & Biebl, W. (1995). Family background and sexual abuse associated with somatization. *Psychotherapy and Psychosomatics, 64*, 82-87.

Loewenstein, R.J. (1994). Diagnosis, epidemiology, clinical course, treatment, and cost-effectiveness of treatment of multiple personality disorder: Report submitted to the Clinton Administration Task Force on Health Care Financing Reform. *Dissociation,7*, 3-12.

Marmar, C.R., Weiss, D.S., Schlenger, W.E., Fairbank, J.A., Jordan, B.K., Kulka, R.A., & Hough, R.L. (1994). Peritraumatic dissociation and posttraumatic stress in male Vietnam theater veterans. *American Journal of Psychiatry, 151*, 902-907.

Mokken, R.J. (1971). *A theory and procedure of scale analysis.* The Hague: Mouton.

Molenaar, I.W. (1986). Een vingeroefening in item response theorie voor drie geordende antwoordcategorieën [An excercise in item response theory for three ordered response categories]. In G.F. Pikkemaat & J.J.A. Moors (eds.): Liber amicorum Jaap Muilwijk. Groningen: Econometrisch Instituut.

Nemiah, J.C. (1989). Janet redivivus: the centenary of L'automatisme psychologique. Editorial. *American Journal of Psychiatry, 146*, 1527-1529.

Nijenhuis, E.R.S. (1990). Somatische equivalenten bij dissociatieve stoornissen [Somatic equivalents with dissociative disorders]. *Hypnotherapie, 12*, 10-21.

Nijenhuis, E.R.S., Spinhoven, P., Van Dyck, R., Van der Hart, O., & Vanderlinden, J. (1996). The development and the psychometric characteristics of the Somatoform Dissociation Questionnaire (SDQ-20). *Journal of Nervous and Mental Disease, 184*, 688-694.

Nijenhuis, E.R.S., Spinhoven, P., Van Dyck, R., Van der Hart, O., & Vanderlinden, J. (1997). The development of the Somatoform Dissociation Questionnaire (SDQ-5) as a screening instrument for dissociative disorders. *Acta Psychiatrica Scandinavica, 96*, 311-318.

Pribor, E.F., Yutzy, S.H., Dean, J.T., & Wetzel, R.D. (1993). Briquet's syndrome, dissociation, and abuse. *American Journal of Psychiatry, 150*, 1507-1511.

Rey, J.M., Morris-Yates, A., & Stanislaw, H. (1992). Measuring the accuracy of diagnostic tests using Receiver Operating Characteristics (ROC) analysis. *International Journal of Methods in Psychiatric Research, 2*, 39-50.

Ross, C.A., Heber, S., Norton, G.R., & Anderson, G. (1989). Somatic symptoms in multiple personality disorder. *Psychosomatics, 30*, 154-160.

Ross, C.A., Heber, S., Norton, G.R., Anderson, B., Anderson, G., & Barchet, P. (1989). The dissociative disorders interview schedule: A structured interview. *Dissociation, 2,* 169-189.

Sainton K., Ellason J., Ross C.A. (1993). Reliability of the new form of the Dissociative Experience Scale (DES) and the Dissociation Questionnaire (DIS-Q). Proceedings of the 10th International Conference on Multiple Personality/Dissociative States, Chicago, November, p. 125.

Saxe, G.N., Chinman, G., Berkowitz, M.D., Hall, K., Lieberg, G., Schwartz, J., & Van der Kolk, B.A. (1994). Somatization in patients with dissociative disorders. *American Journal of Psychiatry, 151,* 1329-1334.

Saxe, G.N., Van der Kolk, B.A., Berkowitz, R., Chinman, G., Hall, K., Lieberg, G. (1993). Dissociative experiences in psychiatric inpatients. *American Journal of Psychiatry, 150,* 1037-1042.

SPSS PC: SPSS Inc./M.J. Norušis (1993). *SPSS for Windows Release 6.0.* Chicago: SPSS Inc.

Steinberg, M. (1993). *Structured Clinical Interview for DSM-IV Dissociative Disorders (SCID-D).* Washington DC: American Psychiatric Press.

Steinberg, M., Cichetti, D.V., Buchanan, J., Hall, P., Rounsaville, B. (1993). Clinical assessment of dissociative symptoms and disorders: The Structured Clinical Interview for DSM-IV Dissociative Disorders. *Dissociation, 6,* 3-16.

Van der Hart, O. & Op den Velde, W. (1995). Posttraumatische stoornissen [Posttraumatic disorders]. In O. Van der Hart (ed.), *Trauma, dissociatie en hypnose* [Trauma, dissociation, and hypnosis] (pp. 103-145). Lisse: Swets & Zeitlinger.

Vanderlinden, J. (1993). *Dissociative experiences, trauma, and hypnosis: Research findings and clinical applications in eating disorders.* Delft: Eburon.

Vanderlinden, J., Van Dyck, R., Vandereycken, W., Vertommen, H., & Verkes, R.J. (1993). The Dissociation Questionnaire: Development and Characteristics of a new self-reporting questionnaire. *Clinical Psychology and Psychotherapy, 1,* 21-27.

Walker, E.A., Gelfand, A.N., Gelfand, R.N., Koss, M.P., & Katon, W.J. (1995). Medical and psychiatric symptoms in female gastroenterology clinic patients with histories of sexual victimization. *General Hospital Psychiatry, 17,* 85-92.

Waller, N.G., Putnam, F.W., & Carlson, E.B. (1996). Types of dissociation and dissociative types: A taxometric analysis of dissociative experiences. *Psychological Methods, 1,* 300-321.

World Health Organization (1992). *The ICD-10 Classification of Mental and Behavioral Disorders. Clinical description and diagnostic guidelines.* Geneva: World Health Organization.

Appendix I
The items of the SDQ-20 and the SDQ-5

It sometimes happens that:

1. I have trouble urinating.
2. I dislike tastes that I usually like (women: apart from pregnancy or monthly periods).
3. I hear sounds from nearby as if they come from far away.
4. I have pain while urinating. *
5. my body, or a part of it, feels numb.
6. people and things look bigger than they actually are.
7. I have an attack that resembles an epileptic fit.
8. my body, or a part of it, is insensitive to pain.*
9. I dislike smells that I usually like.
10. I feel pain in my genitals (apart from sexual intercourse).
11. I cannot hear for a while (as if I am deaf).
12. I cannot see for a while (as if I am blind).
13. I see things around me differently than usual (for example as if looking through a tunnel, or seeing merely a part of an object).*
14. I do not have a cold but yet am able to smell much better or worse than I usually do.
15. it is as if my body, or a part of it, has disappeared.*
16. I cannot swallow, or only with great effort.
17. I cannot sleep for nights on end, but remain very active during daytime.
18. I cannot speak (or merely with great effort) or I can only whisper.*
19. I am paralysed for a while.
20. I grow stiff for a while.

---

*   Items of the SDQ-5

VI

Somatoform Dissociation Discriminates among Diagnostic Categories over and above General Psychopathology*

> *It has been possible to get in touch with a part or fragment, or aspect of the personality which produces and controls the "automatic" movements and to obtain from it an introspective or retrospective account of thinking and feeling expressed in the action.*
> William McDougall, 1926, p.253

Introduction

Most modern empirical studies on dissociation restrict this mental phenomenon to disruptions in memory, consciousness, and identity (Atchison & McFarlane, 1994). As these disruptions involve manifestations of dissociation in psychological variables, we have proposed to name this phenomenon *psychological dissociation* (Nijenhuis, Spinhoven, Van Dyck, Van der Hart, & Vanderlinden, 1996). However, as previously described in 19th century French psychiatry, dissociation also manifests in disturbances of sensation, movement, and other bodily functions (Briquet, 1895; Charcot, 1887; Janet, 1901; Pitres, 1891). We have proposed to call these disruptions *somatoform dissociation* (Nijenhuis et al., 1996).

In 1859 Briquet wrote that "hysteria is a general disease which modifies the whole organism," and in 1887 Charcot recognized that hysteria essentially involves disturbances of perception and control. In his view, those with hysteria somehow are unable to intentionally and consciously feel, hear, see, or hear what they are supposed to perceive, and they lack the usual control over bodily movements. Apart from these functional *losses*, Charcot observed that they also suffer from *intrusion* phenomena. According to Janet (1901), hysteria – a conglomerate of disorders which are dominated by dissociative disorders – essentially involves dissociation. He maintained that dissociative symptoms are often induced by psychological trauma, severe illness, or fatigue (Janet, 1909). Subjects who are exposed to these events may fail to integrate their experiences and

---

* Previously published in the Australian and New Zealand Journal of Psychiatry, 1999, 33, 511-520, as authored by Nijenhuis, E.R.S., Van Dyck, R., Spinhoven, P., Van der Hart, O., Chatrou, M., Vanderlinden, J., & Moene, F. We thank Paul Brown and Kathy Steele for their valued editorial assistence.

reactions, which are instead stored as dissociated "systems of ideas and functions." These systems are totally or partially inaccessible to normal awareness, operate independently of voluntary control, and may include somatoform components of experience, reactions, and functions (Janet, 1901, 1907).

Functional losses, which include kinesthetic, visual, and auditory anesthesia, analgesia, and motor inhibitions, are incurred as a result of a lowering of the mental level and related narrowing of the field of consciousness. Janet (1901) regarded these losses as permanent symptoms of hysteria. They include feelings of incompleteness and lapses of all the mental functions, which he termed *mental stigmata*. As mental stigmata all involve functional losses, these stigmata are currently referred to as negative dissociative symptoms (Nijenhuis et al., 1996; Nijenhuis & Van der Hart, in press). Somatoform dissociation also entails intrusions, such as site-specific pain and changing preferences of taste and smell. These positive dissociative symptoms (Nijenhuis et al., 1996; Nijenhuis & Van der Hart, 1999) relate to periodic reactivations of dissociated systems, which Janet termed *mental accidents*. The manifestation of any given symptom at a particular point in time depends on the dissociative state in which the patient remains. For example, in one state the patient may show negative symptoms, in another state he may display positive symptoms, and in a third state he may be free of such symptoms.

Following Janet, Breuer and Freud (1974) maintained that hysteria involves dissociation, but, unlike Janet, they believed that the condition is exclusively induced by childhood sexual trauma (Brown & Van der Hart, 1998). However, Freud subsequently became convinced that sexual fantasy and forbidden wish fulfilment – not sexual trauma – are involved in the etiology of hysteria. Simultaneously, he began to regard somatoform hysterical symptoms as the result of a process of conversion, i.e., the transformation of unacceptable mental contents into a somatic symptom. Other psychoanalytical oriented authors used the term "somatization" (Stekel, 1908). Since the beginning of this century several definitions of somatization and conversion have been proposed, but all refer to a postulated transformation of psychological problems into somatoform symptoms (Mayou, 1993).

Psychoanalytic views on hysterical somatoform symptoms have been criticized repeatedly on theoretical and clinical grounds (Kihlstrom, 1994; McDougall, 1926; Nemiah, 1991; Van der Hart & Op den Velde, 1991). In line with these criticisms, *the International Classification of Diseases, 10th edition* (World Health Organization, 1992) refers to so-called conversion disorders in terms of *dissociative disorders of movement and sensation*. More generally, however, there continues to be confusion regarding the concepts and the classification of somatization, conversion, and dissociation. For example, in each version of *the Diagnostic and Statistical Manual of Mental Disorders* the conversion, somatization, and dissociative disorders have been categorized differently. In the DSM-IV (American Psychiatric Association, APA, 1994) the symptoms of somatoform dissociation are categorized as symptoms of conversion, somatization, sexual, or pain disorders.

Current scientific interest in psychological manifestations of dissociation is reflected in the development of self-report questionnaires, such as the Dissociative Experiences Scale (DES; Bernstein & Putnam, 1986) and the Dissociation Questionnaire (DIS-Q; Vanderlinden, Van Dyck, Vandereycken, Vertommen, & Verkes, 1993a), as well as the development of structured clinical interviews, such as the Structured Clinical Interview for DSM-IV Dissociative Disorders (SCID-D; Steinberg, 1993; Steinberg, Cichetti, Buchanon, Hall, & Rounsaville, 1993). The above questionnaires and interview schedules all include items that pertain to dissociative amnesia, depersonalization, derealization, identity confusion, and identity fragmentation.

Until recently, no such instrument existed for the measurement of somatoform dissociation, i.e., the partial or complete loss of the normal integration of somatoform components of experience, reactions, and functions. In order to systematically study somatoform dissociation, Nijenhuis et al. (1996, 1998a) developed the 20-item self-report Somatoform Dissociation Questionnaire (SDQ-20). These authors started from a list of 75 items that might reflect instances of the construct, according to clinical experience and expert judgement. Using standard statistical techniques, the items were selected which best discriminated between psychiatric patients with dissociative disorders and patients with other psychiatric disorders. All items of the SDQ-20 describe negative and positive dissociative symptoms. From the SDQ-20 was later derived the SDQ-5, which serves as a brief screening instrument for dissociative disorders (Nijenhuis et al., 1997b, 1998a). The psychometric characteristics of these scales proved very satisfactory. Somatoform dissociation is highly characteristic of dissociative disorders, not otherwise specified (DDNOS; APA, 1994) and dissociative identity disorder (DID; APA, 1994), and somatoform dissociation as measured by the SDQ-20 is highly correlated with psychological dissociation as measured by the DIS-Q (Vanderlinden et al., 1993b).

Among various types of traumatic experiences, somatoform dissociation was best predicted by reported physical and sexual abuse occurring in an emotionally neglectful and abusive social context, as well as by early onset of reported intense, chronic, and multiple traumatization (Nijenhuis, 1998b). Another finding was that somatoform dissociative symptoms that resemble animal defensive reactions to major threat (e.g., analgesia and inhibited motor reactions) are very good predictors of dissociative disorders (Nijenhuis, Spinhoven, Vanderlinden, Van Dyck, & Van der Hart, 1998c). These findings concur with increasing evidence for a link between trauma and dissociation (Lewis, Yeager, Pincus, & Lewis, 1997; Marmar et al., 1994; Ogawa, Sroufe, Weinfeld, Carlson, & Egeland, 1997).

Some authors have argued that a large component of an individual's score on dissociation scales should not be attributed specifically to dissociative pathology, but to psychopathology in general (Tillman, Nash, & Lerner, 1994). Indeed, several studies (for a review see Van IJzendoorn & Schuengel, 1996) have shown that DES scores are substantially associated with general psychopathology, such as measured by the Symptom Checklist-90-R (Derogatis, 1977). These findings suggest that the relative severity of somatoform dissociation in various psychiatric disorders may perhaps result from different degrees of general psychopathology. However, the validity of a separate construct of (somatoform) dissociation would be further supported if the SDQ-20 could differentiate among diagnostic categories with different levels of predicted dissociative pathology before and after statistically controlling for general psychopathology.

We hypothesized that patients belonging to various DSM-IV (APA, 1994) diagnostic categories will report different degrees of somatoform dissociation. Previous findings (Nijenhuis et al., 1996, 1998a) suggested that somatoform dissociation is low in patients with anxiety disorders, depression, adjustment disorders, and bipolar mood disorder (Nijenhuis, Spinhoven, Van Dyck, Van der Hart, De Graaf, & Knoppert, 1997a).

Patients with eating disorders manifested above normal levels of dissociative symptoms as measured by the DIS-Q (Vanderlinden, Vandereycken, Van Dyck, & Vertommen, 1993a) and the DES (Demitrack et al., 1993). A subgroup had dissociative experiences to a high degree (McCarthy, Goff, Baer, Cioffi, & Herzog, 1994; Tobin, Molteni, & Elin, 1995; Vanderlinden et al., 1993a). Therefore, we hypothesized that at least a subgroup of eating disorder patients would obtain significantly increased SDQ-20 scores.

Strong correlations have been found between psychological dissociation and somatization, in particular among subjects who report trauma (Farley & Keaney, 1997; Pribor, Yutzy, Dean, & Wetzel, 1993; Saxe et al., 1994; Walker, Katon, Neraas, Jemelka, & Massoth, 1992). Studying a large sample of traumatized subjects, Van der Kolk et al. (1996) found that PTSD, psychological dissociation, somatization, and affect dysregulation were highly interrelated. Since somatoform dissociative symptoms include pain – the SDQ-20 includes items assessing pelvic pain and pain while urinating – somatoform pain disorder may involve (somatoform) dissociative symptoms in at least some cases. Consistent with this hypothesis, Badura, Reiter, Altmaier, Rhomberg, and Alas (1997) and Walker et al. (1992) found associations among chronic pelvic pain, psychological dissociation, and somatization. In summary, in support for the hypothesis somatoform dissociation would be more severe among a group of patients with somatization disorder, conversion disorder, or somatoform pain disorder, than among patients with eating disorders.

As patients with DDNOS experience severe psychological dissociation (Vanderlinden et al., 1993b) they would probably experience even higher degrees of somatoform dissociation than would subjects with DSM-IV somatoform disorders. Consistent with studies showing that DID is associated with severe psychological dissociation, as well as with our previous findings regarding severe somatoform dissociation in DID (Nijenhuis et al., 1996, 1997b, 1998a) it is hypothesized that DID will be associated with the highest SDQ-20 scores.

Because there may be differences in the relative severity of either somatoform or psychological dissociation within particular diagnostic groups, it is important to compare the relative capacities of the SDQ-20 and the DES to distinguish among these diagnostic groups. Putnam et al. (1996) recently found that elevated dissociation in particular mental disorders (e.g., eating disorders) was due to a subgroup of highly dissociative subjects within the diagnostic category. Therefore, it also seemed important to assess the proportions of subjects within the various diagnostic groups with scores above the cutoff scores on psychological (DES) and somatoform dissociation (SDQ-5) screening instruments for dissociative disorders.

In summary, we hypothesized that: (1) the intercorrelation between somatoform dissociation and general psychopathology is considerable, but lower than the correlation between somatoform and psychological dissociation; (2) SDQ-20 scores and the number of cases obtaining SDQ-5 scores above the cutoff are increasingly higher, beginning with (i) non-dissociative, non-somatoform, and non-eating disorders, then (ii) eating disorders, (iii) DSM-IV somatoform disorders, (iv) DDNOS, and (v) DID; and (3) somatoform dissociation also discriminates among these diagnostic categories after controlling for general psychopathology.

Methods

Subjects

Dissociative disorder patients (n = 44, mean age 38.7, 50 = 8.6 years, range 21 to 59 years, 42 women, 2 men) included patients with DID (n = 23) and DDNOS (n = 21). All were diagnosed using the SCID-D by trained interviewers (Steinberg, 1993; Steinberg et al., 1993).

Somatoform patients consisted of two groups, each recruited in a different center specialized in the assessment and treatment of somatoform disorders (i.e., the Department of Psychosomatic Medicine, Willem Arntzhuis, Utrecht, the Netherlands, and the Outpatient Department of General Psychiatric Hospital "De Grote Rivieren," Dordrecht, the Netherlands). The twenty-one patients of the first center included patients with conversion disorder (n = 5), pain disorder (n = 7), conversion and pain disorder (n = 5), somatization disorder (n = 2), and somatization disorder and pain disorder (n = 2). The second group of somatoform disorders consisted of consecutive cases of DSM-IV conversion disorder (n = 26) who were treated at an inpatient psychiatric unit specialized in the treatment of this condition. The total group consisted of 41 women and 6 men, and the mean age was 39.4, SD = 10.9 years, range, 19 to 68 years. The disorders were assessed by diagnosticians using DSM-IV criteria.

A group of consecutive eating disorder patients (n = 50, mean age, 22.8, SD = 8.4 years, range, 13 to 48 years, 49 women, one man) was recruited from a residential eating disorder unit. The group included patients with anorexia restrictive type (n = 25), anorexia mixed type (n = 11), bulimia (n = 7), and bulimia overweight (n = 7). Patients with bipolar mood disorder (n = 23, mean age, 45.3, SD = 6.3 years, range, 33 to 58 years, 11 women, 12 men) were recruited from a mood disorder clinic. All mood disorder patients were on a maintenance treatment of lithium, except one who received carbamazepine.

Finally, a group of consecutive psychiatric outpatients (n = 45, mean age 34.6, SD = 10.1 years, range 19 to 53 years, 27 women, 18 men) was selected, excluding dissociative disorders, somatoform disorders, eating disorders, and bipolar mood disorder. Diagnoses were given by clinicians according to DSM-IV criteria, and included Axis I anxiety disorders (n = 20), depressive disorders (n = 16), adjustment disorders (n = 10), alcohol abuse (n = 2), polysubstance dependence

($n = 1$), schizophrenia ($n = 1$), bereavement ($n = 2$) and problems of relationship ($n = 3$). Axis II diagnoses included borderline personality disorder ($n = 3$), avoidant personality disorder ($n = 2$), dependent personality disorder ($n = 2$), and personality disorder, NOS ($n = 2$). In the remainder of this paper we will refer to this group as the "mixed psychiatric disorders" group.

As assessed with Chi-Square analysis, there were differences among various diagnostic groups with respect to living apart or with a partner ($\chi^2 = 16.9$, df 4, $p < .002$). More eating disorder patients were living apart, while more bipolar mood disorder patients were living with a partner. There was an imbalance of the gender distribution between groups as men were underrepresented among somatoform disorders patients, and were practically absent in the dissociative disorders and eating disorders groups (Fisher's Exact tests). A one-way analysis of variance revealed group age differences ($F = 32.93$, $df = 4{,}206$, $p < .0001$). According to Tukey's Honestly Significant Difference (HSD) tests, eating disorder patients were younger, and bipolar disorder patients were older than patients from the other diagnostic categories. Finally, the group with somatoform disorders included more individuals who had only received primary school education ($\chi^2 = 36.3$, $df = 16$, $p = .002$) than individuals in the other diagnostic categories.

Instruments

The *Structured Clinical Interview for DSM-IV Dissociative Disorders* (SCID-D) (Steinberg, 1993; Steinberg et al., 1993) is a diagnostic instrument developed for the assessment of DSM-IV dissociative disorders. It assesses five dissociative symptom areas (amnesia, depersonalization, derealization, identity confusion, and identity fragmentation). Good to excellent reliability and validity have been reported both in the US and in the Netherlands (Boon & Draijer, 1993; Steinberg, 1993; Steinberg et al., 1993).

The *Somatoform Dissociation Questionnaire* (SDQ-20) (Nijenhuis et al., 1996, 1998a) is a 20-item self-report questionnaire measuring somatoform dissociation. According to Mokken scale analysis (Mokken, 1971; Molenaar, 1986) the items are strongly scalable on a unidimensional latent scale, the reliability of the instrument is high (Cronbach's alpha = .95), and the scores are not dependent on gender or age. The high intercorrelations with the DIS-Q total and subscale scores support the convergent validity of the SDQ-20. Higher scores of patients with dissociative disorders in comparison with patients with other DSM-IV diagnoses demonstrate criterion-related validity. The construct validity was supported by the finding that the degree of somatoform dissociation in DID and DDNOS was correlated with reported trauma, in particular sexual and physical abuse (Nijenhuis et al., 1998b).

The *SDQ-5* is a 5-item dissociative disorders screening instrument which was derived from the SDQ-20 (Nijenhuis et al., 1997b; 1998a). The scores range from 5 to 25, and the optimal cutoff point in the screening for dissociative disorders is ≥ 8. The SDQ-5 has high sensitivity and specificity, excellent negative predictive value, and satisfactory positive predictive value in predicting cases of dissociative disorders. There were no indications that the SDQ-5 yielded different scores when administered as a separate scale, as opposed to when embedded in the SDQ-20 (Nijenhuis et al., 1998a).

The *Dissociative Experiences Scale* (DES; Bernstein & Putnam, 1986) is a 28-item self-report questionnaire that evaluates psychological dissociation. The scores range from 0 to 100. The DES has adequate test-retest reliability, good internal consistency, and good clinical validity (Bernstein & Putnam, 1996; Carlson et al., 1993; Frischholz et al., 1992). DES scores of ≥ 30 in a North American sample (Carlson & Putnam, 1993), and respectively ≥ 25 in a Dutch sample (Draijer & Boon, 1993) were found to yield optimal sensitivity and specificity in screening for dissociative disorders.

The *Symptom Checklist-90-R* (Derogatis, 1977) is a self-report rating scale with good psychometric properties which measures general psychopathology.

Procedure

All patients completed the SDQ-20 and the SCL-90-R. The patients with bipolar mood disorder, somatoform disorders, and dissociative disorders also completed the DES, except for the conversion disorder patients from the second inpatient unit (where the DIS-Q was used). In all cases informed consent was obtained after presentation of a brochure providing information about the study.

Data Analyses

The associations among the SDQ-20, the SCL-90-R, and the DES were calculated using Pearson product-moment correlations. Analyses of variance (ANOVA) were performed to examine whether the average sum scores on the SDQ-20 and the DES differed among diagnostic groups. Differences among these groups were assessed post hoc with Tukey's HSD tests. ANCOVA, entering the SCL-90-R as a covariate, was applied to assess whether the SDQ-20 and the DES differentiated among diagnostic groups after statistically correcting for general psychopathology. Next, the estimated marginal means on the SDQ-20 and DES of the various diagnostic groups were compared pairwise, and post hoc Bonferroni correction was applied.

The SDQ-5 scores were derived through summation of the relevant SDQ-20 item scores, and subsequently the proportion of cases per diagnostic category that obtained above cutoff scores (≥ 8) was assessed. The proportion of cases according to the recommended DES cutoff score (≥ 25) in the screening for dissociative disorders as found in a Dutch psychiatric sample (Draijer & Boon, 1993) was also calculated.

Statistical analyses were performed with SPSS-PC 7.5 (SPSS Inc., 1997).

Results

The SDQ-20 was strongly intercorrelated with the DES ($r = .85, p < .0001$). The intercorrelations of the SDQ-20 with the SCL-90-R total and subscale scores were more moderate, but still of considerable strength ($.30 ≤ r ≤ .55$; all $p < .0001$).

The associations with the SCL-90-R somatization, agoraphobia, anxiety subscales and the SCL-90-R total scores obtained the highest values (all $r \geq .50$).

According to ANOVA, the SDQ-20 differentiated among diagnostic groups ($F = 57.80$, $df = 5$, 203, $p < .0001$; table 1). Tukey's HSD indicated that somatoform dissociation was significantly higher in DID than in DDNOS. Somatoform dissociation was also significantly higher in both of these dissociative disorders than in the other diagnostic categories. Finally, patients with somatoform disorders obtained significantly higher SDQ-20 scores than patients with mixed psychiatric (without dissociative or somatoform) disorders, or bipolar mood disorder (Table 1).

Table 1
Differences among Several Diagnostic Categories on the SDQ-20 and the DES

	SDQ-20		DES	
	M	SD	M	SD
Bipolar Mood Disorder	21.6	1.93	11.1	9.90
Mixed Psychiatric Group	22.9	3.94	-	-
Eating Disorders	27.7	8.77	-	-
Somatoform Disorders	31.9	9.37	17.4	17.46
Dissociative Disorder NOS	43.0	12.01	39.7	14.78
Dissociative Identity Disorder	55.1	13.47	54.2	15.12

ANCOVA showed that the estimated marginal mean SDQ-20 scores of various diagnostic categories still discriminated among these diagnostic categories when these scores were adjusted for the SCL-90-R total scores as a covariate ($F = 52.49$, $df = 5$, 193, $p < .0001$; Table 2). Pairwise comparison revealed that the adjusted SDQ-20 scores significantly discriminated among the diagnostic groups as did the unadjusted SDQ-20 scores, except that the adjusted scores also discriminated somatoform disorders and eating disorders (Table 2). Applying a post hoc Bonferroni correction, the differences between the mixed group, and eating disorders, as well as bipolar mood disorder, failed to remain statistically significant.

Table 2
Differences on the SDQ-20 among Several Diagnostic Categories after Adjustment for General Psychopathology Using Adjusted Estimated Marginal Means

	M	SE
Mixed Psychiatric Group	22.6	1.18
Eating Disorders	26.1	1.09
Bipolar Mood Disorder	27.2	1.72
Somatoform Disorders	33.9	1.18
Dissociative Disorder NOS	40.3	1.73
Dissociative Identity Disorder	51.2	1.65

The DES scores were significantly different among patients with bipolar mood disorder, somatoform disorders, DDNOS, and DID (ANOVA, $F = 42.71$, $df = 3$, 84, $p < .0001$) (Table 1). As Tukey's HSD indicated, the DES scores of the DID patients significantly exceeded those of the DDNOS patients, and the patients with dissociative disorders had significantly higher scores than did the patients with somatoform disorders or bipolar mood disorder. However, the difference between somatoform disorders and bipolar mood disorder was not significant. ANCOVA demonstrated that the estimated marginal mean DES scores discriminated between these diagnostic categories when the scores were adjusted for the SCL-90-R total scores as a covariate ($F = 19.36$, $df = 3$, 81, $p < .0001$) (Table 3). Finally, Bonferroni corrected pairwise comparisons showed that the indicated differences among groups remained statistically significant after adjustment of the DES scores for the influence of the SCL-90-R scores (Table 3).

Table 3

Differences on the DES among Several Diagnostic Categories after Adjustment for General Psychopathology Using Adjusted Estimated Marginal Means

	M	SE
Somatoform Disorders	18.9	2.67
Bipolar Mood Disorder	21.3	2.94
Dissociative Disorder NOS	34.1	2.78
Dissociative Identity Disorder	47.2	2.71

The proportions of patients from the various diagnostic categories with above cutoff scores on the SDQ-5 and the DES are displayed in Table 4. The diagnostic categories encompassed, in the hypothesized order, increasing proportions of cases with above cutoff scores. None of the patients with bipolar mood disorder, and only one patient of the mixed psychiatric group had scores above the SDQ-5 cutoff. In contrast, 40% of the cases with eating disorder and 64.6% of the patients with somatoform disorder passed the SDQ-5 cutoff, as did most cases of DDNOS and all but one cases of DID. However, only 23.8% of the cases with somatoform disorders had scores which exceeded the DES cutoff. The DES and SDQ-5 screening results with bipolar mood disorder and dissociative disorders yielded comparable results.

As far more female patients than male patients were included in the diagnostic categories DID, DDNOS, and somatoform disorders, the results could have been biased by this imbalance. However, including only women in the analyses did not affect the results. In a meta-analytic validation study on the DES, Van IJzendoorn and Schuengel (1996) remarked that this instrument has many strengths and some weaknesses. One weakness is that DID patients who were unaware of their diagnostic status obtained lower DES scores than DID patients who were knowledgeable of their condition. As the measurement of somatoform dissociation could also be subject to this bias, we compared the SDQ-20 scores

Table 4

Percentages of Cases of Various Diagnostic Categories Scoring Below and Above the Cutoffs on the SDQ-5 and DES

	SDQ-5 D 8		DES D 25
	N	%	%
Bipolar Mood Disorder	23	0	13.0
Mixed Psychiatric Group	45	2.2	n.a.
Eating Disorders	50	40.0	n.a.
Somatoform Disorders	47	64.6	23.8
DDNOS	21	76.2	81.0
DID	23	95.7	100.0

n.a.= not available

of DDNOS and DID patients when the scales were administered by a diagnostic consultant before the diagnosis had been made and shared, or by the treating therapist in a post-diagnostic stage. Interestingly, the patients who were not aware of their diagnosis (DDNOS, $M = 47.6$, $SD = 12.0$; DID, $M = 60.0$, $SD = 14.86$) tended to obtain higher scores than dissociative patients who were aware of their psychiatric status (DDNOS, $M = 35.6$, $SD = 7.9$; DID, $M = 53.0$, $SD = 12.73$).

Since the bipolar mood disorder patients were generally older than the patients from the other groups, and patients with somatoform disorders generally had received less education, we checked for differences in the SDQ-20, DES, and SCL-90-R scores according to age and level of education, but found that they did not influence the present results.

Discussion

Somatoform dissociation was strongly associated with psychological dissociation as measured by the DES. These findings support the convergent validity of the SDQ-20. Other recent studies also found strong correlations between SDQ-20 and DES scores, both among Turkish and North-American psychiatric patients (Dell, 1997; Şar, Kundaçki, Kiziltan, Bahadir, & Aydiner, 1998), and among a non-psychiatric Dutch population (Nijenhuis, Van Dyck, Ter Kuile, Spinhoven, Mourits, & Van der Hart, submitted).

In view of the striking comorbidity displayed by patients with dissociative disorders (Cardeña & Spiegel, 1996; Dell, 1998; Ellason, Ross, & Fuchs, 1996), the considerable correlations between somatoform dissociation and general psychopathology were expected. However, we also predicted that this association would be weaker than the association between somatoform and psychological dissociation. This first hypothesis was supported by the present data. Interestingly, the association of the SDQ-20 with the SCL-90-R somatization subscale was of the same magnitude as the correlation with the SCL-90-R total scale, and the anxiety and agoraphobia subscales. These findings suggest that the SDQ-20 and the somatization subscale of the SCL-90-R assess related, but distinct constructs. It follows that somatoform dissociation cannot be equated with a tendency to report physical complaints.

The SDQ-20 differentiated among most diagnostic groups, and in all cases but one, the differences were as hypothesized. The associations between somatoform dissociation and SCL-90-R total and subscale scores could raise a concern about whether the SDQ-20 would actually be a measure of general psychopathology. However, statistically controlling for the influence of the SCL-90-R total score did not affect the SDQ-20's ability to differentiate among the diagnostic groups. Somatoform dissociation, whether unadjusted or adjusted for general psychopathology, was significantly raised in a stepwise manner beginning with (i) somatoform disorders, then (ii) DDNOS, and finally (iii) DID. These results strongly support the discriminant validity of the SDQ-20, and provide evidence that somatoform dissociation stands apart from general psychopathology.

The mixed psychiatric group and patients with bipolar mood disorder obtained low SDQ-20 scores. This result is in concordance with their low DES scores, the low DES scores of patients with anxiety disorders and affective disorders as assessed in other studies (for a review see Van IJzendoorn & Schuengel, 1996), as well as the low DES scores of bipolar mood disorder patients (Nijenhuis et al., 1997a). Only one patient of the mixed psychiatric group, and none of the bipolar mood disorder patients passed the SDQ-5 cutoff point. We conclude that anxiety disorders, depression, and adjustment disorders are not associated with dissociative pathology, and that the present data strongly contradict Merskey's (1992) assertion that DID would be misdiagnosed bipolar mood disorder.

Consistent with our prediction, somatoform dissociation was elevated in a subgroup of patients with eating disorders. About one third surpassed the SDQ-5 cutoff in the screening for dissociative disorders. This result concurs with earlier findings that a subgroup of patients with eating disorders experienced substantial psychological dissociation (Demitrack et al., 1993; Tobin et al., 1995).

Patients with somatoform disorders reported considerable somatoform dissociation. As many as two thirds of them scored above the SDQ-5 cutoff in the screening for dissociative disorders. This finding suggests that these patients would possibly have a dissociative disorder as a comorbid diagnosis, although in the present study presence of dissociative disorder according to DSM-IV criteria was not assessed. In the ICD-10 (WHO, 1992), so-called conversion disorders, but not pain and somatization disorders, are categorized and labeled as dissociative disorders. The present data suggest that somatoform dissociation may be typical for a substantial subgroup of patients with somatoform disorder.

Somatoform dissociation was high in DDNOS and extreme in DID, which confirms our previous findings (Nijenhuis et al., 1996, 1998a). DDNOS and DID were also associated with, respectively high and extreme levels of psychological dissociation. This result is consistent with the finding that psychological dissociation is highly characteristic of dissociative disorders, and that it increases with the complexity of the dissociative disorder (Hornstein & Putnam, 1993; Ross, Anderson, Fraser, Reagor, Bjornson, & Miller, 1992; Steinberg, 1993; Steinberg et al., 1993; Vanderlinden et al., 1993a).

Psychological dissociation as measured by the DES differentiated among bipolar mood disorder, DDNOS, and DID, both when the scores were unadjusted and adjusted for the influence of general psychopathology. However, the DES did not distinguish somatoform disorder from bipolar mood disorder. About two thirds of the present DSM-IV somatoform disorder patients experienced significant somatoform dissociation, but psychological dissociation was only characteristic of a quarter of them.

Some limitations of this study demand discussion. The eating disorder and the somatoform disorder patients were admitted to inpatient units specialized in the treatment of these conditions. Assuming that as a rule, inpatients would display more psychopathology than outpatients, the scores of the eating disorder and somatoform disorders patients may have been raised for this reason, and, thus, may have influenced the comparisons. On the other hand, the inpatient status of the eating disorder and somatoform disorder patients made it more difficult for the SDQ-20 to differentiate these inpatients from the dissociative disorder outpatients, especially those with DDNOS. A future comparison between consecutive psychiatric outpatients without dissociative disorders or somatoform disorders and somatoform disorder outpatients would nevertheless be important. As the group of patients with somatoform disorder included various diagnostic subcategories (conversion disorder, somatoform pain disorder, and somatization disorder), future work should study somatoform dissociation among homogeneous subgroups of DSM-IV somatoform disorders. Another limitation of this study is that two subgroups (dissociative disorders and eating disorders) almost entirely consisted of women. However, including only women in the analyses did not affect the results. The patients with bipolar mood disorder were older than the patients of some other diagnostic categories, but these differences did not affect the results either.

DID and DDNOS patients who were aware of their diagnostic status did not report more somatoform dissociative phenomena than dissociative disorder patients who were not aware of their diagnosis. The trend was even in the other direction, which could perhaps reflect a positive treatment effect.

Conclusion

The present data support the SDQ-20's convergent, criterion-related, and discriminant validity. The evidence indicates that this instrument measures a unique construct – somatoform dissociation – which is strongly associated with, but not identical to psychological dissociation, and which differs from general psychopathology. The findings confirm our previous conclusion that dissociative disorders are highly characterized by somatoform dissociation. They also suggest that somatoform dissociation is a core feature in many patients with somatoform disorders, and an important symptom cluster in a subgroup of patients with eating disorders.

References

American Psychiatric Association. Author (1994). *Diagnostic and statistical manual of mental disorders, 4th edn.* Washington DC: American Psychiatric Association.

Atchison, M., & McFarlane, A.C. (1994). A review of dissociation and dissociative disorders. *Australian and New Zealand Journal of Psychiatry, 28,* 591-599.

Badura, A.S., Reiter, R.C., Altmaier, E.M., Rhomberg, A., & Elas, D. (1997). Dissociation, somatization, substance abuse and coping in women with chronic pelvic pain. *Obstetrics & Gynecology, 90,* 405-410.

Bernstein, E., & Putnam F.W. (1986). Development, reliability, and validity of a dissociation scale. *Journal of Nervous and Mental Disease, 102,* 280-286.

Boon, S., & Draijer, N. (1993). Multiple personality disorder in The Netherlands: A clinical investigation of 71 patients. *American Journal of Psychiatry, 150,* 489-494.

Breuer, J., & Freud S. (1974). *Studies on hysteria.* Harmondsworth: Penguin Books.

Briquet, P. (1895). *Traité clinique et thérapeutique de l'hystérie* (2 vols.) [Clinical and therapeutic treatise of hysteria]. Paris: J.-P. Baillière & Fils.

Brown, P., & Van der Hart, O. (1998). Memories of sexual abuse: Janet's critique of Freud, a balanced approach. *Psychological Report, 82,* 1027-1043.

Cardeña, E., & Spiegel, D. (1996). Diagnostic issues, criteria, and comorbidity of dissociative disorders. In L.K. Michelson & J.W. Ray (eds.), *Handbook of dissociation: Theoretical, empirical, and clinical perspectives* (pp. 227-250). New York: Plenum Press.

Carlson, E.B., & Putnam, F.W. (1993). An update on the Dissociative Experiences Scale. *Dissociation, 6,* 16-27.

Carlson, E.B., Putnam, F.W., Ross, C.A., Torem, M., Coons, P., Dill, D.L., Loewenstein, R.J., & Braun, B.G. (1993). Validity of the Dissociative Experiences Scale in screening for multiple personality disorder: A multicenter study. *American Journal of Psychiatry, 150,* 1030-1036.

Charcot, J.-M. (1887). Leçons sur les maladies du système nerveux faites à la *Salpêtrière*, Tome III. Paris: Progrès Médical en A. Delahaye & E. Lecrosnie. English edition: Clinical lectures on certain diseases of the nervous system. Detroit: Davies, 1888.

Dell, P.F. (1997). Somatoform dissociation in DID, DDNOS, chronic pain, and eating disorders in a North American sample. Proceedings of the 14th International Conference of the International Society for the Study of Dissociation, november 8-11, 130.

Dell, P.F. (1998). Axis II pathology in outpatients with dissociative identity disorder. *Journal of Nervous and Mental Disease, 186,* 352-356.

Demitrack, M.A., Putnam, F.W., Rubinov, D.R., Pigott, T.A., Altemus, M., Krahn, D.D., & Gold, P.W. (1993). Relation of dissociative phenomena to levels of cerebrospinal fluid monoamine metabolites and beta-endorphin in patients with eating disorders: A pilot study. *Psychiatry Research, 9,* 1-10.

Derogatis, L.R. (1977). *SCL-90: Administration, scoring, and procedures manual-I for the R(evised) version and other instruments of the psychopathology rating scale series.* Baltimore: Clinical Psychometric Research Unit, John Hopkins University School of Medicine.

Draijer, N., & Boon, S. (1993). Trauma, dissociation, and dissociative disorders. In S. Boon & N. Draijer (eds.), *Multiple personality disorder in the Netherlands: A study on reliability and validity of the diagnosis* (pp. 177-193). Amsterdam/Lisse: Swets & Zeitlinger.

Ellason, J.W., Ross, C.A., & Fuchs, D.L. (1996). Lifetime axis I and II comorbidity and childhood trauma history in dissociative identity disorder. *Psychiatry, 59,* 255-266.

Farley, M., & Keaney, J.C. (1997). Physical symptoms, somatization, and dissociation in women survivors of childhood sexual assault. *Women & Health, 25*, 33-45.

Frischholz, E.J., Braun, B.G., Sachs, R.G., Schwartz, D.R., Lewis, J., Shaeffer, D., Westergaard, C., & Pasquotto, J. (1992). Construct validity of the dissociative experiences scale: II. Its relationship to hypnotizability. *American Journal of Clinical Hypnosis, 35*, 145-152.

Hornstein, N.L., & Putnam, F.W. (1993). Clinical phenomenology of child and adolescent disorders. *Journal of American Academic Child and Adolescent Psychiatry, 31*, 1077-1085.

Janet, P. (1901). *The mental state of hystericals*. New York: Putnam and Sons.

Janet, P. (1907). The major symptoms of hysteria. New York: MacMillan. Hafner, 1965.

Janet, P. (1909). Problèmes psychologiques de l'émotion. [Psychological problems of emotion]. *Revue Neurologique, 17*, 1551-1687.

Kihlstrom, J.F. (1994). One hundred years of hysteria In S.J. Lynn & J.W. Rhue (eds.), *Dissociation: clinical and theoretical perspectives* (pp. 365-394). New York: Guilford.

Lewis, D.O., Yeager, C.A., Swica, Y., Pincus, J.H., & Lewis, M. (1997). Objective documentation of child abuse and dissociation in 12 murderers with dissociative identity disorder. *American Journal of Psychiatry, 154*, 1703-1710.

Mayou, R. (1993). Somatization. *Psychotherapy and Psychosomatics, 59*, 69-83.

Marmar, C.R., Weiss, D.S., Schlenger, W.E., Fairbank, J.A., Jordan, B.K., Kulka, R.A., & Hough, R.L. (1994). Peritraumatic dissociation and posttraumatic stress in male Vietnam theater veterans. *American Journal of Psychiatry, 151*, 902-907.

McCarthy, M.K., Goff, D.C., Baer, L., Cioffi, J., & Herzog, D.B. (1994). Dissociation, childhood trauma, and the response to fluoxetine in bulimic patients. *International Journal of Eating Disorders, 15*, 227-235.

McDougall, W. (1926). *An outline of abnormal psychology*. London: Methuen.

Merskey, H. (1992). The manufacture of personalities: The production of multiple personality disorder. *British Journal of Psychiatry, 160*, 327-340.

Mokken, R.J. (1971). *A theory and procedure of scale analysis*. The Hague, Mouton, 1971.

Molenaar, I.W. (1986). Een vingeroefening in item response theorie voor drie geordende antwoordcategorieën. In G.F. Pikkemaat & J.J.A. Moors (eds.), *Liber amoricum Jaap Muilwijk*. Groningen, Econometrisch Instituut, 1986.

Nemiah, J.C. (1991). Dissociation, conversion, and somatization In Tasman, A. & Goldfinger, S.M. (eds.), American Psychiatric Press Annual Review of Psychiatry (Vol 10, pp. 248-260). Washington DC: American Psychiatric Press.

Nijenhuis, E.R.S., Spinhoven, P., Van Dyck, R., Van der Hart, O., De Graaf, A.M.J., & Knoppert, E.A.M. (1997a). Dissociative pathology discriminates between bipolar mood disorder and dissociative disorder. *British Journal of Psychiatry, 170*, 581.

Nijenhuis, E.R.S., Spinhoven P., Van Dyck R., Van der Hart, O., & Vanderlinden, J. (1996). The development and the psychometric characteristics of the Somatoform Dissociation Questionnaire (SDQ-20). *Journal of Nervous and Mental Disease, 184*, 688-694.

Nijenhuis, E.R.S., Spinhoven, P., Van Dyck, R., Van der Hart, O., & Vanderlinden J. (1997b). The development of the Somatoform Dissociation Questionnaire (SDQ-5) as a screening instrument for dissociative disorders. *Acta Psychiatrica Scandinavica, 96*, 311-318.

Nijenhuis, E.R.S., Spinhoven, P., Van Dyck, R., Van der Hart, O., & Vanderlinden J. (1998a). Psychometric characteristics of the Somatoform Dissociation Questionnaire: A replication study. *Psychotherapy and Psychosomatics, 67*, 17-23.

Nijenhuis, E.R.S., Spinhoven, P., Van Dyck, R., Van der Hart, O., & Vanderlinden J. (1998b). Degree of somatoform and psychological dissociation in dissociative disorders is correlated with reported trauma. *Journal of Traumatic Stress, 11*, 711-730.

Nijenhuis, E.R.S., Spinhoven, P., Vanderlinden, J., Van Dyck, R., & Van der Hart, O. (1998c). Somatoform dissociative symptoms as related to animal defensive reactions to predatory threat and injury. *Journal of Abnormal Psychology, 107*, 63-73.

Nijenhuis, E.R.S., Van Dyck, R., Ter Kuile, M., Spinhoven, P., Mourits, M., & Van der Hart O. (submitted). Evidence for associations between somatoform dissociation, psychological dissociation, and reported trauma in chronic pelvic pain patients.

Nijenhuis, E.R.S., & Van der Hart, O. (1999). Somatoform dissociative phenomena: A Janetian Perspective. In J.M. Goodwin & R. Attias (eds.), *Splintered reflections: Images of the body in trauma* (pp. 89-127). New York: Basic Books.

Ogawa, J.R., Sroufe, L.A., Weinfeld, N.C., Carlson, E.A., & Egeland, B. (1997). Development and the fragmented self: Longitudinal study of dissociative symptomatology in a nonclinical sample. *Development and Psychopathology, 9*, 855-879.

Pitres, A. (1891). *Leçons cliniques sur l'hystérie et l'hypnotisme*. Paris: Octave Doin.

Pribor, E.F., Yutzy, S.H., Dean, T., & Wetzel, R.D. (1993). Briquet's syndrome, dissociation, and abuse. *American Journal of Psychiatry, 150*, 1507-1510.

Putnam, F.W., Carlson, E.B., Ross, C.A., Anderson, G., Clark, P., Torem, M., Bowman, E., Coons, P., Chu, J.A., Dill, D.L., Loewenstein, R., & Braun, B.G. (1996). Patterns of dissociation in clinical and nonclinical samples. *Journal of Nervous and Mental Disease, 184*, 673-679.

Ross, C.A., Anderson, G., Fraser, G.A., Reagor, P., Bjornson, L., & Miller, S.D. (1992). Differentiating multiple personality disorder and dissociative disorder not otherwise specified. *Dissociation, 5*, 87-91.

Şar, V., Kundakçi, T., Kiziltan, E., Bahadir, B., & Aydiner, O. (1998). Reliability and validity of the Turkish version of the Somatoform Dissociation Questionnaire (SDQ-20). Proceeding of the International Society of Dissociation 15th International Fall Conference. Seattle, november 14-17.

Saxe, G.N., Chinman, G., Berkowitz, R., Hall, K., Lieberg, G., Schwartz, J., & Van der Kolk, B.A. (1994). Somatization in patients with dissociative disorders. *American Journal of Psychiatry, 151*, 1329-1334.

SPSS PC: SPSS Inc. (1997). *SPSS for Windows Release 7.5*. Chicago, SPSS Inc.

Steinberg, M., (1993). Structured Interview for DSM-IV Dissociative Disorders (SCID-D). Washington DC: American Psychiatric Press.

Steinberg, M., Cichetti, D.V., Buchanan, J., Hall, P., & Rounsaville, B. (1993). Clinical assessment of dissociative symptoms and disorders: The Structured Clinical Interview for DSM-IV Dissociative Disorders. *Dissociation, 6*, 3-16.

Stekel, W. (1908). *Nervöse Angstzustände und ihre Behandlung* [Nervous mental states and their treatment]. Berlin: Urban und Schwarzenbach.

Tillman, J.G., Nash, M.R., & Lerner, P.M. (1994). Does trauma cause dissociative pathology? In S.J. Lynn & J.W. Rhue (eds.), *Dissociation: Clinical and theoretical perspectives* (pp. 395-415). New York: Guilford.

Tobin, D.L., Molteni, A.L., & Elin, M.R. (1995). Early trauma, dissociation, and late onset in the eating disorders. *International Journal of Eating Disorders, 17*, 305-308.

Van der Hart, O., & Op den Velde, W. (1991). Traumatische stoornissen. In O. Van der Hart (ed.), *Trauma, dissociatie en hypnose* (pp. 91-125). Amsterdam: Swets & Zeitlinger.

Van der Kolk, B.A., Pelcovitz, D., Roth, S., Mandel, F.S., McFarlane, A., & Herman J.L. (1996). Dissociation, somatization, and affect dysregulation: The complexity of adaptation to trauma. *American Journal of Psychiatry, Festschrift Supplement, 153*, 83-93.

Vanderlinden, J., Vandereycken, W., Van Dyck, R., & Vertommen, H. (1993a). Dissociative experiences and trauma in eating disorders. *International Journal of Eating Disorders, 13*, 187-194.

Vanderlinden J., Van Dyck, R., Vandereycken, W., Vertommen, H., & Verkes, R.J. (1993b) The Dissociation Questionnaire: Development and characteristics of a new self-reporting questionnaire. *Clinical Psychology and Psychotherapy 1*, 21-27.

Van IJzendoorn, M.H. & Schuengel, C. (1996). The measurement of dissociation in normal and clinical populations: Meta-analytic validation of the Dissociative Experiences Scale (DES). *Clinical Psychology Review, 16*, 365-382.

Walker, E.A., Katon, W.J., Neraas, K., Jemelka, R.P., & Massoth, D. (1992). Dissociation in women with chronic pelvic pain. *American Journal of Psychiatry, 149*, 534-537.

World Health Organization (1992). *The ICD-10 Classification of Mental and Behavioral Disorders: Clinical description and diagnostic guidelines*. Geneva: World Health Organization.

VII
Dissociative Disorders and Somatoform Dissociation: Effects of Indoctrination?*

A correspondence in the British Journal of Psychiatry

> *"How is it that, in all civilized countries,*
> *hystericals should have agreed to simulate the same thing ever*
> *since the Middle Ages to the present day?"*
> Janet, 1907, p. 171

I Dissociative Pathology Discriminates between Bipolar Mood Disorder and Dissociative Disorder

Although Dissociative Identity Disorder (DID) is a prominent diagnostic category in the *DSM-IV*, serious doubt has been voiced about the validity of this diagnosis in this journal (Fahy, 1988; Merskey, 1992). Merskey suggested that so-called dissociative symptoms may be a misinterpretation of bipolar disorder. From this criticism a specific hypothesis can be derived: high scores on instruments pretending to measure dissociative pathology should be typical not only of patients with the diagnosis of dissociative disorder, but would also be found in patients with bipolar disorder.

In order to study this question, we administered the Dissociative Experiences Scale (DES; Bernstein & Putnam, 1989) and the Somatoform Dissociation Questionnaire (SDQ-20; Nijenhuis et al., 1996) to patients with bipolar mood disorder ($n = 51$), DID ($n = 21$), or dissociative disorder NOS (DDNOS; $n = 20$). The DES measures dissociative symptoms, such as dissociative amnesia and identity fragmentation (scores range from 0 to 100). The SDQ-20 measures somatoform manifestations of dissociation, for example, loss of control over sensation and movement (scores range from 20 to 100). The bipolar mood disorder patients were recruited from two mood disorder clinics. All but 4 patients were on a maintenance treatment of lithium, three received carbamaze-

---

* This chapter includes two letters to the editor of the British Journal of Psychiatry. The references are:

1. Nijenhuis, E.R.S., Spinhoven, P., Van Dyck, R., Van der Hart, O., De Graaf, A.M.J., & Knoppert, E.M. (1997). Dissociative pathology discriminates between bipolar mood disorder and dissociative disorder (letter), *170*, 581.
2. Nijenhuis, E.R.S., Van Dyck, R., Van der Hart, O., & Spinhoven, P. (1998). Somatoform dissociation is unlikely to be a result of indoctrination by therapists (letter), *172*, 452.

The citation appears in: P. Janet (1907). *The major symptoms of hysteria.* London & New York: Macmillan.

pine, and one did not tolerate psychopharmacological drugs. The dissociative disorder patients were assessed with the Structured Clinical Interview for Dissociative Disorders (SCID-D; Steinberg et al., 1993).

Bipolar mood disorder was associated with low dissociation scores (DES: 11.6 [SD = 9.8]) (SDQ-20: 22.9 [SD = 3.7]), DDNOS with significant higher scores (DES: 38.6 [SD = 14.3], t = 9.12, 69, p < .0001) (SDQ-20: 42.5 [SD = 12.0], t = 7.14, 20.40, p <.0001), and DID with extreme dissociation (DES: 54.9 [SD = 14.5], t = -3.61, 39, p <.001) (SDQ-20: 55.6 [SD = 14.0], t = -3.19, 39, p <.003).

The DES is also a dissociative disorder screening instrument, as is the SDQ-5 (Nijenhuis et al., 1997), which consists of five SDQ-20 items. Only 9.8% (DES), respectively 4% (SDQ-5) of the bipolar mood disorder patients obtained scores above the cutoff values of these instruments, but 80%, respectively 75% of the DDNOS patients, and 100%, respectively 97% of the DID patients passed the cutoff values.

These results contradict Merskey's hypothesis: while dissociative patients reported extreme dissociation, bipolar mood disorder patients hardly experienced such symptoms.

References

Bernstein, E., & Putnam, F. (1986). Development, reliability, and validity of a dissociation scale. *Journal of Nervous and Mental Disease, 102,* 280-286.

Fahy, T.A. (1988). The diagnosis of multiple personality disorder: A critical review. *British Journal of Psychiatry, 153,* 597-606.

Merskey, H. (1992). The manufacture of personalities: The production of multiple personality disorder. *British Journal of Psychiatry, 160,* 327-340.

Nijenhuis, E.R.S., Spinhoven, P., Van Dyck, R., Van der Hart, O., & Vanderlinden, J. (1996). The development and the psychometric characteristics of the Somatoform Dissociation Questionnaire (SDQ-20). *Journal of Nervous and Mental Disease, 184,* 688-694.

Nijenhuis, E.R.S., Spinhoven, P., Van Dyck, R., Van der Hart, O., & Vanderlinden, J. (1997). The development of the Somatoform Dissociation Questionnaire (SDQ-5) as a screening instrument for dissociative disorders. *Acta Psychiatrica Scandinavica, 96,* 311-318.

Steinberg, M., Cichetti, D.V., Buchanan, J., Hall, P., & Rounsaville, B. (1993). Clinical assessment of dissociative symptoms and disorders: The Structured Clinical Interview for DSM-IV Dissociative Disorders. *Dissociation, 6,* 3-16.

II Merskey's Response

In his response to our letter, Merskey (1997) replied that the hypothesis that dissociative patients are misdiagnosed cases of bipolar mood disorder cannot validly be tested by studying the scores on self-report questionnaires of patients with supposed dissociative disorders and with bipolar affective disorder. Patients with bipolar mood disorder may be misdiagnosed in several ways, he argued. First, the natural phenomena of bipolar mood disorder may be misinterpreted.

Such would apply to cases of double consciousness. Second, therapists may educate suggestible patients with bipolar disorder into producing "dissociative" states. Merskey, therefore, felt that patients with bipolar disorder would only match the dissociative disorder group on self-report dissociation scales if they had been indoctrinated. Consequently, he stated that:

> "Nijenhuis et al. have compared un-indoctrinated subjects with others whom they consider to be dissociative and have obtained highly significant results which are predictable, but not for the reason they suppose. The comparison that has been offered is worthless."

Reference

Merskey, H. (1997). Tests of "dissociation" and mood disorder (letter), British Journal of Psychiatry, 171, 487.

III Somatoform dissociation is unlikely to be a result of indoctrination by therapists

In a previous letter (Nijenhuis, Spinhoven, Van Dyck, Van der Hart, De Graaf, & Knoppert, 1997) we reported that high scores on instruments measuring dissociation were typical of dissociative disorder patients and not of bipolar mood disorder patients. We argued that these data show that dissociative disorders are highly unlikely to be a result of misinterpretation of bipolar disorder. Merskey (1997) commented that our comparison is worthless. Assuming that dissociative disorders result from indoctrination by therapists, he maintained that we have compared un-indoctrinated bipolar patients and indoctrinated "dissociative" patients.

This assumption is incorrect. For the patients with dissociative disorders we had two groups: one received the somatoform dissociation questionnaire (SDQ-20) prior to the administration of the Structured Clinical Interview for Dissociative Disorders (SCID-D) and the diagnosis of DID or DDNOS, and the other after this diagnosis was given and discussed with the patient. The first group cannot possibly have been indoctrinated. Interestingly, patients from the first group who were unaware of their diagnosis tended to obtain *higher* SDQ-20 scores than patients who were aware of their psychiatric status and who were exposed to therapy (Nijenhuis et al., submitted).

Moreover, prior to the publication of our relevant research (Nijenhuis et al., 1996) at which time the data were collected, diagnosticians, therapists, and patients could not be aware that particular somatoform symptoms are manifestations of dissociation. The high scores obtained with our questionnaire, therefore, cannot be satisfactorily explained as an effect of indoctrination.

Although we do not deny that iatrogenic influences and overdiagnosis are possible in clinical practice, it should be noted that systematic studies are lacking which demonstrate, when using a reliable and valid diagnostic instrument such as the SCID-D, that the diagnosis of dissociative disorder does only occur in patients who have been exposed to indoctrination. In the absence of such studies, the a priori assumption that the diagnosis of dissociative disorders must follow from indoctrination seems to be based on prejudice instead of on research findings. In conclusion, our comparison between dissociation in bipolar disorder and dissociative disorders is relevant and of clinical and scientific interest.

References

Merskey, H. (1997). Tests of "dissociation" and mood disorder (letter). *British Journal of Psychiatry, 171*, 487.

Nijenhuis, E.R.S., Spinhoven, P., Van Dyck, R., Van der Hart, & Vanderlinden (1996). The development and the psychometric characteristics of the Somatoform Dissociation Questionnaire (SDQ-20). *Journal of Nervous and Mental Disease, 184*, 688-694.

Nijenhuis, E.R.S., Spinhoven, P., Van Dyck, R., Van der Hart, & Vanderlinden (1997). The development of the Somatoform Dissociation Questionnaire (SDQ-5) as a screening instrument for dissociative disorders. *Acta Psychiatrica Scandinavica, 96*, 311-318.

Nijenhuis, E.R.S., Spinhoven, P., Van Dyck, R., Van der Hart, De Graaf, A.M.J., & Knoppert, E.A.M. (1997). Dissociative pathology discriminates between bipolar mood disorder and dissociative disorder (letter). *British Journal of Psychiatry, 170*, 581.

Nijenhuis, E.R.S., Van Dyck, R., Spinhoven, P., Van der Hart, O., Chatrou, M., Vanderlinden, J., & Moene, F. (submitted). Somatoform dissociation discriminates among diagnostic groups over and above general psychopathology.

PART II

TRAUMA, SOMATOFORM DISSOCIATION, AND DEFENSE

VIII
Degree of Somatoform and Psychological Dissociation in Dissociative Disorder is Correlated with Reported Trauma[*]

"Nous oublions le corps mais le corps ne nous oublie pas.
Maudite mémoire des organes."
Carol Dallaire, 1996

Introduction

Contemporary empirical studies indicate that traumatized individuals, in particular adult survivors of childhood sexual and physical abuse, often manifest dissociative, as well as medically unexplained somatoform symptoms (e.g., Pribor, Yutzy, Dean, & Wetzel, 1993).

These findings suggest that dissociative and somatoform symptoms may be trauma-induced phenomena. Dissociation may be of an everyday type (e.g., daydreaming), which does not imply the formation of disconnected memories, and which would better be labeled absorption, or it may be of a qualitatively different and pathological type (Waller, Putnam, & Carlson, 1996), which is characterized by the formation of dissociative memory structures (Janet, 1907; Van der Hart, Boon, & Op den Velde, 1991; Yates & Nasby, 1989). While this distinction has not consistently been made, many authors have hypothesized that dissociation reaching pathological proportions is trauma-induced as a rule (e.g., Janet, 1909; Spiegel, 1984; Van der Hart et al., 1991). In concurrence with this hypothesis, in several studies high correlations between pathological dissociation and documented, as well as reported trauma, have been found. These studies involved patients with dissociative disorders (e.g., Draijer & Boon, 1993; Hornstein & Putnam, 1992; Ross et al., 1991), posttraumatic stress disorder (PTSD; e.g., Bremner, Steinberg, Southwick, Johnson, & Charney, 1993), eating disorder (Vanderlinden, Vandereycken, Van Dyck, & Vertommen, 1993), and borderline personality disorder (e.g., Herman, Perry, & Van der Kolk, 1989). Dissociative symptoms of borderline personality disorder patients correlated more strongly with childhood trauma than borderline psychopathol-

* This chapter has been published as: Nijenhuis, E.R.S., Spinhoven, P., Van Dyck, R., Van der Hart, O., & Vanderlinden, J. (1998). Degree of somatoform and psychological dissociation in dissociative disorder is correlated with reported trauma. *Journal of Traumatic Stress, 11*, 711-730.

ogy per se (Herman et al., 1989). In a study of patients with *DSM-IV* dissociative identity disorder (DID; American Psychiatric Association, 1994), who display the most complex and pervasive dissociative symptoms, Draijer and Boon (1993) found that dissociation of these patients was best predicted by early onset, duration, and severity of reported sexual and physical abuse, consistent with Janet's (1909) original observations. Furthermore, adult peritraumatic dissociation, that is, dissociative symptoms experienced during or immediately following exposure to a traumatic event and reported in its aftermath, are predictive of later development of posttraumatic stress symptoms (Koopman, Classen, & Spiegel, 1994) and PTSD (e.g., Marmar et al., 1994; Shalev, Peri, Canetti, & Schreiber, 1996).

However, limitations of the evidence for the link between trauma and dissociation have also been put forward. Tillman, Nash, and Lerner (1994) cited some evidence suggesting that high scores of traumatized subjects on measures of dissociation, such as the Dissociative Experiences Scale (DES; Bernstein & Putnam, 1986), may have less to do with dissociation per se than with gross psychopathology. They also mentioned that research in the area of sexual trauma often fails to consider baseline reports of abuse among all patients, and that the research design in studies on the link between sexual trauma and patterns of resulting psychopathology is sometimes weak, as it consists of weak control groups and weak dependent measures. Next, retrospective assessment of trauma may yield selecting false negatives (not reporting trauma when it actually did occur) and false positives (reporting trauma that in fact did not occur). Finally, dissociative symptomatology may involve memory distortion, compromising the validity of reports of trauma in either direction (Brown, 1995; Loftus, 1993): underreporting, overreporting, and reporting mixtures of historically valid and invalid components may occur. Moreover, contextual factors may influence dissociation scores (Van IJzendoorn & Schuengl, 1996).

Existing studies investigating the relationship between trauma and dissociation neglect two major aspects. The first aspect involves the nature of posttraumatic dissociation. Until recently, modern empirical studies on dissociation limited this mental phenomenon to disruptions in memory, consciousness, and identity, which may be called *psychological* dissociation, that is, dissociation manifested in psychological variables. However, the original studies on dissociation, such as Janet's (1901, 1907) studies around the turn of the century, also pertained to phenomena which we proposed to call *somatoform* dissociation, that is, dissociation which is manifested in a loss of the normal integration of somatoform components of experience, bodily reactions and functions (e.g., anesthesia and motor inhibitions; Nijenhuis, Spinhoven, Van Dyck, Van der Hart, & Vanderlinden, 1996). Somatoform dissociation is not a somatic disturbance. Like psychological dissociation, it involves a disturbance of a *mental* function, hence, the adjective somato*form* is used.

The second neglected aspect pertains to the question of whether in childhood traumatization other factors than sexual and physical abuse contribute to posttraumatic dissociation. Some studies (Fromuth, 1986; Nash, Hulsey, Sexton, Harralson, & Lambert, 1993) report evidence that adult psychopathology and dissociation in women with a history of childhood sexual abuse might be a consequence, at least in part, of a pathogenic family structure, rather than of the abuse per se. According to Nijenhuis, Vanderlinden and Spinhoven (1998c), somatoform dissociative reactions such as analgesia and freezing reactions may be similar to animal defense reactions to predatory threat and injury. Evidence consistent with this position has been found (Nijenhuis, Spinhoven, Vanderlinden, Van Dyck, & Van der Hart, 1998b). For this reason, events which involve specific threat to the body, such as sexual and physical abuse, may be more strongly related to somatoform dissociation than variables which pertain to a negative emotional climate.

Several authors report convincing clinical, theoretical, and research findings which support the case for a separate somatoform dissociative category (Kihlstrom, 1994; Nemiah, 1991; Nijenhuis et al., 1996-1998a). Nijenhuis et al. (1996-1998a) found that somatoform dissociative phenomena, such as intermittent analgesia, anesthesia, motoric inhibitions, and pain symptoms, highly characterized dissociative disorder patients. Indirect evidence stems from studies reporting that patients with medically unexplained somatoform symptoms attained high scores on measures of psychological dissociation (Albach, 1993; Pribor et al., 1993; Walker, Gelfand, Gelfand, Koss, & Katon, 1995). Also, patients with DID and dissociative disorder not otherwise specified (DDNOS) manifest many somatoform symptoms (Boon & Draijer, 1993; Ross et al., 1992), and more so than patients with other psychiatric diagnoses (Ross, Heber, Norton, & Anderson, 1989; Saxe et al., 1994). Studying consecutive rape victims at a French forensic center, Darves-Bornoz (1997) found that recent rape, which in a proportion of cases was preceded by other rape, was associated with PTSD, dissociative disorders and somatoform disorders after 6 months in respectively 71%, 69%, and 66% of cases. Many PTSD patients also had dissociative disorder (85%) and somatoform disorder (75%).

For the present study it was hypothesized that (1) compared to patients with other *DSM-IV* diagnoses, those with a dissociative disorder would report more types of traumatic events, and more severe trauma, as defined by earlier onset, longer duration, perpetration by members of the family of origin, and higher subjective ratings of traumatic stress these events imposed; (2) reported emotional neglect, emotional abuse, physical trauma, and sexual trauma would be significant predictors of somatoform and psychological dissociation, but physical trauma and sexual trauma would predict these variables better than emotional neglect and abuse; and (3) reported early onset of trauma would contribute to these predictions relatively more than later trauma.

Methods

Subjects

As a part of their clinical assessment, psychiatric outpatients were interviewed by experienced clinicians using the SCID-D (Steinberg, Cichetti, Buchanan, Hall, & Rounsaville, 1993; described in the next section) upon the observation or reporting of substantial dissociative symptoms. In approximately 75% of cases, this interview was held in the diagnostic phase, or the early stages of treatment by a diagnostician/therapist. In the remaining cases, the interview was held in a later stage of treatment. In some cases, an independent diagnostician was involved. All diagnosticians/therapists were trained in the administration and interpretation of the instrument. Forty five cases were collected who presented a dissociative disorder (2 with depersonalization disorder [DP], 19 with DDNOS, 24 with DID). The DDNOS patients displayed clinical features similar to DID, which failed to meet full *DSM-IV* criteria for this disorder. That is, they encompassed dissociative states, but these did not recurrently take full control of the patient's behavior. The mean age of this group (39 women, 6 men) was 35.3, $SD = 9.9$ years, range = 20 to 58.

The comparison group consisted of a sample of 43 psychiatric outpatients receiving treatment, predominantly behavior therapy, with a non-dissociative *DSM-IV* diagnosis who scored < 2.5 on the Dissociation Questionnaire (DIS-Q; Vanderlinden, 1993; Vanderlinden, Van Dyck, Vandereycken, Vertommen, & Verkes, 1993). Diagnoses were assessed according to *DSM-IV* guidelines and included Axis I anxiety disorders ($n = 24$), depressive disorder ($n = 5$), eating disorders ($n = 8$), somatoform disorders ($n = 3$), adjustment disorder ($n = 5$), and alcohol abuse ($n = 3$). Some patients presented with other conditions described in *DSM-IV* that warranted clinical attention ($n = 5$), e.g., bereavement. Five patients had Axis II diagnoses, and 25 patients displayed traits of personality disorder, predominantly dependent personality disorder. The mean age of the comparison group (33 women, 10 men) was 35.1, $SD = 13.2$ years, range 16 to 79. The distribution of gender, living with or without a partner (chi-square tests), and level of education (Mann-Whitney U test) of dissociative disorder patients compared to comparison patients did not differ.

Instruments

Structured Interview for DSM-IV Dissociative Disorders (SCID-D; Steinberg et al., 1993). The SCID-D is a diagnostic instrument developed for the assessment of dissociative disorders, covering dissociative amnesia, depersonalization, derealization, identity confusion, and identity fragmentation. Good to excellent reliability and validity have been reported both in the US and in The Netherlands (Boon & Draijer, 1993; Steinberg et al., 1993).

Dissociation Questionnaire (DIS-Q; Vanderlinden, 1993; Vanderlinden et al., 1993). The DIS-Q is a 63-item self-report questionnaire measuring psychological dissociation, which includes four factors labeled identity confusion and fragmentation, loss of control, amnesia, and absorption. Reliability is good to excellent, scores are stable over time and the DIS-Q differentiates between patients with dissociative disorders, psychiatric subjects with other diagnoses, and normals.

Somatoform Dissociation Questionnaire (SDQ-20; Nijenhuis et al., 1996, 1998a). This 20-item self-report questionnaire evaluates somatoform dissociation. These items include symptoms of analgesia, anesthesia, motor disturbances, alternating preferences of tastes and smells, pain, and loss of consciousness. Some examples are: ("It sometimes happens that:") "it is as if my body or a part of it has disappeared," "I am paralyzed for a while," "I dislike tastes that I usually like." According to Mokken scale analysis, the items are strongly scalable on a unidimensional latent scale (Loevinger's H = .50). Reliability (Cronbach's α) is high, and SDQ-20 scores are highly correlated with DIS-Q and DES scores. These original findings were replicated (Nijenhuis et al., 1998a). Nonsomatoform disorders and nondissociative disorders were associated with low SDQ-20 scores, these scores were significantly elevated in somatoform disorders, were further elevated in DDNOS, and were extreme in DID (Nijenhuis et al., 1997). The differences between these groups remained statistically significant after controlling for general psychopathology, meaning that gross psychopathology did not explain the results (cf. Tillman et al., 1994).

Traumatic Experiences Questionnaire * (Nijenhuis, Van der Hart, & Vanderlinden, unpublished data). The TEQ is a self-report questionnaire inquiring about 25 types of trauma, their age of occurrence or onset, as well as duration. Further, it inquires after the subjectively rated degree of traumatic stress the trauma presented. With respect to emotional neglect, emotional abuse, physical abuse, sexual harassment, and sexual abuse, the TEQ specifically addresses the setting in which such trauma occurred, that is, the family of origin, the extended family, or any other setting. The questions contain short descriptions that intend to define the events of concern. All items are preceded by the phrase: "Did this happen to you?" An example of a sexual harassment item is: "Sexual harassment (acts of a sexual nature that DO NOT involve physical contact) by your parents, brothers or sisters." A sexual abuse item is: "Sexual abuse (unwanted sexual acts involving physical contact) by your parents, brothers, or sisters." The TEQ also requests information about the number of perpetrators of emotional, physical, and sexual abuse.

All patients completed the DIS-Q, SDQ-20, and TEQ after informed consent was obtained.

Scoring and Data Analysis

Differences between dissociative disorder and comparison patients pertaining to the reported prevalence of various types of specific traumata were analysed with chi-square tests. Attempting to estimate the relationship between the severity of emotional, physical, and sexual trauma and group classification, as well as somatoform and psychological dissociation, trauma composite scores per trauma area (emotional abuse, emotional neglect, physical abuse, sexual harassment, and sexual abuse) in three developmental age periods (0-6 years; 7-12 years; 13-18 years) were created (Weaver & Clum, 1993). These composite scores involved four variables: (a) presence of the event, (b) relationship, indicating whether the event occurred within the constraints of the family of origin, versus those of the extended family or another setting, (c) duration, indicating whether trauma lasted shorter or longer than one year, and (d) subjective response, indicating whether the subject felt not traumatized, or only slightly

---

* See note on p. 148.

traumatized, versus moderately, severely, or extremely traumatized by the event(s). These variables were given a score of 1 if they applied, and a score of 0 if they did not apply. The possible composite score per trauma area in each developmental period, thus, ranged from 0 to 4 (e.g., composite physical abuse 0-6 years = [presence, 1] + [relationship, 1] + [duration, 0] + [subjective response, 1] = 3). Summated composite scores per trauma area were also created, and consisted of the summated composite scores per developmental period (e.g., summated sexual trauma composite score, range 0 to 12). Finally, composite trauma scores per developmental period including emotional neglect, emotional abuse, physical abuse, sexual harassment, and sexual abuse were calculated (e.g., composite trauma score for period 0 to 6 years, range 0 to 20). When subjects could or would not recall, or did not report characteristics of acknowledged trauma for other reasons, the responses were coded as 0. In order to evaluate whether the composite constructs were assessing homogeneous constructs, (point-biserial) correlation coefficients between each composite score per developmental period and their constituting components scores were calculated. Next, differences between dissociative disorder cases and comparison patients with respect to summated composite scores per trauma area and composite scores per developmental period were assessed with Mann-Whitney U tests. Differences between composite scores per developmental period were evaluated with Friedman Two Way Anovas. Multiple regression analyses were used to assess which trauma variables predicted somatoform and psychological dissociation.

Statistical analyses were performed with SPSS-PC 6.0 (1993).

Results

Prevalence of Specific Traumatic Experiences

Dissociative disorder patients reported a significantly higher prevalence of traumatic experiences than comparison patients (Table 1). As measured by the presence of trauma during one or more developmental periods in any setting, dissociative disorder patients reported high rates of emotional neglect (91%), emotional abuse (87%), physical abuse (78%), sexual harassment (78%), sexual abuse (82%), and any type of sexual trauma (93%). As measured by presence of trauma during one or more developmental periods, comparison patients often reported emotional neglect (46%) and emotional abuse (42%). Physical abuse (19%), sexual harassment (14%), sexual abuse (14%), and any type of sexual trauma (23%) were reported less frequently.

Trauma Composite Scores

In order to ensure that the created composite scores were assessing homogeneous constructs, composite score-constituent item score (presence, duration, relationship to the perpetrator, and subjective response) (point-biserial) correlation coefficients were calculated. All correlations were significant ($p < .001$), and ranged from .63 (presence of sexual harassment in the extended family in period

Table 1

Reported Trauma on the TEQ of Patients with Dissociative Disorder and Patients with Other DSM-IV Diagnoses

Reported Events	Dissociative Disorder Patients (n = 45*)	Comparison Patients (n = 43*)	Chi-Square Comparison	
	%	%	χ^{2}**	p
Parentification	68	23	17.67	< .001***
Family burdens	64	37	5.50	.019
Death family member	25	33	0.37	n.s.
Death child/partner	9	2	1.84	n.s.
Severe physical injury	25	9	3.56	n.s.
Life threat (through illness, accident)	36	16	4.51	.033
Life threat (through person)	51	11	15.47	< .001***
Intense pain	70	26	17.54	< .001***
War experiences	9	12	0.12	n.s.
Observed trauma	63	21	15.59	< .001***
Emotional neglect f.o.****	89	44	19.89	< .001***
Emotional neglect f.****	57	14	17.42	< .001***
Emotional neglect o.****	36	9	9.00	.003
Emotional abuse f.o.	84	33	23.81	< .001***
Emotional abuse f.	43	16	7.51	.006
Emotional abuse o.	61	26	11.32	.001***
Physical abuse f.o.	67	9	31.67	< .001***
Physical abuse f.	25	7	5.03	.025
Physical abuse o.	35	17	3.68	.055
Sexual harassment f.o.	46	7	17.47	< .001***
Sexual harassment f.	34	0	17.62	< .001***
Sexual harassment o.	73	12	33.22	< .001***
Sexual abuse f.o.	59	5	30.50	< .001***
Sexual abuse f.	31	2	12.40	< .001***
Sexual abuse o.	67	12	28.02	< .001***

*   Due to missing data, the calculations per TEQ item may not involve all cases

** $df = 1$

*** $\alpha = .05/25 = .002$

****   f.o. = by one or more members of the family of origin

        f. = by one or more other relatives

        0. = by other person(s)

7-12 years) to .99 (traumatic stress imposed by sexual harassment, perpetrated in the extended family in period 7-12).

Dissociative disorder patients obtained higher composite scores per developmental period in each trauma area, as well as summated composite scores per trauma area than comparison patients, Mann-Whitney U tests, $-3.97 \leq z \leq -6.42$, all $p < .0001$. There were no significant differences in any type of trauma area composite scores per developmental period in either dissociative disorder or comparison patients (Friedman Two Way ANOVAS).

Relationship of Trauma Composite Scores to Somatoform and Psychological Dissociation

The zero-order correlations between the composite scores per trauma area were all significant and ranged from r (88) = .34; $p < .001$ (emotional neglect/sexual abuse) to r (88) = .67; $p < .0001$ (emotional neglect/emotional abuse). SDQ-20 and DIS-Q scores were highly correlated r (88) = .73, $p < .0001$, and the correlations between these two measures of dissociation and trauma composite scores ranged from $r = .40$ to $r = .61$ ($p < .0001$).

Table 2 presents the results from the multiple regression analyses predicting somatoform dissociation, as measured by the SDQ-20, in separate runs. Stepwise entrance of the composite scores per trauma area yielded a prediction model, which included physical abuse and sexual harassment. Attempting to statistically disentangle the influence of the emotional climate in which the subject was reportedly raised from physical and sexual abuse experiences, in the next run first both emotional trauma composite scores were forced into the model. Upon additional stepwise entrance of the other trauma composite scores, sexual abuse and sexual harassment delivered independent contributions to the prediction of somatoform dissociation. In the final model, emotional neglect, *beta* = .22, and emotional abuse, *beta* = .03, contributed to that prediction less than sexual abuse, *beta* = .27, and sexual harassment, *beta* = .24.

Reported sexual trauma and early trauma best predicted *psychological* dissociation, as measured by the DIS-Q, with or without forced entrance of emotional neglect and emotional abuse. These predictors largely matched the variables which predicted somatoform dissociation, which is not surprising in view of the strong intercorrelation between psychological and somatoform dissociation.

According to Tabachnick and Fidell (1989), collinearity of independent variables may build spurious associations with a dependent variable in the regression equation. This logical problem may arise with correlations $\geq .70$. As the correlation between the emotional abuse and emotional neglect composite scores was .67, the analyses were repeated entering only the emotional neglect composite score. Comparable results were obtained.

Evaluating whether the developmental age period in which trauma occurred was an important predictor of somatoform dissociation, the five composite scores per developmental period were summated, which gave three complex composites. Of these, only trauma in period 0-6 was selected, *beta* = .61 (Table 2).

Table 2
Multiple Regression Analyses Predicting Somatoform Dissociation

Runs	Total R^2	df	F Ratio for R^2	R^2 Change	p F Change	Beta in final model
1. All composite scores (entered stepwise):						
total equation	.33	2, 85	21.39*			
physical abuse				.26	<.0001	.35
sexual harassment				.07	.0022	.32
2. Sexual and physical abuse while controlling for emotional neglect and emotional abuse:						
total equation	.36	4, 83	11.74*			
emotional neglect/abuse				.23	<.0001	.22**/.03***
sexual abuse				.09	.0008	.27
sexual harassment				.04	.0336	.24
3. Summed composites per developmental period (entered stepwise):						
Trauma in period 0-6 years	.37	1, 86	51.01*		<.0001	.61

* p < .0001; ** emotional neglect; *** emotional abuse

Psychological dissociation was also best predicted by reported trauma during this period.

Age at Onset of Trauma, its Duration, Perpetrators, and Posttraumatic Support

As Table 3 shows, dissociative disorder patients reported early onset of emotional neglect, emotional abuse, physical abuse, sexual harassment, and sexual abuse. The extremely early onset of emotional abuse, neglect, and physical abuse was influenced by the reports of several dissociative patients that trauma, in particular emotional neglect and abuse, or physical abuse, had been going on from birth onwards (e.g., 0-17 years). Several comparison patients also indicated that trauma had started from 0 years onwards. As people do usually not have (reliable) memories before the age of 2-4, we asked some dissociative patients for explanations. Most of them explained that they had experienced trauma "as long as they could remember." It seems unlikely that these imprecisions did unduly affect the composite scores ("duration" scores were dichotomized using the criterion of less or more than one year, and the trauma scores for the earliest developmental period involved the first 6 years of life).

Table 3

Reported Age of Onset, Duration, and Number of Perpetrators of Trauma, and Consolation Received after Trauma by Dissociative Disorder Patients

	Family of Origin	Extended Family	Other Setting
Onset (mean age at onset)			
Emotional neglect	1.8	2.6	7.9
Emotional abuse	2.1	4.2	8.6
Physical abuse	2.0	4.6	9.6
Sexual harassment	4.7	7.2	11.5
Sexual abuse	4.8	7.4	10.0
Duration (mean number of years)			
Emotional neglect	21.7	18.1	15.2
Emotional abuse	19.2	14.8	7.8
Physical abuse	14.0	11.1	6.4
Sexual harassment	10.8	8.0	5.2
Sexual abuse	10.1	7.8	4.5
Number of perpetrators	M	SD	
Emotional trauma	4.1	3.5	
Physical trauma	2.6	2.8	
Sexual trauma	3.5	4.2	
Consolation after trauma	None	Some	Adequate
	100%	0%	0%

The reported traumas generally were of long duration. Neglect and abusive experiences in the family of origin appeared to be of earlier onset and longer duration than they were in the extended family or in other settings. Many dissociative patients reported maltreatment by multiple perpetrators, and all but one, who did not report any trauma, indicated total absence of consolation or support after the occurrence of trauma.

Repeated Analyses with Women Only

Even though there was no statistically significant difference in gender across samples, the proportion women was somewhat higher in the dissociative disorders group ($n = 39$ vs. $n = 6$) than in the comparison group ($n = 33$ vs. $n = 10$). Since more women than men report sexual abuse, this "imbalance" could have influenced the results. Repeating all composite score analyses including only women, however, yielded highly comparable to identical results.

Comparisons between Dissociative Disorder Patients with and without Reported Corroborative Evidence of Traumatic Memories

A subset of dissociative disorder patients reported corroboration of their abuse, which included witness-testimonies, documents, confessions of perpetrators, physical traces of abuse, and incestuous childbirth. Only in some cases, these self-reported sources were checked by the therapist. Corroboration of emotional neglect/abuse, physical abuse, and sexual abuse was reported by 57%, 54%, and 33% of the patients respectively. The patients who did ($n = 23$) and who did not ($n = 21$) report corroboration did not obtain different SDQ-20, DIS-Q totals, or DIS-Q subscale scores (all t tests n.s.), and the groups did not obtain different summated or developmental period composite scores (all Mann-Whitney U tests n.s.).

Repeated Analyses Deleting Subjective Estimation of Impact from the Composite Scores

The composite scores may have been flawed by the inclusion of retrospective estimations of impact of trauma. It could be that this inclusion would index severity of current symptomatology rather than index the original impact of trauma. Deleting this variable from the composite scores, however, did not alter the results.

Discussion

The present retrospective study is subject to methodological limitations restricting causal inferences between reported trauma and dissociation. Therefore, its results should be considered with some caution. It is not warranted to conclude from the present data that one phenomenon is caused by another. Tabachnick and Fidell (1989), as well as Briere and Elliott (1993), have warned that there are limits to the inferences that can be made from the results of partializing statistical methods such as analysis of covariance, or multiple regression analysis. Partializing analyses to infer causality may be misleading, if the design is quasi-experimental and the control variable is not causally antecedent to the independent variables. These issues are most relevant to emotional, sexual and physical trauma research (Briere & Elliott, 1993). For example, sexual and physical abuse can have negative effects on the emotional climate in which the child is raised, family functioning and sexual or physical abuse can have mutually reciprocating impacts, and the subject's perception of family functioning can be affected by his or her sexual/physical abuse history. In this context, the conclusion of Nash et al. (1993) that adult psychopathology and dissociation in women with a history of childhood sexual abuse might be a consequence, at least in part, of a pathogenic family structure, rather than the abuse per se, must also be considered with caution (Briere & Elliott, 1993).

Due to absence of a self-reporting instrument measuring a broad range of traumatic experiences in the Netherlands, it was necessary to use a newly constructed scale. Some dissociative, as well as comparison patients reported that trauma started from "0 years" onwards. In view of infantile amnesia, these indications are unreliable. Imprecision of responding to the TEQ was involved, and a proportion of the subjects may have been distorting their memories. The TEQ instructions should be adapted to reduce the chance of collecting unreliable indications of age at trauma onset. Next, the sexual harassment items may be more open to the patient's judgment and interpretation than the other events. Sexual harassment was considerably correlated with sexual abuse (Spearman correlation coefficient = .50), suggesting that it is a rather common accompanying experience to sexual abuse.

As only the dissociative patients were interviewed using the SCID-D, these patients received different experimental demands than the comparison subjects. This imbalance may have influenced our results, and in future studies the SCID-D should therefore be administered to all subjects. Also, the diagnostic procedure may have communicated that there was an expected relationship between the dissociation questionnaires and the content of the SCID-D. Indeed, dissociation questionnaires seem sensitive to the context of measurement. For example, in a meta-analytic validation study on the DES, Van IJzendoorn and Schuengel (1996) remarked thatDID patients who were unaware of their diagnostic status obtained lower DES scores than DID patients who were knowledgeable of their condition. As the SDQ-20 could also be subject to this bias, we compared scores of DDNOS and DID patients, who were administered the SDQ-20 by a diagnostic consultant before the SCID-D diagnosis had been made and shared, with scores of DID and DDNOS patients, who were administered this instrument by the treating therapist in a post-diagnostic stage (Nijenhuis et al., 1997). DDNOS patients who were aware of their diagnostic status obtained significantly lower SDQ-20 scores, and with DID no between-group differences were found. It, thus, seems that the SDQ-20 is not sensitive to the context of measurement. The lower scores of the DDNOS patients who were in treatment may indicate a positive treatment effect.

The validity of traumatic memories of dissociative disorder patients, especially with regard to childhood sexual abuse, has been questioned (e.g., Frankel, 1993). In particular, recovered adult memories of sexual abuse could be (re)constructions, created by therapists in suggestible patients (Loftus, 1993; Ofshe & Watters, 1994). To date this claim has not been tested among dissociative disorder patients, and memories of abuse of psychiatric patients were found to be equally accurate whether recovered or continuously remembered (Dalenberg, 1996). Analogue studies show that autobiographical memories of mildly stressful events are reconstructive, and open to postevent influences (Loftus, 1993). According to Briere (1995), these studies suffer limitations in generalizability. For example, narrative recollections of stressful events differ from traumatic memories which, at least initially, tend to be retrieved in the form of dissociated mental imprints of sensory and affective elements of the traumatic experience (e.g., Van der Kolk & Fisler, 1995).

On the other hand, corroboration of alleged traumatic events, in particular when they involve secretive events in a distant past, is obviously difficult. Alleged perpetrators have every reason to deny charges, and the innocent may have difficulty proving that abuse did not occur. Another complexity is that corroboration or disproval of a (part of a) traumatic memory does not necessarily verify or falsify other recollections (Kluft, 1996). In spite of these and related obstacles, independent corroboration of dissociative patients' traumatic memories, including formerly dissociated memories, has been found (Coons, 1994; Hornstein & Putnam, 1992; Kluft, 1995; Martínez-Taboas, 1996; Swica, Lewis, & Lewis, 1996). Memory distortion may yield false positive and false negative recall. For example, reports of satanic ritual abuse have remained unverified, and dissociative patients often cling in some of their dissociative states to a fantasized happy life as a defense against authentic trauma (Putnam, 1989).

The memory disturbances and denial symptoms of the dissociative disorder patients may have influenced the results. Some could or would not recall the possible occurrence of a particular kind of trauma, or its date of onset. Others had difficulty judging the validity of some of their recollections. Whenever a patient indicated any doubt whether trauma had occurred, trauma was rated as absent. We did not check to what extent the present reported memories were recovered. As dissociative patients usually have continuous as well as discontinuous (i.e., dissociative state-dependent) traumatic and other memories, a certain proportion may have been of the recovered type. The dissociative patients who did and did not report corroboration of their traumatic memories displayed equal degrees of pathological dissociation. Assuming that the self-reported corroboration was largely valid (in some cases checks were performed), it seems unlikely that the dissociative patients who did not report corroboration would suffer total memory distortion. However, future studies should inquire about the characteristics of traumatic memories, and should include verification of self-reported corroboration.

Hypnotizability is elevated in PTSD, DDNOS, and DID patients (e.g., Frischholz, Lipman, Braun, & Sachs, 1992). Of course, this is in itself not enough to conclude that reported trauma is a product of suggestion in these patients.

Interrogatory suggestibility – that is, misinformation suggestibility plus a constellation of social influence factors ranging from response bias, to source credibility, and especially to some sort of "interpersonal pressure" in a closed social interaction – may be more relevant to the clinical situation than hypnotizability (Brown, 1995). In the only study so far in which interrogatory suggestibility was investigated in patients with recovered memories of sexual abuse, a low interrogatory suggestibility was found (Leavitt, 1997). Also, interrogatory suggestibility was not correlated with DES scores and high levels of psychopathology. These findings suggest that there is reason to doubt that traumatic memories and the major symptoms of dissociative patients would, as a rule, be a mere result of suggestion.

In concordance with our first hypothesis, compared with other psychiatric patients, dissociative disorder patients reported having been exposed to more types of traumatic events and more severe traumatization as defined by presence of a particular type of trauma, its duration, the relationship to the perpetrator(s), and the subjective response. The observed between-group differences pertained to all developmental periods. The high proportion of dissociative disorder patients that recalled child sexual and physical trauma resembled those which were found in other studies (e.g., Draijer & Boon, 1993; Putnam, Guroff, Silberman, Barban, & Post, 1986; Ross et al., 1991). Most dissociative patients also reported emotional neglect and abuse. Reported emotional neglect, emotional abuse, physical abuse, sexual harassment, and sexual abuse were intercorrelated to a considerable extent. Often, more than one alleged perpetrator was involved. They were considerably older than the patient, and they primarily included members of the family of origin. Many dissociative patients also recalled parentification, and family burdens, such as alcoholism of a parent. The reported sexual and physical abuse thus often occurred within a family context which was experienced as traumatic.

The present study is the first to investigate empirically the relationship between somatoform dissociation and reported trauma. The observed association adds to the construct validity of the SDO-20. Consistent with our second hypothesis, created composite scores involving reported physical and sexual trauma abuse best predicted somatoform and psychological dissociation, even after forced entrance of emotional neglect and abuse in the multiple regression model. This result diverges from the finding that dissociation might be a consequence, at least in part, of a pathogenic family structure, rather than childhood sexual abuse per se (Nash et al., 1993). It matches the previous finding that higher levels of clinical dissociation were associated with verified abuse by multiple perpetrators and co-presence of physical abuse independent of sexual abuse (Putnam, Helmers, Horowitz, & Trickett, 1995). It is also consistent with the idea that specific threat to bodily integrity, rather than a negative emotional climate, may evoke somatoform dissociative reactions resembling animal defensive reactions (Nijenhuis et al., 1998a,b). Experienced neglect may play an important role in obstructing the resolution of trauma-induced dissociation: as the present dissociative patients stated, none had ever received consolation or support after the occurrence of traumatic events.

In consonance with the third hypothesis, experienced trauma before 7 years seemed to be of major influence with respect to the prediction of somatoform and psychological dissociation, as well as caseness. These results concur with the finding by Draijer and Boon (1993) that psychological dissociation was best predicted by reported early onset and severity of sexual abuse. As Bryant (1995) found, fantasy proneness (i.e., imaginative involvement in internal events) was correlated with early onset of reported abuse. Could this mean that early memories of abuse are more likely to be false? We agree with Bryant (1995) that causal directions cannot be inferred. Reported early abuse may involve memory distortion, but it is also possible that early trauma induces or promotes imaginative involvement, and the more so when other modes of coping have not yet been developed. Preliminary data indeed suggest that fantasy proneness and absorption are elevated in traumatized individuals compared with non-traumatized individuals (Lynn, Rhue, & Green, 1988). We add that both processes may operate at the same time, yielding traumatic memories which involve true and false elements (Kluft, 1996). Also, imagination may promote false negative, as well as false positive memories of trauma.

Acknowledging the methodological limitations of the present study, its results suggest that somatoform and psychological dissociative symptoms are primarily tied to reported severe, as well as chronic physical and sexual abuse, which according to the subjects started at an early age, and occurred in a disturbed and emotionally neglectful family of origin. The association between somatoform dissociation and reported trauma adds to the construct validity of the SDQ-20. In order to further investigate this relationship, it would be best to assess somatoform dissociation before, during, and after exposure to authentic, highly threatening events.

References

Albach, F. (1993). *Freud's verleidingstheorie: Incest, trauma en hysterie*. [Freud's seduction theory: Incest, trauma and hysteria]. Middelburg: Petra.

American Psychiatric Association (1994). *Diagnostic and statistical manual of mental disorders, 4th edn*. Washington DC: Author.

Bernstein E., & Putnam F.W. (1986). Development, reliability, and validity of a dissociation scale. *Journal of Nervous Mental Disease, 102*, 280-286.

Boon S., & Draijer N. (1993). *Multiple personality disorder in the Netherlands: A study on reliability and validity of the diagnosis*. Amsterdam/Lisse: Swets & Zeitlinger.

Bremner, J.D., Steinberg, M., Southwick, S.M., Johnson, D.R., & Charney, D.S. (1993). Use of the structured clinical interview for DSM-IV dissociative disorders for systematic assessment of dissociative symptoms in posttraumatic stress disorder. *American Journal of Psychiatry, 150*, 1011-1014.

Briere, J. (1995). Science versus politics in the delayed memory debate: A commentary. *Counseling Psychologist, 23*, 290-293.

Briere, J., & Elliott, D.M. (1993). Sexual abuse, family environment, and psychological symptoms: On the validity of statistical control. *Journal of Consulting and Clinical Psychology, 61*, 284-288.

Brown, D. (1995). Pseudomemories: The standard of science and standard of care in trauma treatment. *American Journal of Clinical Hypnosis, 37,* 1-24.

Bryant, R.A. (1995). Fantasy proneness, reported childhood abuse, and the relevance of reported abuse onset. *The International Journal of Clinical and Experimental Hypnosis, 158,* 184-193.

Coons, P.M. (1994). Confirmation of childhood abuse in child and adolescent cases of multiple personality disorder and dissociative disorder not otherwise specified. *Journal of Nervous and Mental Disease, 182,* 461-464.

Dalenberg, C.J. (1996). Accuracy, timing and circumstances of disclosure in therapy of recovered and continuous memories of abuse. *Journal of Psychiatry and Law, 24,* 229-275.

Darves-Bornoz, J.-M. (1997). Rape-related psychotraumatic syndromes. *European Journal of Obstetrics & Gynecology, 71,* 59-65.

Draijer, N. & Boon, S. (1993). Trauma, dissociation, and dissociative disorders. In S. Boon & N. Draijer (eds.), *Multiple personality disorder in the Netherlands: A study on reliability and validity of the diagnosis* (pp. 177-193). Amsterdam/Lisse: Swets & Zeitlinger.

Frankel, F.H. (1993). Adult reconstruction of childhood events in the multiple personality literature. *American Journal of Psychiatry, 150,* 954-958.

Frischholz, E.J., Lipman, L.S., Braun, B.G., & Sachs, R.G. (1992). Psychopathology, hypnotizability, and dissociation. *American Journal of Psychiatry, 149,* 1521-1525.

Fromuth, M.E. (1986). The relationship of childhood sexual abuse with later psychological and sexual adjustment in a sample of college women. *Child Abuse and Neglect, 10,* 5-15.

Herman, J.L., Perry, J.C., & Van der Kolk, B.A. (1989). Childhood trauma in borderline personality disorder. *American Journal of Psychiatry, 146,* 390-395.

Hornstein, N.L., & Putnam, F.W. (1992). Clinical phenomenology of child and adolescent disorders. *Journal of the American Academy of Child and Adolescent Psychiatry, 31,* 1077-1085.

Janet, P. (1901). *The mental state of hystericals.* New York: Putnam & Sons. Reprint: University Publications of America, Washington DC, 1977.

Janet, P. (1907). *Major symptoms of hysteria.* London: Macmillan. Reprint: Hafner, New York, 1965.

Janet, P. (1909). Problèmes psychologiques de l'émotion. [Psychological problems of emotion]. *Revue Neurologique, 17,* 1551-1687.

Kihlstrom, J.F. (1994). One hundred years of hysteria. In S. J. Lynn & J.W. Rhue (eds.) *Dissociation: Clinical and theoretical perspectives* (pp. 365-395). New York: Guilford.

Kluft, R.P. (1995). The confirmation and disconfirmation of memories of abuse in DID patients: A naturalistic clinical study. *Dissociation, 8,* 251-258.

Kluft, R.P. (1996). Treating the traumatic memories of patients with dissociative identity disorder. *American Journal of Psychiatry, Festschrift Supplement, 153,* 103-110.

Koopman, C., Classen, C., & Spiegel, D. (1994). Predictors of posttraumatic stress symptoms among survivors of the Oakland/Berkeley, Calif., Firestorm. *American Journal of Psychiatry, 151,* 888-894.

Leavitt, F. (1997). False attribution of suggestibility to explain recovered memory of childhood sexual abuse following extended amnesia. *Child Abuse and Neglect, 21,* 265-272.

Loftus, E.F. (1993). The reality of repressed memories. *American Psychologist, 48,* 518-537.

Lynn, S.J., Rhue, J.W., & Green, J.P. (1988). Multiple personality and fantasy proneness: Is there an association or dissociation? *British Journal of Experimental and Clinical Hypnosis, 5,* 138-142.

Marmar, C.R., Weiss, D.S., Schlenger, W.E., Fairbank, J.A., Jordan, B.K., Kulka, R.A., & Hough, R.L. (1994). Peritraumatic dissociation and posttraumatic stress in male Vietnam theater veterans. *American Journal of Psychiatry, 151,* 902-907.

Martínez-Taboas, A. (1996). Repressed memories: Some clinical data contributing towards its elucidation. *American Journal of Psychotherapy, 50,* 217-230.

Nash, M.R., Hulsey, T.L., Sexton, M.C., Harralson, T.L., & Lambert, W. (1993). Long-term sequelae of childhood sexual abuse: Perceived family environment, psychopathology, and dissociation. *Journal of Consulting and Clinical Psychology, 61,* 276-283.

Nemiah, J.C. (1991). Dissociation, conversion, and somatization. In A. Tasman & S.M. Goldfinger (eds.), *American Psychiatric Press Annual Review of Psychiatry, Vol. 10.* (pp. 248-260). Washington, DC: American Psychiatric Press.

Nijenhuis, E.R.S., Spinhoven, P., Van Dyck, R., Van der Hart, O., & Vanderlinden, J. (1996). The development and the characteristics of the Somatoform Dissociation Questionnaire (SDQ-20). *Journal of Nervous and Mental Disease, 184,* 688-694.

Nijenhuis, E.R.S., Spinhoven, P., Van Dyck, R., Van der Hart, O., & Vanderlinden, J. (1997). The development of the Somatoform Dissociation Questionnaire (SDQ-5) as a screening instrument for dissociative disorders. *Acta Psychiatrica Scandinavica, 96,* 311-318.

Nijenhuis, E.R.S., Spinhoven, P., Van Dyck, R., Van der Hart, O., & Vanderlinden, J. (1997, April). Wezenlijke kenmerken van somatoforme en dissociatieve stoornissen. [Major symptoms of somatoform and dissociative disorders]. Presentation at the Conference on Somatic Complaints, Conversion and Dissociation, Utrecht, Society of Psychosomatic Medicine.

Nijenhuis, E.R.S., Spinhoven, P., Van Dyck, R., Van der Hart, O., & Vanderlinden, J. (1998a). The psychometric characteristics of the Somatoform Dissociation Questionnaire: A replication study. *Psychotherapy & Psychosomatics, 67,* 17-23.

Nijenhuis, E.R.S., Spinhoven, P., Vanderlinden, J., Van Dyck, R., & Van der Hart, O. (1998b). Somatoform dissociative symptoms as related to animal defensive reactions to predatory threat and injury. *Journal of Abnormal Psychology, 107,* 63-73.

Nijenhuis, E.R.S., Vanderlinden, J., & Spinhoven, P. (1998c). Animal defensive reactions as a model for trauma-induced dissociative reactions. *Journal of Traumatic Stress, 11,* 243-260.

Nijenhuis, E.R.S., Van der Hart, O., & Vanderlinden, J. (Unpublished data). The Traumatic Experiences Questionnaire.

Ofshe, R., & Watters, E. (1994). *Making monsters: False memories, psychotherapy, and sexual hysteria.* New York: Scribner's.

Pribor, E.F., Yutzy, S.H., Dean, J.T., & Wetzel, R.D. (1993). Briquet's syndrome, dissociation, and abuse. *American Journal of Psychiatry, 150,* 1507-1511.

Putnam, F.W. (1989). *Diagnosis and treatment of multiple personality disorder.* New York: Guilford.

Putnam, F.W., Guroff, J.J., Silberman, E.K., Barban, L., & Post, R.M. (1986). The clinical phenomenology of multiple personality disorder. *Journal of Clinical Psychiatry, 47,* 285-293.

Putnam, F.W., Helmers, K., Horowitz, L.A., & Trickett, P.K. (1995). Hypnotizability and dissociativity in sexually abused girls. *Child Abuse and Neglect, 19,* 645-655.

Ross, C.A., Anderson, G., Fraser, G.A., Reagor, P., Bjornson, L., & Miller, S.D. (1992). Differentiating multiple personality disorder and dissociative disorder not otherwise specified. *Dissociation, 5*, 87-91.

Ross, C.A., Heber, S., Norton, G.R., & Anderson, G. (1989). Somatic symptoms in multiple personality disorder. *Psychosomatics, 30*, 154-160.

Ross, C.A., Miller, S.D., Bjornson, M.A., Reagor, P., Fraser, G.A., & Anderson, G. (1991). Abuse histories in 102 cases of multiple personality disorder. *Canadian Journal of Psychiatry, 36*, 97-102.

Saxe, G.N., Chinman, G., Berkowitz, M.D., Hall, K., Lieberg, G., Schwartz, J., & Van der Kolk, B.A. (1994). Somatization in patients with dissociative disorders. *American Journal of Psychiatry, 151*, 1329-1334.

Shalev, A.Y., Peri, T., Canetti, M.A., & Schreiber, S. (1996). Predictors of PTSD in injured trauma survivors: A prospective study. *American Journal of Psychiatry, 153*, 219-225.

Spiegel, D. (1984). Multiple personality disorder as a post-traumatic stress disorder. *Psychiatric Clinics of North America, 7*, 101-110.

SPSS PC/M.J. Norušis (1993). SPSS for Windows Release 6.0. Chicago: SPSS Inc.

Steinberg, M., Cichetti, D.V., Buchanan, J., Hall, P., & Rounsaville, B. (1993). Clinical assessment of dissociative symptoms and disorders: The structured clinical interview for DSM-IV dissociative disorders. *Dissociation, 6*, 3-16.

Swica, Y., Lewis, D., & Lewis, M. (1996). Child abuse and dissociative identity disorder/multiple personality disorder: The documentation of childhood maltreatment and the corroboration of symptoms. *Child and Adolescent Psychiatric Clinics of North America, 5*, 431-447.

Tabachnick, B.G., & Fidell, L.S. (1989). *Using multivariate statistics. 2nd ed.* New York: Harper Collins Publishers.

Tillman, J.G., Nash, M.R., & Lerner, P.M. (1994). Does trauma cause dissociative pathology? In S.J. Lynn & J.W. Rhue (eds.), *Dissociation: Clinical and theoretical perspectives* (pp. 395-415). New York: Guilford.

Van der Hart, O., Boon, S. & Op den Velde, W. (1991). Trauma en dissociatie. [Trauma and dissociation] In O. Van der Hart (ed.), *Trauma, dissociatie en hypnose* [Trauma, dissociation, and hypnosis] (pp. 55-71). Amsterdam/Lisse: Swets & Zeitlinger.

Van der Kolk, B.A., & Fisler, R. (1995). Dissociation and the fragmentary nature of traumatic memories. *Journal of Traumatic Stress, 8*, 505-527.

Vanderlinden, J. (1993). *Dissociative experiences, trauma, and hypnosis: Research findings and clinical applications in eating disorders.* Delft: Eburon.

Vanderlinden, J., Vandereycken, W., Van Dyck, R., & Vertommen, H. (1993). Dissociative experiences and trauma in eating disorders. *International Journal of Eating Disorders, 13*, 187-193.

Vanderlinden, J., Van Dyck, R., Vandereycken, W., Vertommen, H., & Verkes, R.J. (1993). The Dissociation Questionnaire (DIS-Q): Development and characteristics of a new self-report questionnaire. *Clinical Psychology and Psychotherapy, 1*, 21-27.

Van IJzendoorn, M.H., & Schuengl, C. (1996). The measurement of dissociation in normal and clinical populations: Meta-analytic validation of the Dissociative Experiences Scale (DES). *Clinical Psychology Review, 16*, 365-382.

Walker, E.A., Gelfand, A.N., Gelfand, R.N., Koss, M.P., & Katon, W.J. (1995). Medical and psychiatric symptoms in female gastroenterology clinic patients with histories of sexual victimization. *General Hospital Psychiatry, 17*, 85-92.

Waller, N.G., Putnam, F.W., & Carlson, E.B. (1996). Types of dissociation and dissociative types: A taxometric analysis of dissociative experiences. *Psychological Methods, 1*, 300-321.

Weaver, T.L., & Clum, G.A. (1993). Early family environments and traumatic
    experiences associated with borderline personality disorder. *Journal of Consulting and
    Clinical Psychology, 61,* 1068-1075.
Yates, J.L. & Nasby, W. (1993). Dissociation, affect, and network models of memory: An
    integrative proposal. *Journal of Traumatic Stress, 6,* 305-326.

IX
Animal Defensive Reactions as a Model for Trauma-induced Dissociative Reactions[*]

"Starting and looking half round, I saw the lion just in the act of springing upon me. I was on a little height; he caught my shoulder as he sprang and we both came to the ground below together. Growling horribly close to my ear, he shook me as a terrier does a rat. The shock produced a stupor to that which seems to be felt by a mouse after the first shake of a cat. It caused a sense of dreaminess in which there was no sense of pain or feeling of terror, though quite conscious of all that was happening ... This singular condition was not the result of any mental process. The shake annihilated fear, and allowed no sense of horror in looking round at the beast. The peculiar state is probably produced in all animals killed by carnivora; and if so, is a merciful provision by our benevolent Creator for lessening the pain of death."

David Livingstone, 1872, p. 15; cited in Greyson, 1993.

Introduction

Patients with dissociative disorders, especially those with dissociative identity disorder (DID; American Psychiatric Association, 1994), or dissociative disorder not otherwise specified (DDNOS; APA, 1994; Ross et al., 1992), show far-reaching and sudden alterations of behavior, affect, sensation, perception, and knowledge. According to Putnam (1988), these alterations indicate that these patients have developed "highly discrete states of consciousness organized around a prevailing affect, sense of self (including body image), with a limited repertoire of behaviors and a set of state-dependent memories."

Following Wolff (1987), Putnam (1988, 1989) postulated that any human being remains in discontinuous, self-organizing, and self-stabilizing states of behavior, physiology, and consciousness. These states appear to be the fundamental unit of organization of consciousness, and are detectable from the first

* This chapter has also been published as: Nijenhuis, E.R.S., Vanderlinden, J., & Spinhoven, P. (1998). Animal defensive reactions as a model for dissociative reactions. *Journal of Traumatic Stress, 11*, 243-260. We thank Onno Van der Hart and Richard Van Dyck for their valued comments on a previous version. Supported by a grant of the Stichting Dienstbetoon Gezondheidszorg, Soesterberg, Netherlands, number 11.92.

moments following birth in particular. In this view, switches between states are manifest by nonlinear changes in a number of variables, including access to memory, attention and cognition, regulatory physiology, and sense of self. As a result of a normal developmental task, the transitions across states of consciousness are smoothed out with maturation. The infant/child learns to achieve homeostasis in that it learns to modulate state, and it learns to recover from disruptions of state. These achievements presuppose a connectivity between states. In the course of maturation these various states, state-dependent experiences and memories will, thus, become preponderately associated and integrated with one another. They jointly will constitute the relative unity of consciousness, memory, and identity which most people are familiar with, and which characterizes their personality. Traumatization may interfere with these integrative processes (Janet, 1909; Van der Kolk & Van der Hart, 1989). Consistent with this view, dissociative patients as a rule report chronic sexual, physical, and psychological abuse. Further, there is evidence that dissociation of psychophysiological states of consciousness and behavior is a function of severity, duration, repetition of traumatization, and age at its onset, as Janet (1909; Van der Kolk & Van der Hart, 1989) already observed, and as contemporary researchers have confirmed (Boon & Draijer, 1993; Hornstein & Putnam, 1992; Ross et al., 1991).

Putnam (1988) did not explain what determines these diverging but nonetheless characteristic behavioral, physiological, and psychological aspects of various dissociative states. In fact, he remarked that ".. very little is known about the alter personalities and what they truly present" (Putnam, 1993, p. 83). Since there seem to be striking similarities between the animal and human response to major threat, in the current article, the typical reactions of dissociative patients to perceived threat are compared to animal defensive and recuperative states. We will first discuss that animal defensive and recuperative reactions constitute a complex system consisting of various nonlinear sub-states which involve radically different behavioral and physiological reactions adapted to meet variable stages of predatory threat. Next, we will argue that these animal substates can serve as a model for some dissociative responses, and possibly even for some characteristic dissociative states of DID and DDNOS patients.

Animal Defensive States

Timberlake and Lucas (1989) have argued that traditional learning research frequently treated organisms as unorganized bundles of reflexes and random responses. Their behavior *system* approach, however, views an organism as a set of organized and interrelated regulatory systems that precede, support, and constrain learning. Consistent with this view, animals do not respond to aversive, threatening stimuli with single responses, but with qualitatively different behavioral and physiological states that are tuned to optimalize survival chances in successive stages of imminence (Bolles, 1970; Bolles & Fanselow, 1980; Fanselow & Lester, 1988). These states are mutually inhibitive, and there is evidence suggesting that the various defensive subsystems (e.g., affiliative behaviors, freezing, aggression) are mediated by different neurochemical systems (Kalin & Shelton, 1989). Imminence varies in terms of space (physical distance between prey and predator), and time (frequency of previous predatory exposure in a particular location). Different stages of imminence evoke abrupt and specific shifts from one behavioral and physiological state to another, and include *pre-encounter, post-encounter, and circa-strike defensive subsystems* and *recuperation.* These defensive and recuperative behaviors typically are rather primitive and inflexible, less subject to reinforcement than once had been supposed (Bolles, 1970), and highly subject to Pavlovian learning principles (Bolles & Fanselow, 1980).

Pre-encounter Defense

If an animal is not at risk of predation, its behaviors will be organized into the preferred activity patterns (Fanselow & Lester, 1988). Placing an animal at risk during foraging and consumption, these behavioral patterns are modified to reduce this risk (Fanselow & Lester, 1988; Helmstetter & Fanselow, 1993). Most nonaversively motivated behaviors are interrupted, and appetitively motivated behavior is *reorganized.* It appears that the animal's meal pattern varies with the risk of predation. Meal frequency decreases as risk increases, but compensatory increase in meal size defends total daily intake and body weight.

Post-encounter Defensive Behavior: Flight, Freeze, and Fight

When a predator has been spotted, flight is a proper response provided there is a good chance of successful escape. Nevertheless, and maybe contrary to expectation, freezing (behavioral immobility) is the dominant post-encounter response pattern, at least in some species. Freezing does not depend on the (un)availability of physical escape from threat, since it also occurs in the face of a potential escape route. It increases survival chances, even when physical contact has been made, probably because: (1) predators detect moving prey more easily, but have difficulty with noticing immobile objects, (2) the attention of predators may shift to other moving or noisy stimuli, and, (3) movement cues are critical releasing stimuli for predatory behavior, and freezing eliminates these cues (Suarez & Gallop, 1981). Species varying from fish to lions are subject to freezing, which seems related to "animal hypnosis" (cf. Krystal, 1988) or "tonic immobility" (Moore & Amstey, 1962).

Freezing does not merely concern a single response (inhibition of movement), but represents an integrated, functional behavioral and physiological pattern. For example, freezing does not occur arbitrarily, since, for instance, rats in nature as well as in experimental contexts freeze next to walls, usually in corners, and if available, in darker areas or places less strongly associated with threat.

Circa-strike Defense: Analgesia, Emotional Numbing, and the Startle Response

When the animal is about to be attacked, freezing tends to be combined with analgesia, which is functional in that perception of pain (nociception) would divert the attention of the prey from defensive concerns (Bolles & Fanselow, 1980). Analgesia can be evoked by innately recognized predators, odors of stressed conspecifics, learned danger signals, pinches directed to the scruff of the neck, and dorsal constraint (Siegfried, Frischknecht, & Nunez de Souza, 1990). The response can be mediated by endogenous opioids (Fanselow & Lester, 1988; Krystal et al., 1989; Siegfried et al., 1990; Van der Kolk & Greenberg, 1987), as well as non-opioid mechanisms (Siegfried et al., 1990). There is evidence that endogenous opioids are also involved in stress-induced and CS-induced catalepsy or immobility (Amir, Brown, Amit, & Ornstein, 1981; Fanselow, 1986; Teskey, Kavaliers, & Hirst, 1984), reduction of panic and fear (Siegfried et al., 1990; Van der Kolk, 1994), suppression and delay of emotional and panic escape behavior, and inhibition of the production of sounds (e.g., cries for help; Kalin, 1993). These effects inhibit reactions which would compromise optimal defense in this stage of imminence. For example, grooming and licking wounds would attract attention, and would elicit further attack (Siegfried et al., 1990).

When a predator rapidly approaches and comes close, the prey again dramatically changes its behavior (Fanselow & Lester, 1988) in that it suddenly displays an explosive escape response, that is, the potentiated startle response (Hirsch & Bolles, 1980), as well as aggressive behavior (Kalin, 1993). If these responses do not eliminate contact, immobility may return, reducing the likelihood of continued attack (Fanselow & Lester, 1988). Under certain conditions, CS will potentiate the startle response, as well as aggressive behavior (Pynoos, Ritzmann, Steinberg, Goenjian, & Prisecaru, 1996). These effects increase with repeated attack.

Post-strike Behavior: Pain and Recuperation

The recuperative stage may be considered, in part, as a response to nociceptive stimulation arising from injury and tissue damage (Bolles & Fanselow, 1980; Fanselow & Sigmundi, 1982; Siegfried et al., 1990). On the termination of imminence, pain perception returns and instigates recuperative behavior (Bolles & Fanselow, 1980), including behaviors directed at injuries, grooming behavior, and resting behavior serving to promote healing. Other kinds of motivation seem, meanwhile, to be inhibited. Upon recovery, there is a return to preferred nonaversively motivated behaviors.

While stimuli predicting aversive events come to elicit analgesia, the presentation of a safety signal (i.e., a stimulus paired backward with UCS), produced an abrupt change in pain sensitivity, essentially "switching off" conditioned analgesia (Wiertelak, Watkins, & Maier, 1992). It thus is suggested that, just as (conditioned) signals for danger elicit analgesia, (conditioned) signals for safety inhibit (conditioned) analgesia. Nociception, subsequently, evokes recuperative behavior.

Some data suggest that animal pain can be reproduced in absence of external pain induction. It has been found that a formalin-induced nociceptive message induced an enduring trace in the animal central nervous system (Cadet, Aigouy, & Woda, 1993), and long-lasting and site-specific sensitization of animal defensive reflexes following shock and injury have been related to hyperalgesia (Walters, 1987). Conditioned animal hyperalgesia has been observed, but seems rare.

Inescapable Shock

While animal defense consists of *unconditional response-sets* elicited by specific natural threat stimuli, these reactions can also experimentally be induced by electrical shocks. As numerous animal studies have shown, experimental traumatization, operationalized as inescapable shock (IS), evokes defensive reactions which in nature appear in the post-encounter and circa-strike stage (see Fanselow & Lester, 1988). A mild shock may, for example, evoke freezing, whereas a more severe shock results in a sudden burst of activity. Using different rates of electrical shock density, Fanselow and Lester (1988) were even able to model all natural stages of imminence. Low density shock produced pre-encounter defense, medium density shock post-encounter defense, and high density shock circa-strike defense.

Animals that initially learned how to physically escape from shock, unconditionally react with an alarm or startle response (an explosive motor burst) when such escape is prevented. IS is secondarily followed by a state of helplessness, freezing, and analgesia. Remarkably, new possibilities of escape do not instigate physical escape: most animals remain frozen, and passively endure continued shock (Garber & Seligman, 1980; Seligman, 1975). IS thus seems to induce deficits in learning and memory. This passive way of self-defense apparently blocks later acquisition or application of more active defensive strategies, as it is also elicited through exposure to stimuli that are associated with IS. Just one or very few learning trials, in which particular stimuli are saliently associated with the ones that evoke IS-responses naturally, can be sufficient in creating conditioned alarm responses, freezing, analgesia, and increased defecation (Cassens, Kuruc, Roffman, Orsuluk, & Schildkraut, 1981; Desiderato & Newman, 1971; Fanselow, 1980; Fanselow & Lester, 1988). For example, presentation of such conditioned stimuli (CS, i.e., previously neutral stimuli that have come to be associated with an unconditioned stimulus [UCS] in that they signal or refer to an aversive stimulus) made rats stop consuming food and drinks, and evoked freezing (Bouton & Bolles, 1980). The acquired associations between an extreme aversive stimulus (UCS) and other stimuli are extraordinarily resistant to change. Further, after threat exposure, the animals tend to react in exaggerated ways to previously tolerated stressors. This effect seems to indicate a sensitization effect (i.e., response increment without further exposure to threat).

Freezing is controlled by antecedent, not consequent, aversive stimuli. For example, punishment of freezing through shock *increases* this kind of behavior

(Fanselow & Lester, 1988). As rats do in nature, in experimental contexts they also freeze in darker areas or other places less strongly associated with threat, such as next to walls, usually in corners.

There is an abundance of animal research showing that intensity, duration, frequency, uncontrollability, and unpredictability of exposure to aversive stimuli significantly affect IS-outcome (e.g., Anisman, deCatanzaro, & Remington, 1978; Weiss, Stone, & Harrell, 1970; see Foa, Steketee, & Rothbaum, 1989; Mineka & Kihlstrom 1978). According to Van der Kolk (1987), the crucial traumatic ingredient concerns real as well as perceived lack of control, since the behavioral and biochemical sequelae of inescapable shock are the opposite of those of escapable shock.

Defense in Social Conflict Situations, and Pain

Studying nonaggressive mice intruding the territory of aggressive resident conspecifics, Siegfried et al. (1990) were able to largely confirm the assumptions that inhibited pain and movement serve defensive functions, that learned danger signals activate defensive behavior, including analgesia, and that nociception elicits recuperative behavior. As Siegfried et al., and others (cited in Siegfried et al., 1990) found, pain may, however, also precede and elicit analgesia, as well as defensive behavior, and tolerance of analgesia may develop upon continued traumatization. Animal pain can, thus, be evoked in various stages of imminence.

Early Availability and Rapid Maturation of Defensive Responses in Animals

A defensive system which would depend on long-term maturation and extensive trial-and-error learning does not make evolutionary sense. It thus comes as no surprise that this system is available early in life. For example, rats innately, automatically, and rapidly freeze to predators such as cats, snakes, canines, and humans (Fanselow & Lester, 1988). Yet, the effective organization of defense demands a degree of maturation of the brain (cf. Jacobs & Nadel, 1985; LeDoux, 1989). Infant rhesus monkeys as young as 0 to 2 weeks displayed different defensive behaviors, but, not knowing how to coordinate these tendencies, at this age they did not selectively respond to different stages of imminence (Kalin, Shelton, & Takahashi, 1991). By 9 to 12 weeks of age, these infants modulated their type of defensive response to the parameters of the threat when exposed to threat for the *first time*. At this age, rhesus monkeys undergo cognitive and behavioral changes associated with brain development similar to those in human infants 7 to 12 months old, which is the time when human infants engage in complex emotional and behavioral responses. These effects seem to be independent of social experience (Sackett, 1966). Apart from maturation, learning is to some extent involved. As Garcia and Garcia y Robertson (1984) put it: "All organisms inherently possess the basic behavioral patterns that enable them to survive in their niches, but learning provides the fine tuning necessary for successful adaptation." (p. 197)

Symptoms of Traumatized Individuals and Those with Dissociative Disorders as Related to Animal Defensive and Recuperative Response-sets

Some types of human trauma may be compared to predator attack, IS, and animal social conflict. For example, phenomenologically, sexual and physical abuse resemble IS, especially when occurring to children and involving relatives as perpetrators. Such highly aversive, burdening, and painful stimulation is inescapable in that perpetrators often force passive subjugation to sexual abuse (Albach, 1993; Draijer, 1990). It also reflects a loss of control and familiarity.

Since the beginning of this century, several authors have observed a striking analogy between certain animal defensive responses and aspects of trauma-induced psychopathology in humans (Kraepelin, 1913; Kretschmer, 1960; Krystal, 1988; Ludwig, 1983; Rivers, 1920). In these analogies the rapid reflex-like character and evolutionary value of these reactions is emphasized. While Rivers (1920) stressed the *survival value* of freezing, and the concomitant reduction of fear and pain, other authors have described this defensive response pattern as a *surrender* reaction in the face of unavoidable and overwhelming danger, providing a means of painless death (for a review Krystal, 1988). Interestingly, the animal defense model as proposed by Fanselow and Lester (1988) involves two stages of imminence evoking these reactions. At the encounter stage, freezing/analgesia is thought to serve survival. Once a strike has occurred, and aggressive or flight responses prove ineffective, there is a return to freezing. Freezing/analgesia in this stage may still have survival value (Fanselow & Lester, 1988), but at the same time it may be "a merciful provision by our benevolent Creator for lessening the pain of death" (Livingstone, 1872, p. 15, cited in Greyson, 1993).

More recently, the many apparent behavioral and biological similarities between the human response to trauma and the animal response to inescapable shock (IS) led Van der Kolk, Greenberg, Boyd, and Krystal (1985) to propose that the animal model of IS may serve as an appropriate biological model for posttraumatic stress disorder (PTSD) in humans. PTSD involves physiological and behavioral hyperreactivity (positive symptoms: hyperarousal, and intrusive reliving of traumatic events in flash-backs, nightmares), alongside restriction-phenomena (negative symptoms: emotional constriction, social isolation, anhedonia, a sense of estrangement). According to Van der Kolk et al. (Van der Kolk & Greenberg, 1987; Van der Kolk, 1994), both reaction-patterns are due to chronic alterations in the central neurotransmitter systems.

Considering certain similarities between patients with PTSD and with dissociative disorders (Bremner, Southwick, Johnson, Yehuda, & Charney, 1993; Warshaw et al., 1993), we assume that animal defensive state-dependent responses to predators, IS, and aggressive conspecifics are also of relevance with respect to a better understanding of trauma-induced dissociation. More specifically, we suspect that they may shed more light on the roots of characteristic dissociative states, and the typical responses displayed in these discrete states. If there is a phylogenetic parallel between animal defensive and recuperative states on the one hand, and dissociative responses and dissociative states on the other hand, one would expect that dominant pre-encounter, post-encounter, circa-strike, and recuperative animal responses will also appear in traumatized dissociative patients.

The following discussion is not exhaustive. We will focus on freezing, analgesia/anesthesia, and pain, and show that most of these symptoms seem to characterize traumatized subjects, and dissociative disorders patients in particular. We do not consider, for example, disturbed eating patterns, aggressive reactions, and flight.

Freezing

Albach (1993) and Draijer (1990) found that only a minority of adult females reporting childhood sexual and physical abuse actively resisted the perpetrator (also: Gebhard, Gagnon, Pomeroy, & Christenson, 1965), because such defense was perceived as useless, or as eliciting further attack. Passive defense (dissociation and fantasy) increased with severity of abuse, and initial resistance decreased with sustained abuse. Most abused women recalled that they were forced to go along with the abuse by way of psychological and physical aggression, or life threats. Flight responses were shown by about half of these women, but were restricted to hiding in dark corners or under blankets. They tended to freeze at those places. Albach (1993) further found that bodily stiffening was reported by as many as 87%. Fainting and paralysis may represent freezing-related responses, and these symptoms occurred in about a quarter of the cases. In other studies, it was found that a substantial number of women reported freezing and paralysis before and during rape (Brickman & Briere, 1989; Burgess & Holmstrom, 1976; Galliano, Noble, Travis, & Puechl, 1993).

We are not aware of systematic studies of freezing among dissociative patients, although Smit and Takke (1994) found that dissociative patients, in contrast with other psychiatric patients, predominantly, if not exclusively, used passive coping styles. Clinical observation (Putnam, 1989) suggests that traumatized child states, which are frequent in DID (Boon & Draijer, 1993; Putnam, Guroff, Silberman, Barban, & Post, 1986; Ross, Norton, & Wozney, 1989), tend to hide at dark places, freeze there, and prefer to physically disappear when they feel threatened. Adopting a fetal position, they seem to be unresponsive to external stimuli. More generally, upon feeling threatened, adult DID-patients often switch into a trance-like state, freeze, become analgesic, and afterwards report out-of-body experiences, or dissociative amnesia. It is also clinically found that consequent stimuli like punishment do not decrease freezing. On the contrary, as happens with shocked animals, defensive responses then will increase. The behaviors are automatically evoked by environmentally as well as internally presented CS (Janet, 1928; Nijenhuis, 1994, 1995; Van der Hart, Boon, Friedman, & Mierop, 1992). It thus seems that, as with animals, human freezing is controlled by antecedent aversive UCS and CS.

Analgesia, Anesthesia, and Emotional Numbing

A large majority of Albach's (1993) subjects who reported childhood sexual abuse experienced analgesia and kinesthetic anesthesia (insensitivity for touch). In fact, analgesia was the most commonly reported "hysterical" symptom. Most female and male DDNOS and DID patients also present analgesic dissociative states (Boon & Draijer, 1993; Loewenstein & Putnam, 1990). Consistent with a Pavlovian view on symptom formation, analgesia and other traumatic responses seem to be reactivated by salient trauma-associated stimuli, even after a delay of two decades (Van der Kolk, Greenberg, Orr, & Pitman, 1989; Pitman, Van der Kolk, Orr, & Greenberg, 1990). With PTSD patients, this analgesia is reversible by naloxone (Pitman et al., 1990), as is often the case with animals (Siegfried et al., 1990). Analgesia and anesthesia frequently go along with emotional numbing, trance-like states, depersonalization, and derealization (Albach, 1993). Automutilation tends to be accompanied by analgesia. In a later stage, nociception returns, which elicits recuperative behavior.

Further exploration is needed to determine whether analgesia, anesthesia, and psychological numbing as dissociative reactions of dissociative patients are exclusively functions of endogenous opioid and non-opioid neurochemical responses to a traumatic stressor (Van der Kolk et al., 1989). The symptoms involved may, for example, very rapidly change with state, and may be restricted to localized bodily areas unrelated to neurophysiological systems. From a psychological point of view, these effects could also relate to threat-induced restriction of attention (Janet, 1893), which also occurs in threatened prey.

Pain

As a rule, studies on animal trauma-induced pain pertain to acute pain, and chronic animal pain seems to be rare. Traumatized and dissociative human subjects, however, often report chronic, as well as acute pain (e.g., Draijer, 1990; Ross, Heber, Norton, & Anderson, 1989; Saxe et al., 1994; Toomey, Seville, Mann, Abashian, & Grant, 1995; Walker, Katon, Neraas, Jemelka, & Massoth, 1992), which may be state-dependent (McFadden & Woitalla, 1993). The observed difference between species is puzzling.

Early Availability and Maturation of Human Defense

As is likely to be the case with animals, human defensive behaviors seem to be available very early. For example, human infants can display a sudden, catatonoid state when exposed to threat (see Krystal, 1988). Yet, as is the case with animals, maturational processes have a role, because the quality of human infant responses to threatening situations changes with age (Bronson, 1972). For instance, from between 7 and 10 months, infants inhibit their ongoing behavior, or withdraw when exposed to novel or threatening situations and unfamiliar people (Campos, Barrett, Lamb, Goldsmith, & Stenberg 1983; Rothbart, 1988), which changes are likely a consequence of perceptual, sensorimotor, and cognitive maturation (Kagan, 1983). The behavioral tendencies may be stable over time. For example, children who display extremely inhibited responses when they are 2 years of age are likely to be pathologically fearful later in life (Biederman et al., 1990). As the appropriate manipulation of experiences early in life can generate stable and relatively permanent complex individual differences, and modify emotional reactivity (Whimbey & Denenberg, 1966), traumatization at this phase of life may induce chronic traumatic responses.

If this line of reasoning is valid, traumatized children with dissociative disorders should have symptoms which also characterize adult dissociative disorder patients. The available evidence indeed suggests that children with DID display features largely identical to those of adults (Fagan & McMahon, 1984; Hornstein, 1993; Hornstein & Putnam, 1992; Kluft, 1984; Reagor, Kasten, & Morelli, 1992; Tyson, 1992). These include negative symptoms (e.g., amnesia, trance-states, being unresponsive to external stimuli, anesthesia, analgesia, paralysis, and loss of feeling), as well as positive symptoms (e.g., hypervigilance, startle responses, and rapid transitions of state). The appearance of spontaneous trance-like states, in which the children do not seem to pay attention to their surroundings, may be even the most prevalent dissociative symptom of children with DID (Putnam & Trickett, 1993). Furthermore, very young sexually and physically traumatized children have positive symptoms, such as pain symptoms related to the specifics of the abuse (e.g., anal pain, abdominal pain), fears of trauma-related stimuli, display of aggressive and fearful regressive behavior, and dramatic increases in affiliative behavior (Burgess, Hartman, & Baker, 1995). These children also have negative symptoms, such as trance-like states, staring into space, being highly inattentive and detached from others, and refusal to eat, or to feed oneself.

The stress responses exhibited by infants are the product of an immature brain processing threat stimuli and producing infant appropriate responses, while the adult who exhibits infantile responses has a mature brain that, barring stress-related abnormalities in brain development, is capable of exhibiting adult response patterns. However, there is evidence that the adult brain may regress to an infantile state when it is confronted with severe stress (Jacobs & Nadel, 1985; LeDoux, 1996). As LeDoux (1996) argues, the amygdala is essentially involved in very rapidly and automatically instigated physiological and behavioral responses to major threat, as well as the classical conditioning of these threat responses. This conditioning yields probably indelible associations between unconditioned and conditioned stimuli. Extreme stress does not interfere with, and may even amplify, memory processes mediated by the amygdala (Corodimas, LeDoux, Gold, & Schulkin, 1994), but it does hamper hippocampal-neocortical information processing which should inhibit or regulate emotional reactions and memories. Chronic release of stress hormones may even damage the hippocampus. This stress-induced condition resembles the infantile state, which is characterized by functional amygdala and a relatively immature hippocampal-neocortical system. Extreme stress may therefore evoke defensive reactions in adults which are also evoked in young children.

Summary and Discussion

While pathological dissociation has been related to state-dependent learning and memory (Janet, 1889; Putnam, 1988, 1992), it is presently unknown what factors explain the various characteristics of a yet limited range of distinct dissociative states. In this article, a phylogenetic parallel is proposed between characteristic dissociative responses and behavioral and physiological animal defensive and recuperative states. This model obviously is speculative in nature, but it shows promise since some empirical data and clinical observations seem to support its validity, and it may be of heuristic value.

The basic idea is that different stages of imminence may serve as UCS to evoke particular unconditioned responses, which prey and human beings seem to share as a consequence of phylogenetic survival value, and which are available at an early age. The various unconditioned responses are thought to be organized in subsystems of defense and recuperation jointly constituting a complex system (Timberlake & Lucas, 1989). Trauma is likely to evoke substate-bound reaction patterns, providing optimal adaptation to particular stages of imminence. Less adaptive reaction patterns will concomitantly be inhibited. In some cases, the expressions of defensive and recuperative substates may mark dissociative states, or perhaps even subtypes of dissociative states, as apparent in complex dissociative disorders. As traumatization reflects a process of classical conditioning, previously neutral stimuli which are saliently associated with innately aversive stimuli may acquire the capacity to raise an expectancy of threat (Bolles & Fanselow, 1980). Consequently, these CS may posttraumatically reactivate substates of defense and recuperation. More severe, and more frequent, UCS exposure would promote the strength and chronicity of conditioned dissociative reactions.

Testable hypotheses can be derived from the model, and a few of them can be indicated: (1) Dissociative disorder patients would predominantly display quite particular somatoform and psychological dissociative symptoms relating to defense and recuperation, including analgesia, anesthesia, motor inhibitions, and restrictions of perceptual fields. While the research to date suggests that dissociative disorder patients often have these symptoms, they tend to have many other symptoms as well. The present model predicts that the indicated symptoms will characterize these patients best, even when controlling for general psychoneuroticism. (2) Upon exposure to conditioned threat stimuli – including external, as well as internal stimuli (Nijenhuis, 1995) – defensive states, instead of isolated conditioned responses, would tend to be reactivated. That is, CS associated with threat which once appeared in a particular stage of imminence would reactivate the related dissociative reaction patterns, or dissociative substates. Clinical observation does indeed suggest that, for example, a freezing state is reactivated by CS associated with the post-encounter stage, an aggressive state by CS relating to the circa-strike stage of imminence, and recuperative states, after a delay, by (self-inflicted) injury. We are not aware of systematic research in this area. (3) Finally, taking into consideration the evolutionary importance of *rapid* responding to major threat, it would seem odd if dissociative defense were strongly dependent upon the relatively slow cognitive (hippocampal-neocortical) information processing system (LeDoux, 1989). The present model postulates that dissociative defensive reactions are elicited almost instantaneously (LeDoux, 1989; see also, Bremner, Krystal, Southwick, & Charney, 1995), which, therefore, cannot be satisfactorily explained by time-consuming processes such as imagery and autohypnosis (cf. Butler, Duran, Jasiukaitis, Koopman, & Spiegel, 1996). However, hypnotic or hypnotic-like processes may be involved in the *secondary* development of personality-like characteristics of dissociative (identity) states (Nijenhuis, 1995). Such characteristics and dissociative state-dependent memory structures may evolve and be reinforced as a result of retraumatization and CS-evoked reactivations of the relevant states.

According to Fanselow and Lester (1988), (conditioned) fear induces analgesia, and acute animal pain is restricted to the recuperation phase. The finding that (conditioned) safety signals produce acute anti-analgesic effects in animals is supportive of this view. It is, therefore, worthwhile studying whether, and to what extent, acute and chronic analgesia and pain in dissociative disorders depend on (conditioned) danger and safety signals. The role of animal pain may, however, be more complex than Fanselow and Lester have suggested: Acute animal pain may precede and elicit analgesia, not all trauma-related CS may, apart from defensive behavior, evoke analgesia, and repeated social attack may imply return of nociception (Siegfried et al., 1990). The evidence to date suggests that conditioned animal hyperalgesia is rare, but the subject deserves further attention. While there are parallels between acute attack-induced and short-term delayed pain in animals and humans, it is as of yet uncertain whether this similarity can be extended to chronic pain.

References

Albach, F. (1993). *Freud's verleidingstheorie: Incest, trauma en hysterie.* [Freud's seduction theory: Incest, trauma, and hysteria.] Middelburg: Stichting Petra.

American Psychiatric Association (1994). *Diagnostic and statistical manual of mental disorders,* 4th edn. Washington, D.C.: Author.

Amir, S., Brown, Z.W., Amit, Z., & Ornstein, K. (1981). Body pinch induces long lasting cataleptic like immobility in mice: Behavioral characteristics and the effect of naloxone. *Life Sciences, 10,* 1189-1194.

Anisman, H., deCatanzaro, D., & Remington, G. (1978). Escape deficits following exposure to inescapable shock: Deficits in motor response maintenance. *Journal of Experimentology and Behavior Processes, 4,* 197-218.

Biederman, J., Rosenbaum, J.F., Hirschfeld, D.R., Faraone, S.V., Boldue, E.Z., Gersten, M., Menninger, S.R., Kagan, J., Snidman, N., & Reznick, J.S. (1990). Psychiatric correlates of behavioral inhibition in young children of parents with and without psychiatric disorders. *Archives of General Psychiatry, 47,* 21-26.

Bolles, R.C. (1970). Species-specific defense reactions and avoidance learning. *Psychological Review, 77,* 32-48.

Bolles, R.C., & Fanselow, M.S. (1980). A perceptual-defensive-recuperation model of fear and pain. *The Behavioral and Brain Sciences, 3,* 291-301.

Boon, S., & Draijer, N. (1993). *Multiple personality disorder in the Netherlands. A study on reliability and validity of the diagnosis.* Amsterdam/Lisse: Swets & Zeitlinger.

Bouton, M.C., & Bolles, R.C. (1980). Conditioned fear assessed by freezing and by the suppression of three different baselines. *Animal Learning and Behavior, 8,* 429-434.

Bremner, J.D., Krystal, J.H., Southwick, S.M., & Charney, D.S. (1995). Functional neuroanatomical correlates of the effects on memory. *Journal of Traumatic Stress, 8,* 527-555.

Bremner, J.D., Southwick, S.M., Johnson, D.R., Yehuda, R., & Charney, D.S. (1993). Childhood physical abuse and combat-related posttraumatic stress disorder in Vietnam veterans. *American Journal of Psychiatry, 150,* 235-239.

Brickman, J., & Briere, J. (1989). Incidence of rape and sexual assault in an urban Canadian population. *International Journal of Women's Studies, 7,* 195-206.

Bronson, G.W. (1972). Infants' reactions to unfamiliar persons and novel objects. *Monographs of the Society for Research in Child Development, 37* (3, Serial No. 148).

Burgess, A.W., Hartman, C.R., & Baker, T. (1995). Memory presentations of childhood sexual abuse. *Journal of Psychosocial Nursing, 33,* 9-16.

Burgess, A.W., & Holmstrom, A.L.L. (1976). Coping behavior of the rape victim. *American Journal of Psychiatry, 133,* 413-418.

Butler, L.D., Duran, R.E.F., Jasiukaitis, P., Koopman, C., & Spiegel, D. (1996). Hypnotizability and traumatic experience: A diathesis-stress model of dissociative symptomatology. *American Journal of Psychiatry,* Festschrift Supplement, *153,* 42-63.

Cadet, R., Aigouy, L., & Woda, A. (1993). Sustained hyperalgesia can be induced in the rat by a single formalin injection and depends on the initial nociceptive inputs. *Neuroscience Letters, 156,* 43-46.

Campos, J.J., Barrett, K.C., Lamb, M.E., Goldsmith, H.H., & Stenberg, C. (1983). Socio-emotional development. In M. Haith, & J. Campos (eds.), *Handbook of child psychology: Vol. 2: Infancy and developmental psychobiology* (pp. 783-915). New York: Wiley.

Cassens, G., Kuruc, A., Roffman, M., Orsulak, P.J., & Schildkraut, J.J. (1981). Alterations in brain norepinephrine metabolism and behavior induced by environmental stimuli previously paired with inescapable shock. *Behavioral Brain Research, 2,* 387-407.

Corodimas, K.P., LeDoux, J.E., Gold, P.W., & Schulkin, J. (1994). Corticosterone potentiation of learned fear. *Annals of the New York Academy of Sciences, 746,* 392-393.

Desiderato, O., & Newman, A. (1971). Conditioned suppression produced in rats by tones paired with escapable and inescapable shock. *Journal of Comparative and Physiological Psychology, 77,* 427-431.

Draijer, N. (1990). *Seksuele traumatisering in de jeugd: Gevolgen op lange termijn van seksueel misbruik door verwanten* [Sexual traumatization in childhood: Long-term consequences of sexual abuse by relatives]. Amsterdam: SUA.

Fagan, J., & McMahon, P.P. (1984). Incipient multiple personality in children: Four cases. *The Journal of Nervous and Mental Disease, 172,* 26-36.

Fanselow, M.S. (1980). Conditional and unconditional components of postshock freezing. *Pavlovian Journal of Biological Science, 15,* 177-182.

Fanselow, M.S. (1986). Conditioned fear-induced opiate analgesia: A competing motivational state theory of stress analgesia. In D.D. Kelly (ed.), *Stress-induced analgesia* (pp. 40-54). New York: The New York Academy of Sciences.

Fanselow, M.S., & Lester, L.S. (1988). A functional behavioristic approach to aversively motivated behavior: Predatory imminence as a determinant of the topography of defensive behavior. In R.C. Bolles, & M.D. Beecher (eds.), *Evolution and learning* (pp. 185-212). Hillsdale NJ: Lawrence Erlbaum Associates.

Fanselow, M.S., & Sigmundi, R.A. (1982). The enhancement and reduction of defensive fighting by naloxone pretreatment. *Physiological Psychology, 10,* 313-316.

Foa, E.B., Steketee, G., & Rothbaum, B.O. (1989). Behavioral/cognitive conceptualizations of post-traumatic stress disorder. *Behavior Therapy, 20,* 155-176.

Galliano, G., Noble, L.M., Travis, L.A., & Puechl, C. (1993). Victim reactions during rape/sexual assault: A preliminary study of the immobility response and its correlates. *Journal of Interpersonal Violence, 8,* 109-114.

Garber, J., & Seligman, M.E.D. (eds.) (1980). *Human helplessness: Theory and application.* New York: Academic Press.

Garcia, J., & Garcia y Robertson, R. (1984). Evolution of learning mechanisms. In B.L. Hammonds (ed.), *Psychology and learning* (pp. 191-243). Washington D.C.: American Psychological Association.

Gebhard, P.H., Gagnon, J.H., Pomeroy, W.B., & Christenson, C.V. (1965). *Sex offenders: An analysis of types.* New York: Harper & Row.

Greyson, B. (1993). Varieties of near-death experiences. *Psychiatry, 56,* 390-399.

Helmstetter, F.J. & Fanselow, M.S. (1993). Aversively motivated changes in meal patterns of rats in a closed economy: The effects of shock density. *Animal Learning and Behavior, 21,* 168-175.

Hirsch, S.M., & Bolles, R.C. (1980). On the ability of prey to recognize predators. *Zeitschrift für Tierpsychologie, 54,* 71-84.

Hornstein, N. (1993). Recognition and differential diagnosis of dissociative disorders in children and adolescents. *Dissociation, 2/3,* 136-144.

Hornstein, N.L., & Putnam, F.W. (1992). Clinical phenomenology of child and adolescent dissociative disorders. *Journal of the American Academy of Child and Adolescent Psychiatry, 31,* 1077-1085.

Jacobs, W.J., & Nadel, L. (1985). Stress-reduced recovery of fears and phobias. *Psychological Review, 92,* 512-531.

Janet, P. (1889). *L'Automatisme psychologique* [Psychological automatism]. Paris: Félix Alcan. Reprint: Société Pierre Janet, Paris, 1973.

Janet, P. (1893). *L'Etat mental des hystériques: Les stigmates mentaux* [The mental state of hystericals: The mental stigmata]. Paris: Rueff &Cie.

Janet, P. (1909). Problèmes psychologiques de l'émotion [The psychological problems of the emotion]. *Revue de Neurologie,* 1551-1687.

Janet, P. (1928). *L'Evolution de la mémoire et la notion du temps* [The evolution of memory and the notion of time]. Paris: A. Chahine.

Kagan, J. (1983). Stress and coping in early development. In N. Garmezy & M. Rutter (eds.), *Stress, coping and development in children* (pp. 191-216). New York: McGraw-Hill.

Kalin, N.H. (1993). The neurobiology of fear. *Scientific American,* May, 54-60.

Kalin, N.H., & Shelton, S.E. (1989). Defensive behaviors in infant rhesus monkeys: Environmental cues and neurochemical regulation. *Science, 243,* 1718-1721.

Kalin, N.H., Shelton, S.E., & Takahashi, L.K. (1991). Defensive behaviors in infant rhesus monkeys: Ontogeny and context-dependent selective expression. *Child Development, 62,* 1175-1183.

Kluft, R.P. (1984). Multiple personality in childhood. *Psychiatric Clinics of North America, 7,* 121-134.

Kraepelin. (1913). Über Hysterie [On hysteria]. *Zeitschrift für die gesamte Neurologie und Psychiatrie, XVIII,* 261-279.

Kretschmer, E. (1960). *Hysteria, reflex and instinct.* London: Peter Owen.

Krystal, H. (1988). *Integration and self-healing: Affect, trauma, alexithymia*. Hillsdale: Lawrence Erlbaum.

Krystal, J. H., Kosten, T.R., Southwick, S., Mason, J.W., Perry, B.D., & Giller, E.L. (1989). Neurobiologic aspects of PTSD: Review of clinical and preclinical studies. *Behavior Therapy, 20*, 177-198.

LeDoux, J.E. (1989). Cognitive-emotional interactions in the brain. *Cognition and Emotion, 3*, 267-289.

LeDoux, J.E. (1996). *The emotional brain: The mysterious underpinnings of emotional life.* New York: Simon & Schuster.

Loewenstein, R.J., & Putnam, F.W. (1990). The clinical phenomenology of males with MPD: A report of 21 cases. *Dissociation, 3*, 135-143.

Ludwig, A.M. (1983). The psychobiological functions of dissociation. *American Journal of Clinical Hypnosis, 26*, 93-99.

McFadden, I.J., & Woitalla, V.F. (1993). Differing reports of pain perception by different personalities in a patient with chronic pain and multiple personality disorder. *Pain, 55*, 379-382.

Mineka, S., & Kihlstrom, J.F. (1978). Unpredictable and uncontrollable events: A new perspective on experimental neuroses. *Journal of Abnormal Psychology, 87*, 256-271.

Moore, A.U., & Amstey, M.S. (1962). Tonic immobility: Differences in susceptibility of experimental and normal sheep and goats. *Science, 135*, 729-730.

Nijenhuis, E.R.S. (1994). *Dissociatieve stoornissen en psychotrauma* [Dissociative disorders and psychotrauma]. Houten: Bohn Stafleu Van Loghum.

Nijenhuis, E.R.S. (1995). Dissociatie en leertheorie: trauma-geïnduceerde dissociatie als klassiek geconditioneerde defensie [Dissociation and learning theory: Trauma-induced dissociation as classically conditioned defense]. In K. Jonker, J.L.L. Derksen, & F.J. Donker (eds.), *Dissociatie: een fenomeen opnieuw belicht* (pp. 35-61) [Dissociation: A phenomenon illuminated afresh]. Houten: Bohn Stafleu Van Loghum.

Pitman, R.K., Van der Kolk, B.A., Orr, S.P., & Greenberg, M.S. (1990). Naloxone reversible stress induced analgesia in post traumatic stress disorder. *Archives of General Psychiatry, 47*, 541-547.

Putnam, F.W. (1988). The switch process in multiple personality disorder. *Dissociation, 1*, 24-33.

Putnam, F.W. (1989). *Diagnosis and treatment of multiple personality disorder*. New York: Guilford.

Putnam, F.W. (1992). Discussion: Are alter personalities fragments or figments? *Psychoanalytic Quarterly, 12*, 95-112.

Putnam, F.W. (1993). Diagnosis and clinical phenomenology of multiple personality disorder: A North-American perspective. *Dissociation, 2/3*, 80-87.

Putnam, F.W., Guroff, J.J., Silberman, E.K., Barban, L., & Post, R.M. (1986). The clinical phenomenology of multiple personality disorder. *Journal of Clinical Psychiatry, 47*, 285-293.

Putnam, F.W., & Trickett, P.K. (1993). Child sexual abuse: A model of chronic trauma. *Psychiatry, 56*, 82-95.

Pynoos, R.S., Ritzmann, R.F., Steinberg, A.M., Goenjian, A., & Prisecaru, I. (1996). A behavioral animal model of posttraumatic stress disorder featuring repeated exposure to situational reminders. *Biological Psychiatry, 39*, 129-134.

Reagor, P.A., Kasten, J.D., & Morelli, N. (1992). A checklist for screening dissociative disorders in children and adolescents. *Dissociation, 5*, 4-19.

Rivers, W.H.R. (1920). *Instinct and the unconsciousness. A contribution to a biological theory of the psycho-neuroses*. London: Cambridge University Press.

Ross, C.A., Anderson, G., Fraser, G.A., Reagor, P., Bjornson, L., & Miller, S.D. (1992). Differentiating multiple personality disorder and dissociative disorder not otherwise specified. *Dissociation, 5*, 87-91.

Ross, C.A., Heber, S., Norton, G.R., & Anderson, G. (1989). Somatic symptoms in multiple personality disorder. *Psychosomatics, 30*, 154-160.

Ross, C.A., Miller, S.D., Bjornson, L., Reagor, P., Fraser, G.A., & Anderson, G. (1991). Abuse histories in 102 cases of multiple personality disorder. *Canadian Journal of Psychiatry, 36*, 97-101.

Ross, C.A, Norton, G.R., & Wozney, K. (1989). Multiple personality disorder: An analysis of 236 cases. *Canadian Journal of Psychiatry, 34*, 413-418.

Rothbart, M.K. (1988). Temperament and the development of inhibited approach. *Child Development, 59*, 1241-1250.

Sackett, G.P. (1966). Monkeys reared in isolation with pictures as visual input: Evidence for an innate releasing mechanism. *Science, 154*, 1468-1473.

Saxe, G.N., Chinman, G., Berkowitz, M.D., Hall, K., Lieberg, G., Schwartz, J., & Van der Kolk, B.A. (1994). Somatization in patients with dissociative disorders. *American Journal of Psychiatry, 151*, 1329-1334.

Seligman, M.E.D. (1975). *Helplessness: On depression, development and death*. San Francisco: Freeman.

Siegfried, B., Frischknecht, H.R., & Nunez de Souza, R. (1990). An ethological model for the study of activation and interaction of pain, memory, and defensive systems in the attacked mouse: Role of endogenous opioids. *Neuroscience and Biobehavioral Reviews, 14*, 481-490.

Smit, Y.L.S., & Takke, M.J. (1994). Multipele persoonlijkheidsstoornis: Coping met scha(n)delijke gebeurtenissen en dagelijkse problemen [Multiple personality disorder: Coping with noxious and infamous events, and daily problems]. Utrecht: Utrecht University, Department of Clinical Psychology and Health Psychology.

Suarez, S.D., & Gallop, G.G. (1981). An ethological analysis of open-field behavior in rats and mice. *Learning and Motivation, 9*, 153-163.

Teskey, G.C., Kavaliers, M., & Hirst, M. (1984). Social conflict activates opioid analgesic and ingestive behaviors in male mice. *Life Sciences, 35*, 303-315.

Timberlake, W., & Lucas, G.A. (1989). Behavior systems and learning: From misbehavior to general principles. In S.B. Klein & R.R. Mowrer (eds.), *Contemporary learning theories* (pp. 237-275). Hillsdale, NJ: Lawrence Erlbaum.

Toomey, T.C., Seville, J.L., Mann, D., Abashian, S.W., & Grant, J.R. (1995). Relationship of sexual and physical abuse to pain description, coping, psychological distress, and health care utilization in a chronic pain sample. *The Clinical Journal of Pain, 11*, 307-315.

Tyson, G.M. (1992). Childhood MPD/dissociative identity disorder: Applying and extending current diagnostic checklists. *Dissociation, 5*, 20-27.

Van der Hart, O., Boon, S., Friedman, B., & Mierop, V. (1992). De reactivering van traumatische herinneringen [The reactivation of traumatic memories]. *Directieve therapie, 12*, 12-56.

Van der Kolk, B.A. (1987). *Psychological trauma*. Washington D.C.: American Psychiatric Press.

Van der Kolk, B.A. (1994). The body keeps the score: Memory and the evolving psychobiology of posttraumatic stress. *Harvard Review of Psychiatry, 1*, 253-265.

Van der Kolk, B.A., & Greenberg, M.S. (1987). The psychobiology of the trauma response: Hyperarousal, constriction, and addiction to traumatic reexposure. In B.A. Van der Kolk (ed.), *Psychological trauma* (pp. 63-89). Washington, D.C.: American Psychiatric Press.

Van der Kolk, B.A., Greenberg, M.S., Boyd, H., & Krystal, J. (1985). Inescapable shock, neurotransmitters and addiction to trauma: Towards a psychobiology of post traumatic stress. *Biological Psychiatry, 20*, 314-325.

Van der Kolk, B.A., Greenberg, M.S., Orr, S.P., & Pitman, R.K. (1989). Endogenous opioids, stress induced analgesia, and posttraumatic stress disorder. *Psychopharmacalogy Bulletin, 25*, 417-422.

Van der Kolk, B.A., & Van der Hart, O. (1989). Pierre Janet and the breakdown of adaptation in psychological trauma. *American Journal of Psychiatry, 146*, 1530-1540.

Walker, E.A., Katon, W.J., Neraas, K., Jemelka, R.P., & Massoth, D. (1992). Dissociation in women with chronic pelvic pain. *American Journal of Psychiatry, 149*, 534-537.

Walters, E.T. (1987). Site-specific sensitization of defensive reflexes in *Aplysia*: A simple model of long-term hyperalgesia. *The Journal of Neuroscience, 7*, 400-407.

Warshaw, M.G., Fierman, E., Pratt, L., Hunt, M., Yonkers, K.A., Massion, A.O., & Keller, M.B. (1993). Quality of life and dissociation in anxiety disorder patients with histories of trauma or PTSD. *American Journal of Psychiatry, 150*, 1512-1516.

Weiss, J.M., Stone, E.A., & Harrell, N. (1970). Coping behavior and brain norepinephrine levels in rats. *Journal of Comparative and Physiological Psychology, 72*, 153-160.

Whimbey, A.E., & Denenberg, V.H. (1966). Programming life histories: Creating individual differences by the experimental control of early experiences. *Multivariate Behavioral Research*, 279-286.

Wiertelak, E.P., Watkins, L.R., & Maier, S.F. (1992). Conditioned inhibition of analgesia. *Animal Learning and Behavior, 20*, 339-349.

Wolff, P.H. (1987). *The development of behavioral states and the expression of emotions in early infancy*. Chicago: University of Chicago Press.

X

Somatoform Dissociative Symptoms as Related to Animal Defensive Reactions to Predatory Imminence and Injury[*]

I suggest ... that the essential process underlying the instinct of immobility is the suppression of fear and pain. It is possible that the instinctive reaction to danger by means of immobility may have furnished one of the earliest motives for suppression.
(p. 59)

In the case of Man ... we have not only suppression of tendencies and of states of consciousness, but there is definite evidence that the suppressed experience and the tendencies associated therewith, may have a kind of independent existence, and may act indirectly upon or modify consciousness even when incapable of recall by any of the ordinary processes of memory. (p. 69)
Rivers, 1920.

Introduction

The wide range of somatoform symptoms that patients with dissociative identity disorder (DID) and dissociative disorder not otherwise specified (DDNOS; American Psychiatric Association, 1994) have, is remarkable (Ross, Heber, Norton et al., 1989; Saxe et al., 1994). It is equally remarkable that these symptoms can be very changeable and contradictory (Janet, 1889, 1893, 1901, 1907), as they include alternating and opposite phenomena, such as motor inhibitions and excitations, analgesia and pain, restrictive anorexia, and binging. Clinical observation (Kollner, Grothgar, & Vauth, 1994; Putnam, 1989) suggests that these somatoform symptoms often depend on the highly distinct states of consciousness, identity, and memory that patients with DID and DDNOS have developed, each of which also involves a prevailing affect, as well as a limited repertoire of behaviors (Putnam, 1988). Thus, they may represent somatoform manifestations of dissociation. For example, in one state these patients may show

* This chapter has previously been published as: Nijenhuis, E.R.S., Spinhoven, P., Vanderlinden, J., Van Dyck, R., & Van der Hart, O. (1998). Somatoform dissociative symptoms as related to animal defensive reactions to predatory imminence and injury. *Journal of Abnormal Psychology, 107, 1,* 63-73. This study was supported by Grant 11.92 of the Stichting Dienstbetoon Gezondheidszorg, Soesterberg, The Netherlands.

inhibited movement and speech, as well as analgesia, in another state, they may be full of motion, tremble, and suffer pain, and in a third state they may be free of such symptoms. Somatoform dissociation can be described as the partial or complete loss of the normal integration of somatoform components of experience, reactions, and functions. It involves negative symptoms, such as anesthesia, and positive symptoms, such as pain and uncontrolled movements (Kihlstrom, 1994; Nijenhuis, Spinhoven, Van Dyck, Van der Hart, & Vanderlinden, 1996, 1997). Because somatoform dissociative symptoms are often displayed in a context of reactivated traumatic memories, they could be intimately connected with overwhelming experience. This interpretation has been proposed from the 19th century French psychiatry (Janet, 1889, 1893) to the present time (Van der Hart & Friedman, 1989).

Following this view, and noticing that experimental induction of human trauma is obviously excluded, one way of enhancing our comprehension of somatoform dissociation could be to compare animal and human responses to major threat. This comparison seems worthwhile, as from Kraepelin (1913), and particularly Rivers (1920), several authors have observed similarities between the animal and human response to trauma. Following these pioneers, several authors have suggested an evolutionary parallel between animal and human defense, but only a few of them included dissociative reactions in their considerations. Some stressed the survival value of the rapid, reflex-like reactions (Kraepelin, 1913; Kretschmer, 1960; Ludwig, 1983; Pavlov, 1927; Rivers, 1920), others conceptualized them as surrender reactions (e.g., Krystal, 1988), while Seligman (1975) drew a parallel with depression and giving up. Relationships with animal hypnosis, implying tonic immobility (see Krystal, 1988), that is, behavioral inhibition, have also been proposed.

Animal defense has been experimentally studied using inescapable shock. Considering the manyfold similarities between the animal response to inescapable shock and the symptoms in posttraumatic stress disorder (PTSD), these studies are relevant for trauma-induced human psychopathology (Van der Kolk, Greenberg, Boyd, & Krystal, 1985). The parallels include motor inhibitions and deficits in learning to escape novel adverse situations, decreased motivation to learn new contingencies, alterations in catecholamine response, and the development of analgesia (Van der Kolk, Greenberg, Orr, & Pitman, 1989). Since DID and DDNOS may be regarded as complex forms of PTSD (Herman, 1992; Spiegel, 1984; Van der Kolk, Herron, & Hostetler, 1994), explanatory models of PTSD could also be applicable to these dissociative disorders.

The typical inescapable shock procedure models only one stage of natural threat, that is, the stage in which the predator is about to strike. However, animal defense and recuperation is a multifaceted system adapted to meet different stages of predatory imminence as determined by the geographical and temporal relationship of the predator to the prey (Fanselow & Lester, 1988). It consists of distinct and mutually inhibitory motivational substates which involve qualitative as well as quantitative behavioral and biological changes (Bolles & Fanselow, 1980; Fanselow & Lester, 1988; Rivers, 1920; Siegfried, Frischknecht, & Nunez de Souza, 1990; Timberlake & Lucas, 1989). By varying the density of inescapable shock, Fanselow and Lester (1988) succeeded in evoking these different substates.   The substates include pre-encounter defense, post-encounter defense, and circa-strike defense. *Pre-encounter defense* involves elicitation of high arousal, narrowing of attention to potential threat cues, and interruption of preferred activity patterns. For example, eating patterns are immediately reorganized into extended periods of food abstinence and infrequent consumption of meals of increased size. As a result, the prey will be able to detect predatory threat rapidly. *Post-encounter defense* consists of short-lived flight, which is followed by freezing and silencing. The latter reactions increase survival chances probably because predators have difficulty noticing immobile and silent objects, and movement of the prey releases predatory behavior. *Circa-strike defense* is characterized by analgesia, startle response, and short-lived flight and fight reactions. Analgesia and bodily as well as emotional anesthesia promote survival in that pain and panic would divert the attention from defensive concerns. When these behaviors do not avert the attack, there will be a return to freezing. Even in this stage, freezing serves survival as it reduces the likelihood of continued attack (Fanselow & Lester, 1988). Freezing and analgesia constitute the dominant animal defensive reactions. Even though these reactions belong to different subsystems, they are very strongly intercorrelated. Although Fanselow and Lester worked only with rats, species varying from fish to lions (Moore & Amstey, 1962), including monkeys (Kalin, Shelton, & Takahashi, 1991), also display defensive reactions such as freezing.

In line with Rivers's (1920) ideas, Nijenhuis, Vanderlinden, and Spinhoven (1998; also Nijenhuis & Vanderlinden, 1996) recently proposed that as a result of an evolutionary mechanism common to many species there may be a similarity between distinct animal defensive reaction patterns, and certain somatoform dissociative symptoms of traumatized dissociative disorder patients such as analgesia, anesthesia, and motor inhibitions. It may even be that certain characteristic dissociative states relate to animal defensive substates. The basic idea is that various stages of imminence may serve as unconditioned stimuli (UCS) to automatically evoke particular unconditioned response patterns, which are available at an early age, and which provide optimal adaptation to these stages of threat. Less adaptive reaction patterns will be concomitantly inhibited. Although, according to this view, dissociative states are primarily evoked by major threat, personality-like characteristics may become attached to these states as a result of secondary elaboration (e.g., posttraumatic, dissociative state-dependent imagery). Posttraumatic lack of integration of the threat-induced dissociative states, amongst others, results from a phobia of traumatic memories and of dissociative (identity) states that carry these memories (Nijenhuis, 1995).

Some clinical and research findings are consistent with the proposed parallel (for reviews, see Nijenhuis & Vanderlinden, 1996; Nijenhuis, Vanderlinden, & Spinhoven, 1998), although most of the studies addressing somatoform symptoms in dissociative disorders involved rather small numbers of subjects, and none included all symptoms of our concern. Many dissociative patients report severe traumatization (Boon & Draijer, 1993b; Putnam, Guroff, Silberman, Barban, & Post, 1986; Ross, Miller, Bjornson, Fraser, & Anderson, 1991;

Schultz, Braun, & Kluft, 1989), and severe threat may induce dissociative reactions, including analgesia and numbness, and restriction of awareness (e.g., Cardeña et al., in press). In a recent longitudinal study, Darves-Bornoz (1997) found that rape induced PTSD in 71%, dissociative disorders in 69%, and somatoform disorders in 66% of the cases. Pribor, Yutzy, Dean, and Wetzel (1993) reported significant associations between somatization, somatization disorder (Briquet's syndrome), dissociation, and abuse. In patients with PTSD, Van der Kolk, Pelcovitz, et al. (1996) also found high intercorrelations between PTSD, dissociation, somatization, and affect dysregulation. Finally, trauma tends to evoke, relative to its severity and duration, somatic and somatoform symptoms in many children (e.g., Burgess, Hartman, & Baker, 1995; Friedrich & Schafer, 1995; Rimsza, Berg, & Locke, 1988) and adults (e.g., Kimerling & Calhoun, 1994; McFarlane, Atchison, Rafalowicz, & Papey, 1994; also Van der Kolk, McFarlane, & Weisaeth, 1996).

DID and DDNOS patients often display or report freezing, analgesia, and anesthesia (e.g., Boon & Draijer, 1993b). Albach (1993) and Draijer (1990) reported that the majority of the sexually abused women they studied experienced analgesia. Retrospectively assessed freezing, dissociation, and anxiety during incestuous abuse were the best predictors for the development of PTSD (Albach & Everaerd, 1992). Survivors of an earthquake also experienced transient analgesic effects (Cardeña & Spiegel, 1993), and many individuals involved in a disaster at sea did not feel the coldness of the water in which they fell (Cardeña et al., in press). Both PTSD and dissociative patients usually report that freezing, analgesia, and emotional numbing were elicited automatically, and that actively resisting perpetrators was useless or elicited further attack.

Intercorrelations between dissociative and eating disorder symptoms have been found (e.g., Boon & Draijer, 1993a; Demitrack, Putnam, Brewerton, Brandt, & Gold, 1990), but this relationship may be specific for subgroups of eating disorder patients, in particular those reporting trauma, displaying self-harm, and having a dissociative disorder (Demitrack et al., 1990; McCallum, Lock, Kulla, Rorty, & Wetzel, 1992; Vanderlinden, Vandereycken, Van Dyck, & Vertommen, 1993).

Animal defensive reactions, as well as dissociative reactions, can persist far beyond actual threat exposure. Freezing and analgesia are highly sensitive to Pavlovian conditioning (Bouton & Bolles, 1980; Fanselow, 1984b; Fanselow & Lester, 1988). While remaining in traumatized child states, which are frequent in DID (e.g., Boon & Draijer, 1993a), dissociative patients tend to hide and freeze when they feel threatened by salient trauma-associated conditioned stimuli (CS), and analgesia and other traumatic responses may be reactivated by CS even after a delay of two decades (Pitman, Van der Kolk, Orr, & Greenberg, 1990; Van der Kolk et al., 1989). As classical conditioning effects are probably relative to threat severity and repetition, the acquisition of probably indelible (Bouton, 1988) propositional associations between CS and UCS could also contribute to an explanation of the severity and chronicity of dissociative state-dependent reactions.

As a first step towards evaluation of the hypothesized similarity between animal defense and certain somatoform dissociative reactions of dissociative disorder patients, this study aimed to assess the presence of a range of somatoform symptoms, including the animal defenselike reactions, in these patients and comparison patients. The following hypotheses were tested: (a) As, in our view, dissociative processes may pertain to many somatoform reactions and functions, in comparison to psychiatric patients with other diagnoses, dissociative patients report more somatoform dissociative symptoms; among these, clustered symptoms of anesthesia-analgesia, freezing, and disturbed eating as primary and essential dissociative reactions to threat would stand out; (b) in contrast with other somatoform symptoms, these three symptom clusters independently contribute to the prediction of dissociative disorder; (c) as animal defense constitutes a functional system, these three symptom clusters strongly correlate; considering that animal freezing and anesthesia/analgesia depend on different, but highly related defensive subsystems, the analogous symptom clusters correlate most strongly; and (d) between-groups differences in somatoform dissociative symptoms cannot be attributed to differences in level of general psychopathology.

Methods

Participants and Procedure

Psychiatric outpatients suspected to suffer from a dissociative disorder were interviewed by experienced clinicians – in many cases the therapist and in some cases an independent diagnostician – using the Structured Clinical Interview for *DSM-IV* (the fourth edition of the *Diagnostic and Statistical Manual of Mental Disorders*; American Psychiatric Association, 1994) Dissociative Disorders (SCID-D, Steinberg, 1993; Steinberg, Cichetti, Buchanan, Hall, & Rounsaville, 1993). This suspicion had been raised by the display and reporting of dissociative symptoms in the diagnostic phase or in the course of treatment. All interviewers were trained in the administration and interpretation of the instrument. Fifty cases were selected that presented a dissociative disorder (27 with DID, 21 with DDNOS, and 2 with depersonalization disorder [DP]). The mean age of this group (44 women and 6 men) was 34.8 years ($SD = 9.7$ years; range 20 to 57).

The comparison group consisted of 50 psychiatric outpatients with a nondissociative *DSM-IV* (APA, 1994) diagnosis. Patients with eating disorder, somatization disorder, conversion disorder, or PTSD were excluded as these patients may experience dissociative symptoms. Diagnoses included Axis I anxiety disorders ($n = 36$) (social and specific phobia, panic disorder with and without agoraphobia, and obsessive-compulsive disorder), depressive disorder ($n = 10$), hypochondriasis ($n = 1$), body dysmorphic disorder ($n = 1$), adjustment disorder ($n = 5$), and alcohol abuse ($n = 3$). Some patients presented with other conditions described in *DSM-IV* that warranted clinical attention: bereavement ($n = 3$), relational problems ($n = 3$), and phase of life problems ($n = 1$). Axis II diagnoses included borderline personality disorder ($n = 2$), narcissistic personality disorder ($n = 1$), dependent personality disorder ($n = 2$), and personality disorder NOS (n = 1). Further, 26 patients displayed traits of personality disorder (predominantly dependent personality disorder). The mean age of the comparison group (37 women and 13 men) was 36.3 years (SD = 11.4 years; range 16 to 79).

Instruments

In the process of developing a somatoform dissociation questionnaire (Nijenhuis et al., 1996, 1997), a pool of 77 self-report items was formulated, starting from clinically observed manifestations of somatoform dissociation. The items were supplied with a Likert-type 5 point scale. To evaluate face validity, the items were submitted to six clinicians who had experience in dealing with dissociative disorders. An item was included if 4 of 6 experts judged that it possibly reflected a somatoform dissociative symptom. As a result, two items were removed. The items of the remaining pool of 75 items were a priori grouped in twelve symptom clusters addressing nonurogenital pain (n = 13); analgesia and kinesthetic, visual, auditory, gustatory, and olfactory anesthesia (n = 11); freezing (n = 7); alternating responses to medication and alcohol (n = 5); arousal (n = 5); alternating preferences of taste and smell (n = 4); alternating quality or acuity of visual perception (n = 4); urogenital pain (n = 4; two gender-specific urogenital pain items [vaginal pain, pain in penis] from the original item pool were combined into one item); eating disorder symptoms (anorexia-bulimia; n = 3); gastrointestinal symptoms (n = 3); alternating allergic reactions (n = 2); and loss of consciousness (n = 2). Other items that were gender-specific (n = 8) could not be combined and were excluded from the present analyses, as were items which could not be categorized (n = 3).

All items started with the phrase "It sometimes happens that." Anesthesia and analgesia items included "my body, or a part of it, is insensitive to pain," and "it is as if my body, or a part of it, has disappeared." An example of a freezing item is "I grow stiff for a while." It was aimed to assess urogenital pain with items such as "I feel pain in my genitals (apart from sexual intercourse)," and symptoms of disturbed eating with items such as "I for days on end have no appetite and cannot get a bite through my throat." Other items included "I have a headache" (nonurogenital pain), "I have palpitations" (arousal), "I am affected by alcohol unpredictably, for example, I get drunk quickly or slowly, independent of how much I have eaten" (alternating responses to medication and alcohol), "I dislike tastes that I usually like" (alternating preferences of taste and smell), "People and things around me look bigger than they actually are" (alternating quality or acuity of visual perception), "I have cramps in my stomach with diarrhea" (gastrointestinal symptoms), "I am allergic to particular food to which food I am normally not allergic" (alternating allergic reactions), and "I have an attack that resembles an epileptic fit" (loss of consciousness).

The pool of 75 items was further used to develop the Somatoform Dissociation Questionnaire (SDQ-20; Nijenhuis et al., 1996) which measures the construct of somatoform dissociation, and a screening instrument for dissociative disorders that was derived from it (SDQ-5; Nijenhuis et al., 1997).

The SCID-D (Steinberg, 1993) is a diagnostic instrument developed for the assessment of dissociative disorders. It covers five dissociative symptom areas (amnesia, depersonalization, derealization, identity confusion, and identity fragmentation). Severity ratings of the symptom areas range from 1 (*absent*) to 4 (*severe*). The total score ranges from 5-20. Good to excellent reliability and validity have been reported both in the US and in the Netherlands (Boon & Draijer, 1993a, 1993b; Steinberg et al., 1993; Steinberg, Rounsaville & Cichetti, 1990).

Data Analysis

We calculated twelve unweighted symptom cluster scores summing the relevant item scores. In order to assess homogeneity of the constructed symptom clusters, we calculated Pearson product-moment correlation coefficients among their constituent variables and we determined the internal consistency of the symptom clusters by Cronbach's alpha. The symptom cluster sumscores were then entered in separate logistic regression analyses (*p* to enter <.05) to evaluate their ability to discriminate between dissociative disorder (dd) and comparison patients (cp). Next, the probabilities of caseness of dissociative disorder or other psychiatric disorder as predicted by these symptom cluster sumscores were compared with observed outcomes according to the SCID-D. The ratio between predicted disorder (PD) in both groups was calculated as a discriminant index (DI; Othmer & DeSouza, 1985) with the formula:

$$DI = \frac{PC\,/\,N_{\text{Dissociative Disorder Patients}}}{PC\,/\,N_{\text{Comparison Patients}}}$$

In other words, the discriminant index represents the ratio of sensitivity (the proportion of positives that are correctly identified by the test) and 1 minus specificity (the proportion of positives that are incorrectly identified by the test; Altman, 1991).

Further, to assess their independent contributions to the prediction of dissociative disorder, the symptom cluster scores were entered in a stepwise logistic regression analysis using forward selection (*p* to enter < .05) and backward elimination (*p* to remove > .10) based on likelihood ratio estimates. Finally, the associations between the symptom cluster scores assessing disturbed eating, freezing, and anesthesia-analgesia were evaluated with Pearson product-moment correlation coefficients.

Statistical analyses were performed with SPSS-PC 6.0 (SPSS, 1993).

Results

The correlations among the variables of the symptom clusters proved significant for all items (range of correlations from $r = .20$, $p = .045$, $n = 12$ to $r = .90$, $p < .0001$, $n = 4$) but one. This nonurogenital pain item was removed from further analyses. The intercorrelations among the symptom clusters, as well as

Table 1
Pearson Product-Moment Intercorrelations between 12 Symptom Cluster Scores and Symptom Cluster Internal Consistencies (Cronbach's Alpha)

Symptom cluster[a]	1	2	3	4	5	6	7	8	9	10	11	12
1. Anesthesia/analgesia (11)	.91											
2. Urogenital pain (4)	.66	.77										
3. Freezing (7)	.83	.63	.86									
4. Disturbed eating (3)	.74	.55	.61	.69								
5. Alternating smell-taste preferences (4)	.75	.61	.62	.59	.80							
6. Distorted visual perception (4)	.86	.60	.77	.72	.73	.81						
7. Non-urogenital pain (12)	.61	.59	.63	.54	.45	.58	.91					
8. Arousal (5)	.60	.38	.55	.55	.51	.55	.61	.85				
9. Gastrointestinal symptoms (3)	.57	.63	.53	.55	.57	.57	.56	.53	.73			
10. Loss of consciousness (2)	.47	.41	.57	.34	.52	.46	.41	.44	.36	.53		
11. Alternating reactions to alcohol/medication (5)	.52	.44	.51	.45	.45	.53	.55	.53	.38	.46	.82	
12. Allergic reactions (2)	.46	.45	.49	.47	.61	.52	.40	.36	.45	.41	.33	.37
13. Caseness dissociative disorder[b]	.73	.67	.68	.66	.54	.65	.61	.41	.49	.35	.42	.42

Note. All correlations are significant at $p < .002$; coefficients of .36 and greater are significant at $p < .0001$. Coefficients on the diagonal are coefficient alphas.
[a] Number in parentheses indicate number of items. [b] Point-biserial correlations.

the internal consistency reliabilities of all symptom clusters, are displayed in Table 1. These results indicate that the internal consistency of most of the constructed symptom clusters is sufficient (especially anesthesia-analgesia and freezing). However, the high intercorrelations among most of the symptom clusters suggest an underlying dimension of somatoform dissociation.

As predicted, the intercorrelations between disturbed eating symptoms, freezing, and anesthesia-analgesia were high and ranged from $r = .61$ to $r = .83$ (all $ps < .0001$). As was also hypothesized, among these three symptoms clusters, the association between freezing and anesthesia-analgesia reached the highest value ($r = .83$). In particular distorted visual perception was very strongly related to anesthesia-analgesia, reaching the highest overall correlation ($r = .86$), and was strongly associated with freezing ($r = .77$) and disturbed eating ($r = .72$).

The discriminant indices of the symptom cluster scores ranged from 2.2 to 15.5. Table 2 shows that, as hypothesized, freezing, anesthesia-analgesia, and disturbed eating patterns all were highly characteristic of dissociative disorder patients, with discriminant indices of 5 or greater; unexpectedly, however, alternating taste and smell preferences and urogenital pain also showed similarly strong associations with group membership. In particular, arousal and gastro-intestinal symptoms proved less distinctive.

Table 2
Unweighted Symptom Cluster Sumscores of Dissociative Disorder Patients and Comparison Psychiatric Patients

Symptom cluster	Dissociative disorder patients ($n = 50$)		Comparison group ($n = 50$)		Discriminant Index	p-value of β
	M	SD	M	SD		
Alternating taste and smell preferences	1.8	0.8	1.1	0.3	15.5	.0001
Anesthesia/analgesia	2.5	0.8	1.2	0.2	8.2	< .0001
Urogenital pain	2.5	1.0	1.2	0.3	7.6	< .0001
Freezing	2.4	0.9	1.2	0.3	5.9	< .0001
Disturbed eating	2.8	1.0	1.4	0.4	5.6	< .0001
Alternating allergic reactions	1.9	0.8	1.3	0.4	4.7	.0001
Distorted visual perception	2.3	0.9	1.1	0.2	4.2	< .0001
Non-urogenital pain	3.1	0.9	1.9	0.7	3.9	< .0001
Loss of consciousness	1.6	0.9	1.1	0.3	2.9	.0036
Alternating reactions to alcohol and medication	2.0	1.1	1.3	0.5	2.8	.0002
Gastro-intestinal symptoms	2.8	1.1	1.7	0.8	2.5	< .0001
Arousal	3.0	1.1	2.1	0.9	2.2	.0001

Note. The range of sum scores per item is 1 (not applicable) to 5 (highly applicable).
M = cluster score/number of cluster items.

Entering the 12 symptom cluster sumscores into a logistic regression equation with presence of dissociative disorder versus some other psychiatric diagnosis as the dependent variable yielded a model with stepwise entrance of anesthesia/analgesia, urogenital pain, and freezing (Table 3), providing 93% correct classification of cases and non-cases. Disturbed eating symptoms were not included in the final prediction model.

Table 3

Multiple Logistic Regression Analysis Predicting Dissociative Disorders by Somatoform Dissociative Symptom Cluster Scores Using Dissociative Disorder Patients (n = 50) and Comparison Patients (n = 50)

Symptom cluster	β	SE	pr	p
Anesthesia/analgesia	.39	.15	.19	.008
Urogenital pain	.74	.26	.21	.004
Freezing	.35	.17	.13	.036
Disturbed eating	-	-	.06	.110 (ns)
All other symptom clusters	-	-	-	-

Note. The pr expresses the partial correlation between the dependent variable and an independent variable while adjusting for the effects of the other independent variables.

In consonance with the a priori assumption, and as detailed by Nijenhuis, Spinhoven, Van Dyck, Van der Hart and Vanderlinden (1998), the dissociative patients reported high rates of severe sexual (82%), physical (78%), and emotional abuse (87%), as well as emotional neglect (91%), and several other types of trauma. The comparison patients reported sexual abuse (11%), and other types of trauma far less frequently. Some patients with dissociative disorders stated that external corroboration of the reported emotional neglect, emotional abuse, or both (57%), physical abuse (54%), and sexual abuse (33%) was available. This self-reported corroboration consisted of official documents, such as hospital records and legal documents, confessions of perpetrators; testimonies of witnesses including relatives, friends, and neighbors; physical traces of physical and sexual abuse: and childbirth following sexual abuse. Only in some cases did the therapists check these claims.

Patients who did and who did not report corroborative evidence could possibly have obtained different symptom cluster scores. In order to investigate this possibility, the scores of dissociative disorder patients with self-reported corroborated and noncorroborated trauma were compared. Trauma was considered being (partially) corroborated if (a) emotional, physical, and sexual abuse was claimed and the (partial) corroboration involved at least two of these three types of trauma (n = 20); (b) two of these types of trauma were claimed and both were (partially) corroborated (n = 2); or (c) one type of trauma was claimed and (partially) corroborated (n = 1). In cases with less or absent self-reported corroboration, trauma was considered being noncorroborated. The group with self-reported corroboration of trauma consisted of patients with DDNOS (n = 8), DP

($n = 1$), and DID ($n = 14$), and the group with noncorroborated trauma encompassed comparable numbers of patients with DDNOS ($n = 9$), DP ($n = 1$), and DID ($n =11$). Six patients did not complete the trauma questionnaire. The groups did not obtain different symptom cluster scores on 11 of the 12 constructed symptom cluster scores (all t-tests ns), but the group with self-reported corroborated trauma had significantly more symptoms of disturbed eating, t (38.12) = -2.23, $p = .032$.

Considering that the Dissociative Experiences Scale (DES; Bernstein & Putnam, 1986), which measures dissociation of memory, consciousness, and identity, is sensitive to response and experimenter bias (Van IJzendoorn & Schuengel, 1996), it was checked whether the results of this study, which involved assessment of (somatoform) dissociation, were likely to have been influenced by the present theoretical ideas through therapist suggestion. To that end, all 12 symptom cluster scores of patients with DDNOS ($n = 7$) and DID ($n = 7$), who were diagnosed and/or treated by the first author (i.e., the main originator of these theoretical notions) were compared with the scores of DDNOS ($n = 14$) and DID ($n = 22$) patients diagnosed and/or treated by 19 other clinicians who were not knowledgeable of our hypotheses, or did not display this potential bias. No differences were found (all t-tests ns).

Certain aspects of the present results could perhaps reflect overall differences in symptom severity or chronicity between dissociative disorder patients and comparison patients. Using an independent sample, we assessed the influence of symptom severity. This sample consisted of SCID-D diagnosed dissociative disorder outpatients ($n = 41$; mean age 38.9, SD = 8.5 years, range 21 to 59 years; 39 women, 2 men), involving patients with DID ($n = 21$) as well as DDNOS ($n = 20$), and consecutive psychiatric outpatients ($n = 45$, mean age 34.6, SD = 10.1 years, range 19 to 53 years, 27 women, 18 men), who did not have dissociative disorder, somatoform disorder, eating disorder, or posttraumatic stress disorder. Diagnoses were assigned by clinicians according to DSM-IV criteria. This comparison group included Axis I anxiety disorders ($n = 20$) (social and specific phobia, panic disorder with and without agoraphobia, obsessive-compulsive disorder), depressive disorder ($n = 14$), adjustment disorder ($n = 10$), alcohol abuse ($n = 1$), polysubstance dependence ($n = 1$), and schizophrenia ($n = 1$). Some patients presented with other conditions described in DSM-IV that warranted clinical attention: bereavement ($n = 2$) and problems of relationship ($n = 3$). Axis II diagnoses included borderline personality disorder ($n = 3$), avoidant personality disorder ($n = 2$), dependent personality disorder ($n = 2$), and personality disorder NOS ($n = 2$). Personality disorder traits were displayed by 8 patients, and included traits of dependent, histrionic, borderline, and narcissistic personality disorder.

These patients completed the SDQ-20 (Nijenhuis et al., 1996), as well as the Symptom Checklist (SCL-90-R; Derogatis, 1977; adapted Dutch version, Arrindell & Ettema, 1986), which evaluates general psychoneuroticism. Most of the SDQ-20 items assess anesthesia-analgesia (9 items), freezing (4 items), and urogenital pain (2 items). As applied to the first sample, in particular anesthesia-analgesia and freezing were strongly intercorrelated (Table 4). Aiming to select the variables which best predicted caseness of dissociative disorder, a stepwise logistic regression analysis was performed using forward selection (p to enter < .05) and backward elimination (p to remove > .10). Entering the three symptom cluster scores and the SCL-90 total score yielded a regression equation with anesthesia-analgesia and urogenital pain (Table 5).

Table 4

Pearson Product-Moment Intercorrelations between General Psychopathology and Dissociative Defensive Symptom Clusters

	Prediction of dissociative disorder[a]	Anesthesia-analgesia	Freezing	Urogenital pain
Anesthesia-analgesia	.79			
Freezing	.73	.86		
Urogenital pain	.60	.73	.70	
SCL-90-R	.37*	.51	.56	.52

Note. Symptoms were derived from the Somatoform Dissociation Questionnaire (SDQ-20) using SCID-D diagnosed dissociative disorder patients (n = 41) and comparison patients (n = 45). SCID-D = Structured Clinical Interview for DSM-IV Dissociative Disorders; DSM-IV = *Diagnostic and Statistical Manual of Mental Disorders*; SCL-90-R = Symptom Checklist 90-Revised.
[a] Point-biserial correlations; all values significant at p <.0001, except where noted.
* p <.001.

Table 5

Multiple Logistic Regression Analysis Predicting Dissociative Disorder by Three Somatoform Dissociative Cluster Scores

Symptom	β	SE	R	p
1. All variables entered stepwise				
Anesthesia-analgesia	-0.79	0.26	-.26	.002
Urogenital pain	-2.58	1.31	-.13	.048
Freezing	-	-	-	-
SCL-90-R total	-	-	-	-
SCL-90-R subscales	-	-	-	-
2. Anesthesia-analgesia, freezing, and urogenital pain after forced entrance of SCL-90-R				
SCL-90-R	-0.01	0.02	.00	.661
Anesthesia-analgesia	-0.81	0.27	-.27	.002
Urogenital pain	-2.32	1.32	-.10	.079
Freezing	-	-	-	-

Note. Scores were derived from the Somatoform Dissociative Questionnaire (SDQ-20) and a measure of general psychopathology, using an independent sample of dissociative disorder patients (n = 41) and comparison patients (n = 45). SCL-90-R = Symptom Checklist 90-Revised.

These variables correctly classified 96% of the cases. After statistically controlling for the effect of psychopathology by forced entrance of the SCL-90-R scores, the anesthesia-analgesia symptom cluster still proved to be highly predictive of dissociative disorder. Repeated analyses entering the SCL-90-R subscale scores instead of the SCL-90-R total score yielded the same results.

Discussion

We predicted that among a range of somatoform dissociative symptoms and symptoms reflecting general psychopathology, animal defenselike dissociative reactions would discriminate best between dissociative disorder and comparison patients. According to the present model, they would constitute primary and essential reactions to threat to which many dissociative patients reportedly have been exposed.

In concordance with the first hypothesis, the present dissociative disorder patients experienced more somatoform symptoms, as all symptom clusters discriminated between cases and non-cases. This result corroborates previous findings that dissociative disorder patients display a wide range of somatoform symptoms (Ross et al., 1989; Saxe et al., 1994), and expands those findings as a larger range of symptoms was included (Nijenhuis et al., 1996). Examples are alternating taste and smell preferences, various types of anesthesia, and motor inhibitions.

Anesthesia-analgesia, freezing, and disturbed eating, apart from alternating taste and smell preferences and urogenital pain, yielded the highest discriminant indices, which partially fits the first hypothesis. Dissociative patients had high scores on arousal and gastrointestinal symptoms, but these clusters reached the lowest discriminant indices as nondissociative patients also had relatively high scores on these anxiety related somatoform symptoms. Anxiety was thus rather common among these psychiatric patients.

Reviewing the literature, Nijenhuis, Vanderlinden, and Spinhoven (1998) noticed that trauma in humans may evoke, apart from analgesia, acute as well as chronic pain, whereas traumatized animals foremost develop analgesia and then pain in the recuperation stage. Although chronic or conditioned animal pain has been experimentally evoked, it seems to be rare. This difference between species is noteworthy, and the high incidence of chronic urogenital pain among dissociative disorder patients cannot be readily explained by the animal defense model.

Partly consistent with the second hypothesis, two of the three presumed defense-related symptom clusters, apart from urogenital pain, independently contributed to the prediction of caseness of dissociative disorder. Anesthesia-analgesia was selected first, and thus most contributed to the discrimination between cases and non-cases. Urogenital pain and freezing further improved the prediction. These three variables correctly classified 93% of the cases and non-cases, indicating that these symptoms are highly characteristic of dissociative disorders. The association with disturbed eating symptoms did not improve the prediction of caseness after the inclusion of anesthesia-analgesia, urogenital pain, and freezing in the equation model.

The intercorrelations between disturbed eating, freezing, and anesthesia-analgesia were high, which result is consistent with the hypothesis that these reactions may belong to a complex defensive system. According to Fanselow and Lester (1988), animal freezing and analgesia constitute distinct, but temporally and functionally closely related defensive reaction-patterns (Fanselow, 1984a, 1984b). In consonance with this view, and as hypothesized, the correlation between freezing and anesthesia-analgesia among these three animal defenselike dissociative reactions was the strongest. Taking these strong intercorrelations into account, the independent contribution of two of these three clusters to the prediction of caseness is noteworthy. Even though too-high correlations become a statistical problem only at values of $r > .90$ (Tabachnick & Fidell, 1989), multicollinearity cannot be completely ruled out.

The correlations between the 12 symptom cluster scores ranged from moderate to very strong. The suggested underlying dimension of somatoform dissociation demands explanation. The observed associations between the symptom clusters need not be inconsistent with the present model. For example, the particularly strong associations of anesthesia-analgesia with distorted visual perception and alternating taste and smell preferences may reveal a link between perceptual loss and perceptual alteration. We speculate that threat-induced visual anesthesia (e.g., constriction of the visual field) may imply visual distortion (e.g., seeing persons and objects smaller than they really are), and anesthesia is likely to affect taste and smell because, as clinical observation suggests, anesthesia often depends on dissociative state, and it probably promotes state-dependent taste and smell preferences.

The results that were obtained using an independent sample suggested that the findings could not be attributed to symptom severity. Animal defenselike reactions and urogenital pain discriminated the groups of this independent sample considerably better than general psychopathology as measured by the SCL-90-R or its subscales. The findings with this sample were consistent with our first results and showed that anesthesia-analgesia predicted dissociative disorder best.

As animal analgesia and freezing are often, although not exclusively, mediated by endogenous opioids (Siegfried et al., 1990), animal defense probably also involves the inhibition of fear and related emotions. For this reason, it is interesting to note that numbing symptoms (e.g., loss of interest, detachment, and restricted affect) appeared to be particularly important in identifying individuals with PTSD (Foa, Riggs, & Gershuny, 1995), as was suggested by Horowitz (1986). Principal-components factor analysis of the PTSD symptoms showed that numbing symptoms, which Foa et al. related to animal freezing, and arousal/effortful avoidance (e.g., excessive startle reactions, emotional reactivity, and avoiding thoughts and situational reminders of trauma) loaded on separate factors. This result is of relevance for the hypothesis that threat may involve several stages of imminence, each of which evokes distinct defensive reactions (see also Foa, Zinbarg, & Rothbaum, 1992). After all, according to Fanselow and Lester (1988) animal flight, fight (effortful avoidance) and freezing, with subsequent development of analgesia (numbing), are different defensive subsystems.

Consistency of the results with our hypotheses does not necessarily rule out rival explanations. Merskey (1992) suggested that dissociative symptoms could be effects of self-suggestion or suggestion by therapists. Such presumed effects cannot be a priori discarded, but it seems unlikely that this speculation would apply. It should be noted that many of the somatoform symptoms we studied were not at the time of measurement generally known or recognized by the field at large as essential markers of dissociative disorders (Nijenhuis et al., 1996). If iatrogenesis were a principal explanatory factor, a theoretical bias pertinent to the present hypotheses should have influenced the results. The symptom cluster scores of dissociative patients who were treated by the main originator of the present theoretical ideas did, however, not differ from those who were treated by therapists who were presumably less biased in this regard.

The traumatic memories of the present patients were retrospectively assessed (Nijenhuis et al., 1998), which may have introduced a bias. As an instrument measuring a broad range of traumatic memories was unavailable in the Netherlands, the relevant data were gathered using a newly designed inventory, which may also have influenced the results. Neither overreporting (Frankel, 1993) nor underreporting of trauma (Draijer, 1990) can be excluded. Apart from these reservations, it may be cautiously concluded that the findings of this study are consistent with a traumatogenic interpretation of somatoform dissociation: A significant number of dissociative disorder patients reported corroborative evidence of their memories of severe and chronic trauma (Nijenhuis et al., 1998), and all but one of the somatoform symptom cluster scores of dissociative patients who did and who did not report such evidence were of equal size. Although independent evaluation of this evidence was occasionally performed, obviously only systematic checks of self-reported corroboration would allow for firmer conclusions.

The present ideas regarding a similarity between animal defense and human dissociation seem compatible with others. Four examples of models or hypotheses that are likely to contribute to an explanation of our results can be indicated. First, traumatization may interfere with the integration of experiences in consciousness, (autobiographical) memory, and identity, leaving trauma organized in memory on sensorimotor and affective levels (Janet, 1889; Kardiner, 1941; Van der Kolk, 1994; Van der Kolk & Van der Hart, 1991; Van der Kolk, McFarlane, & Weisaeth, 1996). Some retrospective data indeed suggest that traumatic memories of PTSD patients tend to be retrieved, at least initially, in the form of dissociated mental imprints of sensory and affective elements of traumatic experiences, that is, as visual, olfactory, affective, auditory and kinesthetic experiences (Van der Kolk & Fisler, 1995). These findings help to explain why sensorimotor defensive reactions can persist beyond the event that evoked them. It also suggests why urogenital pain was such a prominent symptom cluster in the present patients who reported sexual abuse. In this view, localized pain, as much as anesthesia-analgesia, freezing, and the like, would constitute reactivated somatoform memories.

Second, the results of this study concur with Janet's (1889, 1893, 1901, 1907) observations indicating that anesthesia, analgesia, motor disturbances, and eating disorders belong to the major symptoms of hysteria. According to Janet, these symptoms are related to the twofold basic characteristics of this broad class of dissociative disorders, that is, restriction of the field of consciousness and concurrent dissociation. It has been noticed in both animal and human stress research that exposure to severe stress involves this restriction (e.g., Cardeña & Spiegel, 1993; Christianson, 1992; Christianson, Loftus, Hoffman, & Loftus, 1991; Fanselow & Lester, 1988). Narrowing of attention could be functional in that all attention can be devoted to essential threat stimuli and defensive concerns. According to the present model, apart from this selective inhibition of awareness and perception, major threat may also inhibit behavioral and motivational states, which compromise optimal defense in a particular stage of imminence.

A third theoretical model that may contribute to an explanation of our results is the diathesis-stress model of dissociative symptomatology. It suggests that pathological dissociation arises from an interaction between innate hypnotizability and traumatic experience (Butler, Duran, Jasiukaitis, Koopman, & Spiegel, 1996). In this view, dissociation reflects an autohypnotic process, which is applied to reduce the perception of pain and the personal implications of trauma. However, in both general population and traumatized samples hypnotizability and dissociativity are weakly related constructs, and the weight of the current data indicates that trauma does not alter hypnotizability in most individuals (Putnam & Carlson, 1997). Future research should explore whether, or to what extent, somatoform dissociation in the face of severe threat depends on high hypnotic susceptibility, intentional self-hypnosis, or both.

While our model postulates that defensive reactions are instantaneous and reflexlike phenomena, it does not explain why dissociative states have often adopted names, ages, and other personality-like characteristics. In our view (also Nijenhuis, 1995), dissociative states may incorporate personality-like characteristics as a result of secondary elaborations which are probably promoted by hypnotic-like imagination, state-bound restricted fields of consciousness, and state-dependent needs. For example, these elaborations may, apart from the presumed effects of state-dependent anesthesia, contribute to the development of state-dependent taste and smell preferences. To some extent, secondary shaping of dissociative states by sociocultural (e.g., iatrogenic) influences may also be involved (Gleaves, 1996; Janet, 1929).

Fourth, clinical observation indicates that some somatoform dissociative symptoms may relate to psychodynamic factors as well. For example, bulimia may involve attempts to become sexually unattractive, while anorexia and purging relate to self-afflicted punishment, efforts to clean the dirty body, or fear of oral impregnation (Torem, 1990).

The present model holds that there would be a similarity between animal defensive-like reactions and particular somatoform dissociative symptoms of dissociative disorder patients. Because the results of this study are broadly consistent with this idea, we suggest the animal defense model contributes to our understanding of certain aspects of dissociative disorders.

References

Albach, F. (1993). *Freud's verleidingstheorie: Incest, trauma en hysterie* [Freud's seduction theory: Incest, trauma, and hysteria]. Middelburg, The Netherlands: Stichting Petra.

Albach, F., & Everaerd, W. (1992). Posttraumatic stress symptoms in victims of childhood incest. *Psychotherapy and Psychosomatics, 57,* 143-151.

Altman, D.G. (1991). *Practical statistics for medical research. London:* Chapman & Hall.

American Psychiatric Association (1994). *Diagnostic and statistical manual of mental disorders, fourth edition (DSM-IV).* Washington DC: American Psychiatric Association.

Arrindell, W.A., & Ettema, J.H.M. (1986). *SCL-90: Handleiding bij een multidimensionele psychopathologie indicator* [Manual for a multidimensional psychopathology indicator]. Lisse, The Netherlands: Swets Test Services.

Bernstein, E., & Putnam, F.W. (1986). Development, reliability, and validity of a dissociation scale. *Journal of Nervous and Mental Disease, 102,* 280-286.

Bolles, R.C., & Fanselow, M.S. (1980). A perceptual-defensive-recuperation model of fear and pain. *The Behavioral and Brain Sciences, 3,* 291-301.

Boon, S., & Draijer, N. (1993a). Multiple personality disorder in the Netherlands: A clinical investigation of 71 patients. *American Journal of Psychiatry, 150,* 489-494.

Boon, S., & Draijer, N. (1993b). *Multiple personality disorder in the Netherlands: A study on reliability and validity of the diagnosis.* Lisse, The Netherlands: Swets & Zeitlinger.

Bouton, M.E. (1988). Context and ambiguity in the extinction of emotional learning: Implications for exposure therapy. *Behaviour Research and Therapy, 26,* 137-149.

Bouton, M.E., & Bolles, R.C. (1980). Conditioned fear assessed by freezing and by the suppression of three different baselines. *Animal Learning and Behavior, 8,* 429-434.

Burgess, A.W., Hartman, C.R., & Baker, T. (1995). Memory presentations of childhood sexual abuse. *Journal of Psychosocial Nursing, 33,* 9-16.

Butler, L.D., Duran, R.E.F., Jasiukaitis, P., Koopman, C., & Spiegel, D. (1996). Hypnotizability and traumatic experience: A diathesis-model of dissociative symptomatology. *American Journal of Psychiatry, Festschrift Supplement, 153,* 42-63.

Cardeña, E., Holen, A., McFarlane, A., Solomon, Z., Wilkinson, C., Spiegel, D. (in press). A multisite study of acute-stress reaction to a disaster. In *Sourcebook for the DSM-IV, Vol. IV.* Washington, D.C.: American Psychiatric Press.

Cardeña, E., & Spiegel, D. (1993). Dissociative reactions to the San Francisco Bay Area earthquake of 1989. *American Journal of Psychiatry, 150,* 474-478.

Christianson, S.-A. (1992). Emotional stress and eyewitness memory: A critical review. *Psychological Bulletin, 112,* 284-309.

Christianson, S.-A., Loftus, E.F., Hoffman, H., & Loftus, G.R. (1991). Eye fixations and memory of emotional events. *Journal of Experimental Psychology: Learning, Memory, and Cognition, 17,* 693-701.

Demitrack, M.A., Putnam, F.W., Brewerton, T.D., Brandt, H.A., & Gold, P.W. (1990). Relation of clinical variables to dissociative phenomena in eating disorders. *American Journal of Psychiatry, 147,* 1184-1188.

Darves-Bornoz, J.-M. (1997). Rape-related psychotraumatic syndromes. *European Journal of Obstetrics & Gynecology and Reproductive Biology, 71,* 59-65.

Derogatis, L.R. (1977). *SCL-90: Administration, scoring and procedures manual-I for the R(evised) version and other instruments of the psychopathology rating scale series.* Baltimore: Clinical Psychometric Research Unit, John Hopkins University School of Medicine.

Draijer, N. (1990). *Seksuele traumatisering in de jeugd: Gevolgen op lange termijn van seksueel misbruik door verwanten* [Sexual traumatization in the youth: Long-term consequences of sexual abuse by relatives]. Amsterdam: SUA.

Fanselow, M.S. (1984a). Opiate modulation of the active and inactive components of the postshock reaction: Parallels between naloxone pretreatment and shock intensity. *Behavioral Neuroscience, 98,* 169-177.

Fanselow, M.S. (1984b). Shock-induced analgesia on the formalin test: Effects of shock severity, naloxone, hypophysectomy, and associative variables. *Behavioral Neuroscience, 98,* 79-95.

Fanselow, M.S., & Lester, L.S. (1988). A functional behavioristic approach to aversively motivated behavior: Predatory imminence as a determinant of the topography of defensive behavior. In R.C. Bolles & M.D. Beecher (eds.), *Evolution and learning* (pp. 185-212). Hillsdale NJ: Lawrence Erlbaum Associates.

Foa, E.B., Riggs, D.S., & Gershuny, B.S. (1995). Arousal, numbing, and intrusion: Symptom structure of PTSD following assault. *American Journal of Psychiatry, 152,* 116-120.

Foa, E.B., Zinbarg, R., & Rothbaum, B.O. (1992). Uncontrollability and unpredictability in post-traumatic stress disorder: An animal model. *Psychological Bulletin, 112,* 218-238.

Frankel, F.H. (1993). Adult reconstruction of childhood events in the multiple personality literature. *American Journal of Psychiatry, 150,* 954-958.

Friedrich, W.N., & Schafer, L.C. (1995). Somatic symptoms in sexually abused children. *Journal of Pediatric Psychology, 20,* 661-670.

Gleaves, D.H. (1996). The sociocognitive model of dissociative identity disorder: A reexamination of the evidence. *Psychological Bulletin, 120,* 42-59.

Herman, J.L. (1992). Complex PTSD: A syndrome in survivors of prolonged and repeated trauma. *Journal of Traumatic Stress, 5,* 377-392.

Horowitz, M.J. (1986). Stress-response syndromes: A review of posttraumatic and adjustment disorders. *Hospital and Community Psychiatry, 37,* 241-249.

Janet, P. (1889). *L'Automatisme psychologique* [Psychological automatism]. Paris: Félix Alcan. Reprint: Société Pierre Janet, Paris, 1973.

Janet, P. (1893). *L'Etat mental des hystériques: Les stigmates mentaux* [The mental state of hystericals: The mental stigmata]. Paris: Rueff & Cie.

Janet, P. (1901). *The mental state of hystericals.* New York: Putnam & Sons. Reprint D.N. Robinson (ed.), Significant contributions to the history of psychology 1750-1920, volume II. Series C. Medical Psychology. Washington DC: University Publications of America, 1977.

Janet, P. (1907). *The major symptoms of hysteria.* London/New York: Macmillan. Reprint of second edition: Hafner, New York, 1965.

Janet, P. (1929). *L'Evolution psychologique de la personnalité* [The psychological evolution of the personality]. Paris: Chahine. Reprint: Société Pierre Janet, Paris, 1984.

Kalin, N.H., Shelton, S.E., & Takahashi, L.K. (1991). Defensive behaviors in infant rhesus monkeys: Ontogeny and context-dependent selective expression. *Child Development, 62,* 1175-1183.

Kardiner, A. (1941). *The traumatic neuroses of war.* New York: Paul Hoeber.

Kihlstrom, J.F. (1994). One hundred years of hysteria. In S.J. Lynn & J.W. Rhue (eds.), *Dissociation: Clinical and theoretical perspectives* (pp. 365-394). New York: Guilford.

Kimerling, R., & Calhoun, K.S. (1994). Somatic symptoms, social support, and treatment seeking among sexual assault victims. *Journal of Consulting and Clinical Psychology, 62,* 333-340.

Kollner, V., Grothgar, B., & Vauth, R. (1994). Cognitive behavioral group therapy for female patients with a history of sexual abuse in early childhood. Paper presented at the 20th European Conference on Psychosomatic Research. Gent, Belgium. August 24-27.

Kraepelin, E. (1913). Über Hysterie [On hysteria]. *Zeitschrift für die gesamte Neurologie und Psychiatrie, XVIII*, 261-279.

Kretschmer, E. (1960). *Hysteria, reflex and instinct*. London: Peter Owen.

Krystal, H. (1988). *Integration and self-healing. Affect, trauma, alexithymia*. Hillsdale: Lawrence Erlbaum.

Ludwig, A.M. (1983). The psychobiological functions of dissociation. *American Journal of Clinical Hypnosis, 26*, 93-99.

McCallum, K.E., Lock, J., Kulla, M., Rorty, M., & Wetzel, R.D. (1992). Dissociative symptoms and disorders in patients with eating disorders. *Dissociation, 5*, 227-235.

McFarlane, A.C., Atchison, M., Rafalowicz, E., & Papay, P. (1994). Physical symptoms in post-traumatic stress disorder. *Journal of Psychosomatic Research, 38*, 715-726.

Merskey, H. (1992). The manufactury of personalities: The production of multiple personality disorder. *British Journal of Psychiatry, 160*, 327-340.

Moore, A.U., & Amstey, M.S. (1962). Tonic immobility: Differences in susceptibility of experimental and normal sheep and goats. *Science, 135*, 729-730.

Nijenhuis, E.R.S. (1995). Dissociatie en leertheorie: Trauma-geïnduceerde dissociatie als klassiek geconditioneerde defensie [Trauma-induced dissociation as classically conditioned defense]. In K. Jonker, J. Derksen, & F. Donker (eds.), *Dissociatie: Een fenomeen opnieuw belicht* (pp. 35-61) [Dissociation: A phenomenon illuminated afresh]. Houten, The Netherlands: Bohn Stafleu Van Loghum.

Nijenhuis, E.R.S., Spinhoven, P., Van Dyck, R., Van der Hart, O., & Vanderlinden, J. (1996). The development and psychometric characteristics of the Somatoform Dissociation Questionnaire (SDQ-20). *Journal of Nervous and Mental Disease, 184*, 688-694.

Nijenhuis, E.R.S., Spinhoven, P., Van Dyck, R., Van der Hart, O., & Vanderlinden, J. (1997). The development of the Somatoform Dissociation Questionnaire (SDQ-5) as a screening instrument for dissociative disorders. *Acta Psychiatrica Scandinavica, 96*, 311-318.

Nijenhuis, E.R.S., Spinhoven, P., Van Dyck, R., Van der Hart, O., & Vanderlinden, J. (1998). Degree of somatoform and psychological dissociation in dissociative disorders is correlated with reported trauma. *Journal of Traumatic Stress, 11*, 711-730.

Nijenhuis, E.R.S., & Vanderlinden, J. (1996). Dierlijke defensie als model voor dissociatieve reacties op psychotrauma [Animal defense as a model for dissociative reactions to psychotrauma]. *Tijdschrift voor Psychiatrie, 38*, 123-135.

Nijenhuis, E.R.S., Vanderlinden, J., & Spinhoven, P. (1998). Animal defensive reactions as a model for trauma-induced dissociative reactions. *Journal of Traumatic Stress, 11*, 243-260.

Othmer, E. & DeSouza, C. (1985). A screening test for somatization disorder (hysteria). *American Journal of Psychiatry, 142*, 1146-1149.

Pavlov, I.P. (1927). *Conditioned reflexes*. London: Oxford University Press.

Pitman, R.K., Van der Kolk, B.A., Orr, S.P., & Greenberg, M.S. (1990). Naloxone reversible stress induced analgesia in post traumatic stress disorder. *Archives of General Psychiatry, 47*, 541-547.

Pribor, E.F., Yutzy, S.H., Dean, J.T., & Wetzel, R.D. (1993). Briquet's syndrome, dissociation, and abuse. *American Journal of Psychiatry, 150*, 1507-1511.

Putnam, F.W. (1988). The switch process in multiple personality disorder. *Dissociation, 1*, 24-33.

Putnam, F.W. (1989). *Diagnosis and treatment of multiple personality disorder.* New York: Guilford.

Putnam, F.W., Guroff, J.J., Silberman, E.K., Barban, L. & Post, R.M. (1986). The clinical phenomenology of multiple personality disorder. *Journal of Clinical Psychiatry, 47*, 285-293.

Putnam, F.W., & Carlson, E.B. (in press). Hypnosis, dissociation and trauma: Myths, metaphors and mechanisms. In J.D. Bremner & C. Marmar (eds.), *Trauma, memory, and dissociation.* Washington, DC: American Psychiatric Press.

Rimsza, M.E., Berg, R.A., & Locke, C. (1988). Sexual abuse: Somatic and emotional reactions. *Child Abuse and Neglect, 12*, 201-208.

Rivers, W.H.R. (1920). *Instinct and the unconsciousness: A contribution to a biological theory of the psycho-neuroses.* London: Cambridge University Press.

Ross, C.A., Heber, S., Norton, G.R., & Anderson, G. (1989). Somatic symptoms in multiple personality disorder. *Psychosomatics, 30*, 154-160.

Ross, C.A., Miller, S.D., Bjornson, L., Reagor, P., Fraser, G.A., & Anderson, G. (1991). Abuse histories in 102 cases of multiple personality disorder. *Canadian Journal of Psychiatry, 36*, 97-101.

Saxe, G.N., Chinman, G., Berkowitz, M.D., Hall, K., Lieberg, G., Schwartz, J., & Van der Kolk, B.A. (1994). Somatization in patients with dissociative disorders. *American Journal of Psychiatry, 151*, 1329-1334.

Schultz, R., Braun, B.G., & Kluft, R.P. (1989). Multiple personality disorder: Phenomenology of selected variables in comparison to major depression. *Dissociation, 2*, 45-51.

Seligman, M.E.P. (1975). *Helplessness.* San Francisco: W.H.Freeman.

Siegfried, B., Frischknecht, H.R., & Nunez de Souza, R. (1990). An ethological model for the study of activation and interaction of pain, memory, and defensive systems in the attacked mouse: Role of endogenous opioids. *Neuroscience and Biobehavioral Reviews, 14*, 481-490.

Spiegel, D. (1984). Multiple personality disorder as a post-traumatic stress disorder. *Psychiatric Clinics of North America, 7*, 101-110.

SPSS PC: SPSS Inc./M.J. Norušis (1993). *SPSS for Windows Release 6.0.* Chicago: SPSS Inc.

Steinberg, M. (1993). *Structured Clinical Interview for DSM-IV Dissociative Disorders (SCID-D).* Washington DC: American Psychiatric Press.

Steinberg, M., Rounsaville, B.J., & Cichetti, D.V. (1990). The Structured Clinical Interview for DSM-III-R Dissociative Disorders: Preliminary report on a new diagnostic instrument. *American Journal of Psychiatry, 147*, 76-82.

Steinberg, M., Cichetti, D.V., Buchanan, J., Hall, P., & Rounsaville, B. (1993). Clinical assessment of dissociative symptoms and disorders: The Structured Clinical Interview for DSM-IV Dissociative Disorders. *Dissociation, 6*, 3-16.

Tabachnick, B.G., & Fidell, L.S. (1989). *Using multivariate statistics,* Second edition. Northridge: Harper Collins Publishers.

Timberlake, W., & Lucas, G.A. (1989). Behavior systems and learning: From misbehavior to general principles. In S.B. Klein & R.R. Mowrer (eds.), *Contemporary learning theories* (pp. 237-275). Hillsdale, NY: Lawrence Erlbaum.

Torem, M.S. (1990). Covert multiple personality underlying eating disorders. *American Journal of Psychotherapy, XLIV*, 357-368.

Van der Hart, O., & Friedman, B. (1989). A reader's guide to Pierre Janet on dissociation: A neglected intellectual heritage. *Dissociation, 2*, 3-16.

Van der Kolk, B.A. (1994). The body keeps the score: Memory and the evolving psychology of posttraumatic stress. *Harvard Review of Psychiatry, 1*, 253-265.

Van der Kolk, B.A., & Fisler, R. (1995). Dissociation and the fragmentary nature of traumatic memories: Overview and exploratory study. *Journal of Traumatic Stress, 8*, 505-525.

Van der Kolk, B.A., Greenberg, M.S., Boyd, H., & Krystal, J. (1985). Inescapable shock, neurotransmitters and addiction to trauma: Towards a psychobiology of post traumatic stress. *Biological Psychiatry, 20*, 314-325.

Van der Kolk, B.A., Greenberg, M.S., Orr, S.P., & Pitman, R.K. (1989). Endogenous opioids, stress induced analgesia, and posttraumatic stress disorder. *Psychopharmacology Bulletin, 25*, 417-422.

Van der Kolk, B.A., Herron, N., & Hostetler, A. (1994). The history of trauma in psychiatry. *Psychiatric Clinics of North America, 17*, 583-600.

Van der Kolk, B.A., McFarlane, A.C., & Weisaeth, L. (eds.)(1996). *Traumatic stress: The overwhelming experience on mind, body, and society.* New York: Guilford, 1996.

Van der Kolk, B.A., Pelcovitz, D., Roth, S., Mandel, F.C., McFarlane, A.C., & Herman, J.L. (1996). Dissociation, somatization, and affect dysregulation: The complexity of adaptation to trauma. *American Journal of Psychiatry, 153 (Festschrift Supplement)*, 83-93.

Van der Kolk, B.A., & Van der Hart, O. (1991). The intrusive past: The flexibility of memory and the engraving of trauma. *American Imago, 48*, 425-454.

Vanderlinden, J., Vandereycken, W., Van Dyck, R., & Vertommen, H. (1993). Dissociative experiences and trauma in eating disorders. *International Journal of Eating Disorders, 13*, 187-194.

Van IJzendoorn, M.H., & Schuengel, C. (1996). The measurement of dissociation in normal and clinical populations: Meta-analytic validation of the Dissociative Experiences Scale (DES). *Clinical Psychology Review, 16*, 365-382.

XI

Evidence for Associations Among Somatoform Dissociation, Psychological Dissociation, and Reported Trauma in Chronic Pelvic Pain Patients*

"Je reconnus enfin que l'hystérie n'était pas cette maladie honteuse dont le nom seul rappelle au monde étranger à la médecine, et à beaucoup de médecins ce vers de notre grand poëte tragique: C'est Vénus tout entière attachée à sa proie, mais qu'elle était au contraire due à l'existence, chez la femme, des sentiments les plus nobles et les plus dignes d'admiration, sentiments qu'elle seule est capable d'éprouver."
Paul Briquet, August 1859

Introduction

Chronic pelvic pain (CPP) is among the most common somatic complaints, both in the general population (Kroenke, 1991) and in patients presenting at primary care clinics (Walker, Katon, Jemelka, Bowers, & Strenchever, 1991), especially in women. A clear, specific organic etiology is only found in a minority of cases (Kroenke, 1991). Psychological and social factors may be involved, as high rates of psychopathology and distress have been reported for women with CPP with and without organic pathology (for a meta-analytic review McGowan, Clark-Carter, & Pitts, 1998). However, such findings are common among patients with other types of chronic pain as well, and may (partly) reflect consequences of the experience of chronic pain (for a review Savidge & Slade, 1997).

Various studies have found high lifetime prevalence rates of reported sexual abuse among women with CPP, ranging from about 50% to 60% (e.g., Badura, Reiter, Altmaier, Rhomberg, & Elas, 1997; Walker et al., 1995; Walling, Reiter, O'Hara, Milburn, Lilly, & Vincent, 1994b). However, Fry, Crisp, Beard, and McGuigan (1993) found that the prevalence of reported sexual abuse (32%) among CPP patients did not convincingly exceed the base rate in the general population, estimated at about 25% among women (Finkelhor, 1986). These authors concluded that: "sexual abuse is unlikely to be a specific etiological factor in the development of CPP though it may yet be found to be important in subsets of the population" (p. 566).

* This research was performed in collaboration with R. Van Dyck, M. Ter Kuile, M. Mourits, P. Spinhoven, and O. Van der Hart. I kindly thank M. Hueting, I. Groenendijk, and M. van Kraaikamp for their contributions, and K. Steele for her linguistic assistance. This research was supported by a grant of the Stichting Dienstbetoon, Soesterberg, The Netherlands; grantnumber 11.92.

Walling et al. (1994b) suggested that sexual abuse which involves genital or abdominal contact/pain may perhaps better predict CPP than milder types of sexual abuse. Consistent with this prediction, these authors found that more women with CPP reported major sexual abuse, involving penetration or contact with genitals (53%) than either women with chronic headache (33%), or those without pain (28%). However, Walker et al. (1995) reported that any childhood sexual abuse, any adult abuse, severe childhood sexual abuse, and severe adult sexual abuse all differentiated between women with and women without CPP. The most striking findings of Walling, O'Hara, Reiter, Milburn, Lilly, and Vincent (1994a) were the global, major abuse histories of many women with CPP (42%), and the fact that childhood physical abuse, not childhood sexual abuse, predicted depression, anxiety, and somatization among women with CPP ($n = 64$), women with chronic headache ($n = 42$), and women without chronic pain complaints ($n = 46$). Rapkin, Kames, Darke, Stampler, and Naliboff (1990) found evidence for an association between CPP and physical abuse. However, this association may apply to chronic pain in general: as Walling et al. (1994a) reported, the lifetime prevalence of physical abuse did not differ significantly between CPP and chronic headache groups.

There is accumulating evidence for a link between trauma and dissociation (e.g., Lewis, Yeager, Swica, Pincus, & Lewis, 1997; Marmar et al., 1994). Consistent with these findings, associations of CPP, dissociation, and reported abuse have been found among patients who presented at a multidisciplinary pelvic pain clinic (Badura et al., 1997). Walker, Katon, Neraas, Jemelka, and Massoth (1992) also found that, compared with randomly selected women without a history of CPP, women with this symptom were significantly more likely to report psychological manifestations of dissociation as measured by the Dissociative Experiences Scale (DES; Bernstein & Putnam, 1986). These symptoms involve dissociative amnesia, depersonalization, derealization, and identity fragmentation. Considering the association between CPP and psychological dissociation, it seems possible that a proportion of CPP patients have DSM-IV dissociative disorder. To date the prevalence of these disorders among CPP patients has not been studied systematically.

Associations of trauma and somatization (Saxe et al., 1994), as well as somatization and CPP have also been reported. For example, Walker et al. (1995) found that medically unexplained somatic symptoms, DSM-III somatization disorder, and high distress were more common in women with CPP than in women who were pain-free. The number of medically unexplained somatic symptoms was among the three variables entered into the logistic regression equation which correctly classified 82% of the subjects into groups. Other investigators reported comparable findings (Badura et al., 1997; Reiter & Milburn, 1992).

Some of these somatic symptoms may involve somatoform manifestations of dissociation, which can be described as the partial or complete loss of the normal integration of somatoform components of experience, reactions, and functions (Nijenhuis, Spinhoven, Van Dyck, Van der Hart, & Vanderlinden, 1996, 1997). Somatoform dissociation involves negative symptoms, such as anesthesia of various sensory modalities (e.g., tunnel vision, apparent disappearance of body parts, bodily numbing), analgesia, and inhibited movement (e.g., stiffening of the body), as well as positive symptoms, such as site-specific pain (e.g., pain while urinating, pain in genitals), uncontrolled movements, and changing preferences of smells and tastes. The severity of somatoform dissociation can be evaluated with the self-report *Somatoform Dissociation Questionnaire* (SDQ-20; Nijenhuis et al., 1996, 1998a).

A considerable group of patients with mental disorders first present in medical care with somatic symptoms. Costs on the part of the subject and the society seem avoidable to the extent that differential diagnostic procedures can be improved. Evaluation of somatoform dissociation and screening for dissociative disorder in gynecology care using an instrument which involves somatic symptoms may perhaps contribute to this objective. In this regard, the SDQ-20 and the SDQ-5, a screening instrument for dissociative disorders which was derived from the SDQ-20 (Nijenhuis et al., 1997, 1998a), could be of service.

Studying patients with dissociative disorders and psychiatric comparison patients, correlations between somatoform and psychological dissociation (Nijenhuis et al., 1996, 1998a), and reported abuse (Nijenhuis et al., 1998b) have been found. The best predictor of somatoform dissociation among these patients was the total score on the Traumatic Experiences Checklist* (TEC; Nijenhuis, Van der Hart, & Vanderlinden, 1994) which evaluates 25 types of traumatic experiences. Among various types of interpersonal trauma, physical abuse and sexual harassment best predicted somatoform dissociation. Interestingly, the SDQ-20 includes three items assessing urogenital pain, which as a cluster strongly correlated with presence of dissociative disorder (Nijenhuis, Spinhoven, Vanderlinden, Van Dyck, & Van der Hart, 1998c). It seems possible that a subset of CPP patients will experience somatoform dissociation, that some may even have a dissociative disorder, and that these symptoms will intercorrelate with reported trauma, in particular physical and sexual abuse.

The primary aim of this study was to investigate somatoform as well as psychological dissociation, somatization, and reported trauma among patients with CPP. More specifically, we tested the hypotheses that (1) there will be a positive association of self-reported somatoform dissociation with features of DSM-IV dissociative disorders; (2) this association will be stronger than the association of self-reported psychological dissociation with features of dissociative disorder; (3) women with CPP who report more serious psychic trauma, in particular sexual and physical abuse, will experience more somatoform and psychological dissociation than women with CPP reporting less trauma, or no trauma at all; and (4) the association of somatoform dissociation and reported trauma will be stronger than the association of psychological dissociation and trauma.

---

* Initially this instrument was labeled the *Traumatic Experiences Questionnaire* (TEQ). As we later discovered the existence of the Traumatic Events Questionnaire, also abbrieviated to TEQ, to avoid a confusion of abbrieviations, we decided to rename the scale the Traumatic Experiences Checklist (TEC).

Methods

Subjects

The present sample consisted of women with pelvic pain ($n = 52$), with a duration of at least 6 months, involving women who were consecutively referred to the gynecology department of two Dutch Academic Hospitals, i.e., Groningen and Leiden Universitary Medical Centers ($n = 27$), and women who had been treated at these centers, but whose pain had remained ($n = 25$). The mean age of this group was 37.8 years ($SD = 9.7$). Of the women, 35 (68.3%) were married or living together with a partner, 5 (9.6%) were divorced, and 12 (23. 1%) were single. The distribution of their educational level was representative of the Dutch general population. There were no differences between the samples of both sites as to mean age (t-test), educational level, and marital status (*Chi-Square* test). The newly referred cases and the treatment resistant pain cases were comparable as to age (t-test) and marital status (*Chi-Square* test), but the educational level of the newly referred sample was higher (*Fisher's Exact*, $p = .012$).

Half of the present CPP sample ($n = 26$) endorsed three or more symptoms of somatization disorder, i.e., the cutoff for this disorder as recommended by Othmer and DeSouza (1985). However, only two patients met sufficient DSM-IV criteria for this disorder, and only one patient met sufficient criteria for DSM-IV conversion disorder.

Measurements

The *Somatoform Dissociation Questionnaire* (SDQ-20; Nijenhuis et al., 1996, 1998a) is a 20-item self-report questionnaire measuring somatoform dissociation. The scores range from 20 to 100. The items are strongly scalable on a unidimensional latent scale, the reliability of the instrument is high, and the scores are not dependent on gender or age. Strong intercorrelations with measures of psychological dissociation supported the scale's convergent validity. Higher scores of patients with dissociative disorders in comparison with patients with other DSM-IV diagnoses demonstrated its criterion-related Validity, in particular since the SDQ-20 discriminated among diagnostic categories over and above general psychopathology (Nijenhuis et al., 1999). Correlations with reported trauma, in particular sexual and physical abuse supported the construct validity (Nijenhuis et al., 1998b).

The *SDQ-5* is a 5-item dissociative disorders screening instrument which was derived from the SDQ-20 (Nijenhuis et al, 1997, 1998a). The items describe pain while urinating, analgesia, visual anesthesia, kinesthetic anesthesia, and inability or difficulty to speak. The scores range from 5 to 25, and the optimal cutoff point in the screening for dissociative disorders is ≥ 8. Among psychiatric patients, the SDQ-5 has high sensitivity and specificity, excellent negative predictive value, and satisfactory positive predictive value in predicting cases of dissociative disorder.

The *Dissociative Experiences Scale* (DES; Bernstein & Putnam, 1986) is a 28-item self-report questionnaire which evaluates psychological dissociation. The scores range from 0 to 100. The DES has adequate test-retest reliability, good internal consistency, and good clinical validity (Bernstein & Putnam, 1986; Carlson et al., 1993). DES scores of ≥ 30 in a North American sample (Carlson et al., 1993), respectively ≥ 25 in a Dutch sample (Draijer & Boon, 1993) were found to yield optimal sensitivity and specificity in the screening for dissociative disorders.

The *Traumatic Experiences Checklist* (TEC; Nijenhuis et al., 1998b) is a self-report questionnaire inquiring about 25 types of trauma, amongst others loss of significant others; life threat by disease or assault; war experience; and emotional, physical, and sexual trauma. With respect to emotional neglect, emotional abuse, physical abuse, sexual harassment, and sexual abuse, the TEC specifically addresses the setting in which such trauma occurred, that is, the family of origin, the extended family, or any other setting. Further, it rates the subjective and current degree of traumatic stress associated with the trauma. The questions contain short descriptions that intend to define the events of concern. All items are preceded by the phrase: "Did this happen to you?" An example of a sexual harassment item is: "Sexual harassment (acts of a sexual nature that DO NOT involve physical contact) by your parents, brothers or sisters." A sexual abuse item is: "Sexual abuse (unwanted sexual acts involving physical contact) by your parents, brothers, or sisters."

Trauma was defined by the TEC item scores in terms of a positive score by respondents. The impact of trauma was further qualified by current ratings by respondents. If an event was not reported, the score "1" was given; if the item was endorsed, it received the score "2." When the event had no impact or minor impact, no additional score was applied; when it had considerable, severe, or very severe impact, a score of "1" was added, yielding a total item score of "3." The total TEC score was obtained by summating the composite itemscores.

The *Structured Clinical Interview for DSM-IV Dissociative Disorders* (SCID-D; Steinberg, 1993; Steinberg, Cichetti, Buchanan, Hall, & Rounsaville, 1993) is a diagnostic instrument developed for the assessment of DSM-IV dissociative disorders. It covers five dissociative symptom areas (amnesia, depersonalization, derealization, identity confusion, and identity fragmentation). The total score ranges from 5 to 20, the subscale scores from 1 to 4. Good to excellent reliability and validity have been reported both in the US and in the Netherlands (Boon & Draijer, 1993; Steinberg et al., 1993).

The *Hospital Anxiety and Depression Scale* (HADS; Zigmond & Snaith, 1983) contains two 7-item scales, one for anxiety and one for depression, both with a score range of 0 to 21. As reported by Spinhoven, Ormel, Sloekers, Kempen, Speckens, and Van Hemert (1998), evidence for a two factor structure was found, although both scales were strongly intercorrelated. Homogeneity and test-retest reliability of the total scale and subscales were good, and the dimensional structure and reliability of the scale were stable across medical settings and age groups.

The *Screening Test for Somatization Disorder* (STSD; Othmer & DeSouza, 1985) is a 7-item self-report questionnaire. The items pertain to dysmenorrhea, lump in throat, vomiting, shortness of breath, burning of sex organs, painful extremities, and amnesia (not induced by alcohol or drugs). Endorsement of three items constitutes the recommended cutoff, yielding a sensitivity in the original sample of 87%, and a specificity of 95%. With an independent sample these values were 73%, respectively 94%.

Procedure

After their written informed consent had been obtained, the patients completed − in this order − the STSD, HADS, SDQ-20, DES, TEC, and SDQ-5. Next, all patients were interviewed using the SCID-D by one of two experienced clinicians who were trained in the administration of the instrument, and who were blind as to the patients' scores on the self-report instruments. Each clinician rated approximately one half of the subjects. They also assessed somatization disorder and conversion disorder according to DSM-IV criteria (APA, 1994).

Data Analysis

Because the distribution of the DES, SDQ-20, HADS and SCID-D total and subscale scores were skewed (skewness > 1), logaritmic transformations to base e of these measurements were performed.

The associations among the SDQ-20, DES, STSD, HADS scores, the TEC composite item scores, and the SCID-D total and subscale scores were calculated using Pearson product-moment correlations. To assess their independent contributions in the prediction of the SCID-D total score, the SDQ-20, DES, HADS, and STSD scores were entered in a stepwise multiple regression analysis using forward selection (p to enter < .05) and backward elimination (p to remove > .10) based on likelihood ratio estimates.

Estimating the types of trauma which best predicted somatoform and psychological dissociation among CPP patients, stepwise multiple regression analyses were performed, entering a reduced number of TEC variables. These included emotional maltreatment (encompassing emotional neglect and emotional abuse in various social contexts, as well as parentification); physical abuse (involving physical abuse in various social contexts, and life threat posed by a person); sexual trauma (sexual harassment and sexual abuse in various social contexts); death of significant others (death of parents as a child, death of child or partner), and some items that could not be combined into one of the forementioned categories. In order to control for the influence of anxiety, depression and intense pain on somatoform and psychological dissociation, regression analyses were executed, using forced entrance of the HADS scores and the TEC composite itemscore assessing intense current or previous pain, before stepwise adding the other trauma variables in a second phase.

Cases which obtained scores above the SDQ-5 cutoff ($\geq$ 8) and scores above the optimal DES cutoff ($\geq$ 25) in the screening for dissociative disorders were compared to the results of the SCID-D assessment.

Statistical analyses were performed with SPSS-PC 7.5 (SPSS PC, 1996).

Results

The mean SDQ-20 score was 25.7 (SD = 9.31), and the mean DES score was 8.6 (SD = 11.98). As Table 1 shows, both measures of dissociation were strongly intercorrelated (r = .58, p < .0001). The intercorrelations among somatoform dissociation and estimates of anxiety and depression (HADS), as well as symptoms of somatization disorder (STSD) were considerable to strong, in particular the intercorrelations between the SDQ-20 and STSD. The associations between the DES on the one hand, and the HADS scores, as well as the STSD scores on the other hand, were modest.

Table 1
Pearson product-moment intercorrelations between somatoform and psychological dissociation, anxiety, depression, and somatization among 52 patients with chronic pelvic pain

	1	2	3
1. SDQ-20			
2. DES	.58		
3. STSD	.72	.33*	
4. HADS total	.46**	.26*	.53

all p <. 0001 except ** p < .001, and * p < .05

Fourteen patients (26.9%) had psychological dissociative symptoms warranting scores on the SCID-D. Most subjects of this subgroup had very modest SCID-D scores of 6 (n = 5) or 7 (n = 6), but three patients obtained higher scores (8, 11, and 15). Only the patient with the highest SCID-D score met criteria for a DSM-IV dissociative disorder diagnosis, i.e., dissociative disorder, NOS, possibly dissociative identity disorder. The two other patients with higher scores were considered to have significant dissociative symptoms, but neither met sufficient DSM-IV criteria for one of the dissociative disorders. Four patients had scores on the SCID-D amnesia subscale, 12 had scores on the depersonalization subscale, and only one subject obtained a score on the derealization subscale. Four patients displayed significant symptoms of identity confusion, and 4 patients had identity fragmentation.

Table 2 presents the intercorrelations between the SDQ-20, DES, HADS, and STSD on the one hand, and the SCID-D total and subscale scores on the other. Consistent with our first hypothesis, somatoform dissociation and psychological dissociation were positively associated with the SCID-D total score. This also applied to the amnesia subscales, as well as to the identity fragmentation and the identity confusion subscales (SDQ-20). There were weaker to absent associations between SDQ-20 and DES scores on the one hand, and SCID-D assessed depersonalization and derealization on the other hand. In particular the HADS had positive associations with the SCID including the total and all except the derealization subscale scores. The derealization subscale score did not correlate with any of the four self-report measures. The STSD score was also correlated with the SCID-D total and several subscale scores.

Table 2

Pearson product-moment intercorrelations between somatoform and psychological dissociation, anxiety, depression, and somatization as self-reported by patients with chronic pelvic pain, and psychological dissociation, as assessed by structured clinical interview

	DES	SDQ-20	HADS	STSD
SCID-D:				
total	.43**	.45***	.55***	.40**
amnesia	.46***	.53***	.35*	.34*
depersonalization	.33*	.23	.43***	.25
derealization	.05	−.02	.13	.03
identity confusion	.31*	.51***	.56***	.45***
identity fragmentation	.39**	.37**	.42**	.35*

$p < .001;$ $^{**}p < .01;$ $^{*}p < .05$

Contrary to our second hypothesis, not somatoform dissociation as measured by the SDQ-20, but self-reported anxiety and depression (HADS; selected into the regression equation first; *Beta* in final model .47) and psychological dissociation (DES; selected in a second step; *Beta* in final model .31) best predicted the SCID-D total score (final model: $F = 15.772$, df 2,49, $p < .0001$; adjusted $R^2 = .37$, S.E. $= 0.15$). However, amnesia as measured by the SCID-D was best predicted by somatoform dissociation, *Beta* .46. Identity confusion was best predicted by anxiety and depression, *Beta* .41, and somatoform dissociation, *Beta* .32.

The sensitivity of the SDQ-5 and DES to predict SCID-D assessed DSM-IV dissociative disorder was 100%: both the SDQ-5 (score: 19) and the DES (score: 69) correctly predicted the dissociative disorder case. The specificity of these instruments to predict absence of dissociative disorder was 90.2% (SDQ-20) and 94,1% (DES) respectively. The SDQ-5 and DES incorrectly suggested dissociative disorder in 5 and 3 cases, respectively. Two patients had scores at the SDQ-5 cutoff($\geq$ 8), one scored 9, and another 10 (who related her SDQ-5 symptoms to her diagnosed epilepsy). Still another patient scored 13. This patient had subthreshold somatization disorder, and reported analgesia, both on the SDQ-5 and the SCID-D, as well as occasional amnesia for recent events. She also scored above the DES cutoff($\geq$ 25), i.e., 30.7. Two patients scored 27.1 on the DES. In this sample, scores at, or slightly above, the recommended SDQ-5 and DES cutoffs, thus, did not indicate dissociative disorder, whereas higher scores correctly suggested dissociative symptomatology or dissociative disorder.

Perhaps not surprisingly in this sample of CPP patients, among all types of reported trauma, experienced intense pain was most prevalent (48.1%; Table 3). About one third experienced emotional trauma in the nuclear family. Emotional neglect, emotional abuse, physical abuse, sexual harassment, and sexual abuse *in any setting* were reported by 38.5%, 48.1%, 28.8%, 28.8%, and 32.7% of the subjects respectively. Twenty-seven percent recalled being subjected to three or more types of emotional, physical, or sexual trauma (items 11 to 25, Table 3), and 50% endorsed 4 or more TEC items.

Table 3
Reported traumatic experiences by 52 women with chronic pelvic pain, as correlated with somatoform and psychological dissociation*

	%	SDQ-20	DES
1. Taking care of parents/brothers/sisters as a child	26.9	.19	.06
2. Family burdens (poverty, alcohol/drug addiction parent or psychiatric disorder family member[s])	25.0	.43*	.27
3. Death of a significant other as a child	17.3	.39*	.32*
4. Death of a child or partner	5.8	.47***	.29*
5. Severe physical injury	17.3	.27	.29*
6. Life threat posed by illness, operation, or accident	13.5	.05	.09
7. Life threat posed by a person	15.4	.50***	.42*
8. Intense pain	48.1	.40*	.09
9. War experiences	9.6	.01	.01
10. Witnessing trauma in other persons	21.2	.18	.17
11. Emotional neglect in nuclear family	34.6	.47***	.24
12. Emotional neglect in extended family	9.6	.59***	.28*
13. Emotional neglect in other social contexts	13.5	.60***	.43**
14. Emotional abuse in nuclear family	38.5	.33*	.13
15. Emotional abuse in extended family	13.5	.57***	.30*
16. Emotional abuse in other social contexts	17.3	.22	.28*
17. Physical abuse in nuclear family	19.2	.40*	.22
18. Physical abuse in extended family	5.8	.80***	.49***
19. Physical abuse in other social contexts	13.5	.46**	.40*
20. Sexual harassment in nuclear family	11.5	.59***	.25
21. Sexual harassment in extended family	11.5	.67***	.30*
22. Sexual harassment in other social contexts	21.2	.35*	.27
23. Sexual abuse in nuclear family	17.3	.36*	.21
24. Sexual abuse in extended family	7.7	.61***	.33*
25. Sexual abuse in other social contexts	21.2	.29*	.33*
Total TEC score		.69***	.44**

*The measures of dissociation were correlated, using Pearson product-moment intercorrelations, with reported presence of events, qualified by their impact as currently rated by the respondent
*** $p < .0001$; ** $p \leq .001$; * $p < .05$

Comparing the TEC scores of the current CPP patients with those of mixed psychiatric patients as found in a previous study (Nijenhuis et al., 1998b), emotional neglect, emotional abuse, physical abuse, and sexual harassment were reported as frequent among both groups, but CPP patients more often reported sexual abuse (psychiatric patients 14%; $t = 2.10$, df 83.31, $p = .039$). Obviously apart from intense pain, the proportion of psychiatric patients who reported other types of trauma were largely comparable to the scores of the present CPP patients.

Consistent with our third hypothesis, somatoform dissociation was strongly correlated with the total TEC score ($r = .69$, $p < .0001$). As inspection of Table 3 shows, there was a strong correlation between somatoform dissociation and emotional neglect and abuse, as well as physical abuse, sexual harassment, sexual abuse in the extended family, and life threat by a person. To a lesser extent, the total TEC scores were also associated with psychological dissociation ($r = .44$, $p = .001$), notably physical abuse. The correlations of these dissociation scales with separate types of reported trauma, qualified by the rated impact, are displayed in Table 4. Anxiety and depression as measured by the HADS ($r = .43$, $p = .001$), and somatization symptoms as measured by the STSD ($r = .41$, $p = .002$) were also correlated with the total TEC score.

Table 4

Pearson product-moment intercorrelations between composite traumascores and somatoform as well as psychological dissociation

Composite scores	SDQ-20		DES	
	r	p	r	p
emotional neglect	.70	< .0001	.40	.003
emotional abuse	.48	< .0001	.29	.038
physical abuse	.67	< .0001	.45	.001
sexual harassment	.65	< .0001	.34	.013
sexual abuse	.54	< .0001	.39	.004
all composites combined	.67	< .0001	.41	.003

Entering somatoform and psychological dissociation, as well as anxiety, depression and somatization symptoms into a stepwise multiple regression analysis, the SDQ-20 was the only variable entered into the regression equation that predicted the total TEC score ($F = 46.13$, df 1, 50, $p < .0001$; adjusted $R^2 = .47$, S.E. $= 6.54$). This result supports our fourth hypothesis, which stated that somatoform dissociation would be a better predictor of reported trauma among CPP patients than psychological dissociation.

In order to assess which types of endorsed traumatic experiences, as qualified by their impact as currently rated by the respondent, best predicted somatoform dissociation, the clustered scores on death of significant others (items 3 and 4 in Table 3), emotional maltreatment (items 1; 11 to 16), physical abuse and life threat by a person (items 7; 17 to 19), sexual trauma (items 20 to 25), as well as TEC items which could not be meaningfully clustered in the forementioned categories (items 2; 5; 6; 8; 9; 10) were entered into in a stepwise multiple regression analysis. The resulting regression equation (final model: $F = 20.63$, df 3,48, $p < .0001$; adjusted $R^2 = .54$, S.E. $= .17$) involved physical abuse/life threat by a person (*Beta* = .43), sexual trauma (*Beta* = .30), and intense pain (*Beta* = .22). Entering the same set of independent variables, psychological dissociation was predicted by physical abuse/life threat by a person (*Beta* = .47; F = 14.33, df 1,50, p < .0001; adjusted R^2 = .21; *S.E.* = .76).

Next, it was explored to what extent somatoform dissociation and psychological dissociation were predicted by reported trauma after statistically controlling for the influence of anxiety, depression, as well as intense current and previous pain (presumably pelvic pain). To that end, the HADS total scores and reported intense pain were forced into the regression equation in a first step, and the remaining variables were entered in a stepwise manner next. Apart from the HADS, *Beta* = .25, and intense pain, *Beta* = .21, somatoform dissociation was best predicted by physical abuse/life threat by a person, *Beta* = .55 (final model: F = 20.56, df 3,48, p < .0001; adjusted R^2 = .54, *S.E.* = .17). Psychological dissociation was predicted by physical abuse/life threat by a person only, *Beta* = .44 (F = 5.08, df 3,48, p <.004; adjusted R^2 = .19, *S.E.* = .76). The power of reported physical abuse and life threat to predict dissociation, thus, could not (with the DES), or not completely (with the SDQ-20) be accounted for by associations with anxiety, depression, or intense pain.

Discussion

In this first study of somatoform dissociation among CPP patients, three of the four hypotheses were supported by the evidence. Consistent with the first hypothesis, a significant positive association was found between somatoform dissociation (as measured with the SDQ-20) and pathological psychological dissociative symptom clusters, i.e., total score, amnesia, identity confusion and identity fragmentation (as assessed with the SCID-D). Dissociative disorder, however, was also associated with anxiety and depression, as well as psychological dissociation as measured by the DES, i.e., the set of variables which best predicted dissociative disorder. The strong correlation between the SDQ-20 and DES matched the values found in our studies among psychiatric patients (Nijenhuis et al., 1996, 1997, 1999) and strengthens our previous conclusion that somatoform and psychological dissociation are manifestations of a common construct.

The considerable DES scores among CPP patients as found by Badura et al. (1997) and Walker et al. (1993) – in particular among those patients who reported sexual and physical abuse (Badura et al., 1997) – suggested that perhaps a proportion of CPP patients would have a dissociative disorder. However, among the current sample of CPP patients who attended a gynecology department of a general medical center, the prevalence of DSM-IV dissociative disorders was very low: few CPP patients obtained considerable SCID-D scores, and, according to the SCID-D criteria, only one patient had DSM-IV dissociative disorder. The skewed distributions of the DES and SDQ-20 suggested that psychological and somatoform dissociation were only elevated in a small subsample. These findings fit recent data showing that elevated mean dissociation scores in particular diagnostic groups are due to the proportion of subjects within these groups who were highly dissociative (Putnam et al., 1996).

As was indicated by the DES scores, psychological dissociation was low among the majority of the present sample (8.6, $SD = 11.98$). For example, the average DES score among the general adult population was 11.57, $SD = 10.63$ ($n = 1458$ from 7 studies) and among anxiety disorder patients 10.32, $SD = 9.99$ ($n = 407$ from 3 studies) (Van IJzendoorn & Schuengl, 1996). Walker et al. (1992), however, found a higher average psychological dissociation score among CPP patients attending a university women's clinic ($M = 19.0$, $SD = 14.9$). These scores approach the mean score of borderline personality disorder patients ($M = 21.6$, $SD = 15.4$). The discrepancy in the low DES scores in the present sample is difficult to explain.

Somatoform dissociation among the present CPP patients was modest, and rather comparable to the severity of somatoform dissociation among eating disorder patients ($M = 27.7$, $SD = 8.77$; Nijenhuis et al., 1999). It seemed slightly increased compared to somatoform dissociation among patients with mixed psychiatric disorders, mainly anxiety disorder, depression, and adjustment disorder ($M = 22.9$, $SD = 3.94$; Nijenhuis et al., 1999).

Contrary to the second hypothesis, somatoform dissociation as measured by the SDQ-20, predicted the SCID-D total score less well than did psychological dissociation. However, the best predictor of the total SCID-D score was anxiety and depression as measured by the HADS; amnesia was best predicted by somatoform dissociation; and identity confusion by anxiety, depression, and somatoform dissociation. The difference in the predictive power of the DES and SDQ-5 was not large. This study, thus, provides no evidence that among CPP patients somatoform dissociation is more indicative of DSM-IV dissociative disorder, or features thereof, than psychological dissociation.

The SDQ-5, as well as the DES, were sensitive in selecting the case of dissociative disorder as diagnosed with the SCID-D. At the recommended cutoffs, the specifity of these screening instruments was less satisfactory. As most false positives scored slightly above these cutoffs, and as the case of dissociative disorder obtained an extreme score, the present data suggest that raising the cutoffs in the screening for dissociative pathology among CPP patients increases specificity without losing sensitivity. For example, a SDQ-5 cutoff score ≥ 10 among the present sample would have yielded a more satisfactory specificity of 96%. With regard to the SDQ-5, in some cases the elevated scores were perhaps due to true somatic disease, as was probably the case with the patient who reported medically assessed epilepsy. Screening for dissociative pathology among CPP patients obviously demands thoughtful consideration of all relevant somatic, somatoform, and psychological factors. However, if the low prevalence rate of dissociative disorders among CPP patients as found in the current study would be corroborated by other studies, routine screening for dissociative disorders in this diagnostic category is not indicated.

Traumatic experiences were rather common in this sample, as about a quarter of the women recalled being subjected to three or more types of emotional, physical, or sexual trauma, and 50% reported a substantial number of TEC items. These results are consistent with the global level of abuse among CPP patients as found by Walling et al. (1994b). The proportion of the present CPP patients reporting sexual abuse was of the same magnitude as was found by Fry et al. (1993), and was lower than in other studies (e.g., Badura et al., 1997). Compared with the scores of mixed psychiatric patients (Nijenhuis, 1998b), a larger proportion of the present CPP patients reported sexual abuse. More generally, both groups reported comparable proportions of various types of trauma.

The observed links between somatoform and psychological dissociation on the one hand, and reported trauma on the other hand, were as hypothesized. The hypothesis that among CPP patients the association between somatoform dissociation and reported trauma would be stronger than the association between psychological dissociation and reported trauma was also supported by the findings. Considering the relatively small sample size compared to the number of trauma variables entered into the relevant multiple regression analyses, the results of these calculations must be interpreted with some caution. Keeping this reservation in mind, the best statistical predictor of both somatoform and psychological dissociation was physical abuse/life threat posed by a person. Somatoform dissociation was additionally predicted by sexual trauma and intense pain. The association with physical abuse and life threat by a person predicted somatoform dissociation over and above the influence of anxiety, depression, and intense pain. Thus, although having chronic pain often was a traumatizing experience, it was not the best predictor of the observed dissociative symptoms. Even though emotional neglect and emotional abuse were also often endorsed, these types of trauma were not the best predictor of pathological dissociation either. Considering that physical abuse and sexual abuse best predicted somatoform dissociation among psychiatric patients as well (Nijenhuis et al., 1998b), the present findings are probably not due to chance.

In conclusion, in particular women with CPP who reported physical abuse, life threat posed by a person, and sexual trauma had somatoform and psychological dissociative symptoms. Although correlational data cannot reveal causal relationships, the associations between physical abuse, sexual trauma, and somatoform dissociation are consistent with the idea that specifically threat to, and violation of, body integrity may evoke somatoform dissociative symptoms (cf. Nijenhuis et al., 1998c; Nijenhuis, Vanderlinden, & Spinhoven, 1998). While a group of patients with mental disorders first present in medical care with somatic symptoms, only a small subgroup of women with CPP reported considerable dissociative symptoms, and DSM-IV dissociative disorders among CPP patients seem rare. CPP patients who score amply above the recommended SDQ-5 and DES cutoffs, should be administered the SCID-D to diagnose or exclude dissociative disorder and other trauma-related disorders.

References

American Psychiatric Association (1994). *Diagnostic and statistical manual of mental disorders, 4th edn.* Washington DC: Author.
Badura, A.S., Reiter, R.C., Altmaier, E.M., Rhomberg, A., & Elas, D., (1997). Dissociation, somatization, substance abuse, and coping in women with chronic pelvic pain. *Obstetrics & Gynecology, 90,* 405-410.

Bernstein, E., & Putnam F. W. (1986). Development, reliability, and validity of a dissociation scale. *Journal of Nervous Mental Disease, 102,* 280-286.

Boon, S., & Draijer, N. (1993). *Multiple personality disorder in the Netherlands: A study on reliability and validity of the diagnosis.* Amsterdam/Lisse: Swets & Zeitlinger.

Carlson, E.B., Putnam, F. W., Ross, C.A., Torem, M., Coons, P., Dill, D.L., Loewenstein, R.J., & Braun, B.G. (1993). Validity of the Dissociative Experiences Scale in screening for multiple personality disorder: A multicenter study. *American Journal of Psychiatry, 150,* 1030-1036.

Draijer, N., & Boon, S. (1993). Trauma, dissociation, and dissociative disorders. In S. Boon & N. Draijer, *Multiple personality disorder in the Netherlands: A study on reliability and validity of the diagnosis* (pp. 177-193). Amsterdam/Lisse: Swets & Zeitlinger.

Finkelhor, D., & Associates (1986). *A sourcebook on child sexual abuse,* Beverly Hill: Sage.

Fry, R.P.W., Crisp, A.H., Beard, R.W., & McGuigan, S. (1993). Psychosocial aspects of chronic pelvic pain, with special reference to sexual abuse: A study of 164 women. *Postgraduate Medical Journal, 69,* 566-574.

Lewis, D.O., Yeager, C.A., Swica, Y., Pincus, J.H., & Lewis, M. (1997). Objective documentation of child abuse and dissociation in 12 murderers with dissociative identity disorder. *American Journal of Psychiatry, 154,* 1703-1710.

Kroenke, K. (1991). Symptoms in medical patients: An untended field. *American Journal of Medicine, 92* (supplement 1 A), 3s-6s.

Marmar, C.R., Weiss, D.S., Schlenger, W.E., Fairbank, J.A., Jordan, B.K., Kulka, R.A., & Hough, R.L. (1994). Peritraumatic dissociation and posttraumatic stress in male Vietnam theater veterans. *American Journal of Psychiatry, 151,* 902-907.

McGowan, P.A., Clark-Carter, D.D., & Pitts, M.K. (1998). Chronic pelvic pain: a meta-analytic review. *Psychology and Health, 13,* 937-951.

Nijenhuis, E.R.S., Spinhoven, P., Van Dyck, R., Van der Hart, O., & Vanderlinden, J. (1996). The development and the characteristics of the Somatoform Dissociation Questionnaire (SDQ-20). *Journal of Nervous and Mental Disease, 184,* 688-694.

Nijenhuis, E.R.S., Spinhoven, P., Van Dyck, R., Van der Hart, O., & Vanderlinden, J. (1997). The development of the Somatoform Dissociation Questionnaire (SDQ-5) as a screening instrument for dissociative disorders. *Acta Psychiatrica Scandinavica, 96,* 311-318.

Nijenhuis, E.R.S., Spinhoven, P., Van Dyck, R., Van der Hart, O., & Vanderlinden, J. (1998a). The psychometric characteristics of the Somatoform Dissociation Questionnaire: A replication study. *Psychotherapy & Psychosomatics, 67,* 17-23.

Nijenhuis, E.R.S., Spinhoven, P., Van Dyck, R., Van der Hart, O., & Vanderlinden, J. (1998b). Degree of somatoform and psychological dissociation in dissociative disorders is correlated with reported trauma. *Journal of Traumatic Stress, 11,* 711-730.

Nijenhuis, E.R.S., Spinhoven, P., Vanderlinden, J., Van Dyck, R., & Van der Hart, O. (1998c). Somatoform dissociative symptoms as related to animal defensive reactions to predatory threat and injury. *Journal of Abnormal Psychology, 107,* 63-73.

Nijenhuis, E.R.S., Van Dyck, R., Spinhoven, P., Van der Hart, O., Chatrou, M., Vanderlinden, J., & Moene, F. (1999). Somatoform dissociation discriminates between diagnostic categories over and above general psychopathology. *Australian and New Zealand Journal of Psychiatry, 33,* 511-520.

Nijenhuis, E.R.S., Vanderlinden, J., & Spinhoven, P. (1998). Animal defensive reactions as a model for trauma-induced dissociative reactions. *Journal of Traumatic Stress, 11,* 243-260.

Othmer, E., & De Souza, C. (1985). A screening test for somatization disorder (hysteria). *American Journal of Psychiatry, 142,* 1146-1149.

Putnam, F.W., Carlson, E.B., Ross, C.A., Anderson, G., Clark, P., Torem, M., Bowman, E.S., Coons, P., Chu, J.A., Dill, D.L., Loewenstein, R.J., & Braun, B.G. (1996). Patterns of dissociation in clinical and nonclinical samples. *Journal of Nervous and Mental disease, 184,* 673-679.

Rapkin, A.J., Kames, L.D., Darke, L.L., Stampler, F.M., & Naliboff, B.D. (1990). History of physical and sexual abuse in women with chronic pelvic pain. *Obstetrics & Gynecology, 76,* 92-96.

Reiter, R.C., & Milburn, A. (1992). Management of chronic pelvic pain. *Postgraduate Obstetrics and Gynecology, 12,* 1-7.

Savidge, C.J., & Slade, P. (1997). Psychological aspects of chronic pelvic pain. *Journal of Psychosomatic Research, 42,* 433-444.

Saxe, G.N., Chinman, G., Berkowitz, M.D., Hall, K., Lieberg, G., Schwartz, J., & Van der Kolk, B.A. (1994). Somatization in patients with dissociative disorders. *American Journal of Psychiatry, 151,* 1329-1334.

Spinhoven, P., Ormel, J., Sloekers, P.P., Kempen, G.I., Speckens, A.E., Van Hemert, A.M. (1998). A validation study of the Hospital Anxiety and Depression Scale (HADS) in different groups of Dutch subjects. *Psychological Medicine, 27,* 363-370.

SPSS PC/M.J. Norušis (1993). SPSS for Windows Release 6.0. Chicago: SPSS Inc.

Steinberg, M. (1993). *Structured Clinical Interview for DSM-IV Dissociative Disorders (SCID-D).* Washington DC: American Psychiatric Press.

Steinberg, M., Cichetti, D.V., Buchanan, J., Hall, P., & Rounsaville, B. (1993). Clinical assessment of dissociative symptoms and disorders: The structured clinical interview for DSM-IV dissociative disorders. *Dissociation, 6,* 3-16.

Van IJzendoorn, M.H., & Schuengel, C. (1996). The measurement of dissociation in normal and clinical populations: Meta-analytic validation of the Dissociative Experiences Scale (DES). *Clinical Psychology Review, 16,* 365-382.

Walker, E.A., Katon, W.J., Jemelka, R.P., Bowers, A.H., & Strenchever, M.A. (1991). The prevalence of chronic pelvic pain and irritable bowel syndrome in two university clinics. *Journal of Psychosomatic Obstetrics and Gynecology, 12,* 65-75.

Walker, E.A., Katon, W.J., Neraas, K., Jemelka, R.P., & Massoth, D. (1992). Dissociation in women with chronic pelvic pain. *American Journal of Psychiatry, 149,* 534-537.

Walker, E.A., Katon, W.J., Hansom, J., Harrop-Griffiths, J., Holm, L., Jones, M.L., Hickok, L.R., & Russo, J. (1995). Psychiatric diagnoses and sexual victimization in women with chronic pelvic pain. *Psychosomatics, 36,* 531-540.

Walling, M.K., O'Hara, M.W., Reiter, R.C., Milburn, A.K., Lilly, G., & Vincent, S.D. (1994a). Abuse history and chronic pain in women: II. A multivariate analysis of abuse and psychological morbidity. *Obstetrics & Gynecology, 84,* 200-206.

Walling, E.A., Reiter, R.C., O'Hara, M.W., Milburn, A.K., Lilly, G., & Vincent, S.D. (1994b). Abuse history and chronic pain in women. I. Prevalences of sexual and physical abuse. *Obstetrics & Gynecology, 84,* 193-199.

Zigmond, A.S., & Snaith, R.P. (1983). The Hospital Anxiety and Depression Scale. *Acta Psychiatrica Scandinavica, 67,* 3-9.

XII
Peritraumatic Somatoform and Psychological Dissociation in Relation to Recall of Childhood Sexual Abuse

"The immediate reactions to shock or fright deserve our attention, particularly because of the sequelae we see in the chronic cases."
Kardiner, 1941, p. 38

Introduction

Beginning with the works of Briquet (1859) and Janet (1889, 1909), there have been consistent clinical observations that overwhelming events can evoke dissociative phenomena which manifest in both psychological and somatoform variables (Brown, 1919; Cardeña & Spiegel, 1993; Kretschmer, 1960; Myers, 1916, 1940). Dissociation during or immediately following exposure to terrifying events has recently been labeled peritraumatic dissociation (Marmar, Weiss, & Metzler, 1998). Marmar and his colleagues have recognized that peritraumatic dissociation is exhibited in psychological phenomena, including dissociative amnesia, depersonalization, derealization, and identity fragmentation, but they have not assessed somatoform manifestation of peritraumatic dissociation, with the exception of one item. Analogous to our distinction between current psychological and somatoform dissociation (Nijenhuis, 1999; Nijenhuis, Spinhoven, Van Dyck, Van der Hart, & Vanderlinden, 1996), we propose to refer to these exhibited phenomena as peritraumatic psychological and somatoform dissociation.

Some research data suggest that overwhelming events can evoke somatoform symptoms, some of which may be dissociative. For example, in their study of acute reactions to an earthquake, Cardeña and Spiegel (1993) presented some effects related to dissociative somatoform disturbances, such as trouble swallowing and general bodily numbness. In another study, Cardeña, Holen, McFarlane, Solomon, Wilkinson, and Spiegel

---

* This chapter has previously been published as: Nijenhuis, E.R.S. (2001). Peritraumatic Somatoform and Psychological Dissociation in Relation to Recall of Childhood Sexual Abuse. *Journal of Trauma and Dissociation*, 2(3), 49–68.

(1998) assessed symptoms of bodily anesthesia among individuals involved in a disaster at sea. However, a systematic study of a wide range of peritraumatic somatoform dissociative phenomena has not yet been performed.

Thus, the current retrospective study investigates the extent to which traumatized individuals report both peritraumatic psychological and somatoform dissociation, and tests whether hypothesized strong association between these phenomena exists. Furthermore, because of indications that the severity of both current and peritraumatic psychological dissociative symptoms correlates with the severity of trauma (Marmar et al., 1998), we hypothesized that a similar association (between severity of trauma and severity of symptoms) would also apply to peritraumatic somatoform dissociation.

A related phenomenon that warrants extended study is dissociative amnesia. Since amnesia for trauma is included as one of the peritraumatic dissociative phenomena (Eriksson & Lundin, 1996), delayed or partial recall of overwhelming events could be related to peritraumatic dissociation, at least in some cases. Current and peritraumatic psychological and somatoform dissociation, threat to bodily integrity, and recall of trauma require additional discussion below.

Current and Peritraumatic Psychological Dissociation and Trauma

Contemporary studies have found associations among current psychological dissociative symptoms, documented trauma, and reported trauma, mainly related to sexual abuse, though not exclusively so. These associations apply to patients with dissociative disorders (Draijer & Boon, 1993; Hornstein & Putnam, 1992; Nijenhuis, Spinhoven, Van Dyck, Van der Hart, & Vanderlinden, 1998b; Ross et al., 1991), posttraumatic stress disorder (PTSD; Bremner, Steinberg, Southwick, Johnson, & Charney, 1993), eating disorders (Vanderlinden, Vandereycken, Van Dyck, & Vertommen, 1993; Waller et al., 2000), and borderline personality disorder (Herman, Perry, & Van der Kolk, 1989). There are correlations between psychological dissociation and reported trauma among patients who present for care in medical settings (Nijenhuis, Van Dyck, Ter Kuile et al., 1999; Walker, Katon, Neraas, Jemelka, & Massoth, 1992) and among nonclinical samples (Marmar et al., 1998; Putnam & Carlson, 1998). Models proposing that trauma can evoke dissociative reactions have been strongly supported by retrospective and prospective studies of peritraumatic psychological dissociation (Koopman, Classen, & Spiegel, 1994; Marmar et al., 1994; Marmar, Weiss, Metzler, Ronfeldt, & Foreman, 1996; Marmar, Weiss, Metzler, & Delucchi, 1996; Shalev, Peri, Canetti, & Schreiber, 1996; Titchenor, Marmar, Weiss, Metzler, & Ronfeldt, 1996; Weiss, Marmar, Metzler, & Ronfeldt, 1995)

Janet (1909) postulated that the disintegrating effects of trauma are in proportion to the severity of the trauma – its intensity, duration, and repetition. More recently, it has also been hypothesized that young children are particularly prone to dissociation and other trauma-related psychopathology (Putnam, 1997). Several studies have provided supportive evidence for these hypotheses (Draijer & Boon, 1993; Nijenhuis et al., 1998b).

Current and Peritraumatic Somatoform Dissociation and Threat to Bodily Integrity

Attention has been directed toward current somatoform dissociation only recently. Current somatoform dissociation has been correlated with reported trauma among patients with dissociative disorders from various countries and cultures, gynecology patients with chronic pelvic pain (Nijenhuis, 2000), and nonclinical subjects (Waller et al., 2000).

Several authors have postulated an evolutionary parallel between human and animal defensive reactions to major threat, but only a few included dissociative reactions in their considerations. Some authors stressed the survival value of rapid, reflex-like reactions (Kraepelin, 1913; Kretschmer, 1960; Ludwig, 1983; Pavlov, 1927; Rivers, 1920), others conceptualized some reactions as surrender responses (Krystal, 1998); still others (Seligman, 1975) drew a parallel between defensive reactions, depression and "giving up."

We have developed a model that postulates a similarity between somatoform dissociative reactions – such as motor inhibitions and analgesia – and animal defensive reactions to life threat (Nijenhuis, Spinhoven, Vanderlinden, Van Dyck, & Van der Hart, 1998; Nijenhuis, Vanderlinden, & Spinhoven, 1998). For instance, in our model, Seligman's concept of "giving up" would relate to total submission to the predator and total anesthesia after other defensive maneuvers failed or were inappropriate. In support of this model, all correlational studies to date that have assessed trauma and somatoform dissociation [using the Somatoform Dissociation Questionnaire (SDQ-20; Nijenhuis, 1999; Nijenhuis et al., 1996; Nijenhuis, Van Dyck, Spinhoven et al. 1999)] found that somatoform dissociation was most strongly associated with reported physical abuse (Nijenhuis et al., 1998b; Van Duyl, p.c.; Waller et al., 2000). More specifically, Nijenhuis, Spinhoven, Vanderlinden et al. (1998) found that dissociative disorder patients and patients with other mental disorders were correctly classified by symptom clusters evaluating current anesthesia, analgesia, motor inhibitions, and pain in 94% of the initial sample and in 96% of a cross-validation sample. According to this model, threat to the integrity of the body will produce animal-defense–like somatoform dissociative reactions (Nijenhuis, Vanderlinden, & Spinhoven, 1998; Nijenhuis, Vanderlinden, Spinhoven et al., 1998), in proportion to trauma severity, age of the victim, and degree of prior traumatization. More specifically, the model proposes that since freezing and anesthesia are the major defensive reactions of prey animals, particular reactions among the wide range of somatoform dissociative reactions will be more prominent: the inability to move and speak, anesthesia of various perceptual modalities, such as lack of pain perception (analgesia), tunnel vision, and bodily numbing (tactile and kinesthetic anesthesia). Thus, dissociative states or parts of the personality would not be random imaginative creations to escape reality, but would primarily represent nonintegrated defensive states (Nijenhuis & Van der Hart, 1999).

Consistent with this model, several studies have found associations between recent trauma and somatization, i.e. somatic complaints that cannot be fully explained by any known general medical condition or the direct effects of a substance (APA, 1994). For example, Darves-Bornoz (1997) reported that six months following a recent rape, victims displayed PTSD (71%), dissociative disorders (69%), and somatoform disorders (66%). Many PTSD patients in this sample also had dissociative disorders (85%) and somatoform disorders (75%). Threat to life, whether due to natural or manmade causes, may induce analgesia and numbness (Cardeña, Holen, McFarlane, Solomon, Wilkinson, & Spiegel, 1998; Cardeña & Spiegel, 1993; Pitman, Van der Kolk, Orr, & Greenberg, 1990; Van der Kolk, Greenberg, Orr, & Pitman, 1989). Such indications of consistent peritraumatic somatoform dissociation revealed the need to systematically assess these symptoms extensively.

Peritraumatic Dissociation and Recall of Trauma

Several researchers have distinguished three patterns of recall related to traumatic experiences (Brewin & Andrews, 1998; Harvey & Herman, 1994; Herman & Harvey, 1997). Continuous recall (CR) refers to some individuals who can access the memories of their traumatic experiences on a continuous basis. However, as supported by data from a large number of retrospective studies and some prospective, longitudinal studies (Brown, Scheflin, & Whitfield, 1999), others have only partial memories of their trauma(s) for a shorter or longer period of time, known as partial recall (PR). Still others fail to access trauma memories either temporarily or persistently (Van der Hart & Brom, 2000), leading to delayed recall (DR). In the aftermath of trauma, some individuals find themselves even unable to access some or all of their life prior to the trauma (Markowitsch et al., 1997; Van der Hart, Nijenhuis, & Brown, 2001). With respect to childhood sexual abuse (CSA), data-based studies have indicated that such traumatic events (or parts of them) can be subject to partial or delayed recall. Brown et al. (1999) reviewed 68 retrospective and prospective studies, including studies pertaining to clinical, forensic, nonclinical and random samples. Since then, the 69th study has been published (Chu, Frey, Ganzel, & Matthews, 1999). Brown et al. (1999) concluded that "the current rapidly accumulating body of data-based studies has adequately settled the question that an important minority of individuals substantially forget and later recover memories of childhood abuse and traumas." (p. 126)

Several studies suggest a positive correlation between the severity and/or frequency of CSA and partial or delayed recall (Briere & Conte, 1993; Chu & Dill, 1990; Chu et al., 1999; Ensink, 1992; Herman & Schatzow, 1987; Hunter & Andrews, 1999; Williams, 1994). To some extent the failure to access memories of trauma may be due to several factors of encoding, storage, and retrieval, all of which have been studied experimentally (Spinhoven, Nijenhuis, & Van Dyck, 1999). However, phenomena such as diminished rehearsal, intentional forgetting, encoding specificity, and implicit memory "... do not seem to provide an adequate explanation of the changeable memory phenomena that patients with, for example, PTSD and dissociative disorders display" (Spinhoven et al., 1999, p. 264). Therefore, although there is still much to learn about the ways in which dissociation relates to the disruption of the integrative functions of consciousness and memory (American Psychiatric Association, 1994), it can be hypothesized that partial or delayed recall of trauma is associated with peritraumatic dissociation.

In summary, the current retrospective study aimed to test the hypotheses that peritraumatic psychological and somatoform dissociation are associated with each other, with delayed recall of CSA, and with CSA severity. It was additionally hypothesized that peritraumatic somatoform dissociation would be specifically correlated with childhood physical abuse. In an attempt to document whether the reported CSA pertained to veridical events, it was explored to what extent continous, partial, and delayed CSA memories were reported to be corroborated by independent sources.

Methods

Participants

The female members of a Dutch national organization against CSA who reported a history of CSA were invited to take part in the study with the assistance of the organization. Thirty-four women (mean age = 42.68 years, SD = 8.58, range 27 to 67 years) were included. Nineteen participants (55.9%) were married or lived with a partner, 5 participants (14.7%) were divorced, and 10 participants (29.4%) were single. Twenty-one participants (61.8%) had children. Eight participants (23.5%) reported an elementary level of education, 9 participants (26.5%) reported an intermediate level of education, and 17 participants (50%) reported an advanced level of education. At the time of the interview, 6 participants (17.6%) were unemployed, 20 participants (58.8%) had a paid employment, and 8 participants (23.5%) had voluntarily employment. All participants had been in therapy because of reported CSA. Various types of therapies were involved: psychotherapy (64.7%), psychosocial counseling (23.5%), group psychotherapy (44.1%), self-help group (52.9%), and alternative therapy (47.1%).

Instruments

Traumatic Experiences Checklist (TEC; Nijenhuis, Van der Hart & Vanderlinden, unpublished data; Nijenhuis, 1999; Nijenhuis et al., 1998b; Nijenhuis, Van der Hart, & Kruger, 2002). The TEC is a self-report questionnaire about 29 types of trauma. All items address the impact of the trauma with a subjective rating. Items evaluating emotional neglect, emotional abuse, physical abuse, sexual harassment, and sexual abuse address the setting in which such trauma occurred. The questions contain short descriptions that intend to define the events of concern. An example of sexual harassment is: "Disturbing sexual overtures (that DO NOT result in physical contact) by your parents, brothers, or sisters." The internal consistency, test-reliability, convergent validity, and construct validity of the TEC are satisfactory (Nijenhuis, Van der Hart, & Kruger, 2002).

The severity of emotional, physical, and sexual trauma can be estimated by calculating trauma composite scores. Composite scores are assessed for each area of trauma – emotional neglect, emotional abuse, physical abuse, sexual harassment, and sexual abuse – and during three developmental periods (0-6 years, 7-12 years, 13-18 years). The composite scores involve four variables: (a) occurrence of the traumatic event; (b) relationship to the perpetrator, indicating whether the event occurred within the confines of the family of origin, within the extended family, or in another setting;(c) duration of the trauma, indicating whether the trauma occurred during a period shorter or longer than one year; and (d) subjective response, indicating whether the respondent did not feel traumatized, felt only slightly traumatized, or whether she or he felt moderately, severely, or extremely traumatized by the event(s).

Peritraumatic Dissociation Experiences Questionnaire (PDEQ; Marmar, Weiss, & Metzler, 1998). The PDEQ is a 10-item self-reporting questionnaire about psychological dissociative experiences, such as derealization, depersonalization, and amnesia, during or immediately after an overwhelming event. Respondents are instructed to recall a particular traumatic event and to rate the intensity of each peritraumatic dissociative reaction on a 5-point Likert scale (1 = not at all true, 5 = extremely true). The PDEQ total score ranges from 10 to 50. The internal consistency of the PDEQ is satisfactory (Cronbach's $\alpha = 0.80$), and its discriminative, convergent, construct, and predictive validity have been demonstrated in several studies (Marmar et al., 1994; Marmar, Weiss, Metzler, & Delucchi, 1996; Marmar, Weiss, Metzler, Ronfeldt et al., 1996; Shalev et al., 1996; Titchenor et al., 1996).

Somatoform Peritraumatic Dissociation Questionnaire (SDQ-P; Nijenhuis & Van der Hart, unpublished document). The SDQ-P is a newly constructed self-report questionnaire that evaluates somatoform manifestations of dissociation during or immediately following an overwhelming event. The items were derived from clinical observations, clinical reports in psychiatric literature, and the SDQ-20 (Nijenhuis et al., 1996; Nijenhuis, Van Dyck, Spinhoven et al., 1999), which assesses the severity of current somatoform dissociation. The original SDQ-P item pool ($n = 10$) was reduced by selecting items that correlated with the total scale score at a level of $r > 0.60$, which yielded a scale of 11 items. Examples of SDQ-P items include: "During (a part of) the event and/or immediately afterward: It was as if my body, or a part of it, had disappeared; I was paralyzed or stiff for a while; my body moved in coordinated ways which I could not control (for example, it was as if my body walked by itself in a particular direction)."

Traumatic Memory Inventory (TMI; Van der Kolk, 1990). The TMI is a 60-item structured interview which assesses the circumstances and characteristics of memory retrieval of a target traumatic event and a target memory of an emotional, but nontraumatic, event. The TMI evaluates (1) the nature of the trauma; (2) the duration of the trauma; (3) whether the respondent has always been aware that the trauma occured, and if not, when s/he became conscious of it; (4) the sensory modalities in which the trauma was (and is) experienced; (5) the nature of nightmares and flashbacks, if applicable; (6) the ways in which recollections are avoided; and (7) availability of corroboration of the trauma. These data were collected for three time periods: immediately after the trauma, over the course of time, and currently. For the present study, the TMI was slightly modified. Questions about the target memory of an emotional, but nontraumatic, event were removed and a question about the reported severity of CSA, in terms of the acts involved, was added. In this article we describe the corroboration data of the TMI.

Procedure

Candidate participants were informed about the procedure, its estimated duration, and the purpose of the study. It was stated that their participation would contribute to increasing the understanding of the consequences of CSA and the efficacy of CSA treatment programs. The participants were also informed that they would be interviewed at a location of their choosing and it was stressed that they could pause or withdraw from the project at any time. When written informed consent was obtained, the participants were randomly assigned to one of four female trained interviewers. In the course of the study, to promote standardization, the interviewers consulted regularly with each other and with the senior investigators (Nijenhuis/Van der Hart) about the administration of the TMI. At the start of the interview, the participants were asked permission to record the interview on audiotape. Prior to the interview, half of the participants completed a demographic inventory in this order: TEC, PDEQ, and SDQ-P. In order to control for possible order effects, the other half completed the SDQ-P prior to the PDEQ. Next, the participants were asked whether they had first remembered the CSA in the form of CR, PR, or DR. Finally, the TMI was administered. When a participant reported more than one type of traumatic recall, the PDEQ and SDQ-P were completed, and the TMI was administered for each type of recall.

Data Analysis

The participants were asked whether they had first remembered CSA in the form of CR, PR, or DR. When a participant reported more than one type of traumatic recall, only the data that pertained to a less complete level of recall were considered. For example, when a participant reported both CR and DR, only the data relating to DR were entered into the analyses. This decision was made because (1) too few participants reported more than one type of recall to allow for worthwhile comparisons of various types of recall within participants, and (2) we wanted to compare participants with less complete levels of recall to participants with more complete levels of recall.

The relationship between peritraumatic psychological and somatoform dissociation was calculated using Pearson's product moment correlation coefficient. The relationship between peritraumatic psychological and somatoform dissociation and the different types of recall were evaluated with Kruskall-Wallis tests and Mann-Whitney tests. To test the hypothesis that peritraumatic psychological and somatoform dissociation are associated with reported CSA severity (in terms of the acts involved) and that peritraumatic somatoform dissociation would be specifically correlated with reported CPA, Pearson's product moment correlation was used. In addition, a multiple regression analysis was performed to estimate the capacity of reported CSA severity and reported CPA to predict peritraumatic somatoform dissociation.

Results

The SDQ-P

The internal consistency of the SDQ-P was high (Cronbach's $\alpha = 0.90$). As hypothesized, peritraumatic psychological dissociation and peritraumatic somatoform dissociation were strongly intercorrelated, with Pearson's product moment $r = 0.62$, $p < 0.0001$. The items of the original item pool were also correlated with the PDEQ ($r = 0.54$, $p < 0.001$).

Prevalence of Types of CSA Recall and the Relationship of Recall with Peritraumatic Dissociation

Fourteen participants (41.2%) reported CR, 12 participants (35.3%) reported PR, and 21 participants (61.8%) reported DR. Ten participants (29.4%) reported more than one type of recall of the CSA. One subject reported CR and PR; 3 participants reported PR and DR, 3 participants reported CR and DR, and three participants reported CR, PR, and DR. Application of the indicated selection criterium (i.e., when a participant reported more than one type of traumatic recall, only the data that pertained to a less complete level of recall were considered) yielded 7 participants with CR, 6 participants with PR, and 21 participants with DR. There was no statistically significant difference among participants with CR, PR, and DR as to the age of CSA onset (CR = 9.7 years, PR = 7.5 years, DR = 6.0 years; Kruskall-Wallis test, $\chi^2 = 3.939$, df 2, n.s.).

The types of CSA recall were associated with the severity of peritraumatic psychological dissociation (Kruskall-Wallis test, $\chi^2 = 6, 113$, df 2, $p < 0.05$) and peritraumatic somatoform dissociation (Kruskall-Wallis test,

Figure 1

Peritraumatic Dissociation and Types of Recall
cr = continuous recall
pr = partial recall
dr = delayed recall
PDEQ = peritraumatic psychological dissociation
SDQ-P = peritraumatic somatoform dissociation

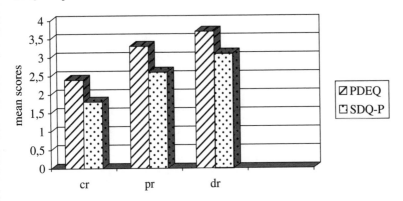

$\chi^2 = 6,031$, *df* 2, $p < 0.05$; see Figure 1). A Mann-Whitney test was performed post hoc, and showed more severe peritraumatic dissociation among participants with DR than among participants with CR (PDEQ: $z = 27.5$, $p < 0.05$; SDQ-P: $z = 28.0$, $p < 0.05$).

Prevalence of Trauma, Composite Trauma Scores, and Types of Recall

The mean of the total TEC score was 11.5 (range: 4-21). Because the total TEC score represents the number of trauma types recalled by the participant, this result suggests that the current sample had been traumatized in many ways. In addition to reporting childhood sexual abuse, 91.2% of the participants reported emotional neglect, 94.1% emotional abuse, 64.7% physical abuse, and 85.3% sexual harassment. Table 1 presents the combined composite scores over five trauma areas (emotional neglect, emotional abuse, physical abuse, sexual harassment, and sexual abuse) per developmental period, as well as the composite trauma scores over all three developmental periods.

CR, PR, and DR were not associated with statistically significant differences among the composite trauma scores per developmental period or among composite trauma scores across all developmental periods (all Kruskall-Wallis tests n.s.).

Composite Trauma Scores and Peritraumatic Dissociation

Among the three composite trauma scores for each developmental level, both the PDEQ (*rho* $= 0.39$, $p < 0.05$) and the SDQ-P (*rho* $= 0.34$,

Table 1

Composite Trauma Scores (TEC) of CSA Reporting Women ($n = 34$)

Total Scores (possible range 0-20)	M	SD	range
0-6 years	10.79	5.74	0-19
7-12 years	13.88	4.84	3-20
13-18 years	13.08	5.06	0-20
total (possible range 0-60)	37.76	12.38	8-54

Emotional Neglect (possible range 0-4)	M	SD	range
0-6 years	2.67	1.82	0-4
7-12 years	3.00	1.65	0-4
13-18 years	3.41	1.31	0-4
total (possible range 0-12)	9.03	3.98	0-12

Emotional Abuse (possible range 0-4)	M	SD	range
0-6 years	3.03	1.71	0-4
7-12 years	3.44	1.31	0-4
13-18 years	3.32	1.42	0-4
total (possible range 0-12)	9.79	3.80	0-12

Physical Abuse (possible range 0-4)	M	SD	range
0-6 years	1.47	1.91	0-4
7-12 years	2.26	1.94	0-4
13-18 years	1.91	1.98	0-4
total (possible range 0-12)	5.65	3.80	0-12

Sexual Harassment (possible range 0-4)	M	SD	range
0-6 years	1.24	1.71	0-4
7-12 years	2.06	1.67	0-4
13-18 years	1.97	1.68	0-4
total (possible range 0-12)	5.24	4.11	0-12

Sexual Abuse (possible range 0-4)	M	SD	range
0-6 years	2.23	1.89	0-4
7-12 years	2.97	1.55	0-4
13-18 years	2.59	1.76	0-4
total (possible range 0-12)	7.77	3.68	1-12

$p < 0.05$) were associated with the composite trauma scores of the developmental period from 7-12 years. When the composite trauma scores per developmental level per trauma area were examined, it was found that measures of peritraumatic dissociation were not associated with emotional neglect, emotional abuse, and sexual harrasment. However, peritraumatic somatoform dissociation was correlated with the composite score related to physical abuse over the three developmental periods at the trend level ($rho = .34$, $p = 0.052$), and at a statistically significant level for the composite score for the developmental period of 7-12 years ($rho = 0.41$, $p < 0.05$). As to the presence of the various types of reported trauma in different settings, the only statistically significant correlation was between peritraumatic somatoform dissociation and reported physical abuse ($rho = 0.46$, $p < 0.01$). Peritraumatic psychological dissociation correlated with reported sexual abuse in the period of 7-12 years at a trend level ($rho = 0.33$, $p = 0.053$).

Peritraumatic Dissociation and Reported Severity of Childhood Sexual Abuse: Interview Data

The total severity score of reported CSA as assessed by the TMI was associated with peritraumatic somatoform dissociation ($rho = 0.37$, $p < 0.05$). Peritraumatic psychological dissociation was correlated with CSA severity at a trend level ($rho = 0.33$, $p = 0.054$). As to the separate CSA severity levels, the PDEQ was associated with intermediate severity (perpetrator[s] touched or stimulted the participant's bare breasts and genitalia; $rho = 0.48$, $p < 0.01$), whereas the SDQ-P tended to be associated with very severe abuse (perpetrator[s] penetrated the participants's vagina and anus with penis, digits or objects; $rho = 0.34$, $p = 0.052$).

Peritraumatic Somatoform Dissociation, Reported CSA, and Reported Physical Abuse

To estimate the ability of reported CSA severity and reported physical abuse to predict peritraumatic somatoform dissociation, a multiple-regression analysis was performed. In a first step, the total CSA severity score, assessed in the interview, was forced into the regression equation and reported physical abuse was then entered stepwise. Reported physical abuse delivered an independent contribution to the prediction of peritraumatic somatoform dissociation. In the final model, the reported severity of CSA contributed to that prediction less ($beta = 0.27$, $p = 0.092$) than reported physical abuse ($beta = 0.43$, $p = 0.009$; total adjusted $R^2 = 0.26$).

Corroboration of Reported Childhood Sexual Abuse

The reported corroborative evidence consisted of reported confessions by the perpetrator ($n = 6$), reports of witnesses ($n = 11$), entries in childhood diaries ($n = 3$), statements in medical and judicial files ($n = 5$), reports of another victim of the same perpetrator ($n = 5$), and other sources ($n = 3$). Three of the 7 participants (42.6%) who reported CR looked for external corroboration of the reported sexual abuse. All 3 reported having found such data. Among 3 of the 6 women (50%) who reported PR and who looked for external corroboration, 2 of them (33.3%) found it. Finally, among the 14 of the 21 women (66.7%) who reported DR and who attempted to find corroborative data, 10 (47.6%) were successful. Finding corroboration was independent of the type of recall (Kruskall-Wallis, $\chi^2 = 1.203$, df 1, n.s.).

Discussion

The SDQ-P—whose internal consistency was very satisfactory—was strongly associated with the PDEQ, a measure of peritraumatic psychological dissociation. This result supports the convergent validity of the SDQ-P. Like the SDQ-20 (Nijenhuis et al., 1996), which evaluates current somatoform dissociation, the items of the SDQ-P predominantly include symptoms of anesthesia, motor disturbances, analgesia, pain, and loss of consciousness. These items describe reactions that are similar to the defensive reactions of animals to major threat (Nijenhuis, Vanderlinden, & Spinhoven, 1998; Nijenhuis, Spinhoven, Vanderlinden et al., 1998; Rivers, 1920).

The present study also explored the relationships between peritraumatic dissociation and different types of recall of CSA. About 60% of the present sample reported DR and only about 20% of the total sample had never forgotten the abuse. Among women with DR, a substantial subgroup also reported CR or PR of other traumatic events. Corresponding to the findings of Hunter and Andrews (1999), we found that in comparison with CR, DR was more strongly associated with peritraumatic dissociation.

Obviously, prospective studies are needed to test whether these types of dissociation cause or promote DR. To the extent that DR is a dissociative phenomenon, the current findings are consistent with those from a longitudinal study by Marmar, Weiss, Metzler, Delucchi, Best, and Wentworth (1999), who found that peritraumatic dissociation accounted for significant increments in current general dissociative tendencies.

Apart from CSA, practically all women in this study reported a wide range of other types of trauma, foremost emotional abuse and neglect. Reported physical abuse accompanied the reported CSA in about two-thirds of the cases. Thus, according to the participants, CSA did not occur in isolation, but within a neglectful and abusive social context. This finding concurs with the results of longitudinal (Widom, 1999) and cross-sectional studies (Draijer & Langeland, 1999; Nijenhuis et al., 1998b), suggesting that CSA and CPA tend to occur in an emotionally abusive and neglectful social context.

As hypothesized, peritraumatic psychological and somatoform dissociation were associated with the severity of reported CSA. Peritraumatic dissociation was associated with the severity of the reported CSA as assessed in the interview by posing direct questions regarding the nature of the sexual acts. More specifically, peritraumatic psychological dissociation correlated with intermediate levels of CSA severity, and peritraumatic somatoform dissociation correlated with the total severity score, and at a trend level with very severe CSA. This is an indication that peritraumatic somatoform dissociation may be particularly associated with severe threat of the integrity of the body. Emotional abuse and neglect did not correlate with peritraumatic dissociation. This concurs with our finding that current somatoform and psychological dissociation correlated with emotional neglect and abuse less strongly than with sexual trauma and physical abuse in patients with dissociative disorders (Nijenhuis et al., 1998b).

Peritraumatic somatoform dissociation, but not peritraumatic psychological dissociation, was especially associated with reported physical abuse. In fact, reported physical abuse predicted peritraumatic somatoform dissociation over and above the severity of CSA. This finding adds to the body of data that suggests a particular association between somatoform dissociation and threat to the integrity of the body. In concurrence with this association, most SDQ-P items describe animal-defense–like reactions such as freezing and total submission. Thus, the results of this study are consistent with the model, which holds that threat to the integrity of the body can evoke dissociative reactions that are manifestations of animal-defense–like, emotional psychobiological systems (Nijenhuis, Van der Hart, & Steele, 2000).

The accuracy of the CSA memories was explored by including an item about corroboration in the interview. About two-thirds of the participants looked for external corroboration and about three-quarters of this subgroup found it. Whether or not corroboration for (aspects of) the CSA was found did not depend on the type of recall. This result concurs with data from other studies suggesting that delayed memories of CSA are as reliable as continuously accessible memories of CSA (Dalenberg, 1996; Williams, 1995). Finding corroboration of delayed memories of abuse is not uncommon. For example, in a study by Chu et al. (1999), 90% of the participants with complete amnesia who sought confirmation of their abuse were able to find some evidence that confirmed it. These data obviously do not suggest that all reports of delayed CSA memories are accurate. Inaccuracies may exist in some reports and in the peripheral details of other reports.

A major methodological limitation of the present study was the use of retrospective data. Thus, the current data could be subject to memory distortions and inaccuracies. However, Marmar et al. (1999) found that reports of peritraumatic dissociation were stable over time in a longitudinal study and that the results of prospective longitudinal studies of peritraumatic dissociation (Koopman et al., 1994; Shalev et al., 1996) converged with the results from retrospective studies. Due to the modest number of participants, the power of the statistical tests is limited. Another limitation is that all participants were members of a Dutch national organization against CSA, which could affect the applicability of the study to other populations. Finally, no attempt was made to assess the validity of the reported independent corroboration of CSA memories.

In conclusion, while somatoform dissociation has been rediscovered in the last decade, this is the first article to systematically address a wide range of peritraumatic somatoform dissociative phenomena. Our understanding of acute trauma responses and their role in the development of posttraumatic psychopathology can be enhanced by including peritraumatic somatoform dissociation in future research.

References

American Psychiatric Association (1994). *Diagnostic and Statistic Manual of Mental Disorders, 4th ed.* Washington DC: American Psychiatric Association.

Bolt. H., & Van der Hart, O. (1994). *Traumatic Memory Inventory*, Dutch edition. Utrecht: Department of Clinical and Health Psychology, Utrecht University. (Unpublished report)

Bremner, J.D., Steinberg, M., Southwick, S.M., Johnson, D.R., & Charney, D.S. (1993). Use of the structured clinical interview for DSM-IV dissociative disorders for systematic assessment of dissociative symptoms in posttraumatic stress disorder. *American Journal of Psychiatry, 150*, 1011-1014.

Brewin, C.R., & Andrews, B. (1998). Recovered memories of trauma: Phenomenology and cognitive mechanisms. *Clinical Psychology Review, 18*, 949-970.

Briere, J., & Conte, J. (1993). Self-reported amnesia for abuse in adults molested as children. *Journal of Traumatic Stress, 6*, 21-31.

Briquet, P. (1859). *Traité Clinique et Thérapeutique de L'Hystérie*. Paris: J.-P. Baillière & Fils.

Brown, W. (1919). Hypnosis, suggestion, and dissociation. *The British Medical Journal, 191*, 734-736.

Brown, D., Scheflin, A.W., & Whitfield, C.L. (1999). Recovered memories: The current weight of the evidence in science and in the courts. *Journal of Psychiatry & Law, 27*, 5-156.

Cardeña, E., Holen, A., McFarlane, A., Solomon, Z., Wilkinson, C., & Spiegel, D. (1998). A multisite study of acute stress reaction to a disaster. In *Sourcebook for the DSM-IV, IV*. Washington DC: American Psychiatric Association.

Cardeña, E., & Spiegel, D. (1993). Dissociative reactions to the San Fransisco Bay Area Earthquake of 1989. *American Journal of Psychiatry, 150*, 474-478.

Chu, J.A., & Dill, D.L. (1990). Dissociative symptoms in relation to childhood physical and sexual abuse. *American Journal of Psychiatry, 147*, 887-892.

Chu, J.A., Frey, L.M., Ganzel, B.L., & Matthews, J.A. (1999). Memories of childhood abuse: Dissociation, amnesia, and corroboration. *American Journal of Psychiatry, 156*, 749-755.

Dalenberg, C.J. (1996). Accuracy, timing, and circumstances of disclosure in therapy of recovered and continuous memories of abuse. Journal of Psychiatry and Law, 24, 229-275.

Darves-Bornoz, J.-M. (1997). Rape-related psychotraumatic syndromes. *European Journal of Obstetrics & Gynecology, 71*, 59-65.

Draijer, N., & Boon, S. (1993). Trauma, dissocation, and dissociative disorders. In S. Boon & N. Draijer (eds.), *Multiple personality disorder in the Netherlands: A study on reliability and validity of the diagnosis* (pp. 177-193). Amsterdam/Lisse: Swets & Zeitlinger.

Draijer, N., & Langeland, W. (1999). Childhood trauma and perceived parental dysfunction in the etiology of dissociative symptoms in psychiatric inpatients. *American Journal of Psychiatry, 156*, 379-385.

Ensink, B.J. (1992). *Confusing realities: A study on childhood sexual abuse and psychiatric symptoms*. Amsterdam: VU University Press.

Eriksson, N.-G., & Lundin, T. (1996). Early traumatic stress reactions among Swedish survivors of the MS Estonia disaster. *British Journal of Psychiatry, 169,* 713-716.

Feldman-Summers, S., & Pope, K.S. (1994). The experience of forgetting childhood abuse: A national survey of psychologists. *Journal of Consulting and Clinical Psychology, 62,* 636-639.

Harvey, M.R., & Herman, J.L. (1994). Continuous memory, amnesia, and delayed recall of childhood trauma: A clinical typology. *Consciousness and Cognition, 3,* 261-271.

Herman, J.L., & Harvey, M.R. (1997). Adult memories of childhood trauma: A naturalistic clinical study. *Journal of Traumatic Stress, 10,* 557-571.

Herman, J.L., Perry, J.C., & Van der Kolk, B.A. (1989). Childhood trauma in borderline personality disorder. *American Journal of Psychiatry, 146,* 390-395.

Herman, J.L., & Schatzow, E. (1987). Recovery and verification of memories of childhood sexual trauma. *Psychoanalytic Psychology, 4,* 1-14.

Hornstein, N.L., & Putnam, F.W. (1992). Clinical phenomenology of child and adolescent disorders. *Journal of the American Academy of Child and Adolescent Psychiatry, 31,* 1077-1085.

Hunter, E., & Andrews, B. (1999). Childhood contextual correlates and adult psycho-social consequences of the forgetting of childhood sexual experience. Abstract, 6th European Conference on Traumatic Stress (Istanbul, Turkey, June 5-8, 1999), 46-47.

Janet, P. (1889). *L'automatisme psychologique.* Paris: Félix Alcan. Reprint: Société Pierre Janet, 1973.

Janet, P. (1909). Problèmes psychologiques de l'emotion. *Revué Neurologique, 17,* 1551-1687.

Kardiner, A. (1941). *The traumatic neuroses of war.* Washington DC: National Research Council.

Kluft, R.P. (1995). The confirmation and disconformation of memories of abuse in DID patients: A naturalistic clinical study. *Dissociation, 8,* 251-258.

Koopman, C., Classen, C., & Spiegel, D. (1994). Predictors of posttraumatic stress symptoms among survivors of the Oakland/Berkeley, California, firestorm. *American Journal of Psychiatry, 151,* 888-894.

Kraepelin, E. (1913). Uber Hysterie. *Zeitschrift für die gesamte Neurologie und Psychiatrie, 18,* 261-279.

Kretschmer, E. (1960). *Hysteria, reflex, and instinct.* London: Peter Owen.

Krystal, H. (1988). *Integration and self-healing. Affect, trauma, alexithymia.* Hillsdale: Lawrence Erlbaum.

Ludwig, A.M. (1983). The psychobiological functions of dissociation. *American Journal of Clinical Hypnosis, 26,* 93-99.

Markowitsch, H.J., Calabrese, P., Fink, G.R., Durwen, H.F., Kessler, J., Härting, C., König, M., Mirzaian, E.B., Heiss, W.-D., Heuser, L., & Gehlen, W. (1997). Impaired episodic memory retrieval in a case of probable psychogenic amnesia. *Psychiatry Research Neuroimaging Section, 74,* 119-126.

Marmar, C.R., Weiss, D.S., Schlenger, W.E., Fairbank, J.A., Jordan, B.K., Kulka, R.A., & Hough, R.L. (1994). Peritraumatic dissociation and posttraumatic stress in male Vietnam theater veterans. *American Journal of Psychiatry, 151,* 902-907.

Marmar, C.R., Weiss, D.S., Metzler, T.J. , Ronfeldt, H.M., & Foreman, C. (1996). Stress responses of emergency services personnel to the Loma Prieta earthquake Interstate-880 freeway collapse and control traumatic incidents. *Journal of Traumatic Stress, 9,* 63-85.

Marmar, C.R., Weiss, D.S., Metzler, T.J., & Delucchi, K. (1996). Characteristics of emergency services personnel related to peritraumatic dissociation during critical incident exposure. *American Journal of Psychiatry, 153*, 94-102.

Marmar, C.R., Weiss, D.S., & Metzler, T.J. (1998). Peritraumatic dissociation and posttraumatic stress disorder. In J.D. Bremner & C.R. Marmar (eds.), *Trauma, memory, and dissociation* (pp. 229-252). Washington, DC: American Psychiatric Press.

Marmar, C.R., Weiss, D., Metzler, T.J., Delucchi, K., Best, S.R., & Wentworth, K.A. (1999). Longitudinal course and predictors of continuing distress following critical incident exposure in emergency services personnel. *Journal of Nervous and Mental Disease, 187*, 15-22.

Myers, C.S. (1915). A contribution to the study of shell shock: Being an account of three cases of loss of memory, vision, smell, and taste, admitted into the Duchess of Westminster's War Hospital, Le Touquet. *The Lancet*, February 13, 316-320.

Myers, C.S. (1940). *Shell shock in France 1914-18.* Cambridge: Cambridge University Press.

Nijenhuis, E.R.S. (1999). *Somatoform dissociation: Phenomena, measurement, and theoretical issues.* Assen, the Netherlands: Van Gorcum.

Nijenhuis, E.R.S. (2000). Somatoform dissociation: Major symptom of dissociative disorders. *Journal of Trauma and Dissociation, 1*, 7-32.

Nijenhuis, E.R.S., Spinhoven, P., Vanderlinden, J., Van Dyck, R., & Van der Hart, O. (1998). Somatoform dissociative symptoms as related to animal defensive reactions to predatory threat and injury. *Journal of Abnormal Psychology, 107*, 63-73.

Nijenhuis, E.R.S., Spinhoven, P., Van Dyck, R., Van der Hart, O., & Vanderlinden, J. (1996). The development and psychometric characteristics of the somatoform dissociation questionnaire (SDQ-20). *Journal of Nervous and Mental Disease, 184*, 688-694.

Nijenhuis, E.R.S., Spinhoven, P., Van Dyck, R., Van der Hart, O., & Vanderlinden, J. (1998a). Psychometric characteristics of the Somatoform Dissociation Questionnaire: A replication study. *Psychotherapy & Psychosomatics, 67*, 17-23.

Nijenhuis, E.R.S., Spinhoven, P., Van Dyck, R., Van der Hart, O., & Vanderlinden, J. (1998b). Degree of somatoform and psychological dissocation in dissociative disorders is correlated with reported trauma. *Journal of Traumatic Stress, 11*, 711-730.

Nijenhuis, E.R.S. & Van der Hart, O. (1999). Forgetting and re-experiencing trauma: From anaesthesia to pain. In J.M. Goodwin & R. Attias (eds.), *Splintered reflections: Images of the body in trauma* (pp. 39-65). New York: Basic.

Nijenhuis, E.R.S., Van der Hart, O., & Kruger, K. (2002). The psychometric characteristics of the Traumatic Experiences Checklist (TEC): First findings among psychiatric outpatients. *Clinical Psychology and Psychotherapy, 9*(3), 200-210.

Nijenhuis, E.R.S., Van der Hart, O., & Steele, K. (2004). Strukturelle Dissoziation der Persönlichkeitsstruktur, traumatischer Ursprung, phobische Residuen. In: L. Reddemann, A. Hofmann, & U. Gast (eds.), *Psychotherapie der dissoziativen Störungen* (pp. 47-69). Stuttgart: Thieme.

Nijenhuis, E.R.S., Vanderlinden, J., & Spinhoven, P. (1998). Animal defensive reactions as a model for trauma-induced dissociative reactions. *Journal of Traumatic Stress, 11*, 243-260. (d)

Nijenhuis, E.R.S., Van Dyck, R., Ter Kuile, M., Mourits, M., Spinhoven, P., & Van der Hart, O. (1999). Evidence for associations between somatoform dissociation, psychological dissociation, and reported trauma in chronic pelvic pain patients. In Nijenhuis, E.R.S., *Somatoform dissociation: Phenomena, measurement, and theoretical issues* (pp. 146-160). Assen, the Netherlands: Van Gorcum.

Nijenhuis, E.R.S., Van Dyck, R., Spinhoven, P., Van der Hart, O., Chatrou, M., Vanderlinden, J., & Moene, F. (1999). Somatoform dissociation discriminates among diagnostic categories over and above general psychopathology. *Australian and New Zealand Journal of Psychiatry, 33,* 512-520.

Pavlov, I.P. (1927). *Conditioned reflexes.* London: Oxford University Press.

Pitman, R.K., Van der Kolk, B.A., Orr, S.P., & Greenberg, M.S. (1990). Naloxone reversible stress induced analgesia in post traumatic stress disorder. *Archives of General Psychiatry, 47,* 541-547.

Putnam, F.W. (1997). *Dissociation in children and adolescents: A developmental perspective.* New York: Guilford.

Putnam, F.W., & Carlson, E.B. (1998). Hypnosis, dissociation, and trauma: Myths, metaphors, and mechanisms. In J. D. Bremner & C.A. Marmar (eds.), *Trauma, memory, and dissociation* (pp. 27-56). Washington DC: American Psychiatric Press.

Rivers, W.H.R. (1920). *Instinct and the unconsciousness: A contribution to a biological theory of the psycho-neuroses.* London: Cambridge University Press.

Ross, C.A., Miller, S.D., Bjornson, L., Reagor, P., Fraser, G.A., & Anderson, G. (1991). Abuse histories in 102 cases of multiple personality disorder. *Canadian Journal of Psychiatry, 36,* 97-101.

Sar, V., Kundakci, T., Kiziltan, E., Bakim, B., & Bozkurt, O. (2000). Differentiating dissociative disorders from other diagnostic groups through somatoform dissociation in Turkey. *Journal of Trauma and Dissociation, 1,* 67-80.

Seligman, M.E.P. (1975). *Helplessness.* San Fransisco: W.H. Freeman.

Shalev, A.Y., Peri, T., Canetti, L., & Schreiber, S. (1996). Predictors of PTSD in injured trauma survivors: A prospective study. *American Journal of Psychiatry, 153,* 219-225.

Spinhoven, P., Nijenhuis, E.R.S., & Van Dyck, R. (1999). Can experimental memory research adequately explain memory for trauma? *Psychotherapy, 36,* 257-267.

Titchenor, V., Marmar, C.R., Weiss, D.S., Metzler, T.J., & Ronfeldt, H.M. (1996). The relationship of peritraumatic dissociation and posttraumatic stress: Findings in female Vietnam veterans. *Journal of Consulting and Clinical Psychology, 64,* 1054-1059.

Van der Hart, O., & Brom, D. (2000). When the victim forgets: Trauma-induced amnesia and its assessment in Holocaust survivors. In A. Shalev, R. Yehuda, & A.C. McFarlane (eds.), *International handbook of human response to trauma* (pp. 233-248). New York: Kluwer Academic/Plenum.

Van der Hart, O., Nijenhuis, E.R.S., & Brown, P. (2001). Loss and recovery of different memory types in generalized dissociative amnesia. *Australian and New Zealand Journal of Psychiatry, 35*(5), 589-600.

Van der Kolk, B.A. *Traumatic Memory Inventory.* Boston: unpublished report.

Van der Kolk, B.A., Greenberg, M.S., Orr, S.P., & Pitman, R.K. (1989). Endogenous opioids, stress induced analgesia, and posttraumatic stress disorder. *Psychopharmacology Bulletin, 25,* 417-422.

Vanderlinden, J., Vandereycken, W., Van Dyck, R., & Vertommen, H. (1993). Dissociative experiences and trauma in eating disorders. *International Journal of Eating Disorders, 13,* 187-194.

Walker, E.A., Katon, W.J., Neraas, K., Jemelka, R.P., & Massoth, D. (1992). Dissociation in women with chronic pelvic pain. *American Journal of Psychiatry, 149,* 534-537.

Waller, G., Hamilton, K., Elliott, P., Lewendon, J., Stopa, L. Waters, A., Kennedy, F., Chalkley, J., F., Lee, G., Pearson, D., Kennerley, H., Hargreaves, I., & Bashford, V. (2000). Somatoform dissociation, psychological dissociation, and specific forms of trauma. *Journal of Trauma and Dissociation, 1,* 81-98.

Weiss, D.S., Marmar, C.R., Metzler, T.J. & Ronfeldt, H.M. (1995). Predicting symtomatic distress in emergeny services personel. *Journal of Consulting and Clinical Psychology, 63*, 361-368.

Widom, C.S. (1999). Posttraumatic stress disorder in abused and neglected children grown up. *American Journal of Psychiatry, 156*, 1223-1229.

Williams, L.M. (1994). Recall of childhood trauma: A prospective study of women's memories of child sexual abuse. *Journal of Consulting and Clinical Psychology, 62*, 1167-1176.

Williams, L.M. (1995). Recovered memories of abuse in women with documented child sexual victimization histories. *Journal of Traumatic Stress, 8*, 649-673.

XIII
The Psychometric Characteristics of the Traumatic Experiences Checklist (TEC): First Findings Among Psychiatric Outpatients[*]

"We found a strong graded relationship between the breadth of exposure to abuse or household dysfunction during childhood and multiple risk factors for several of the leading causes of death in adults."
Felitti, V.J. et al., 1998, 245-258

Introduction

There is mounting evidence for, and growing awareness of, substantial associations between several forms of psychopathology and corroborated as well as uncorroborated reported exposure to overwhelming events (Brown et al., 1998; Van der Kolk et al., 1996). Retrospective and prospective studies have established, or have strongly suggested, that overwhelming events – ranging from one-time incidents to chronic traumatization – may induce posttraumatic stress disorder (PTSD), dissociative disorders, somatoform disorders, and other forms of trauma-related psychopathology in a substantial proportion of individuals (Darves-Bornoz, 1997; Darves-Bornoz et al., 1998; Macfie et al., 2001; Marmar et al., 1994, 1998; Ogawa et al., 1997; Nijenhuis et al., 2001; Shalev et al., 1996; Van der Hart et al., 2000). For example, it has been reported that 60% of men and 51% of women experience at least one traumatic experience in their lifetimes and 8% and 20%, respectively, develop PTSD (Davidson, 2000). Disproportionate numbers of patients with borderline personality disorder (Herman et al., 1989), dissociative disorders (Draijer and Boon, 1993; Hornstein and Putnam, 1992; Nijenhuis et al., 1998b), eating disorders (Vanderlinden et al., 1993), disorders of extreme stress (Roth et al., 1997), and severe mental illness (Mueser, et al.,

[*] This chapter has previously been published as: Nijenhuis, E.R.S., Van der Hart, O., & Kruger, K. (2002). The psychometric characteristics of the Traumatic Experiences Questionnaire (TEC): First findings among psychiatric outpatients. *Clinical Psychology and Psychotherapy, 9*(3), 200–210.

1998) also report one or more types of childhood traumatization, including emotional neglect, sexual, physical, and emotional abuse.

Systematic assessment of a wide range of potential traumatic experiences is often inherent in trauma research and mandatory in clinical practice (Carlson, 1997). Given limits on time and funding, the conduction of extensive trauma interviews may remain beyond reach in many research studies and beyond routine application in most clinical settings. Administration of retrospective self-report questionnaires can be an acceptable, time-efficient, and cost-effective alternative. Moreover, some patients may be less inhibited to report traumatic experiences in self-report measures than in the context of face-to-face trauma interviews (Carlson, 1997). For practical purposes, it is advisable to assess recalled trauma using self-report instruments as a first step and to subsequently conduct trauma interviews with patients who have high scores and who can emotionally cope with detailed trauma-related items (Carlson, 1997).

The *Traumatic Experiences Checklist*, or TEC (Nijenhuis et al., 1999a) is a self-report questionnaire that was developed in the context of a research study which aimed to assess the correlations among a wide range of reported traumatic experiences, including emotional neglect and abuse, and somatoform, as well as psychological, manifestations of dissociation (Nijenhuis et al., 1998b). Consistent with the wording of the DSM-IV (American Psychiatric Association, 1994) criterion A of posttraumatic stress disorder (PTSD), the self-report measures that were available at the time, for example, the *Trauma Assessment for Adults* (Resnick, 1996); the *Trauma History Questionnaire* (Green, 1996); and the *Traumatic Stress Schedule* (Norris, 1990) do not include items that assess emotional neglect and emotional abuse. Other self-report questionnaires, such as the *Childhood Trauma Questionnaire* (Bernstein et al., 1994) include items that assess emotional neglect and abuse, but do not address traumatic experiences that may happen to adults. Some studies have suggested that adult psychopathology may be related to a pathogenic family structure rather than to a specific trauma such as physical and sexual abuse (Fromuth, 1986; Nash et al., 1993). Thus, the TEC includes items that address emotional neglect, emotional abuse, parentification, and extraordinary family burdens, such as poverty, psychiatric illness, alcoholism, or drug addiction of one or both parents.

The TEC involves questions that assess events that are not necessarily traumatizing to every individual, as is true for any self-report trauma questionnaire. At the same time, experiences that are not traumatic to most individuals can be quite traumatic to others. When the aim is to discover most, if not all, lifetime traumatic experiences of respondents, it is important to use a measure that includes a wide range of potentially traumatizing experiences. Thus, the TEC was developed to do so. It is important to stress that when the expression "reported traumatic experience" or similar expressions are used in the remainder of this chapter, they should be understood as "reported potential traumatic experience."

This study assessed the psychometric characteristics of the TEC among psychiatric outpatients. More specifically, the TEC's internal consistency, test-retest reliability, concurrent validity, and criterion-related validity were studied. Theoretical models (Nijenhuis et al., 2001) as well as several empirical studies (Breslau et al., 1999; Draijer and Boon, 1993; Nijenhuis et al., 1998b) have suggested that the degree of traumatization relates to the severity of posttraumatic stress symptoms, and psychological as well as somatoform manifestations of dissociation. According to the DSM-IV (American Psychiatric Association, 1994) dissociation manifests in disturbances of memory, consciousness, identity, and altered perception of the environment; these phenomena have been subsumed under the generic label of psychological dissociation (Nijenhuis et al., 1996). Somatoform as well as psychological manifestations of dissociation both result from mental processes. Thus, to avoid confusion, Van der Hart et al. (2000) recently proposed relabelling psychological dissociation as psychoform dissociation. We adopt this proposal here.

In several studies positive associations have been found between (reported) trauma and peritraumatic dissociation (i.e., dissociation during and immediately following an emotionally traumatizing event) that was retrospectively as well as prospectively assessed (Marmar et al., 1994, 1998). Numerous studies found a substantial correlation between current psychoform dissociation and recalled – and sometimes partly corroborated – traumatic experiences among patients with dissociative disorders (Draijer and Boon, 1993; Hornstein and Putnam, 1992; Nijenhuis et al., 1998b), PTSD (Bremner et al., 1993), eating disorders (Vanderlinden et al., 1993), and borderline personality disorder (Herman et al., 1989).

An evaluation of the criterion-related validity of a trauma measure should include an assessment of its association with somatoform dissociation. Until recently it has been largely ignored that dissociation also manifests in somatoform phenomena such as anesthesia, analgesia, motor disturbances, and pain (Nijenhuis, 1999, 2000; Sar et al., 2000; Waller et al., 2000; World Health Organization, 1992). However, these somatoform manifestations were acknowledged as major dissociative symptoms in the nineteenth century (Janet, 1893, 1901) and were frequently observed in traumatized World War I soldiers (Van der Hart et al., 2000). Somatoform dissociation, as we have labeled this category of dissocative phenomena (Nijenhuis et al., 1996), was correlated with reported trauma in patients with dissociative disorders (Nijenhuis et al., 1998b), in psychiatric outpatients (Waller et al., 2000), and in gynecology patients with chronic pelvic pain (Nijenhuis et al., 1999c). Moreover, retrospective assessment of peritraumatic somatoform dissociation was associated with severity of recalled childhood physical and sexual abuse in a sample of women who reported these types of trauma (Nijenhuis et al., in press b). Among a wide range of reported traumatizing events, both current and peritraumatic somatoform dissociation were associated most strongly with physical abuse and threat to life from a person (Nijenhuis 1999, 2000; Waller et al., 2000).

Methods

Demographics

Because it was assumed that the relationships among trauma reporting, dissociation, and posttraumatic stress symptoms apply to psychiatric patients generally, a clinical sample was taken from new referrals – patients who were in outpatient treatment as well as patients who were in day treatment – and assessed in a general psychiatric outpatient department. However, only psychiatric patients assessed by the attending clinicians as able to complete trauma and dissociation self-report questionnaires were invited to participate in the study. Thus, very low functioning patients were excluded from entering the study.

Of the 153 total participants, 53 were new referrals and 45 were patients in regular care (they attended once every week or two weeks for one hour of treatment). An additional 27 patients had more intensive treatment on an outpatient basis (at least two hours or more per week). The remaining 28 patients received full-day treatment. The patients came from a number of mental health care institutions in the Netherlands.

The new referrals (35% of the sample) were referrals to a general psychiatric outpatient department. Referrals to this institution involve the spectrum of DSM-IV diagnoses. In 43% of the other cases, the DSM-IV diagnoses of the participants were available. The diagnoses included a broad range of mental disorders (anxiety disorders, phobias, eating disorders, depersonalization disorder, bipolar mood disorder, schizophrenia, and borderline personality disorder).

The sample involved 92 women, 57 men, and 4 participants who did not state their gender. The mean age of the sample ($n = 153$) that completed the TEC at the initial administration was 35.01, $SD = 11.23$, range 18-69. Of the test group (not the retest group, which was smaller), 8.7% had primary education, 56.7% completed intermediate education, and 34.7% had higher education. Single respondents numbered 38.2%, 32.2% were married, 16.1% were co-habitating, 12.8% were divorced, and 0.7% were widowed.

There were no significant differences in the age, gender, educational level, socioeconomic status, mean number of reported traumatic events, and psychoform and somatoform dissociation between the patients who completed the TEC in the test and retest phase of the study and the patients ($n = 39$) who did not complete or return the TEC in the retest phase (see below). Significant differences with respect to any of the TEC trauma composite scores were absent as well.

Instruments

Traumatic Experiences Checklist (TEC; Nijenhuis et al., 1999a). The TEC is a self-report questionnaire about 29 types of potential trauma, including criterion A events of PTSD ("the person experienced, witnessed, or was confronted with an event or events that involved actual or threatened death or serious injury, or a threat to the physical integrity of self or others;" American Psychiatric Association, 1994, p. 427) as well as other potential overwhelming events: loss of significant others; life threat by disease or assault; war experience; emotional neglect, emotional abuse, physical abuse, sexual harassment, and sexual trauma. The TEC total score ranges from 0 to 29. With respect to emotional neglect, emotional abuse, physical abuse, sexual harassment, and sexual abuse, the TEC specifically addresses the setting in which such trauma occurred – i.e., the nuclear family, or family of origin, extended family, or any other setting. It rates the subjective and current degree of traumatic stress associated with the trauma. The questions contain short descriptions that are intended to define the events of concern. All items are preceded by the phrase: "Did this happen to you?" An example of sexual harassment is: "Sexual harassment (acts of a sexual nature that DO NOT involve physical contact) by your parents, brothers, or sisters." A sexual abuse item is: "Sexual abuse (unwanted sexual acts involving physical contact) by your parents, brothers, or sisters."

The format of the TEC allows for calculating trauma area presence scores with respect to emotional trauma (emotional neglect and emotional abuse in various social settings, 6 items), sexual trauma (sexual harassment and sexual abuse in various social settings, 6 items), and bodily threat (physical abuse in various social settings, intentional threat to life from a person, bizarre punishment, intense pain, 6 items). The TEC format also allows for calculating trauma area severity scores using four variables: (a) presence of the event; (b) age at onset, indicating whether trauma had occurred or started in the first six years of life or thereafter; (c) duration of the trauma, indicating whether trauma had lasted shorter or longer than one year; and (d) subjective response, indicating whether the subject felt not traumatized or only slightly traumatized, versus moderately, severely, or extremely traumatized by the event(s). These variables are given a score of 1 if they apply and a score of 0 if they do not apply. The scores are calculated for each setting in which the trauma occurred; that is, in the family of origin, in the extended family, or in other settings. Next, these scores are added up. As to life threat from a person, pain, or bizarre punishment, the TEC does not specifically assess the setting in which the event occurred. The composite scores for life threat from a person, pain, and bizarre punishment are added to the physical abuse composite score for the indicated three settings. Thus, the possible trauma area severity scores range from 0 to 12 for emotional neglect, emotional abuse, physical abuse, sexual harassment, and sexual abuse, and from 0 to 24 for bodily threat. In a previous study involving patients with dissociative and other DSM-IV disorders, these trauma area severity scores proved to be homogeneous constructs (however, physical abuse instead of bodily threat was calculated in this study; Nijenhuis et al., 1998a).

In previous studies the criterion-related validity of the TEC was supported by moderate to strong associations of the TEC total score and trauma

area severity scores, in particular physical and sexual abuse, and current psychoform and somatoform dissociation. These associations were found when
studying psychiatric outpatients with dissociative disorders and other mental disorders (Nijenhuis et al., 1998b), gynecology patients with chronic
pelvic pain (Nijenhuis et al., 1999b), and women who reported childhood
sexual abuse (Nijenhuis et al., in press b).

   Stressful Life Events Screening Questionnaire (SLESQ; Goodman et al.,
1998). The SLESQ was developed as a general traumatic event screening
questionnaire. The SLESQ showed good test-retest reliability (0.89), with
a median kappa of 0.73. The median kappa between the SLESQ items and
an interview two weeks later was 0.64. Thus, the convergent validity of the
SLESQ seemed adequate. As to concurrent validity, the prevalence rates of
the various types of trauma assessed by the SLESQ were similar to the rates
that were assessed in comparable samples.

   The SLESQ and the TEC are similar yet different types of general traumatic experience screening questionnaires. One of the differences is that
the wording of the SLESQ items is more specific than the wording of the
TEC items, which address rather broad categories.

   Somatoform Dissociation Questionnaire (SDQ-20; Nijenhuis et al., 1996,
1998a). The SDQ-20 is a 20-item self-report questionnaire measuring somatoform manifestations of dissociation. The items are strongly scalable on
a unidimensional latent scale and the internal consistency of the instrument
is high (Cronbach's alpha = 0.95). The test-retest reliability is very satisfactory (Sar et al., 2000) and the scores are not dependent on gender or age.
The high intercorrelations with measures of psychoform dissociation support the convergent validity of the SDQ-20 (Nijenhuis et al., 1996, 1998a;
Sar et al., 2000). Higher scores of patients with dissociative disorders compared with patients with other DSM-IV diagnoses demonstrate the scale's
criterion-related validity (Nijenhuis et al., 1999b; Sar et al., 2000). Discriminant validity was supported by the finding that the SDQ-20 scores discriminated among diagnostic groups over and above general psychopathology
(Nijenhuis et al., 1999b). The criterion-related validity was supported by
the finding that the degree of somatoform dissociation in DID and DDNOS
was correlated with reported trauma, in particular childhood physical and
sexual abuse (Nijenhuis et al., 1998b).

   The *Dissociative Experiences Scale* (DES; Bernstein and Putnam, 1986) is
a 28-item self-report questionnaire that evaluates psychoform dissociation.
The scores range from 0 to 100. The DES has adequate test-retest reliability,
good internal consistency, and good clinical validity (Bernstein and Putnam,
1996; Carlson et al., 1993; Frischholz et al., 1992). DES scores of $\geq$ 30 in a
North American sample (Carlson and Putnam, 1993) and $\geq$ 25 in a Dutch
sample (Draijer and Boon, 1993) were found to yield optimal sensitivity
and specificity in screening for dissociative disorders.

   PTSD-self scoring (PTSD-ss; Carlier et al., 1996) is a self-report screening
instrument for DSM-IV posttraumatic stress disorder. The 21 items of the
scale evaluate the severity of re-experiencing, avoidance, and hyperarousal

symptoms. The internal consistency of the three symptom groups was, respectively, $\alpha = 0.88$, $\alpha = 0.88$, and $\alpha = 0.93$. The convergent validity was satisfactory, sensitivity 86%, and specificity 80%.

Procedure

After informed consent, the participants completed the TEC, DES, SLESQ, and SDQ-20, in that order. Counterbalancing was not applied because the indicated order was considered the least stressful for the participants. Most participants ($n = 115$) completed the TEC for the second time after a delay of three to four weeks and the PTSD-ss.

Data Analysis

In order to assess the reliability of the TEC and the TEC trauma area presence and severity scores, Cronbach's α were calculated, as well as the Pearson product moment test-retest correlations. The separate item scores on the TEC test and the retest were compared using kappa. To evaluate the homogeneity of the TEC trauma area presence and severity scores, trauma area total score/constituent item score (point-biserial) correlations were computed. Concurrent validity was assessed by calculating the Pearson product moment correlation between the TEC and SLESQ total scores.

To evaluate the criterion-related validity of the trauma scales, the associations among the TEC, SLESQ, PTSD-ss, DES, and SDQ-20 were calculated using Pearson product moment correlations. Because the distribution of the DES and SDQ-20 were skewed (skewness > 1), logaritimic transformations to base e of these measurements were performed on these two variables.

Statistical analyses were performed with SPSS-PC 9.0 (SPSS PC, 1998).

Results

TEC Reliability

The reliability of the TEC was supported by satisfactory indices of the scale's internal consistency – which provides a lowerbound of reliability – and of the scale's test-retest reliability. Cronbach's α for the first administration of the TEC was 0.86, and 0.90 for the TEC retest. In comparison, Cronbach's α for the SLESQ was 0.66. The test-retest reliability of the TEC total score was $r = 0.91$. The prevalence of the various types of reported trauma assessed by the TEC and comparisons between the test-retest scores for the separate TEC items are shown in Table 1. There was no evidence that repeated inquiry about trauma promoted increased trauma reporting.

Only 9.8% of the sample did not report trauma, and 7.2% reported only one traumatic experience. The mean number of traumas reported was 6 ($SD = 5,11$).

Table 1

Prevalences of Various Trauma Types, and Test-retest Stability for Separate TEC Items

	Reported Trauma Prevalence		
	Test %	Retest %	Kappa*
Parentification	30.7	28.1	.661
Family problems (e.g., parent with alcohol or psychiatric problems, poverty)	38.6	31.6	.650
Divorced parents	21.9	19.3	.866
Own divorce	20.2	18.4	.887
Loss of own child or partner in adulthood	1.8	0.9	.837
Loss of member of family of origin in childhood	11.4	13.2	.663
Severe bodily injury (e.g., loss of limb, burns)	16.7	12.3	.753
Intense pain (from injury, surgery)	30.7	28.1	.744
Threat to life from illness, surgery, accident, torture	20.2	21.1	.812
Deliberate threat to life from another person (e.g., during a crime)	24.6	21.1	.772
Witnessing others undergo trauma	41.2	36.8	.589
War-time experiences	5.3	2.6	.424
Second generation warvictim	10.5	11.4	.775
Emotional neglect by member family of origin	40.4	41.2	.728
Emotional neglect by other family member	18.4	18.4	.532
Emotional neglect by nonfamily members	14.9	8.8	.456
Emotional abuse by member family of origin	29.8	27.2	.825
Emotional abuse by other family member	9.6	8.8	.423
Emotional abuse by nonfamily members	25.4	19.3	.470
Physical abuse by member family of origin	21.1	22.8	.795
Physical abuse by other family member	7.0	7.0	.731
Physical abuse by nonfamily member	18.4	18.4	.591
Bizarre punishment	8.8	11.4	.661
Sexual harassment by member family of origin	12.3	7.9	.759
Sexual harassment by other family member	5.3	7.0	.696
Sexual harassment by nonfamily member	29.8	27.2	.718
Sexual abuse by member family of origin	10.5	10.5	.907
Sexual abuse by other family member	2.6	1.8	.387
Sexual abuse by nonfamily member	20.2	21.2	.812

*All Kappa's statistically significant at approximate sig. <.0001

Reported Trauma Among Men and Women

As shown in Table 2, women generally reported more trauma than men. With respect to the various trauma areas assessed by the TEC, reported emotional neglect (35.1% vs. 55.4%), sexual harassment (14% vs. 48.9%), and sexual abuse (3.5% vs. 37%) were more prominent among women. No

Table 2
Reported Trauma on the TEC and Gender

	Z^*	p
Parentification	−1.630	n.s.
Family problems	−1.593	n.s.
Loss of a family member in childhood	−0.817	n.s.
Loss of own child or partner in adulthood	−0.863	n.s.
Severe bodily injury	−0.249	n.s.
Divorced parents	−0.874	n.s.
Own divorce	−0.638	n.s.
Threat to life from illness, surgery, accident, torture	−0.917	n.s.
Deliberate threat to life from another person, e.g., during crime	−1.553	n.s.
Intense pain from illness, medical treatment, etc.	−1.219	n.s.
War experience	−0.045	n.s.
Second generation warvictim	−0.059	n.s.
Witnessing others undergo trauma	−0.888	n.s.
Emotional neglect by member family of origin	−1.861	n.s
Emotional neglect by other family member	−2.616	.009
Emotional neglect by nonfamily member	−1.272	n.s.
Emotional abuse by member family of origin	−1.630	n.s
Emotional abuse by other family member	−1.139	n.s.
Emotional abuse by nonfamily member	−0.603	n.s.
Physical abuse by member family of origin	−1.820	n.s.
Physical abuse by other family member	−1.590	n.s.
Physical abuse by nonfamily member	−1.243	n.s.
Bizarre punishment	−0.980	n.s.
Sexual harassment by member family of origin	−3.147	.002
Sexual harassment by other family member	−1.325	n.s.
Sexual harassment by nonfamily member	−3.372	.001
Sexual abuse by member family of origin	−3.195	.001
Sexual abuse by other family member	−1.113	n.s.
Sexual abuse by nonfamily member	−3.848	<.0001
Total scale score, initial administration	−2.049	.04
Total scale score, repeated administration	−2.330	.02

*Mann Whitney U-tests; statistically significant differences indicate higher scores for women

gender differences were observed as to reported emotional abuse, physical abuse, and threat to life from a person.

TEC Concurrent Validity

The correlation between the TEC and SLESQ total scores was strong, $r = 0.77 (p < 0.0001)$, which suggests that both instruments assess a highly

Table 3

Pearson Product-moment Correlations among Reported Trauma, Symptoms of Posttraumatic Stress, Psychoform Dissociation, and Somatoform Dissociation

	PTSS-ss r^*	DES r^*	SDQ-20 r^*
TEC test	.53	.43	.57
TEC retest	.59	.43	.66
SLESQ total score	.47	.36	.46
DES	.49		
SDQ-20	.47	.63	

*All p <.0001

similar construct. The summated item scores of the TEC and the SLESQ that assess physical abuse, deliberate threat to life from a person, and sexual trauma were also correlated, i.e., $r = 0.54$, and $r = 0.78$, respectively (both $p < 0.0001$).

TEC Criterion-Related Validity

As Table 3 indicates, the TEC total score was moderately to strongly correlated with the PTSD-ss, DES, and, in particular, with SDQ-20 scores. The SLESQ total score was also associated with these measures.

Consistent with the results of various previous studies, psychoform and somatoform dissociation were strongly intercorrelated (Table 3). Both measures of dissociation were associated with posttraumatic stress symptoms as well. Apart from reporting more trauma, women also had higher PTSD-ss, DES, and SDQ-20 scores than men (Table 4).

TEC Trauma Area Presence Scores

Cronbach's α for the presence of emotional trauma was 0.78, 0.65 for sexual trauma, and 0.77 for bodily threat. All cluster score/constituent item score correlations were significant and ranged from $r = 0.60$ to $r = 0.77$

Table 4

Posttraumatic Stress-Symptoms and Dissociation in Men and Women

	men M	SD	women M	SD	t-test t	df	p
DES	11.1	10.4	15.6	13.2	−2.164	145	.032
SDQ-20	24.0	4.9	26.4	8.1	−2.240	141.9	.027
PTSD-ss	32.1	9.8	39.3	10.4	−3.429	99	<.001

for emotional trauma; from $r = 0.57$ to $r = 0.72$ for bodily threat from a person/intense pain; and from $r = 0.31$ to $r = 0.75$ for sexual trauma (all $p < 0.0001$). The correlations among the trauma area presence composites ranged from $r = 0.56$ (bodily threat from a person/intense pain vs. sexual trauma) to $r = 0.64$ (bodily threat from a person/intense pain vs. emotional trauma). The strength of these correlations suggests that the indicated trauma area scores were related but of different constructs.

The test-retest for the trauma area presence scores were as follows: emotional trauma, $r = 0.80$; bodily threat/intense pain, $r = 0.86$; sexual trauma, $r = 0.88$ (all $p < 0.0001$).

Trauma Area Severity Scores

In order to study whether the TEC trauma area severity scores assess homogeneous constructs, severity score/constituent item scores (i.e., presence, age at onset of traumatization, duration, subjectively rated impact) (point biserial) correlation coefficients were calculated. All correlations were significant ($p < 0.0001$), and ranged from 0.51 (subjectively rated impact of sexual abuse by a member of the extended family) to 0.99 (duration of bizarre punishment).

The test-retest reliability for the trauma area severity scores were for emotional trauma, $r = 0.83$; for bodily threat from a person/intense pain, $r = 0.88$; and for sexual trauma, $r = 0.93$ (all $p < 0.0001$). The trauma area severity scores were moderately to strongly correlated (range $r = 0.33$, $p = 0.001$, for emotional trauma vs. sexual trauma, to $r = 0.58$, $p < 0.0001$, for sexual trauma vs. bodily threat from a person/intense pain).

As to criterion-related validity, the correlations of the trauma area severity scores with psychoform dissociation, somatoform dissociation, and post-traumatic stress symptoms ranged from $r = 0.25$ (psychoform dissociation vs. bodily threat from a person/intense pain, $p = 0.007$) to $r = 0.48$ (somatoform dissociation vs. bodily threat from a person/intense pain, $p < 0.0001$).

Deletion of the retrospective estimations of impact of trauma from the TEC trauma area severity scores did not alter the results with respect to reliability and criterion-related validity.

Discussion

The results of the current preliminary study suggest that the psychometric characteristics of the TEC are good. The internal consistency of the TEC items was satisfactory, both for the test and the retest. This is particularly true because the TEC assesses a wide range of potentially traumatic experiences, and the internal consistency of the SLESQ, which assesses a smaller range of potentially traumatic experiences, was more moderate. The test-retest reliability of the TEC total score and of the separate items scores were satisfactory as well.

The internal consistency, the cluster score/constituent item score correlations, and the test-retest reliability of the trauma area presence scores with respect to emotional neglect, emotional abuse, bodily threat from a person/intense pain, and sexual trauma were acceptable to good. The internal consistency, cluster score/constituent item score correlations, and test-retest reliability of the trauma area severity scores were satisfactory.

The current study suggests that the convergent and criterion-related validity of the TEC are good to excellent. The convergent validity of the TEC was high, as demonstrated by the strong correlation with the SLESQ. The intercorrelations between the trauma area scores on the TEC and SLESQ that involved reported sexual trauma and physical abuse were also quite strong. The criterion-related validity of the TEC total score and trauma area severity scores were supported by the hypothesized associations with symptoms of posttraumatic stress symptoms, psychoform dissociation, and somatoform dissociation.

Some authors have suggested that repeated inquiry about traumatic experiences may inflate trauma reporting (Brown et al., 1998). However, the repeated administration of the TEC yielded quite similar proportions of trauma reporting. This finding pertained to the reporting of all types of trauma.

Compared with men, women reported more sexual harassment and sexual abuse. Women also reported more emotional neglect. These higher levels of trauma reporting coincided with higher levels of posttraumatic stress symptoms, psychoform dissociation, and somatoform dissociation.

A limitation of the present study is that the external validity of the reported traumatic experiences on the TEC and SLESQ was not assessed. The documented correlation of reported traumatic experiences to actual trauma and subsequent assessment of under- and overreporting of trauma on the TEC are important future goals. However, no matter how meticulously performed, retrospective assessment of trauma will remain open to a degree of imprecision. This imperfection is due to the nature of encoding, storage, and retrieval of trauma memories, as well as psychological mechanisms that affect trauma reporting such as denial, dissociation, fantasy proneness, suggestion, social influence (Spinhoven et al. 1999), and biological factors that affect memory of traumatic experiences (McGaugh, 1990; Perry, 1999; Perry et al., 1995).

To assess the convergent validity, the TEC was correlated with the SLESQ. This decision was based on the consideration that the SLESQ also evaluates a rather broad range of potentially traumatic experiences of children and adults. However, we were unable to find a trauma questionnaire that also evaluates emotional neglect and abuse in various social settings. Both instruments are designed to serve as relatively brief questionnaires. In order to avoid an undue, long list of items, the TEC evaluates many types of trauma by one item only. Further study on to what extent this poses constraints on the reliability is needed, especially with regard to the wording of items that may be somewhat ambiguous or open to the judgment of the patients (e.g., parentification: "Having to look after your parents and/or brothers and sisters when you were a child"). Future study should also compare trauma reporting on the TEC with trauma reported during a structured trauma interview, assess TEC scores among patients with selected psychiatric disorders, and also address how the TEC performs in samples drawn from the general population.

Another limitation of the present study pertains to the small sample size relative to the number of TEC items. To evaluate the criterion-related validity of the TEC more extensively, future studies should assess relationships among the TEC and a wider range of trauma-related psychopathology, such as general psychopathology, depression, self-mutilation, and substance abuse.

In sum, current preliminary findings suggest that the TEC is a reliable and valid self-report instrument that can be used in clinical practice and research. In clinical practice systematic assessment of the patient's trauma history is a relatively neglected area. Highly vulnerable individuals should not be exposed to self-report trauma questionnaires or untimely trauma interviews. However, assessment of trauma history, even if stressful, is appreciated by most patients and helpful to clinicians (Walker et al., 1997).

References

American Psychiatric Association (1994). *Diagnostic and Statistical Manual of Mental Disorders,* 4th ed. (DSM-IV). Washington DC: American Psychiatric Association.

Bernstein, D.P., Fink, L., Handelsman, L., Foote, J., Lovejoy, M., Wenzel, K., Sarapeto, E., & Ruggiero, J. (1994). Initial reliability and validity of a new retrospective measure of child abuse and neglect. *American Journal of Psychiatry, 151,* 1132-1136.

Bernstein, E., & Putnam, F.W. (1986). Development, reliability, and validity of a dissociation scale. *Journal of Nervous Mental Disease, 102,* 280-286.

Bremner, J.D., Steinberg, M., Southwick, S.M., Johnson, D.R., & Charney, D.S. (1993). Use of the Structured Clinical Interview for DSM-IV Dissociative Disorders for systematic assessment of dissociative symptoms in posttraumatic stress disorder. *American Journal of Psychiatry, 150,* 1011-1014.

Breslau, N., Chilcoat, H.D., Kessler, R.C., & Davis, G.C. (1999). Previous exposure to trauma and PTSD effects of subsequent trauma: Results from the Detroit area survey of trauma. *American Journal of Psychiatry, 156,* 902-907.

Brown, D., Scheflin, A.W., & Hammond, D.C. (1998). *Memory, Trauma Treatment, and the Law.* New York: W. W. Norton & Company.

Carlier IV, E., Van Uchelen, J.J., Lamberts, R.D., & Gersons, B.P.R. (1996). Een korte screeningstest voor de diagnose posttraumatische stress-stoornis. *Tijdschrift voor Psychiatrie, 8,* 624-629.

Carlson, E.B. (1997). *Trauma Assessments: A Clinician's Guide.* New York: Guilford.

Carlson, E.B., & Putnam, F.W. (1993). An update on the Dissociative Experiences Scale. *Dissociation, 6,* 16-27.

Carlson, E.B., Putnam, F.W., Ross, C.A., Torem, M., Coons, P., Dill, D.L., Loewenstein, R.J., & Braun, B.G. (1993). Validity of the Dissociative Experiences Scale in screening for multiple personality disorder: A multicenter study. *American Journal of Psychiatry, 150,* 1030-1036.

Darves-Bornoz, J-M. (1997). Rape-related psychotraumatic syndromes. *European Journal of Obstetrics and Gynecology, 71*, 59-65.

Darves-Bornoz, J-M., Lepine, J-P., Choquet, M., Berger, C., Degiovanni, A., & Gaillard, P. (1998). Predictive factors of chronic post-traumatic stress disorder in rape victims. *European Psychiatry, 13*, 281-287.

Davidson, J.R.T. (2000). Trauma: The impact of post-traumatic stress disorder. *Journal of Psychopharmacology, 14*, Supplement, S5-S12.

Draijer, N., & Boon, S. (1993). Trauma, dissociation, and dissociative disorders. In Boon, S., Draijer, N. (eds.). *Multiple personality disorder in the Netherlands: A study on reliability and validity of the diagnosis.* Amsterdam/Lisse: Swets and Zeitlinger: 177-193.

Felitti, V.J., Anda, R.F., Nordenberg, D., Williamson, D.F., Spitz, A.M., Edwards, V., Koss, M.P., & Marks, J.S. (1998). Relationship of childhood abuse and household dysfunction to many of the leading causes of death in adults: The adverse childhood experiences study (ACE) study. *American Journal of Preventive Medicine, 14*, 245-258.

Frischholz, E.J., Braun, B.G., Sachs, R.G., Schwartz, D.R., Lewis, J., Shaeffer, D., Westergaard, C., & Pasquotto, J. (1992). Construct validity of the dissociative experiences scale: II. Its relationship to hypnotizability. *American Journal of Clinical Hypnosis, 35*, 145-152.

Fromuth, M.E. (1986). The relationship of childhood sexual abuse with later psychological and sexual adjustment in a sample of college women. *Child Abuse and Neglect, 10*, 5-15.

Goodman, L.A., Corcoran, C., Turner, K., Yuan, N., & Green, B. (1998). Assessing traumatic event exposure: General issues and preliminary findings for the Stressful Life Events Screening Questionnaire. *Journal of Traumatic Stress, 11*, 521-542.

Green, B.L. (1996). Trauma History Questionnaire. In *Measurement of stress, trauma, and adaptation,* Stamm, B.H. (ed.) Lutherville, MD: Sidran, 366-369.

Herman, J.L., Perry, J.C., & Van der Kolk, B.A. (1989). Childhood trauma in borderline personality disorder. *American Journal of Psychiatry, 146*, 490-495.

Hornstein, N.L., & Putnam, F.W. (1992). Clinical phenomenology of child and adolescent dissociative disorders. *Journal of the American Academy of Child and Adolescent Psychiatry, 31*, 1077-1085.

Janet, P. (1893). *L' Etat mental des hystériques: Les stigmates mentaux.* Paris: Rueff & Cie.

Janet, P. (1977). *The mental state of hystericals.* Washington DC: University Publications of America, 1977.

Macfie, J., Cichetti, D., & Toth, S.L. (2001). The development of dissociation in maltreated preschool-aged children. *Development and Psychopathology, 13*, 233-254.

Marmar, C.R., Weiss, D.S., Schlenger, W.E., Fairbank, J.A., Jordan, K., Kulka, R.A., & Hough, R.L. (1994). Peritraumatic dissociation and posttraumatic stress in male Vietnam theater veterans. *American Journal of Psychiatry, 151*, 902-907.

Marmar, C.R., Weiss, D.S., & Metzler, T.J. (1998). Peritraumatic dissociation and posttraumatic stress disorder. In *Trauma, memory, and dissociation,* Bremner, J.D., Marmar, C.R. (eds.) Washington DC: American Psychiatric Press, 229-252.

McGaugh, J.L. (1990). Significance and remembrance: The role of neuromodulatory systems. *Psychological Science, 1*, 15-25.

Mueser, K.T., Goodman, L.B., Trumbetta, S.L., Rosenberg, S.D., Osher, F., Vidaver, R., Auciello, P., & Foy, D.W. (1998). Trauma and posttraumatic stress disorder in severe mental illness. *Journal of Consulting and Clinical Psychology, 66*, 493-499.

Nash, M.R., Hulsey, T.L., Sexton, M.C., Harralson, T.L., & Lambert, W. (1993). Long-term sequelae of childhood sexual abuse: Perceived family environment, psychopathology, and dissociation. *Journal of Consulting and Clinical Psychology, 61,* 276-283.

Nijenhuis, E.R.S. (1999). *Somatoform dissociation: Phenomena, measurement, and theoretical issues.* Assen, the Netherlands: Van Gorcum.

Nijenhuis, E.R.S. (2000). Somatoform dissociation: Major symptoms of dissociative disorders. *Journal of Trauma and Dissociation, 1*(4), 7-32.

Nijenhuis, E.R.S., Spinhoven, P., Van Dyck, R., Van der Hart, O., & Vanderlinden, J. (1996). The development and psychometric characteristics of the Somatoform Dissociation Questionnaire (SDQ-20). *Journal of Nervous and Mental Disease, 184,* 688-694.

Nijenhuis, E.R.S., Spinhoven, P., Van Dyck, R., Van der Hart, O., & Vanderlinden, J. (1998). Psychometric characteristics of the Somatoform Dissociation Questionnaire: A replication study. *Psychotherapy and Psychosomatics, 67,* 17-23. (a)

Nijenhuis, E.R.S., Spinhoven, P., Van Dyck, R., Van der Hart, O., & Vanderlinden, J. (1998). Degree of somatoform and psychological dissociation in dissociative disorder is correlated with reported trauma. *Journal of Traumatic Stress, 11,* 711-730. (b)

Nijenhuis, E.R.S., Van der Hart, O., & Steele, K. (2004). Strukturelle Dissoziation der Persönlichkeitsstruktur, traumatischer Ursprung, phobische Residuen. In: L. Reddemann, A. Hofmann, & U. Gast (eds.), *Psychotherapie der dissoziativen Störungen* (pp. 47-69). Stuttgart: Thieme.

Nijenhuis, E.R.S., Van der Hart, O., & Vanderlinden, J. (1999). The Traumatic Experiences Checklist (TEC). In *Somatoform dissociation: Phenomena, measurement, and theoretical issues,* Nijenhuis, E.R.S. (ed.). Assen, the Netherlands: Van Gorcum. (a) Included as Appendix 3, pp. 223–229 in this book.

Nijenhuis, E.R.S., Van Dyck, R., Spinhoven, P., Van der Hart, O., Chatrou, M., Vanderlinden, J., & Moene, F. (1999). Somatoform dissociation discriminates among diagnostic categories over and above general psychopathology. *Australian and New Zealand Journal of Psychiatry, 33,* 512-520. (b)

Nijenhuis, E.R.S., Van Dyck, R., Ter Kuile, M., Mourits, M., Spinhoven, P., & Van der Hart, O. (1999). Evidence for associations between somatoform dissociation, psychological dissociation, and reported trauma in chronic pelvic pain patients. In *Somatoform dissociation: Phenomena, measurement, and theoretical issues,* Nijenhuis, E.R.S. (ed.). Assen, the Netherlands: Van Gorcum: 146-160. (c)

Nijenhuis, E.R.S., Van Engen, A., Kusters, I., & Van der Hart, O. (2001). Peritraumatic somatoform and psychological dissociation in relation to recall of childhood sexual abuse. *Journal of Trauma and Dissociation, 2*(3), 49-68. (b) Included as Chapter XII in this book.

Norris, F.H. (1990). Screening for traumatic stress: A scale of use in the general population. *Journal of Applied Social Psychology, 20,* 1704-1718.

Ogawa, J.R., Sroufe, L.A., Weinfield, N.S., Carlson, E.A., Egeland, B. (1997). Development and the fragmented self: A longitudinal study of dissociative symptomatology in a normative sample. *Development and Psychopathology, 9,* 855-879.

Perry, B.D. (1999). The memory of states: How the brain stores and retrieves traumatic experience. In J. Goodwin, & R. Attias (eds.) *Splintered reflections: Images of the body in trauma treatment* (pp. 9-38). New York: Basic Books.

Perry, B.D., Pollard, R.A., Blakely, T.L., Baker, W.L., & Vigilante, D. (1995). Childhood trauma, the neurobiology of adaptation, and "use dependent" development of the brain: How "states" become "traits". *Infant Mental Health Journal, 16,* 271-291.

Resnick, H. (1996). Psychometric review of the Trauma Assessment for Adults (TAA). In B.H. Stamm (ed.) *Measurement of stress, trauma, and adaptation,* (pp. 362-365). Lutherville, MD: Sidran.

Roth, S., Newman, E., Pelcovitz, D., Van der Kolk, B., & Mandel, F.S. (1997). Complex PTSD in victims exposed to sexual and physical abuse: results from the DSM-IV Field Trial for Posttraumatic Stress Disorder. *Journal of Traumatic Stress, 10,* 539-555.

Sar, V., Kundakci, T., Kiziltan, E., Bahadir, B., & Aydiner, O. (1998). Reliability and validity of the Turkish version of the Somatoform Dissociation Questionnaire (SDQ-20). Proceeding of the International Society of Dissociation 15th International Fall Conference. Seattle, November 14-17.

Sar, V., Kundakci, T., Kiziltan, E., Bakim, B., & Bozkurt, O. (2000). Differentiating dissociative disorders from other diagnostic groups through somatoform dissociation in Turkey. *Journal of Trauma and Dissociation, 1*(4), 67-80.

Shalev, A.Y., Freedman, S., Peri, T., Brandes, D., & Sahar, T. (1977). Predicting PTSD in trauma survivors: Prospective evaluation and self-report and clinicial-administrated instruments. *British Journal of Psychiatry, 170,* 558-564.

Shalev, A.Y., Peri, T., Canetti, L., & Schreiber, S. (1996). Predictors of PTSD in injured trauma survivors: a prospective study. *American Journal of Psychiatry, 153,* 219-225.

Spinhoven, P., Nijenhuis, E.R.S., & Van Dyck, R. (1999). Can experimental memory research adequately explain memory for trauma? *Psychotherapy, 36,* 257-267.

SPSS PC: SPSS Inc. (1998). *SPSS for Windows Release 9.0.* Chicago: SPSS Inc.

Van der Hart, O., Van Dijke, A., Van Son, M.J.M., & Steele, K. (2000). Somatoform dissociation in traumatized World War I combat soldiers: A neglected clinical heritage. *Journal of Trauma and Dissociation, 1*(4), 33-66.

Van der Kolk, B.A., McFarlane, A.C., & Weisaeth, L. (1996). *Traumatic stress: The effects of overwhelming experience on mind, body, and society.* New York: Guilford.

Vanderlinden, J., Vandereycken, W., Van Dyck, R., & Vertommen, H. (1993). Dissociative experiences and trauma in eating disorders. *International Journal of Eating Disorders, 13,* 187-193.

Walker, E.A., Newman, E., Koss, M., & Bernstein, D. (1997). Does the study of victimization revictimize the victims? *Psychiatry and Primary Care, 19,* 403-410.

Waller, G., Hamilton, K., Elliott, P., Lewendon, J., Stopa, L., Waters, A., Kennedy, F., Chalkley, J.F., Lee, G., Pearson, D., Kennerley, H., Hargreaves, I., & Bashford, V. (2000). Somatoform dissociation, psychological dissociation and specific forms of trauma. *Journal of Trauma and Dissociation, 1*(4), 81-98.

World Health Organization, Division of Mental Health, (1992). *The ICD-10 Classification of mental and behavioral disorders: Clinical descriptions and diagnostic guidelines.* Geneva, Switzerland: World Health Organization.

XIV
Summary, Discussion, and Future Directions

> *"Integration is not a function of the self,*
> *integration is what the self is."*
> Loevinger, 1976, as paraphrased by Ogawa, 1997

As was described in the introductory chapter, according to 19th century French psychiatry and contemporary clinical observations, dissociation pertains to both psychological and somatoform components of experience, reactions, and functions. Because systematic research of the somatoform manifestations of dissociation was lacking, we aimed at studying what we proposed to call somatoform dissociation. Part I focused on the measurement of the construct and the prevalence of somatoform dissociation in various diagnostic categories; Part II explored relationships between somatoform dissociation, trauma, and defense.

Part I

The Somatoform Dissociation Questionnaire

In Chapter II we presented a Janetian view on the major symptoms of hysteria, the 19th century category of psychiatric disorders which prominently included the current DSM-IV (American Psychiatric Association, 1994), as well as ICD-10 (World Health Organization, 1992) dissociative disorders. Maintaining that psyche and soma are inseparable, Janet refrained from distinguishing between psychological and somatoform dissociative symptoms. Although we subscribe to this position, we also insisted that making a phenomenological distinction among these various symptoms can be clarifying and may highlight the largely forgotten, or ignored, clinical observation that dissociation also pertains to the body.

According to Janet, hysteria is essentially characterized by mental stigmata and mental accidents. In our view, all these stigmata involve losses, and thus represent negative dissociative symptoms: loss of knowledge, sensation, perception, affect, mobility, and control over ideas. The accidents are intrusions, and thus represent positive dissociative symptoms. They reflect manifestations of lost personal experiences, that is, dissociated knowledge, sensations, affects, and motor responses, (control over) other functions that intrude into consciousness from time to time. With severe dissociation, intrusions may even take the form of complete alterations of (dissociative identity) state. These clinical observations indicate that negative and positive dissociative symptoms are highly intertwined phenomena. A case presentation illustrated that according to contemporary clinical observation, somatoform dissociative symptoms that characterize 19th century hysterical patients also manifest in current patients with dissociative disorders. The case example also indicated the clinically observed connectivity between negative and positive dissociative symptoms.

In order to study somatoform dissociation more systematically, there was a need for an instrument assessing the construct. The development of a somatoform dissociation self-report questionnaire constituted the core of Part I. As described in Chapter II, patients with dissociative disorders and with other DSM-IV (APA, 1994) psychiatric diagnoses completed a list of 75 items that according to clinical experience and expert judgement could reflect instances of somatoform dissociation. Separate logistic analyses and determination of discriminant indices per item revealed 20 items that best discriminated between cases and non-cases. Mokken analysis showed that these items are strongly scalable on a unidimensional latent scale interpreted to measure somatoform dissociation. Reliability of the scale was high. Construct validity was supported by high intercorrelations with the Dissociation Questionnaire (DIS-Q; Vanderlinden, Van Dyck, Vandereycken, Vertommen, & Verkes, 1993), which measures psychological dissociation, and by higher SDQ-20 scores of patients with dissociative identity disorder (DID) compared to patients with dissociative disorder not otherwise specified (DDNOS) or depersonalization disorder. These results demonstrated that the Somatoform Dissociation Questionnaire (SDQ-20) is a scale of good psychometric quality which measures somatoform dissociation. The symptoms pertain to negative and positive dissociative phenomena which were also characteristic of 19th century patients with hysteria.

If Janet was right that somatoform dissociative symptoms, such as anesthesia and motor disturbances, belong to the major symptoms of hysteria (dissociative disorders), then it should be possible to construct a brief somatoform dissociation screening instrument for this category of disorders. The development of the SDQ as a screening device for DSM-IV dissociative disorders was described in Chapter IV. Entering the SDQ-20 items in a stepwise forward logistic analysis, five items were detected that, as a group, provided optimal discrimination between patients with dissociative disorders and other psychiatric diagnoses. At an estimated prevalence rate of 10% for dissociative disorders among psychiatric patients sensitivity of this 5-item SDQ-5 would be 94%, specificity 96%, positive predictive value 72%, and negative predictive value 99%. Cross-validation in an independent sample ($n = 33/42$) largely corroborated the first findings. It was concluded that the SDQ-5 could serve as a brief screening instrument for dissociative disorders. Its items pertain to visual and kinesthetic anesthesia, analgesia, motor inhibitions, and pelvic pain: four negative symptoms and one positive symptom.

Calculating the positive predictive prevalence of the SDQ-5 among both independent samples of psychiatric outpatients, we assumed that this prevalence rate would be 10%. Using the SCID-D, in the only study to date of the prevalence of dissociative disorders among consecutive psychiatric outpatients, a prevalence rate of 13.3% was found: 2.5% had DID, 9.6% DDNOS, and 1.4% dissociative amnesia(Şar et al., 1999). Estimations of the prevalence of dissociative disorders among psychiatric inpatients across studies have varied from about 8% to 17%. Using the Dissociative Disorders Interview Schedule (DDIS; Ross, Miller, Reagor, Bjornson, Fraser, & Anderson, 1990) as the "gold standard," Horen, Leichner, and Lawson (1995) found that DSM-IV dissociative disorders were present in 17% of an adult psychiatric inpatient sample. Dissociative disorder diagnoses were applied when the subjects had one of the DSM-IV dissociative disorders as assessed with the DDIS (Ross et al., 1990), as well as the SCID-D (Steinberg, 1993; Steinberg, Cichetti, Buchanan, Hall, & Rounsaville, 1993). Using the DDIS, Saxe et al. (1993) found that 15% of their sample had a DSM-IV dissociative disorder. The sample consisted of 110 patients consecutively admitted to a state hospital. In these three studies, the structured interviews were administered to all subjects who scored over 25 on the DES. Studying Dutch psychiatric inpatients, Friedl & Draijer (2000) recently reported that 8% of the sample had a DSM-IV dissociative disorder.

There are few data on the prevalence of dissociative disorders among psychiatric outpatients. Because the prevalence of dissociative disorders among psychiatric outpatients may be lower than the prevalence among psychiatric inpatients, the predictive values of the SDQ-5 were reanalysed, this time applying a conservative estimated prevalence rate of 5%. The positive predictive values of the SDQ-5 corrected for this prevalence rate were 55% (sample 1), and 26% (sample 2).

Chapter V involved a study that aimed to replicate the findings of both previous studies. To that end, an independent sample of patients with dissociative disorders and consecutive psychiatric outpatients with other DSM-IV diagnoses completed the SDQ-20 and SDQ-5, as well as the DIS-Q, which evaluates the severity of psychological dissociation. Mokken scale analysis showed that the items of the SDQ-20 are strongly scalable on a latent unidimensional scale, internal consistency was high, and the SDQ-20 convergent validity was supported by high intercorrelations with the DIS-Q. Dissociative patients obtained significantly higher scores than comparison patients, and patients with DID scored significantly higher compared to patients with DDNOS. These results confirmed the concurrent and criterion-related validity of the SDQ-20.

Sensitivity (93%) and specificity (98%) of the SDQ-5 were very satisfactory, as were positive predictive value (84%) and negative predictive value (99%) at an estimated prevalence rate of dissociative disorders 10% among psychiatric patients. Reanalyzing the data using a prevalence rate of 5%, the positive predictive value was 71%. Averaged over the two samples described in Chapter IV and the sample presented in Chapter V, the positive predictive value of the SDQ-5 at an estimated prevalence rate of 5% was 51%. This figure suggests that one in two subjects with an SDQ-5 score of$\geq$ 8 is likely to have a DSM-IV dissociative disorder.

While the SDQ-5 did well in the screening for dissociative disorders, it seems possible that combining the 5 items of the SDQ-5 with the 8 items of the

DES-T (Waller, Putnam, & Carlson, 1997), or the — yet to be selected — best discriminating items of the DIS-Q (Vanderlinden et al., 1993), would yield even better results. This is an empirical question which deserves study.

In conclusion, all results of the study which were presented in Chapter V replicated the first findings (Chapter III and IV), and therefore corroborated the conclusion that the SDQ-20 and SDQ-5 are instruments of sound psychometric quality, and that somatoform dissociative phenomena are core symptoms of dissociative disorders.

Somatoform Dissociation in Various Diagnostic Categories and Among Various Cultures

Having developed the SDQ, we could evaluate the severity of somatoform dissociation in various diagnostic groups. This work was the subject of Chapter VI. As it was possible that the SDQ-20 measures general psychopathology rather than somatoform dissociation, a next goal was to test the hypothesis that somatoform dissociation would differentiate between specific diagnostic categories over and above general psychopathology. To that end DSM-IV cases of dissociative disorders, somatoform disorders, eating disorders, bipolar mood disorder, and a group of consecutive psychiatric outpatients with other psychiatric disorders, which mainly included anxiety disorders, depression, and adjustment disorder, completed three self-report questionnaires. In addition to the SDQ-20, these instruments involved the Dissociative Experiences Scale (DES; Bernstein & Putnam, 1986), which evaluates psychological manifestations of dissociation, and the SCL-90-R (Derogatis, 1977), which measures general psychopathology.

The SDQ-20 significantly differentiated between diagnostic groups in the hypothesized order of increasing somatoform dissociation, both before and after statistically controlling for general psychopathology: somatoform dissociation was extreme in DID, high in DDNOS, and increased in somatoform disorders, as well as in a subgroup of patients with eating disorders. In contrast with somatoform dissociation, psychological dissociation did not discriminate between bipolar mood disorder and somatoform disorders. These results revealed that somatoform dissociation is a unique construct which discriminates among diagnostic categories.

Our consistent finding that somatoform dissociation is extremely characteristic of DSM-IV dissociative disorders, in particular DID (see Chapters III, V, and VI), has recently been largely corroborated by findings in some other countries and cultures. In the USA, Chapperon (personal communication, September 1996) found high somatoform dissociation ($M = 50.7$, $SD = 10.7$) among DID patients ($n = 11$), and Dell (1997a) reported that DID patients had significantly higher scores than patients with DDNOS, eating disorders, or pain disorder.

Yar, Kundakçi, Kiziltan, Bakim, and Aydmer (1998) translated the SDQ-20 into Turkish. Sar et al. (2000) studied the psychometric characteristics of this version. The reliability of this version of the SDQ-20 was excellent. Including 299 subjects (175 nonclinical subjects and 124 psychiatric patients, including dissociative disorder patients), Cronbach's alpha was 0.94 with item-total score correlations reaching values between 0.50 and 0.78. The test-retest reliability was calculated using Pearson correlations from the scale scores of 35 subjects, including 9 dissociative disorder cases, who completed the scale on two occasions separated by an average interval of 33.2 days ($SD = 14$, range of total scale scores 21-76). The test-retest reliability was $r = 0.95$ for the total score ($p < .0001$), and the test-retest correlations for the individual variables varied between $r = 0.63$ and $r = 0.93$ with a significance of at least $p < .0001$, apart from one item which reached a correlation of $r = 0.37 (p < .05)$.

Among the Turkish sample, the SDQ-5 did somewhat less well as a screening instrument for dissociative disorders than the SDQ-20. The sensitivity of the SDQ-5 at a cutoff value of 9 was extremely good (97%), but the specificity was 85%, yielding a positive predictive value of 42% corrected for prevalence of dissociative disorders estimated at 10%. Using the SDQ-20 at a cutoff value of 40, the sensitivity was 93%, and the specificity 95%, which gave a positive predictive value of 67%.

Studying various diagnostic categories, Sar et al. (2000) obtained results which are remarkably similar to ours (see in particular Chapter VI and VII): somatoform dissociation was extreme in DSM-IV dissociative disorders($M = 58.1, SD = 17.0, n = 30$), quite modest in anxiety disorder($M = 26.8, SD = 6.4, n = 25$), major depression ($M = 28.7, SD = 8.3, n = 23$), and schizophrenia($M = 27.1, SD = 9.5, n = 23$), and low in bipolar mood disorder ($M = 22.7, SD = 3.5, n = 22$). Yar et al. (1998) additionally studied somatoform dissociation among a sample of the general Turkish population, and found a mean score of $27.4 (SD = 8.2, n = 175)$.

Also consistent with our data, both Dell (1997a) and Sar et al. (2000) found strong intercorrelations of SDQ-20 and DES scores ($r = .61$ and $r = .79$ respectively), which results closely match ours. Jointly, the Dutch, Flemish, North American and Turkish data strongly suggest that somatoform dissociation is highly characteristic of dissociative disorders, and that somatoform and psychological dissociation are closely related constructs. These data also indicate that the severity of somatoform dissociation among dissociative disorder patients from these cultures is largely comparable.

The findings of our studies better fit the ICD-10 (WHO, 1992), which includes dissociative disorders of movement and sensation, than the DSM-IV, which classificatory system restricts dissociation to its psychological manifestations and regards the somatoform manifestations of dissociation as "conversion" symptoms. However, the SDQ-5 is as effective as the DES in the screening for DSM-IV dissociative disorders. Maintaining that the items of the SDQ involve conversion implies saying that complex dissociative disorders essentially involve conversion, which is nonsensical.

Other recent studies also suggest that somatoform dissociation is strongly correlated with psychological dissociation, and that somatoform dissociation is characteristic of DSM-IV conversion disorder (Kuyk, Spinhoven, Van Emde Boas, & Van Dyck, 1999; Spitzer, Freyberger, Kessler, & Kompf, 1994; Spitzer et al., 1998). For example, Kuyk et al. (1999) assessed the severity of somatoform and psychological dissociation in a subtype of DSM-IV conversion disorder, i.e. conversion disorder with seizures or convulsions. In the ICD-10 this disorder is labeled dissociative convulsions, and it is categorized as a dissociative disorder of movement and sensation. Partly consistent with the ICD-10 classification, previous studies suggested that a subgroup of patients with pseudo-epileptic seizures have a disorder involving psychological dissociative symptomatology (Bowman, 1993; Kuyk, Van Dyck & Spinhoven, 1996). Kuyk et al. (in press) found that patients with pseudo-epileptic seizures scored significantly higher on the DIS-Q (Vanderlinden et al., 1993) than patients with epileptic seizures or temporal lobe epilepsy. Their SDQ-20 scores ($M = 29.8, SD = 7.5$) exceeded the SDQ-20 scores of patients with epileptic seizures (SDQ-20: $M = 25.6, SD = 7.3$) or temporal lobe epilepsy ($M = 24.3, SD = 6.8$) as well. Interestingly, however, only somatoform dissociation discriminated between these diagnostic groups after statistical correction for the influence of general psychoneuroticism, as assessed with the SCL-90 (Derogatis, 1977). Kuyk et al. (in press) concluded that somatoform dissociation, not psychological dissociation, is characteristic for patients with pseudo-epileptic seizures.

In conclusion, relabeling conversion somatoform dissociation, and categorizing the DSM-IV conversion disorders as dissociative disorders is indicated. The same applies to somatization disorder if it would be predominantly characterized by somatoform dissociation. Such findings would promote a reinstitution of the 19th century category of hysteria (under the general label dissociative disorders), which included the current dissociative disorders, conversion disorder (c.q., ICD-10 dissociative disorders of movement and sensation), and somatization disorder. On the other hand, analysis of somatoform dissociation in DSM-IV somatization disorder may also reveal the existence of various subgroups. For example, it could be that a subgroup of patients with somatization disorder has severe somatoform dissociation, whereas another subgroup obtains low SDQ-20 scores. Although somatoform dissociation was significantly increased in DSM-IV somatoform disorders, it should not escape attention that the latter category encompasses a range of disorders which significantly differ from each other. As it seems doubtful that for example conversion disorder and hypochondriasis relate to similar pathology, study of somatoform dissociation in the various somatoform disorders is needed.

An issue which also deserves study is the extent to which dissociative disorder and borderline personality disorder (BPD) patients experience different degrees of somatoform dissociation. Instruments measuring psychological dissociation are not efficient in differentiating dissociative disorders from BPD (e.g., Vuchelen, Vanderlinden, Vandereycken, & Pieters, 1996), because BPD may involve substantial psychological dissociation (Brodsky, Cloitre, & Dulit, 1995; Vuchelen et al., 1996). It may appear that BPD is also associated with somatoform dissociation. Although the DSM-IV does not mention that this disorder is associated with somatoform (dissociative) symptoms, it is known that some BPD patients experience analgesia in the context of automutilation, in particular those who report sexual abuse and psychological dissociation (Russ, Shearin, Clarkin, Harrison, & Hull, 1993). In executing this proposed research, it will be essential to administer the SCID-D to all subjects, as some BPD cases may have dissociative disorder as a co-morbid diagnosis.

The SDQ-20 as a Therapy Evaluation Instrument

Our clinical observations suggest that the SDQ-20 may also serve as a therapy evaluation instrument. Dissociative patients who according to clinical standards were successfully treated, or who made significant progress, obtained low SDQ-20 scores, whereas those who had not, or had not yet, reached these improvements still had high scores on this instrument. These observations invite systematic study of the subject.

Somatoform Dissociation and Iatrogenesis

Some authors have argued that dissociative disorders, in particular DID, are artificial constructions, resulting from indoctrination by therapists. Misdiagnosis and suggestive shaping of bipolar mood disorder would be involved (Merskey, 1992). In this view, suggestible patients learn to play a role. Chapter VI and Chapter VII provided empirical data showing that this hypothesis is very unlikely to be the best explanation of somatoform dissociation and dissociative disorders. Bipolar mood disorder was associated with low dissociation scores, DDNOS with far higher scores, and DID with extreme dissociation, whether or not the influence of general psychoneuroticism was taken into account. Moreover, in contrast with dissociative disorder patients, only a few bipolar mood disorder patients obtained scores above the cutoff values of the SDQ-5 and DES.

No evidence was found that the high dissociation scores of the DDNOS and DID patients resulted from indoctrination of bipolar mood disorder patients by diagnosticians or therapists. We also remind readers that the present author's theoretical bias concerning animal defense and somatoform dissociation did not affect the somatoform dissociation scores of dissociative disorder patients (Chapter X). This obviously is far from saying that dissociative disorder patients are immune to suggestion, or denying that there are factitious dissociative disorder cases, but it seems warranted to state that suggestion does not explain the findings of our studies.

Part II

Somatoform Dissociation and Trauma

Part II opened with Chapter VIII, in which the prevalence and severity of traumatic experiences as reported by patients with dissociative disorders and with other DSM-IV psychiatric diagnoses were compared. Furthermore, the predictive value of emotional, physical, and sexual trauma with respect to somatoform and psychological dissociation was analyzed. In contrast with comparison patients, dissociative disorder patients reported severe as well as multifaceted traumatization. Physical and sexual trauma predicted somatoform dissociation, and sexual trauma predicted psychological dissociation.

Dissociative disorder patients reported that this abuse usually occurred in an emotionally neglectful and abusive social context. Pathological dissociation was best predicted by early onset of reported intense, chronic and multiple traumatization. These findings supported the construct validity of the SDQ-20. Methodological limitations restricting causal inferences between memories of trauma and dissociation were discussed.

Future studies on trauma and dissociation using the TEC should include an evaluation of the scale's total score (which involves the summation of the endorsed types of trauma; range from 0 to 29). Reanalysing the data of the study which was summarized above, we recently entered this total score into a separate regression analysis, and found that it explained 48% of the variance of somatoform dissociation ($R^2 = .483$), which exceeded the variance explained by reported physical and sexual abuse (Chapter VIII). This additional finding suggests that somatoform dissociation is strongly associated with reporting multiple types of trauma: a finding which fits the results of recent research into the occurrence of verified multiple and chronic traumatization of DID patients (Coons, 1994; Hornstein & Putnam, 1992; Kluft, 1995; Lewis, Yeager, Swica, Pincus, & Lewis, 1997).

When the study presented in Chapter VIII was performed, the psychometric characteristics of the TEC were unknown. These features, explored in a later stage, appeared to be quite satisfactory, and are presented in Chapter XIII.

Preliminary findings (Dell, 1997b) indicated particularly strong correlations of somatoform dissociation and reported sexual abuse ($r = .51$), sexual harassment ($r = .49$), physical abuse ($r = .49$), and lower correlations with reported emotional neglect ($r = .25$) and emotional abuse ($r = .31$). Reported early onset of traumatization was somewhat more strongly associated with somatoform dissociation than was recalled trauma in later developmental periods, and among all variables tested the total TEC score was associated with somatoform dissociation most strongly ($r = .63$). These results are consistent with our findings, and confirm the construct validity of the SDQ-20.

Somatoform Dissociation and Defense

Patients with DID or related types of DDNOS remain in alternating psycho-physiological states which are discrete, discontinuous, and resistant to integration. According to clinical observation, these states are associated with particular somatoform dissociative symptoms (Chapter II). In Chapters IX and X, we explored the roots of these dissociative states and phenomena. In Chapter IX, a parallel was drawn between animal defensive and recuperative states that are evoked in the face of variable predatory imminence and injury, and characteristic somatoform dissociative responses of trauma-reporting patients with dissociative disorders. Empirical data of research with animals and humans, as well as clinical observations, were reviewed. These data fit the idea that there are similarities between disturbances of normal eating-patterns and other normal behavioral patterns in the face of diffuse threat; freezing and stilling when serious threat materializes; analgesia and anesthesia when strike is about to occur; and acute pain when threat has subsided and recuperation is at stake.

Chapter X involved a first test of the hypothesized similarity between animal defensive reactions and certain somatoform dissociative symptoms of trauma-reporting dissociative disorder patients. Twelve somatoform symptom clusters consisting of clinically observed somatoform dissociative phenomena were constructed. All clusters discriminated between patients with dissociative disorders and patients with other psychiatric diagnoses. Those expressive of the hypothesized similarity — freezing, anesthesia-analgesia, and disturbed eating — belonged to the five most characteristic symptoms of dissociative disorder patients. Anesthesia-analgesia, urogenital pain and freezing symptom clusters independently contributed to predicted caseness of dissociative disorder. An independent sample showed that anesthesia-analgesia best predicted caseness after controlling for symptom severity. These results were largely consistent with the hypothesized similarity.

The above data are consistent with the idea that traumatic events may induce defensive states which involve particular somatoform dissociative responses. Our theoretical model can be further tested in several ways. One possibility would be to explore whether exposure to traumatic events, in particular those which involve threat to the body and life, tends to evoke anesthesia, analgesia, motor inhibitions, submission, and delayed pain. For this purpose, Nijenhuis and Van der Hart (1998) have started to develop a *Peritraumatic Somatoform Dissociation Questionnaire* (SDQ-P), which aims to measure somatoform dissociative responses as evoked by traumatic events. In a retrospective study with women recalling childhood sexual trauma (and in many cases physical abuse, emotional abuse, and emotional neglect as well) ($n = 32$), presented in Chapter XII, Nijenhuis, Van Engen, Kusters, and Van der Hart (2001) found that peritraumatic somatoform dissociation was strongly correlated with the severity of sexual abuse (Spearman's rho $= .70; p < .0001$), and was correlated with physical abuse and emotional neglect as well. The study suggests that traumatic experiences that involved serious threat to the integrity of the body may evoke somatoform dissociation.

Another possibility would be to develop a standardized and systematized behavioral challenge test designed to assess behavioral, affective, somatoform, and physiological responses to perceived threat of dissociative patients who have been exposed to physical or sexual abuse (apart from those of other psychiatric patients, and subjects who simulate dissociative disorder). Phasic approach of a person who aims to enter a designated territorium of the patient, may model predatory (perpetrator) imminence. We predict that in DID different dissociative identities, defensive responses, and physiological reactions will be evoked by the modeled preencounter, postencounter, near-strike, strike, and post-strike phases of imminence. This research is now in progress (Nijenhuis, Matthews, & Kirsch).

One may object that this project would hardly be ethical. On the other hand, it is well known that many dissociative patients are prone to retraumatization. As we have clinically observed, they may be unable to defend themselves against psychological and physical threat in ways that fit present contexts. Many freeze, become anesthetic, and submit. For example, in the course of her therapy, Lisa (Chapter II) discovered that during particular amnestic episodes, she was still frequently "raped." A man who had started abusing her sexually when she was 12 years, still came to her house. His appearance reactivated a dissociative identity which time and again froze and submitted, without any apparent resistance, to sexual intercourse. As the therapist discovered upon testing, Lisa consistently froze when she was physically approached. Stimulated by increased cooperation of various identities as well as subsequent behavioral rehearsal involving exposure to "physical threat" by the therapist, Lisa acquired the ability to defend herself in more appropriate, assertive ways. This helped her to stop the unwanted sexual encounters (note: the perpetrator confessed to the events as described). This example may illustrate that systematic observation and therapeutic rehearsal of defensive behavior of dissociative disorder patients can be fruitfully combined and can be appropriate.

A third possibility to test the model that animal defense and dissociation are related would be to systematically study the kind of identities that DID patients have developed. We would predict that DID patients who have been exposed to severe physical threat at an early age will encompass identities who, as a rule, either take care of daily routines (execution of a job, raising children), display disturbed eating patterns, flee, freeze, fight, submit to threat, or engage in recuperative behaviors. In fact, if the model is correct, these states should be prominent among the major identity states of these patients.

The animal survival system also encompasses attachment. Among other behaviors and responses, attachment involves calling for help when alone and in potential danger. This behavior should only be emitted when predators have not yet appeared on the scene, as calling for help may attract the attention of natural enemies (Kalin, 1993; Kalin & Shelton, 1989; Kalin, Shelton, & Takahashi, 1991). Kalin and his colleagues indeed found that neurophysiological changes rapidly follow environmental changes of this kind. Different hormones are released which yield totally different behavioral patterns. Attachment also involves seeking parental comforting when stressed. Favorable experiences of this kind should in the long run provide the ability to self-modulate arousal and emotional states (Putnam, 1997).

But what if trauma is perpetrated by caregivers? Studies into human attachment have recently identified an insecure-disorganized/disoriented attachment category (Main & Morgan, 1996), which is highly relevant for our theoretical model. Disorganized/disoriented attachment amongst others involves sequential or simultaneous display of contradictory behavioral patterns. For example, the infant first approaches a caregiver, but suddenly, although slowly, moves away from the caregiver to still and freeze with blank gazing, expressionless face and eyes half-closed for periods up to 45 seconds. Aggressive-like behavior may appear. In a later stage, the infant shifts back to approach behavior. It seems likely that infants who are abused by their caregivers are confronted with a paradox in that the caregiver has become a stimulus for both affiliative behavior and fear (Main & Hesse, 1990). Affiliative needs stimulate the infant to approach the caregiver, whereas this approach elicits defensive flight, freeze, and fight. These irresolvable tendencies may promote dissociation (Liotti, 1992). In our terms, then, the caregiver-abuser would represent an unconditioned, as well as conditioned stimulus evoking incompatible unconditioned and conditioned responses which promote dissociative state-dependent functioning, and in the case of chronic parental abuse, the emancipation of various affiliative and defensive states.

Consistent with this interpretation, about 80% of parentally maltreated infants in high-risk samples were disorganized (Carlson, Cichetti, Barnett, & Braunwald, 1989; Lyons-Ruth, Repacholi, McLeod, & Silva, 1991), and disorganized attachment in infancy was a predictor of dissociative behavior in both the elementary and high school setting (Ogawa, Sroufe, Weinfeld, Carlson, & Egeland, 1997). Consistent with the interpretations that dissociation becomes less normative with age, and that disorganized attachment is a risk factor for dissociation, the correlation between disorganized attachment and dissociation increased with age. The age of onset, chronicity, and severity of trauma were all strongly correlated and predicted dissociation. These prospective findings support our retrospectively assessed associations between somatoform and psychological dissociation and trauma-reporting.

These accumulating data suggest that progress in the study of dissociation demands careful study of children who are abused by caretakers and close relatives (Silberg, 1998). This work would include the study of somatoform dissociative phenomena, and the defensive behavioral and mental states with which these responses are associated. For this reason, the development of a structured interview for somatoform dissociation and defensive reactions suitable for children and adolescents is important.

Chronic Pelvic Pain, Somatoform Dissociation, and Reported Trauma

The work so far revealed powerful associations between somatoform dissociation, dissociative disorder, and reported trauma among psychiatric patients. In order to test the generalizability of these findings, it was important to explore whether these relationships would also hold among a nonpsychiatric population. According to the literature chronic pelvic pain (CPP) is one of the somatic symptoms which, at least among a subgroup of gynecology patients, relates to reported trauma and dissociation. Considering that patients who present in somatic health care may be more inclined to report somatic symptoms than psychological symptoms, we hypothesized that somatoform dissociation would be more indicative of (features of) dissociative disorder among CPP patients than psychological dissociation. We also hypothesized that, in particular, trauma-reporting CPP patients experience somatoform dissociation, and that somatoform dissociation statistically predicts trauma better than psychological dissociation in this diagnostic category.

In order to study these hypotheses, a sample of CPP patients first completed self-report questionnaires which evaluate dissociative symptoms and/or screen for dissociative disorder, somatization, anxiety, depression, and traumatic experiences. To assess or exclude dissociative disorder, next a structured clinical interview for DSM-IV dissociative disorders was administered.

Psychological dissociation and somatoform dissociation were significantly assiciated with (features of) DSM-IV dissociative disorders, as measured by the

SCID-D. Anxiety, depression, and psychological dissociation best predicted the SCID-D total score, whereas amnesia was best predicted by somatoform dissociation, as was identity confusion by anxiety/depression and somatoform dissociation. These findings ran partly contrary to the hypothesis that somatoform dissociated among CPP patients would be more predictive of dissociative disorder than psychological dissociation.

Considering that patients with psychosomatic conditions initially prsent in medical care, and that many dissociative disorder patients have urogenital pain, we suspected that a subset of gynecology patients with chronic pelvic pain would have dissociative pathology (Chapter I and XI). However, our data suggested that dissociative disorders among CPP patients are rare (Chapter XI): the sample included only one case. This finding casts doubt on the idea that dissociative disorder patients (initially) present in medical care, and suggests that assistance-seeking behavior of dissociative disorder patients warrants study. Of particular interest is assistance-seeking of these patients when they were young: several studies, including ours, indicate that dissociative disorders are associated with enduring traumatization starting in early childhood, and according to clinical experience, dissociative disorders in childhood can be treated much faster and with less effort than dissociative disorders among adults (Putnam, 1997; Silberg, 1996). Therefore, early detection and treatment of dissociative disorders is important.

The sensitivity of somatoform and psychological dissociation screening instruments for dissociative disorders was 100%. The specificity was 90.2% (SDQ-5) and 94.1% (DES) respectively. When scores at, or slightly above, the recommended cutoff values were applied, somatoform and psychological dissociation screening instruments for dissociative disorders overpredicted dissociative disorder in a few cases. According to the results of this study, raising the SDQ-5 and DES cutoffs among CPP patients yields increased specificity without loss of sensitivity. Patients who obtain scores in the higher regions are more likely to have dissociative disorder. When using dissociative disorder screening instruments among gynecology patients with CPP, the positive and negative predictive values of dissociative disorder screening instruments must be corrected for the observed low prevalence rate of dissociative disorders among this group.

About half of the CPP patients reported substantial trauma. In consonance with our hypotheses, somatoform dissociation was strongly associated with, and best predicted, reported trauma. Among the various types of trauma physical abuse, life threat posed by a person, sexual trauma, and intense pain best predicted somatoform dissociation. After statistically controlling for the influence of anxiety, depression, and intense pain, physical abuse/life threat posed by a person remained the best predictor of somatoform dissociation.

In conclusion, this study demonstrated a strong association between somatoform dissociation and reported trauma in a nonpsychiatric population, as well as a considerable association between somatoform dissociation and features of dissociative disorders. These results are consistent with our findings among psychiatric patients, and, therefore, strengthen our thesis that somatoform dissociation, (features of) dissociative disorder, and reported trauma are strongly intercorrelated phenomena. Future work should include studying somatoform dissociation and trauma, as well as the screening capacity of the SDQ-5, among other medical diagnoses that have been empirically related to considerable trauma reporting. These disorders include irritable bowel syndrome (Walker, Gelfand, Gelfand, Green, & Katon, 1996) and fibromyalgia (Alexander et al., 1998; Amir, Neumann. Sharabani, Shani, & Buskila, 1997; Walker et al., 1997). In view of the current low prevalence rate of dissociative disorders among gynecology patients with CPP, the prevalence of dissociative disorders among patients with irritable bowel syndrome, fibromyalgia and other psychosomatic conditions who present in medical care may also be low.

Dissociation: A Dimensional or Typological Phenomenon?

Since the beginning of this decade, there is a repetition of the discussion whether dissociation is best conceptualized as a dimensional or a typological phenomenon. Whereas Janet (1889) maintained that dissociation involves a pathological discontinuity in awareness, which is typical of hysterical patients, James (1890/ 1983) and Prince (1905/1978) argued that dissociation is a continuous or quantitative variable present to a greater or lesser extent in everyone.

Criticizing the tendency of modern authors to regard rather common trance-like experiences as instances of dissociation, Van der Hart, Boon and Op den Velde (1991) warned that the dissociation construct loses its former specificity. Van der Hart et al. remind that in Janet's view dissociation involves systems of ideas and functions that escape normal integration and later manifest as intrusions or complete changes of state. In contrast, trance-like experiences are not stored as separate mental states.

The authors of the Dissociative Experiences Scale (DES; Bernstein & Putnam, 1986) originally assumed that their scale assessed a dimensional construct, but more recently a different picture has been put forward. Using taxometric statistical methods for distinguishing typological from dimensional constructs, Waller, Putnam, and Carlson (1996) found evidence for the existence of two types of experiences, which they labeled "non-pathological" and "pathological" dissociation. "Non-pathological" dissociation essentially concerns absorption and imaginative involvement, which experiences are manifestations of a trait. "Pathological" dissociation involves amnesia, depersonalization, derealization, and identity fragmentation, and excludes absorption-like phenomena. Pathological dissociation seems to represent a latent class variable that can be measured by the 8-item DES-Taxon (DES-T) (i.e., 8 of the 28 DES items; Waller et al., 1996). Interestingly, the SCID-D assesses amnesia, depersonalization, derealization, and identity fragmentation as well, and does not include items referring to non-pathological dissociation. Data reported by Waller and Ross (1997) also suggest that absorption-like phenomena are less indicative of dissociative disorder patients. As they found, the DES-T is a better screening instrument for dissociative disorders than the DES because of the higher specificity of the DES-T.

Systematic inquiry into the nature of dissociative phenomena among dissociative disorder patients has also been used to claim that dissociation is a typological variable. For example, according to Boon and Draijer (1993) the results of their SCID-D validation study revealed that:

"the nature and quality of the dissociative experiences of patients without a dissociative disorder were found to be different from those of patients with a dissociative disorder." (p. 203)

In their view, the experiences of dissociative disorders patients are difficult to conceptualize along a dissociative continuum, because they are qualitatively different from the experiences of patients with other mental disorders.

Finally, some empirical data have been understood to indicate that dissociation among clinical subjects is of a different order compared to dissociation among normal subjects. In their prospective longitudinal study with young children at risk for traumatization, Ogawa et al. (1997) found that the largest difference was between the clinical dissociative group and the normal group as a whole, which consisted of low and high dissociative normal subjects. They argued that if the clinical group were merely the high end of a distribution of dissociation scores then one would expect that discriminant analyses would differentiate the low normal group, the largest group, from the two smaller high dissociation groups.

How about somatoform dissociation? According to Janet (1901), the proper somatoform mental stigmata, i.e., anesthesia, analgesia, and motor inhibitions, appear exclusively in hysteria (Chapter II), and therefore would qualify as typological phenomena. Consistent with Janet's view, our studies have revealed that the items of the SDQ-20 and SDQ-5 predominantly involve mental stigmata, or negative dissociative symptoms. Since somatoform dissociation is strongly correlated with dissociative amnesia, depersonalization, and identity fragmentation, and less strongly correlated with absorption, one could be inclined to suspect that somatoform dissociation is a latent class variable.

On the other hand, Mokken scale analysis showed that the items of the SDQ-20 are strongly scalable on a latent unidimensional scale (Chapters III and V). These findings suggest that the SDQ-20 measures a dimensional construct. Considering that somatoform dissociation was correlated with reported trauma both among patients with and patients without DSM-IV dissociative disorders (see Chapters VIII and XI), a dimensional aspect is suggested by these data as well.

The idea that dissociation is a typological variable can be critized (Braude, 1995). Apart from differences between pathological and more usual manifestations of dissociation, both phenomena have properties in common. For example, consider the conformities between hypnotic dissociation and pathological dissociation: hypnotic and pathological analgesia both involve perceptive failure. As the philosopher Braude (1995, p. 95) states:

"... no evidence uncovered so far suggests that the phenomena considered dissociative are totally unprecedented among organic (or just cognitive) capacities, even if they are distinctive in certain respects. Hence, it is reasonable to begin by assuming that features found generally in human (or other organic) capacities are likely to be found also in the case of dissociation. Let us call this the *non-uniqueness assumption*."

Braude goes on to argue that capacities and abilities vary from one person to another. These may vary from moderate to extreme, from adaptive to nonadaptive, and often take forms highly idiosyncratic to the subject. One would therefore expect that dissociation also assumes a variety of forms, and varies along several continua (pervasiveness, frequency, severity, completeness, retrievability, etc). Braude calls this the *diversification assumption*.

There is no doubt that qualitative differences between dissociative phenomena among dissociative disorder patients and normal subjects exist. However, considering that qualitative differences may result from dimensional alterations, this diversity in itself does not prove that dissociation would not be dimensional. For example, pathological lying has properties in common with ordinary lying, and panic attacks are qualitatively different from more mundane manifestations of anxiety, but yet are taken to represent extreme fear, not a separate category (Braude, personal communication; Van Dyck, personal communication).

The view that pathological dissociation is a typological variable is problematic for another reason as well. As Wittgenstein (1976) has demonstrated, categorizations are not imposed upon us by the world: there are no privileged or inherently preferred categorizations. The value of a particular categorization depends on the needs and interests it is intended to serve in a particular context (Braude, personal communication), thus, on the (practical, personal, political) advantages it offers. It is a better or worse tool for a specified purpose. For example, although there is no doubt that posttraumatic stress disorder (PTSD) involves significant dissociative psychopathology, in the DSM-IV, PTSD is not categorized as a dissociative disorder. Whether this disorder will be seen as a dissociative disorder in the future, depends on various interests, including political ones. Using respectively clinical and statistical analyses, Janet and Waller et al. (1996) have shown that there are some grounds for regarding nonpathological and pathological dissociation as significantly different. However, it is our position that acknowledging the differences between both forms is compatible with the existence of other grounds for regarding them as continuous in important respects. As Braude (1995, p. 120) has demonstrated, nonpathological and pathological dissociation fit the reasonably stringent criteria of dissociation he proposed:

(1)(a) x is an occurrent or dispositional state of a human being S, or else a system of states (as in traits, skills, and alternate personalities), and
   (b) y is either a state or system of states of S, or else the person S.
(2) y may or may not be dissociated from x (i.e., dissociation is a nonsymmetrical relation).
(3) x and y are separated by a phenomenological or epistemological barrier (e.g., amnesia, anesthesia) erected by the subject S.
(4) S is not consciously aware of erecting the barrier between x and y.

(5)   The barrier between x and y can be broken down, at least in principle.
(6)   Third- and first-person knowledge of x may be as direct as (respectively) third- and first-person knowledge of the subject's non-dissociated states.

While most modern dissociation theories assume a variable *capacity* to dissociate (i.e., to erect a barrier between x and y), Janet held that hysterical patients are characterized by a *weakness* or *failure* of the capacity to synthesize, integrate and realize components of mental and behavioral functioning. Would both views be incompatible? It does not seem that way, because capacities developed and applied to their extremes may yield psychopathology. For example, the capacity to be orderly is valuable in many contexts, but extreme orderliness equals being compulsive. Likewise, dissociation can be adaptive when applied within limits (e.g., of time and context), but is maladaptive when applied in extreme degrees. For example, quickly shifting from one discrete defensive state to another is highly adaptive in many threat contexts (Chapter IX and X). However, failure to integrate these various state-dependent experiences into consciousness, identity, and memory when threat has subsided, may be at the basis of PTSD and dissociative disorders. As applies to DID, dissociation may become a life style in that even minor threat or stress evokes dissociative responding. Strengths may become weaknesses, assets may become symptoms.

Are Dissociative Symptoms State-Dependent?

Janetian dissociation theory, Putnam's behavioral states model of DID (Putnam, 1997), as well as our defensive states model, predict that a range of responses and symptoms of dissociative disorder patients are dissociative (identity) state-dependent. Several clinical examples of Chapter II are consistent with this hypothesis. For example, remaining in some of her identities, Lisa experienced negative symptoms (e.g., anesthesia), whereas in other states, she reported positive symptoms (e.g., pain).

However, in spite of the clinically observed (limited) dissociative state-dependent symptomatology, the major symptoms of dissociative disorders can be documented using self-report questionnaires while disregarding the dissociative state in which the patient remains when completing the items of these instruments. Does this empirical fact contradict the hypothesized dissociative state-dependency? In our view, several arguments suggest that both observations are not mutually exclusive. (1) While some identities of DID and DDNOS patients claim being ignorant of the existence of (mental "contents" of) other identities, this does not apply to most of them, in any case not to all. As described in Chapter II, the barriers among most dissociative states are far from absolute. Dissociative identities may influence one another in multiple ways, as is revealed by the intrusion symptoms (e.g., hearing voices, receiving commands, being influenced by the emotions, intentional motor acts, and sensations of other states). To an extent, identities also share knowledge, memories, skills, and character traits. Hence, within limits, there can be, and usually will be transfer of, or shared access to, information among dissociative states (see Braude's [1995, p. 120] above quoted definition of dissociation). Indeed, while completing self-report questionnaires and responding to diagnostic interview schedules, dissociative patients either spontaneously, or when asked, may report that their responses result from a mixture of sources. In addition to the experience of personalized symptoms, these sources include knowledge of symptoms experienced by other identities, reception of commands from other identities to respond in particular ways (as when hearing imperative voices), and outcomes of struggles among various identities (as when some identities inform the responding state that the symptom applies, whereas other identities deny its occurrence); (2) It may be that while completing self-report questionnaires and responding to structured clinical interviews, dissociative disorder patients, as a rule, remain in identity states which perform functions in daily life (this hypothesis can be systematically studied). Clinical experience suggests that these identities are dominated by negative symptoms, which would partly explain why the SDQ-20 and SDQ-5 mainly include items involving these negative symptoms; (3) Negative symptoms are far less variable than positive symptoms, as the latter apparently depend on accidental factors. For example, a positive symptom like pain in a body part may depend on whether the body, and more specifically the relevant body part, was hurt in a traumatic experience. As a result, the discriminant indices of most positive symptoms would be of a lower magnitude than the discriminant indices of negative symptoms: Chapter III provided data consistent with this hypothesis; (4) Considering that most dissociative disorder patients report negative symptoms, Janet (1901) overstated the issue when he claimed that hysterical patients often are unaware of mental stigmata. According to our clinical experience they are often initially (e.g., prior to treatment) consciously aware of these symptoms, or their severity, *within limits*, but the extent of this awareness may depend on (identity) state.

The hypothesized state-dependent nature of somatoform dissociation cannot be studied with the regular use of the SDQ-20 and SDQ-5, which disregards state-dependency, but must be analysed using other methods. One approach would be repeated administration of the SDQ to DID patients while they remain in different identity states, as well as to DID simulating controls who role-play various dissociative identity states and imagine that they remain in different identity states. The controls should include subjects from the normal population, as well as anxiety disorder patients. More important approaches, however, involve the study of somatoform dissociative symptoms while DID patients remain in various identities as they are experimentally exposed to memories of trauma or trauma-related cues.

Conclusion

Somatoform dissociation is a unique construct that can be measured with the SDQ. The construct is strongly correlated with psychological manifestations of dissociation, as well as reported trauma, and is highly characteristic of dissociative disorders. Having assessed these associations, and seeking to learn more about dissociation as a *process*, research into somatoform dissociation must now be expanded to include prospective and longitudinal, as well as experimental research.

References

Alexander, R.W., Bradley, L., Alarcón, G.S., Triana-Alexander, M., Aaron, L.A., Alberts, K., Martin, M.Y., & Steward, K.E. (1998). Sexual and physical abuse in women with fybromyalgia: Association with outpatient health care utilization and pain medication usage. *Arthritis Care and Research, 11*, 102-115.

American Psychiatric Association (1994). *Diagnostic and statistical manual of mental disorders, 4th ed. (DSM-IV)*. Washington DC: Author.

Amir, M., Kaplan, Z., Neumann, L., Sharabani, R., Shani, N., & Buskila, D. (1997). Posttraumatic stress disorder, tenderness, and fybromyalgia. *Journal of Psychosomatic Research, 42*, 607-613.

Bernstein, E.M., & Putnam, F.W. (1986). Development, reliability, and validity of a dissociation scale. *Journal of Nervous and Mental Disease, 174*, 727-735.

Boon, S., & Draijer, N. (1993). *Multiple personality disorder in the Netherlands. A study on reliability and validity of the diagnosis.* Amsterdam/Lisse: Swets & Zeitlinger.

Bowman, E.S. (1993). The etiology and clinical course of pseudoseizures: Relationship to trauma, depression, and dissociation. *Psychosomatics, 34*, 333-342.

Braude, S. E. (1995). *First person plural: Multiple personality and the philosophy of mind.* Revised edition. Lanham: Rowman & Littlefield.

Brodsky, B.S., Cloitre, M., & Dulit, R.A. (1995). Relationship of dissociation to self-mutilation and childhood abuse in borderline personality disorder. *American Journal of Psychiatry, 152*, 1788-1792.

Carlson, V., Cichetti, D., Barnett, D., & Braunwald, K. (1989). Disorganized/disoriented attachment relationships in maltreated infants. *Developmental Psychology, 25*, 525-531.

Coons, P.M. (1994). Confirmation of childhood abuse in child and adolescent cases of multiple personality disorder and dissociative disorder not otherwise specified. *Journal of Nervous and Mental Disease, 182*, 461-464.

Dell, P.F. (1997a). Somatoform dissociation in DID, DDNOS, chronic pain, and eating disorders in a North American sample. Proceedings of the 14th International Conference of the International Society for the Study of Dissociation, November 8-11, p. 130.

Dell, P.F. (1997b). Somatoform dissociation and reported trauma in DID and DDNOS. Proceedings of the 14th International Conference of the International Society for the Study of Dissociation, November 8-11, p. 130.

Derogatis, L.R. (1977). *Administration, scoring and procedures manual-I for the (R)evised version.* Baltimore: John Hopkins University School of Medicine, Clinical Psychometrics Research Unit.

Friedl, H. C., & Draijer, N. (2000). Dissociative Disorders in Dutch psychiatric patients. *American Journal of Psychiatry, 157*, 1012-1013.

Horon, S.A., Leichner, P.P, & Lawson, J.S. (1995). Prevalence of dissociative symptoms and disorders in an adult psychiatric inpatient population in Canada. *Canadian Journal of Psychiatry, 40*, 185-191.

Hornstein, N.L., & Putnam, F.W. (1992). Clinical phenomenology of child and adolescent dissociative disorders. *Journal of American Academic Child and Adolescent Psychiatry, 31*, 1077-1085.

James, W. (1983). *The principles of psychology*. Cambridge, MA: Harvard University Press. Original publication: 1905.

Janet, P. (1889). *L'Automatisme psychologique*. Paris: Félix Alcan.

Janet, P. (1893). *L'Etat mental des hystériques. Les stigmates mentaux*. Paris: Rueff & Cie.

Janet, P. (1901). *The mental state of hystericals*. New York: Putnam and Sons.

Kalin, N.H. (1993). The neurobiology of fear. *Scientific American*, May, 54-60.

Kalin, N.H., & Shelton, S.E. (1989). Defensive behaviors in infant rhesus monkeys: Environmental cues and neurochemical regulation. *Science, 243*, 1718-1721.

Kalin, N.H., Shelton, S.E., & Takahashi, L.K. (1991). Defensive behaviors in infant rhesus monkeys: Ontogeny and context-dependent selective expression. *Child Development, 62*, 1175-1183.

Kluft, R.P. (1995). The confirmation and disconfirmation of memories of abuse in DID patients: A naturalistic clinical study. *Dissociation, 8*, 251-258.

Kuyk, J., Spinhoven, P., Van Emde Boas, M.D., & Van Dyck, R. (1999). Dissociation in temporal lobe epilepsy and pseudo-epileptic seizure patients. *The Journal of Nervous and Mental Disease, 187* (12), 713-720.

Kuyk, J., Van Dyck, R. & Spinhoven, P. (1996). The case for a dissociative interpretation of pseudo-epileptic seizures: A review. *Journal of Nervous and Mental Disease, 184*, 468-474.

Lewis, D.O., Yeager, C.A., Swica, Y., Pincus, J.H. & Lewis, M. (1997). Objective documentation of child abuse and dissociation in 12 murderers with dissociative identity disorder. *American Journal of Psychiatry, 154*, 1703-1710.

Liotti, G. (1992). Disorganized/disoriented attachment in the etiology of the dissociative disorders. *Dissociation, 4*, 196-204.

Loevinger, J. (1976). *Ego development*. San Francisco: Jossey-Bass.

Lyons-Ruth, K., Repacholi, B., McLeod, S., & Silva, E. (1991). Disorganized attachment behavior in infancy: Short-term stability, maternal and infant correlates, and risk-related subtypes. *Development and Psychopathology, 3*, 397-412.

Main, M. & Morgan, H. (1996). Disorganization and disorientation in infant strange situation behavior. In L.K. Michelson & W.J. Ray (eds.), *Handbook of dissociation: Theoretical, empirical and clinical perspectives* (pp. 107-138). New York: Plenum Press.

Merskey, H. (1992). The manufacture of personalities: The production of multiple personality disorder. *British Journal of Psychiatry, 160*, 327-340.

Nijenhuis, E.R.S., & Van der Hart, O. (1998). The Peritraumatic Somatoform Dissociation Questionnaire (SDQ-P). Unpublished manuscript.

Nijenhuis, E.R.S., Van Engen, A., Kusters, I., & Van der Hart, O. (2001). Peritraumatic somatoform and psychological dissociation in relation to recall of childdhood sexual abuse. *Journal of Trauma and Dissociation, 2*(3), 49-68. (b) Included as Chapter XII.

Ogawa, J.R., Sroufe, L.A., Weinfeld, N.C., Carlson, E.A., & Egeland, B. (1997). Development and the fragmented self: Longitudinal study of dissociative symptomatology in a nonclinical sample. *Development and Psychopathology, 9*, 855-879.

Prince, M. (1978). *The dissociation of a personality*. New York: Oxford University Press. Original publication: 1905.

Putnam, F.W. (1997). *Dissociation in children and adolescents: A developmental perspective*. New York: Guilford.

Ross, C.A., Miller, S.D., Reagor, P., Bjornson, L., Fraser, G.A., & Anderson, G. (1990). Structured interview data on 102 cases of multiple personality disorder from four centers. *American Journal of Psychiatry, 147*, 596-601.

Russ, M.J., Shearin, E.N., Clarkin, J.F., Harrison, K., & Hull, J.W. (1993): Subtypes of self-injurious patients with borderline personality disorder. *American Journal of Psychiatry, 150*, 1869-1871.

Şar, V., Kundakci, T., Kiziltan, E., Bakim, B., & Bozkurt, O. (2000). Differentiating dissociative disorders from other diagnostic groups through somatoform dissociation in Turkey. *Journal of Trauma and Dissociation, 1*(4), 67-80.

Şar, V., Kundakçi, T., Kiziltan, E., Yargiç, I.L., Tutkun, H., Bakim, B., Ayudiner, O., Özpulat, T., Keser, V., & Özdemir, Ö. (1999). Frequency of dissociative disorders among psychiatric outpatients with borderline personality disorder. *Proceedings of the 6th European Conference on Traumatic Stress: Psychotraumatology, clinical practice, and human rights*. Istanbul, Turkey, June 5-8, p. 115.

Saxe, G.N., Van der Kolk, B.A., Berkowitz, R., Chinman, G., Hall, K., Lieberg, G., & Schwartz, J. (1993). Dissociative disorders in psychiatric inpatients. *American Journal of Psychiatry, 150*, 1037-1042.

Silberg, J.L. (1996). *The dissociative child*. Lutherville: Sidran.

Silberg, J. (1998). Dissociative symptomatology in children and adolescents as displayed on psychological testing. *Journal of Personality Assessment 71*, 421-439.

Spitzer, C., Freyberger, H.J., Kessler, C., & Kompf, D. (1994). Comorbidity of dissociative disorders in neurology. *Nervenarzt, 65*, 680-688.

Spitzer, C., Freyberger, H.J., Steiglitz, R.D., Carlson, E.B., Kuhn, G., Magdeburg, N., & Kessler, C. (1998). Adaptation and psychometric properties of the German version of the Dissociative Experiences Scale. *Journal of Traumatic Stress, 11*, 799-809.

Steinberg, M. (1993). *Structured Interview for DSM-IV Dissociative Disorders (SCID-D)*. Washington DC: American Psychiatric Press.

Steinberg, M., Cichetti, D.V., Buchanan, J., Hall, P., & Rounsaville B. (1993). Clinical assessment of dissociative symptoms and disorders: The Structured Clinical Interview for DSM-IV Dissociative Disorders. *Dissociation, 6*, 3-16.

Van der Hart, O., Boon, S., & Op den Velde, W. (1991). Trauma en dissociatie [Trauma and dissociation]. In O. van der Hart (ed.). *Trauma, dissociatie en hypnose [Trauma, dissociation, and hypnosis]* (pp. 55-71). Amsterdam: Swets & Zeitlinger.

Vanderlinden, J., van Dyck, R., Vandereycken, W., Vertommen, H., & Verkes, R.J. (1993). The Dissociation Questionnaire (DIS-Q): Development and characteristics of a new self-report questionnaire. *Cinical Psychology and Psychotherapy, 1*, 21-27.

Vuchelen, S., Vanderlinden, J., Vandereycken, W., & Pieters, G. (1996). Trauma en dissociatie bij borderline persoonlijkheidsstoornis [Trauma and dissociation in borderline personality disorder]. *Tijdschrift voor Psychiatrie, 38*, 123-135.

Walker, E.A., Gelfand, A.N., Gelfand, M.D., Green, C., & Katon, W.J. (1996). Chronic pelvic pain and gynecological symptoms in women with irritable bowel syndrome. *Journal of Psychosomatic Obstetrics & Gynecology, 17*, 39-46.

Walker, E.A., Keegan, D., Gardner, G., Sullivan, M., Bernstein, D., & Katon, W.J. (1997). Psychosocial factors in fibromyalgia compared with rheumatoid arthitis: II. Sexual, physical, and emotional abuse and neglect. *Psychosomatic Medicine, 59*, 572-577.

Waller, N.G., Putnam, F.W., & Carlson, E.B. (1996). Types of dissociation and dissociative types: A taxometric analysis of dissociative experiences. *Psychological Methods, 1*, 300-321.

Waller, N.G., & Ross, C.A. (1997). The prevalence and biometric structure of pathological dissociation in the general population: Taxometric and behavior genetic findings. *Journal of Abnormal Psychology, 106*, 499-510.

Wittgenstein, L. (1976). *Philosophical investigations*. Oxford: Basil Blackwell.

World Health Organization (1992). *The ICD-10 Classification of Mental and Behavioural Disorders. Clinical descriptions and diagnostic guidelines.* Geneva: Author.

Ÿar, V., Kundakçi, T., Kiziltan, E., Bahadir, B., & Aydiner, O. (1998). Reliability and validity of the Turkish version of the Somatoform Dissociation Questionnaire (SDQ-20). Proceedings of the International Society of Dissociation 15th International Fall Conference. Seattle, U.S.A., November 14-17.

Appendices

Appendix 1
S. D. Q. – 20

This questionnaire asks about different physical symptoms or body experiences, which you may have had either briefly or for a longer time.
Please indicate to what extent these experiences apply to you *in the past year*.

For each statement, please circle the number in the first column that best applies to YOU. The possibilities are:

1 = this applies to me NOT AT ALL
2 = this applies to me A LITTLE
3 = this applies to me MODERATELY
4 = this applies to me QUITE A BIT
5 = this applies to me EXTREMELY

If a symptom or experience applies to you, please indicate whether a *physician* has connected it with a *physical disease*.
Indicate this by circling the word YES or NO in the column "Is the physical cause known?"
If you wrote YES, please write the physical cause (if you know it) on the line.

Example:

	Extent to which the symptom or experience applies to you	Is the physical cause known?
Sometimes:		
my teeth chatter	1 2 3 4 5	NO YES, namely ....
I have cramps in my calves	1 2 3 4 5	NO YES, namely ....

If you have circled a 1 in the first column (i.e., This applies to me NOT AT ALL), you do NOT have to respond to the question about whether the physical cause is known.

On the other hand, if you circle 2, 3, 4, or 5, you MUST circle NO or YES in the "Is the physical cause known?" column.

Please do not skip any of the 20 questions.
Thank you for your cooperation.

Source: Nijenhuis, Van der Hart & Vanderlinden, Assen-Amsterdam-Leuven.

Here are the questions:

1 = this applies to me NOT AT ALL
2 = this applies to me A LITTLE
3 = this applies to me MODERATELY
4 = this applies to me QUITE A BIT
5 = this applies to me EXTREMELY

	Extent to which the symptom or experience applies to you	Is the physical cause known?	

Sometimes:

1. I have trouble urinating — 1 2 3 4 5 — No — Yes, namely ....

2. I dislike tastes that I usually like (women: at times OTHER THAN pregnancy or monthly periods) — 1 2 3 4 5 — No — Yes, namely ....

3. I hear sounds from nearby as if they were coming from far away — 1 2 3 4 5 — No — Yes, namely ....

4. I have pain while urinating — 1 2 3 4 5 — No — Yes, namely ....

5. My body, or a part of it, feels numb — 1 2 3 4 5 — No — Yes, namely ....

6. People and things look bigger than usual — 1 2 3 4 5 — No — Yes, namely ....

7. I have an attack that resembles an epileptic seizure — 1 2 3 4 5 — No — Yes, namely ....

8. My body, or a part of it, is insensitive to pain — 1 2 3 4 5 — No — Yes, namely ....

9. I dislike smells that I usually like — 1 2 3 4 5 — No — Yes, namely ....

10. I feel pain in my genitals (at times OTHER THAN sexual intercourse) — 1 2 3 4 5 — No — Yes, namely ....

11. I cannot hear for a while (as if I am deaf) — 1 2 3 4 5 — No — Yes, namely ....

12. I cannot see for a while (as if I am blind) — 1 2 3 4 5 — No — Yes, namely ....

Source: Nijenhuis, Van der Hart & Vanderlinden, Assen-Amsterdam-Leuven.

1 = this applies to me NOT AT ALL
2 = this applies to me A LITTLE
3 = this applies to me MODERATELY
4 = this applies to me QUITE A BIT
5 = this applies to me EXTREMELY

	Extent to which the symptom or experience applies to you	Is the physical cause known?	
Sometimes:			
13. I see things around me differently than usual (for example as if looking through a tunnel, or seeing merely a part of an object)	1 2 3 4 5	No	Yes, namely ....
14. I am able to smell much BETTER or WORSE than I usually do (even though I do *not* have a cold)	1 2 3 4 5	No	Yes, namely ....
15. It is as if my body, or a part of it, has disappeared	1 2 3 4 5	No	Yes, namely ....
16. I cannot swallow, or can swallow only with great effort	1 2 3 4 5	No	Yes, namely ....
17. I cannot sleep for nights on end, but remain very active during daytime	1 2 3 4 5	No	Yes, namely ....
18. I cannot speak (or only with great effort) or I can only whisper	1 2 3 4 5	No	Yes, namely ....
19. I am paralysed for a while	1 2 3 4 5	No	Yes, namely ....
20. I grow stiff for a while	1 2 3 4 5	No	Yes, namely ....

Source: Nijenhuis, Van der Hart & Vanderlinden, Assen-Amsterdam-Leuven.

Before continuing, will you please check whether you have responded to all 20 statements?

You are asked to fill in and place an X beside what applies to you.

21. Age: ....   years

22. Sex: ....   female
                          ....   male

23. Marital status: ....   single
                          ....   married
                          ....   living together
                          ....   divorced
                          ....   widower/widow

24. Education: ....   number of years

25. Date: ....

26. Name: ....

Source: Nijenhuis, Van der Hart & Vanderlinden, Assen-Amsterdam-Leuven.

Appendix 2
S. D. Q. – 5

This questionnaire asks about different physical symptoms or body experiences, which you may have had either briefly or for a longer time.
Please indicate to what extent these experiences apply to you *in the past year*.

For each statement, please circle the number in the first column that best applies to YOU. The possibilities are:

1 = this applies to me NOT AT ALL
2 = this applies to me A LITTLE
3 = this applies to me MODERATELY
4 = this applies to me QUITE A BIT
5 = this applies to me EXTREMELY

If a symptom or experience applies to you, please indicate whether a *physician* has connected it with a *physical disease*.
Indicate this by circling the word YES or NO in the column "Is the physical cause known?"
If you wrote YES, please write the physical cause (if you know it) on the line.

Example:

	Extent to which the symptom or experience applies to you	Is the physical cause known?

Sometimes:

my teeth chatter	1 2 3 4 5	NO	YES, namely ....
I have cramps in my calves	1 2 3 4 5	NO	YES, namely ....

If you have circled a 1 in the first column (i.e., This applies to me NOT AT ALL), you do NOT have to respond to the question about whether the physical cause is known.

On the other hand, if you circle 2, 3, 4, or 5, you MUST circle NO or YES in the "Is the physical cause known?" column.

Please do not skip any of the 5 questions.
Thank you for your cooperation.

Source: Nijenhuis, Van der Hart & Vanderlinden, Assen-Amsterdam-Leuven.

Here are the questions:

1 = this applies to me NOT AT ALL
2 = this applies to me A LITTLE
3 = this applies to me MODERATELY
4 = this applies to me QUITE A BIT
5 = this applies to me EXTREMELY

	Extent to which the symptom or experience applies to you	Is the physical cause known?	

Sometimes:

1.	I have pain while urinating	1 2 3 4 5	No	Yes, namely ....
2.	My body, or a part of it, is insensitive to pain	1 2 3 4 5	No	Yes, namely ....
3.	I see things around me differently than usual (for example as if looking through a tunnel, or seeing merely a part of an object)	1 2 3 4 5	No	Yes, namely ....
4.	It is as if my body, or a part of it, has disappeared	1 2 3 4 5	No	Yes, namely ....
5.	I cannot speak (or only with great effort) or I can only whisper	1 2 3 4 5	No	Yes, namely ....

Source: Nijenhuis, Van der Hart & Vanderlinden, Assen-Amsterdam-Leuven.

Before continuing, will you please check whether you have responded to all 5 statements?

You are asked to fill in and place an X beside what applies to you.

    6. Age: ....   years

    7. Sex: ....   female
                                         ....   male

    8. Marital status: ....   single
                                       ....   married
                                       ....   living together
                                       ....   divorced
                                       ....   widower/widow

    9. Education: ....   number of years

10. Date: ....

11. Name: ....

Source: Nijenhuis, Van der Hart & Vanderlinden, Assen-Amsterdam-Leuven.

Appendix 3
T. E. C.

People may experience a variety of traumatic experiences during their life. We would like to know three things: 1) if you have experienced any of the following 29 events, 2) how old you were when they happened, and 3) how much of an impact these experiences had on you.

A) In the *first column* (i.e., Did this happen to you?), indicate whether you had each of the 29 experiences by circling YES or NO.

B) For each experience where you circled YES, list *in the second column* (i.e., Age) your age when it happened.
    If it happened more than once, list ALL of the ages when this happened to you.
    If it happened for years (e.g., age 7-12), list the age range (i.e., age 7-12).

C) In the *final column* (i.e., How much impact did this have on you?), indicate the IMPACT (by circling the appropriate number): 1, 2, 3, 4, or 5.

1 = none
2 = a little bit
3 = a moderate amount
4 = quite a bit
5 = an extreme amount

Example:

	Did this happen to you?	Age	How much impact did this have on you?
You were teased	no yes	....	1 2 3 4 5

Thank you for your cooperation.

Source: Nijenhuis, Van der Hart & Vanderlinden, Assen-Amsterdam-Leuven.

	Did this happen to you?	Age	How much impact did this have on you? 1 = none 2 = a little bit 3 = a moderate amount 4 = quite a bit 5 = an extreme amount
1. Having to look after your parents and/or brothers and sisters when you were a child.	no yes	....	1 2 3 4 5
2. Family problems (e.g., parent with alcohol or psychiatric problems, poverty).	no yes	....	1 2 3 4 5
3. Loss of a family member (brother, sister, parent) when you were a CHILD.	no yes	....	1 2 3 4 5
4. Loss of a family member (child or partner) when you were an ADULT.	no yes	....	1 2 3 4 5
5. Serious bodily injury (e.g., loss of a limb, mutilation, burns).	no yes	....	1 2 3 4 5
6. Threat to life from illness, an operation, or an accident.	no yes	....	1 2 3 4 5
7. Divorce of your parents.	no yes	....	1 2 3 4 5
8. Your own divorce.	no yes	....	1 2 3 4 5
9. Threat to life from another person (e.g., during a crime).	no yes	....	1 2 3 4 5
10. Intense pain (e.g., from an injury or surgery).	no yes	....	1 2 3 4 5

Source: Nijenhuis, Van der Hart & Vanderlinden, Assen-Amsterdam-Leuven.

	Did this happen to you?	Age	How much impact did this have on you? 1 = none 2 = a little bit 3 = a moderate amount 4 = quite a bit 5 = an extreme amount
11. War-time experiences (e.g., imprisonment, loss of relatives, deprivation, injury).	no yes	....	1 2 3 4 5
12. Second generation war-victim (war-time experiences of parents or close relatives).	no yes	....	1 2 3 4 5
13. Witnessing others undergo trauma.	no yes	....	1 2 3 4 5
14. Emotional neglect (e.g., being left alone, insufficient affection) by your parents, brothers or sisters.	no yes	....	1 2 3 4 5
15. Emotional neglect by more distant members of your family (e.g., uncles, aunts, nephews, nieces, grandparents).	no yes	....	1 2 3 4 5
16. Emotional neglect by non-family members (e.g., neighbors, friends, step-parents, teachers).	no yes	....	1 2 3 4 5
17. Emotional abuse (e.g., being belittled, teased, called names, threatened verbally, or unjustly punished) by your parents, brothers or sisters.	no yes	....	1 2 3 4 5

Source: Nijenhuis, Van der Hart & Vanderlinden, Assen-Amsterdam-Leuven.

	Did this happen to you?	Age	How much impact did this have on you? 1 = none 2 = a little bit 3 = a moderate amount 4 = quite a bit 5 = an extreme amount
18. Emotional abuse by more distant members of your family.	no yes	....	1 2 3 4 5
19. Emotional abuse by non-family members.	no yes	....	1 2 3 4 5
20. Physical abuse (e.g., being hit, tortured, or wounded) by your parents, brothers, or sisters.	no yes	....	1 2 3 4 5
21. Physical abuse by more distant members of your family.	no yes	....	1 2 3 4 5
22. Physical abuse by non-family members.	no yes	....	1 2 3 4 5
23. Bizarre punishment If applicable, please describe:	no yes	....	1 2 3 4 5
24. Sexual harassment (acts of a sexual nature that DO NOT involve physical contact) by your parents, brothers, or sisters.	no yes	....	1 2 3 4 5
25. Sexual harassment by more distant members of your family.	no yes	....	1 2 3 4 5

Source: Nijenhuis, Van der Hart & Vanderlinden, Assen-Amsterdam-Leuven.

	Did this happen to you?	Age	How much impact did this have on you? 1 = none 2 = a little bit 3 = a moderate amount 4 = quite a bit 5 = an extreme amount

26. Sexual harassment by non-family members.   no yes 1 2 3 4 5

27. Sexual abuse (unwanted sexual acts involving physical contact) by your parents, brothers, or sisters.   no yes 1 2 3 4 5

28. Sexual abuse by more distant members of your family.   no yes 1 2 3 4 5

29. Sexual abuse by non-family members.   no yes 1 2 3 4 5

30. If you were mistreated or abused, how many people did this to you?

   A) Emotional maltreatment (if you answered YES to any of the questions 11-16).

      Numbers of persons: ....

   B) Physical maltreatment (if you answered YES to any of the questions 17-19).

      Number of persons: ....

   C) Sexual harassment (if you answered YES to any of the questions 20-22).

      Number of persons: ....

   D) Sexual abuse (if you answered YES to any of the questions 23-25).

      Number of persons: ....

Source: Nijenhuis, Van der Hart & Vanderlinden, Assen-Amsterdam-Leuven.

31. Please describe your relationship with each person mentioned in your answer to question 30 (e.g., father, brother, friend, teacher, stranger, etc.), and add if the person(s) was (were) at least 4 years older than you at the time when the experience(s) occurred. For example, write "friend (−)" if this friend was less than 4 years older than you. Write "uncle (+)" if this uncle was more than 4 years older than you.

A) Emotional neglect ....
....

B) Emotional abuse ....
....

C) Physical abuse ....
....

D) Sexual harassment ....
....

E) Sexual abuse ....
....

32. Please describe any OTHER traumatic events that had an impact on you.
....
....
....
....

33. If you have answered YES to any of the questions 1-29, how much support did you receive afterwards? (give the number of the question and the level of support)

Question number	Level of support (0 = none, 1 = Some, 2 = Good)
....	....
....	....
....	....
....	....
....	....

Source: Nijenhuis, Van der Hart & Vanderlinden, Assen-Amsterdam-Leuven.

You are asked to fill in and place an X beside what applies to you.

34. Age: ....   years

35. Sex: ....   female
                                     ....   male

36. Marital status: ....   single
                                     ....   married
                                     ....   living together
                                     ....   divorced
                                     ....   widower/widow

37. Education: ....   number of years

38. Date   ....

39. Name: ....

Thank you very much for your cooperation.

Source: Nijenhuis, Van der Hart & Vanderlinden Assen-Amsterdam-Leuven

Index

absent-mindedness, 14, 17
absorption, 61, 89, 103, 208
absorption scale, 33
abulia, 12, 16, 27
adaptation, 5–6, 210–11
adjustment disorders
  and animal-like responses, 129
  and diagnostic categories, 69,
    70–71, 76
  and replication study, 57
adversity, 126
affect dysregulation
  correlates, 69, 128
  and hysteria, 27
  and PTSD, 138
  SDQ-20 and DES, 76
  see also emotional numbing
age
  disorganized attachment, 205
  and instruments, 71, 77
  at sexual harassment, 94–96
  and threat response, 33
  at traumatization, 96–99, 100, 103,
    169–71, 202
  see also children; infancy
aggressive behavior, 111, 117, 204
agoraphobia, 75, 129
alcohol, 40*t*, 70–71, 129
American Psychiatric Association
  (APA), 1, 5, 29, 33, 90, 108,
  164, 165, 182–83
amnesia
  in case example, 22
  dissociative, 43, 61

  for Janet, 16
  and pelvic pain, 147
  and pretraumatic life, 164
  and somatoform dissociation,
    157
amygdala, 117
analgesia
  as animal-like response, 34,
    111–14, 119, 127, 202–3
  in BPD, 201
  in case example, 21
  discriminant index, 38*t*
  as human defense, 116, 119, 128,
    133–34, 137, 202–3
  for Janet, 50
  predictive value, 136, 137–38,
    202–3
  and questionnaires, 68
  and repeated traumatization,
    113
  and safety signals, 111, 119
  and sexual abuse, 128
  see also pain
anesthesia
  as animal response, 127, 133, 137,
    202–3
  auditory, 16
  in case example, 21
  discriminant index, 38*t*
  and fixed ideas, 23
  genital, 15
  as human response, 34, 116
  kinesthetic, 15, 20 (*see also* motor
    control)

anesthesia (*cont.*)
  predictive value, 136, 137–38,
    202–3
  visual, 15–16, 21, 47, 50, 138
animals, 109–13
  circa-strike, 127
  and human symptoms, 128–40
  phylogenesis, 109–19, 126,
    202–3
  pre- and post-encounter, 127
  recuperation, 112–13, 137,
    201–5
  surrender, 126
anxiety, 147, 153
anxiety disorders, 60, 69, 70–71, 75,
    198–99
APA. *see* American Psychiatric
    Association
arousal, 133, 137, 203–4
assertiveness, 204
assistance-seeking, 205–6
ataxia, 15, 21
attachment, disorganized, 203–5
attention. *see* field of consciousness
auditory anesthesia, 16
auditory hallucinations, 18
autosuggestion, 17, 33–34,
    139–40
avoidance, 138
awareness, 82–85, 100, 203–4,
    210–212

behavioral challenge test, 202–4
behaviors
  aggressive, 111, 117, 204–5
  assertiveness, 204–5
  assistance-seeking, 205–6
  disorganized attachment, 204–5
  escape, 111, 126
  in infancy, 113, 116–17, 204–5
  in novel adversity, 126
  recuperative, 111–13, 137,
    201–5
  rehearsal of, 203–4
  repertoire, 108
  see also animals

bias. *see* iatrogenic factor
bipolar disorder
  and dissociation, 69, 73, 74,
    82–85, 198–99, 200–1
  and SCID-D, 84
  and SDQ-20, 76
blindness, temporary, 21
blood pressure, 40t
bodily integrity
  organic anesthesia, 15, 16–17, 20,
    21, 22, 47, 50
  threat to, 91, 102, 163, 183, 189
body dysmorphic disorder, 129
borderline personality disorder
    (BPD), 89–90, 129–30,
    199–201
Briquet's syndrome. *see* somatization
    disorder

caregivers, 203–5
  see also family
case example, 20–23
caseness, predictors of, 137–38,
    202–3
catalepsy, 16–17, 22
catecholamine response, 126
character traits, 12
children
  and caregivers, 203–5
  dissociation in, 207–8
  dissociative disorders in, 117
  traumatization, 6, 89–91, 103, 114,
    128, 147, 162–63
    in case example, 21
common stigmata, 13–14
complex dissociative identity states,
    14, 19–20, 23
conditioning, 112–13, 118, 128,
    204–5
consciousness
  altered states, 14
  double, 83–84
  experience integration, 139
  in hysterical attacks, 19
  and states, 108–9
  see also field of consciousness

consolation, 99, 102, 203–4
contractures, 17, 18, 22
control, 113
conversion disorders, 50–51, 69, 70,
    199–200
conversion hysteria, 42
convulsions, 199–200

daydreaming, 89
DDIS. *see* Dissociative Disorders
    Interview Schedule
DDNOS. *see* dissociative disorders,
    not otherwise specified
death
    of family member, 95
    threat of, 155–56, 158, 164, 181,
        183, 206–7
deliriums, 14, 20
denial, 101
dependent personality disorder,
    129–30
depersonalization, 61, 116, 147
depersonalization disorder, 28, 92
depression
    and animal-like response, 129
    and pelvic pain, 153
    predictive value, 147
    and somatoform dissociation, 69,
        70–71, 76, 198–99
    and surrender, 126
derealization, 61, 116, 147
DES. *see* Dissociative Experiences
    Scale
detachment, 138
development. *see* age
*Diagnostic and Statistical Manual of
    Mental Disorders,* 2nd ed.
    (DSM-II) on dissociative
    disorders, 42
*Diagnostic and Statistical Manual of
    Mental Disorders,* 3rd ed.
    revised (DSM-III-R), 4, 11, 51
*Diagnostic and Statistical Manual of
    Mental Disorders,* 4th ed.
    (DSM-IV) on BPD, 200–1
dissociation symptoms, 181

on dissociative disorders, 11,
    41–42, 54
and instruments, 27–28
and PTSD, 210
and SDQ-5, 198–200
somatoform disorders, 42, 52,
    199–200
somatoform dissociation
    symptoms, 67
diagnostic category study, 71–78
DID. *see* dissociative identity disorder
differential diagnosis, 71–78
disasters, 128, 161
discriminant indices, 38–40*t*, 131,
    133–34, 211–12
DIS-Q. *see* Dissociation
    Questionnaire
dissociation
    adaptiveness, 209–11
    and animal defenses, 114–14
    in at-risk children, 207–8
    and bipolar disorder, 69, 73, 74,
        82–85, 199, 200–1
    defined, 12
    and DES, 90
    versus dissociative disorders, 207–8
    hypnotic, 208–9
    ICD-10 on, 2–3, 11–12
    for Janet, 26–27, 66–67, 140
    non-pathological, 61, 103,
        206–11
    pathological, 89, 206–11
    peritraumatic, 90, 164–65
        instrument (PDEQ), 166,
        169–70, 171, 172
    predictive factors, 204–5
    prevalence, 49, 51, 196–97
    psychological (*see* psychological
        dissociation)
    qualitative *versus* quantitative view,
        206–11
    and somatization, 51
    and trauma, 5–6, 68, 147
Dissociation Questionnaire (DIS-Q)
    and DES, 29, 57
    and eating disorders, 69

Dissociation Questionnaire (DIS-Q)
 (*cont.*)
 factor structure, 27–28, 29
 and psychological dissociation,
  42–43, 68
 and replication study, 57
 and SDQ-5, 44, 50, 51, 197–98
 and SDQ-20, 32*t*, 33, 55, 59, 61,
  196
 and seizures, 199–200
 in trauma study, 92
dissociation theory, 209–11
dissociative disorders
 and animal defenses, 202–3
 and BPD, 199–201
 in children, 117
 comorbidity, 76
 differential diagnosis
 versus dissociation, 207–8
 in DSM-III-R, 11
 in DSM-IV, 11, 41–42, 54
 essential symptoms, 2, 54
 in ICD-10, 2–3, 42
 indoctrination effect, 77, 82–85,
  201 (*see also* iatrogenic factor)
 and instruments, 57–58, 59,
  60–61, 68, 211–12
  SCID-D, 152, 207–8
 and pelvic pain, 156–57, 205–6
 prediction, 136
 presentation, 205–6
 prevalence, 49, 51, 196–97
 and psychological dissociation, 76,
  77
 and PTSD, 91, 114–15
 and rape, 128
 and somatoform dissociation,
  41–42, 61–62, 69, 70, 73,
  197–98, 206–7, 208–9
 and trauma, 89–103, 201–2
dissociative disorders, not otherwise
 specified (DDNOS)
 and animal-like responses, 129–35
 versus bipolar disorder, 82–85
 diagnostic category, 69, 73, 74–75,
  76, 77

dissociation in, 200–1
 patient awareness, 82–85, 100,
  210–11
 and questionnaires, 28, 57–58,
  60–61, 68
  SDQ-20, 100, 196, 197
 symptoms, 108
 and trauma, 92
Dissociative Disorders Interview
 Schedule (DDIS), 27–28,
 196–97
Dissociative Experiences Scale (DES)
 and anxiety, bipolar, and affective
  disorders, 76
 bipolar disorder, 76, 82–83
 DES-Taxon(DES-T), 61, 197–98,
  207–8
 diagnostic category study, 69–70,
  72, 74
 and DIS-Q, 29, 57
 and dissociation, 90, 205–7
  qualitative *versus* quantitative
  view, 208
 and dissociative identity, 74, 100
 and eating disorders, 69
 and gender, 188
 and iatrogenic factor, 135
 and pelvic pain, 147, 149–50, 152,
  153, 205–7
 positive/negative symptoms, 27–28
 and psychological dissociation, 68,
  75, 77, 149–50
 and psychopathology, 68
 and SDQ-5, 49, 51, 61, 74, 153
 and SDQ-20, 72–73, 198–99
 and somatoform dissociation,
  42–43, 75
 and TEC study, 184
dissociative identity disorder (DID)
 animal response, 129–35
 awareness, 74, 77, 82–85, 100,
  200–1, 210–12
 case example, 20–23
 and DES, 74, 100
 diagnostic category, 7, 73, 74–75,
  76

hypnotic processes, 119
personalities, 12, 14, 104, 119,
    140, 203–4, 210–11
and questionnaires, 28, 211–12
    SDQ-20, 100, 196, 196–97
retraumatization, 203–4
and somatization disorder, 51
and state-dependence, 210–12
symptoms, 108
threats, 115
dissociative psychotic episodes, 14,
    20
dissociative states
barriers between, 211
struggles between, 18
see also state-dependence
dissociative symptoms
categorization, 13t
and childhood trauma, 89–90
in children, 117
negative, 14–17, 21–22, 28t,
    147–48, 195, 208–9, 211–12
positive, 17–20, 22–23, 29–30t,
    67, 148, 195–96
reporting, 147
state-dependence, 125–26, 211–12
    (see also state dependence)
see also animals
dizziness, 40t
double consciousness, 83–84
DSM-II. see Diagnostic and Statistical
    Manual of Mental Disorders,
    2nd ed.
DSM-III-R. see Diagnostic and
    Statistical Manual of Mental
    Disorders, 3rd ed. revised
DSM-IV. see Diagnostic and Statistical
    Manual of Mental Disorders,
    4th ed.

earthquake, 128
eating, 18–19, 22, 38t, 40t
and animal response, 127, 133,
    137–38
eating disorders
and dissociative disorders, 128

and somatization disorder, 51
and somatoform dissociation, 69,
    70, 76, 77, 140
emotional abuse
age factor, 96–99, 170t
and dissociative disorders, 91
and pelvic pain, 153–55
as setting, 201–2
severity, 189
and TEC, 93, 95t, 183, 189
emotional neglect
and animal response, 134
and other abuse, 94, 102
see also emotional abuse
emotional numbing, 111, 116, 128,
    138
see also affect dysregulation
endogenous opioids, 111, 116,
    138
epilepsy, 157
see also seizures
escape, 111, 126

family
caregivers, 204–5
consolation, 203–4
death in, 95t
incest, 128
parentification, 102, 190–91
pathogenic, 90–91, 102
and pelvic pain study, 153–55
perception of, 100
as perpetrators, 95t, 102, 114,
    203–5
sexual harassment in, 94–96
and TEC, 95t, 183, 190
fantasies, 103
fatigue, 15, 38t
fear, 21, 117
see also threat
fetal position, 115
fibromyalgia, 206–7
field of consciousness, 14, 17, 50, 67,
    140
fixed ideas, 17–19, 22, 23, 27
single versus multiple, 18

flight and fight reactions, 110, 115,
   127
freezing
   and animal response, 110–11, 127,
      128, 133, 134, 137, 202–3
   in DID sexual abuse victim, 203–4
   predictive value, 136, 137–38,
      202–3
   see also immobility

gastrointestinal symptoms, 40t, 133,
   137, 206–7
gender
   diagnostic category study, 71, 74,
      77
   and PTSD, 188
   and SDQ-20, 33, 55, 58, 188
   TEC study, 186–87, 188
   trauma study, 90–91, 99
genital anesthesia, 15
genital pain
   and animal response, 133–34, 137,
      138, 202–3
   discriminant index, 39t
   predictive value, 136, 202–3
   and SDQ-20, 6
   and sexual abuse, 139, 147
   see also pelvic pain

HADS. see Hospital Anxiety and
      Depression Scale
hallucinations, 18, 22
headache, 39t, 147
hearing, 16, 38t
helplessness, 112, 113
hiding, 115, 128
hippocampus, 117
hormones, 117, 204
Hospital Anxiety and Depression
      Scale (HADS), 150, 152–53,
      156
hospitalizations, 43
hyperesthesia, 18, 22
hypnotic dissociation, 209
hypnotic processes, 119
hypnotizability, 101–2, 140

hypochondriasis, 129
hysteria
   Charcot on, 66
   Janet on, 11, 12, 17, 42, 50, 66–67,
      139–40, 195–96
   and SDQ-5, 50
   see also dissociative disorders
hysterical accidents, 18
hysterical amnesia, 16
hysterical attacks, 14, 18, 19, 20, 22
hysterical psychosis, 20

iatrogenic factor, 33–34, 101–2, 135,
      140, 200–1
ICD-10. see International
      Classification of Diseases,
      10th ed.
identity
   alteration, 61
   and body parts, 15 (see also bodily
      integrity)
   experience integration, 139
   and pelvic pain, 147
   structured interview, 43
   see also dissociative identity
      disorder; personality
identity confusion, 153, 157, 205–6
imagination, 61
imminence, 111, 113, 127, 138,
      203–4
immobility, 21, 22, 68, 110–11, 127
   paralysis, 16, 18, 115
impotency, 38t
incest, 128
indoctrination. see iatrogenic factor
inertness, 19
inescapable shock, 112–13, 126
infancy
   behavioral responses, 113, 116–17,
      204–5
   caregiver relationship, 203–5
   regression to, 117
   trauma in, 98, 100
inhibitions, 33
integration, 2–3, 108–9, 139,
      209–11

interest, loss of, 138
International Classification of Diseases, 10th ed. (ICD-10)
conversion disorders, 67, 76, 199–200
dissociation, 2–3, 11–12
dissociative disorder, 2–3, 42, 198–99
pseudoseizures, 13
somatoform dissociation, 42
intrusions, 12, 17–19, 22–23, 27, 67
irritable bowel syndrome, 206–7

kinesthetic anesthesia, 15, 50
see also motor disturbances

Lasegue's syndrome, 15, 16, 21
learning, 126
life threat, 164, 183, 206–7
see also under threat
limbs, 15, 16–17, 21
lithium, 70, 82–83
Loevinger's coefficient, 30

Mann-Whitney test, 30, 32
medication, response to, 40t
memory
loss of (see amnesia)
posttraumatic, 127
and stress, 101, 117
of trauma (see also iatrogenic factor)
from childhood, 90, 101, 103, 201–2
complete, partial or delayed, 164–74
corroboration, 99, 101, 134–35, 171–72, 173
experience integration, 139
state dependence, 211–12
menstruation, 23, 39t, 40t
mental accidents, 12–14, 17–20, 22–23, 27, 67, 195–96
and instruments, 28
mental function, 14, 17, 90

mental stigmata, 12, 13–17, 21–22, 27, 67, 195–96, 208–9, 211–12
and instruments, 21–22, 27, 208–9, 211–12
monoideism, 18, 19
mood disorders, 70
see also bipolar disorder; depression
motivation, 126, 138, 140
motor control
catalepsy, 16–17, 22
discriminant indices, 38t
and fixed ideas, 18
and ICD-10, 12
immobility, 21, 22, 68, 110–11, 127
involuntary acts, 22, 33, 39t

narcissistic personality disorder, 129
neglect. see emotional neglect
neurotransmitters, 114
nociception, 111–12
see also analgesia; pain
novel adverse conditions, 126
numbing. see analgesia; anesthesia; emotional numbing

obsessive compulsive disorder, 57, 129
organic anesthesia, 15, 21
organization, level of, 139
overdiagnosis, 82–85

pain
and animal defenses, 111–12
in body part, 211–12
chronic, 116, 119, 137
insensibility to, 15, 47, 50
as intrusion, 18
in joints, 39t
and somatoform dissociation, 206–7
and trauma history, 22, 117
types, discriminant indices, 38–40t
see also analgesia; genital pain; pelvic pain; urination

pain disorder, 70, 76
    somatoform, 69
panic attacks, 209
panic disorders, 51, 57
paralysis, 16, 18, 115
    see also freezing
parentification, 102, 190–91
passivity, 15, 115, 163, 203–4
    catalepsy, 16–17
    submission, 126, 203–4
PDEQ. see Peritraumatic Dissociation
    Experiences Questionnaire
pelvic pain
    anesthesia, 21
    discriminant index, 39t
    predictive value, 204–7
    and psychological dissociation, 13,
        69
    study, 148–58, 205–6
    and trauma, 181
    see also genital pain; urination
perceptions
    of family, 99–100
    gaps in, 14, 138
    as intrusion, 12
    of present, 19
    sensory, 15–16, 18, 138
Peritraumatic Dissociation
    Experiences Questionnaire
    (PDEQ), 166, 169–70, 171,
    172
Peritraumatic Somatoform
    Dissociation Questionnaire
    (SDQ-P), 202–3
personality disorders
    and animal-like response study,
        129–30
    diagnostic category study,
        71
    and replication study, 57
    see also borderline personality
        disorder
personality(ies)
    interruptions of, 14, 17, 26–27
    secondary, 12, 119, 140, 203–4,
        210–11

    see also dissociative identity
        disorder
phobias, 57, 129
phylogenesis, 109–19, 126, 202–3
physical abuse
    age at occurrence, 170t
    and animal-like response study,
        134
    and family, 95t, 99–100
    and other abuse types, 102
    and pelvic pain, 147, 153–56, 158,
        181
    and peritraumatic somatoform
        dissociation, 165, 170–73, 181
    as predictor, 68, 89–90, 147
    prevalence, 94
    reporting, 171, 188–89, 190
    setting, 93
    and somatoform dissociation,
        201–2, 206–7
polyideism, 18, 19
posttraumatic stress disorder (PTSD)
    and animal responses, 34, 114,
        126, 138
    APA on, 182–83
    and dissociative disorders, 91,
        114–15
    in DSM-IV, 210
    and emotional numbing, 128
    and gender, 188
    predictors, 90, 128
    questionnaire, 184–85
    and rape, 164
    and somatoform disorder, 91
    and trauma severity, 181
    traumatic memories, 139
presentation, 3–4, 76, 206
prevalence, 49, 51, 196–97
proper stigmata, 13–14
pseudo-hallucinations, 22
psychological dissociation, 12–13,
        23, 66, 67–68
    diagnostic category study, 77
    and dissociative disorders, 76
    and general psychopathology,
        77

and pelvic pain, 12–13, 147, 157
peritraumatic, 162–71, 173
questionnaires, 67–68
screening for, 205–7
and somatization, 69
and somatoform dissociation,
    12–13, 23, 66, 67–68, 69, 75,
    90, 155–56, 188
terminology, 66
and trauma, 90, 96, 158, 168, 189,
    201–2
psychopathology, 68, 70, 73, 75–77,
    90, 92, 197–98
psychotic episodes, 14, 20
PTSD. see posttraumatic stress
    disorder
PTSD-self scoring (PTSD-ss),
    184–85, 188
punishment, 115

reactive dissociative psychosis, 20
reality, 13t, 27
    derealization, 61
recall, 90, 101, 103, 201–2
    see also memory
recuperative behavior, 111–13, 137,
    201–5
reexperiencing, 18, 20
rehearsal, 203–4
relationship problems, 71, 129
repetition
    of testing, 188–89, 190
    of trauma, 113, 119, 128, 201–2,
        203–4
reporting
    of dissociative symptoms, 147
    of physical complaints, 76
    of physical/sexual abuse, 171,
        188–89, 190
    of trauma, 171, 190, 201–2
retraumatization, 119, 203–4

safety signal, 111, 119
satanic ritual, 101
schizophrenics, 51, 57, 71,
    198–99

SCID-D. see Structured Clinical
    Interview for DSM-III-R/-IV
    Dissociative Disorders
SCL-90-R. see Symptom
    Checklist-90-R
screening instruments, 3–4, 27–34,
    49
Screening Test for Somatization
    Disorder (STSD), 150–50
SDQ-5
    and conversion disorders, 50–51
    and DES, 51, 61, 74, 153
        DES-T, 197–98
    development, 43–47, 130
    diagnostic category study, 71–72
    and DIS-Q, 44, 50, 51, 198
    and DSM-VI, 198–200
    efficacy, 47–50, 55, 153, 157
    future testing, 50–51
    and mental stigmata, 208–9,
        211–12
    pelvic pain study, 148, 149, 153,
        157
    predictive value, 55, 60t, 61, 153,
        157, 196–97, 205–7
    questions, 65, 221–23
    replication study, 57, 59–62
    and SCID-D, 50, 73, 150, 197
    and SDQ-20, 49–50, 55, 58–61
    and severity, 69–70
    specificity, 205–7
    Turkish translation, 198–99
    uses, 62, 196–97
SDQ-20
    and animal responses, 135–36
    and bipolar disorder, 82–83
    and DES, 72–73, 76, 198–99
    development, 28–30, 130
    and diagnostic category, 71–77
    and DIS-Q, 32t, 33, 55, 59, 61
    future research, 34
    and gender, 33, 55, 58, 188
    and general psychopathology, 76,
        90
    and negative symptoms, 208–9,
        211–12

SDQ-20 (*cont.*)
  and patient awareness, 100
  pelvic pain study, 148, 149, 152,
    157
  predictive value, 59, 68, 135–36
  questions, 65, 217–20
  replication study, 57, 59–62
  and SCID-D, 157
  and SCL-90-R, 72–73, 75–76
  and seizures, 199–200
  and severity, 69–70, 148
  and somatization disorder,
    199–200
  and somatoform dissociation,
    197–98, 208–9
  and TEC, 184
  in trauma study, 92–93, 100, 102
  Turkish translation, 198–98
  uses, 62, 200–1
  validity, 30–32, 55, 59–62, 76, 196,
    201–2
SDQ-P. *see* Peritraumatic Somatoform
    Dissociation Questionnaire
secondary existences, 12, 14, 104,
    119, 140, 211
seizures, 13, 33, 38t, 200
self, sense of, 14, 108–9
  see also identity
self-modulation, 203–4
self-mutilation, 21
self-organization, 108
self-suggestion, 17, 33–34, 139
sensation, loss of, 12, 15–16
sexual abuse
  age factor, 170t
  and analgesia, 128
  and animal-like response study,
    134
  and family, 99
  incest, 128
  as inescapable shock, 114
  and pelvic pain, 139, 147, 153–55,
    158
  and peritraumatic dissociation,
    170t, 171
  as predictor, 68, 89–90, 95t

prevalence, 94
recall type, 164–74
reporting, 171, 188–89, 190
resubmission, 203–4
setting, 93
severity, 171, 172–73, 189, 202–3
and somatoform dissociation,
    201–2, 206–7
and TEC, 183
sexual assault, 91, 128, 158, 164,
    206–7
sexual harassment
  age factor, 170t
  defined, 93, 94–96
  and pelvic pain, 153–55
  and sexual abuse, 100
  and TEC, 183
sexual trauma
  and dissociative disorder, 94
  and genital pain, 6
  and pelvic pain, 153–55, 158
skills, loss of, 16, 22
sleep, 18, 40t
  somnambulisms, 14, 19–20, 23
SLESQ. *see* Stressful Life Events
    Screening Questionnaire
smell, sense of
  anesthesia, 16
  and animal responses, 133, 138,
    140
  preferences, 33–34, 38t, 39t
social phobia, 57, 129
sociocultural factors, 140
somatization
  and dissociation, 51
  and psychological dissociation,
    69
somatization disorder
  history, 1–2
  and pelvic pain, 147
  and PTSD, 128
  and SDQ-5, 50–51
  and SDQ-20, 152
  and somatoform dissociation, 69,
    70
  subgroups, 200

somatoform disorders
  diagnostic category study, 74, 76,
    77
  in DSM-IV, 42
  and PTSD, 91
  and rape, 128
  somatoform dissociation
    subcategories, 77
somatoform dissociation
  low levels, 69
  patient awareness, 74–75, 77,
    82–85
  peritraumatic
    and physical abuse, 170–71,
    173
    and recall, 168–69, 172–73,
    202–3
  terminology, 3, 54
Somatoform Dissociation
  Questionnaires. see SDQ-5;
  SDQ-20
somatoform pain disorder, 69
Somatoform Peritraumatic
  Dissociation Questionnaire
  (SDQ-P), 166–67, 168,
  169–70, 172
somnambulisms, 14, 19–20, 23
sounds, 111
speech, 18, 22, 33–34, 47, 50
startle response, 111, 138
state dependence
  and animal responses, 6
  and caregivers, 205
  and complex dissociative state,
    19–20
  DID, 21
  of dissociative symptoms, 125–26,
    210–12
  and fixed ideas, 27
  integration and disruption, 108–9,
    209–11
  and motor skill loss, 16
  and personality-like
    characteristics, 140
  and questionnaires, 212
  as reactivation, 67

response types, 40t
  and trauma memory, 101
stiffening, of body, 21, 22
stigmata, 13–14
  see also mental stigmata
stimuli
  and experience integration, 139
  and imminence, 127
  trauma-associated, 128
  and visual anesthesia, 15–16
stress, 101, 117
Stressful Life Events Screening
  Questionnaire (SLESQ), 184,
  185, 187–88, 190–91
Structured Clinical Interview for
  DSM-IV Dissociative
  Disorders (SCID-D)
  in animal response study, 129, 131,
    136
  and bipolar disorder, 84
  description, 131
  and diagnostic categories, 71–73
  and dissociation, 207–8
  and dissociative disorder, 29, 43,
    152
  and pelvic pain, 150, 152
  and positive/negative symptoms,
    27–28
  and psychological dissociation,
    67–68
  reliability, 5
  and SDQ-5, 50, 73, 157, 197
  and SDQ-20, 72–73
    replication study, 56, 57
  and trauma study, 91–92, 100
STSD. see Screening Test for
  Somatization Disorder
subconscious acts, 14
subconscious fixed ideas, 17–19, 22,
  23
substance dependence, 57, 70–71
suggestibility, 101–2, 139–40
  see also autosuggestion; awareness;
    iatrogenic factor
surrender, 114, 126, 203–4
swallowing, 22, 33–34, 161

Symptom Checklist-90-R
    (SCL-90-R), 68, 72, 75–76,
    135–37
symptoms. *see* dissociative
    symptoms

tactile anesthesia, 15, 21
taste, sense of, 16, 33–34, 38*t*, 39*t*
    and animal response, 133, 138, 140
TEC. *see* Traumatic Experiences
    Checklist
TEQ. *see* Traumatic Experiences
    Questionnaire
thirst, 15
threat
    animal response, 109–13, 134
    to bodily integrity, 91, 102, 163,
        183, 189
    human responses
        and animal responses, 114–19
        and autohypnosis, 139–40
        of dissociative patients, 128
        factors, 163
        in infancy, 116–17
    imminence, 111, 113, 127, 138,
        203–4
    to life, 164, 183, 206–7
        and pelvic pain, 155–56, 158,
            181
    and TEC, 183
tics, 18
TMI. *see* Traumatic Memory
    Inventory
touch, sense of, 15, 21
trance-like states, 116, 117
trauma
    and adaptiveness, 5–6, 210–11
    age at occurrence (*see* age)
    animal responses, 109–13, 134
    case example, 20–23
    in childhood (*see* children; family;
        infancy)
    and conditioning, 112–13, 118,
        204–5
    corroboration, 99, 101, 134–35,
        171–72, 173

disasters as, 128
and dissociation, 5–6, 68, 90, 147,
    164–65
    psychological, 90, 96, 158, 168,
        189, 201–2
    somatoform, 96, 103, 139, 155,
        201–2, 206–7
and dissociative disorders, 89–103,
    201–2
duration, 98–99, 113
emotional abuse and neglect, 91,
    93, 95*t*, 96–99, 102
integration, 2–3, 108–9, 139,
    209–11
versus milder stress, 101
multiple types, 153–54, 201–2
outcome determinants, 113
perpetrators, 102, 114,
    203–5
reexperiencing, 18, 20
repetitions, 113, 119, 128, 201–2,
    203–4
reporting, 90, 113, 171, 188–89,
    190, 201–2
retrospective estimations, 99
and SCID-D, 91–92, 100
and SDQ-20, 34, 62
setting, 183, 190, 201–2
severity, 171, 172–73, 181, 183,
    189, 202–3
see also emotional neglect; physical
    abuse; sexual abuse; sexual
    harrassment; threat
Traumatic Experience Questionnaire.
    see Traumatic Experience
    Checklist (TEC)
Traumatic Experiences Checklist
    (TEC)
    background, 180
    content, 224–30
    future, 201–2
    pelvic pain, 148, 150, 151,
        155
    peritraumatic study, 165–66,
        169–71
    psychometric study, 182–91

repeated testing, 188–89, 190
trauma study, 93
Traumatic Memory Inventory (TMI),
    167
tremors, 18, 39t
tunnel vision, 15, 21, 47

unconscious acts, 14
urinary needs, awareness of,
    15
urination
    difficult, 38t
    need to, 15
    pain on
        and animal response, 136, 137,
            138, 203

discriminant index, 33–34, 39t,
    47, 133–34
hysteria, 50
in SDQ-20, 69
and sexual abuse, 139

vision, 15–16, 21, 33, 47, 138
visual anesthesia, 15–16, 21, 47, 50,
    138

walking, 16
whispering, 47
will, loss of, 12, 16, 27
women. see gender
writhing, 19
writing, 16